CONTROL SYSTEM
INTERFACES
Design and Implementation
Using Personal Computers

MICHAEL F. HORDESKI

PRENTICE HALL, Englewood Cliffs, New Jersey 07632

Library of Congress Cataloging-in-Publication Data

HORDESKI, MICHAEL F.
   Control system interfaces : design and implementation using personal computers / Michael F. Hordeski.

   Includes bibliographical references and index.
   ISBN 0-13-456823-0
   1. Automatic control.   2. Microcomputers.   3. Computer interfaces.
   I. Title.
TJ223.M53H65 1992   91-6955
629.8′9--dc20   CIP

Editorial/production supervision
  and interior design: BARBARA MARTTINE
Cover designer: Wanda Lubelska
Manufacturing buyer: KELLY BEHR/SUSAN BRUNKE
Acquisitions editor: GEORGE KUREDJIAN

 © 1992 by Prentice-Hall, Inc.
A Simon & Schuster Company
Englewood Cliffs, New Jersey 07632

The publisher offers discounts on this book when ordered
in bulk quantities. For more information, write:

   Special Sales/College Marketing
   Prentice-Hall, Inc.
   College Technical and Reference Division
   Englewood Cliffs, New Jersey 07632

Printed in the United States of America

10 9 8 7 6 5 4 3 2 1

ISBN   0-13-456823-0

PRENTICE-HALL INTERNATIONAL (UK) LIMITED, *London*
PRENTICE-HALL OF AUSTRALIA PTY. LIMITED, *Sydney*
PRENTICE-HALL CANADA INC., *Toronto*
PRENTICE-HALL HISPANOAMERICANA, S.A., *Mexico*
PRENTICE-HALL OF INDIA PRIVATE LIMITED, *New Delhi*
PRENTICE-HALL OF JAPAN, INC., *Tokyo*
SIMON & SCHUSTER ASIA PTE. LTD., *Singapore*
EDITORA PRENTICE-HALL DO BRASIL, LTDA., *Rio de Janeiro*

Contents

9

Other Interface Boards   252

Preface

The applications for the personal computer (PC) and related software packages have grown well beyond their initial beginnings in office and business automation. Today, in addition to word processing and accounting, there are applications in engineering computation and analysis, production and quality control, and computer-aided design. One of the fastest-growing application areas is measurement and control. This relates to the use of PCs in the laboratory, collecting data, and monitoring the status of processes and equipment. The introduction of specialized software has made it possible to apply microcomputers directly in control or indirectly through programmable or process controllers.

The major application of PCs in industrial plants is in configuring control systems. The next largest application is data acquisition, either as a front end to programmable logic controllers (PLCs) or process controllers or in direct connection to a process through input/output (I/O) boards or I/O processors.

Since most PCs cannot handle real-time applications, they are used primarily to monitor and control relatively simple processes. In the future, they can be expected to be used along with and in place of other major types of monitoring and control devices, such as PLCs or process controllers.

Most applications software is aimed at the IBM-PC family because of its greater market share and its availability in industrial versions capable of surviving the characteristics of plant environments. IBM compatibility will continue to be a strong consideration for PC selection into the future.

In the late 1970s, a number of companies were marketing PCs, including Apple and Commodore. During this time period, the use of PCs in data acquisition and industrial control was not even a distant consideration. Apple may have unknowingly started a trend for applications like data acquisition when it began incorporating extra slots into the chassis for adding extra memory or peripheral devices.

The IBM-PC, when it was introduced in 1981, also featured expansion slots that could be used for analog interfaces. Shortly after the introduction of the IBM-PC, several companies began offering add-in accessory boards including analog input/output and IEEE-488 interfaces. Most of these initial offerings supported Apple personal computers. Today many companies provide analog interfaces for several different PCs, most of these are designed for the IBM-PC family. These vendors have adopted the IBM-PC format for their analog interfaces, mostly due to the acceptance of the IBM-PC family in scientific and engineering applications.

As new data acquisition hardware and software products appear, they feature higher performance, lower cost, and ease of use. There have been improvements in speed, number of channels, resolution, ruggedness, and processing intelligence. These systems tend to compete with specialized test, measurement, and control systems. Declining costs and more powerful software are resulting in new applications for PCs.

Personal computers are becoming part of a move to construct fully integrated data handling systems. These generally parallel the physical processes being controlled. The PC would be one of the fundamental building blocks in these systems.

PCs are often used as an operator interface for PLC applications. Here, they are used to change set points, start and stop motors, and control valves. The PC with the proper software can be used to replace control and graphic panels as well as annunciators. PCs are particularly useful in those parts of processes which are subject to frequent major adjustments, the pilot plant, start-up, and laboratory environment.

Due to the real-time limitations of PC disk operating system (PC-DOS), PCs were more often used for process monitoring rather than control applications. They are found in nontime-dependent control situations where high-speed response is not critical. PCs are often used to perform precalculations on data.

PCs are excellent training devices, and once users become familiar with the methods of using computers, they can quickly learn revised procedures.

This book presents the tools needed for such an implementation. It provides the background to apply PCs to automation and process control applications. Chapter 1 shows how the PC evolved in noncontrol applications. Spreadsheets and database packages were widely used for everything from parts lists and maintenance inventory control to storage and the manipulation of local data. Graphics packages for the PC are also widely used. Although the graphics available for the smaller machines may be limited, their ability to display data in a readily usable format and to assist in such tasks as the production of diagrams continues to grow. Word processing software is used for text editing, such as specification creation and revision. Statistical packages and project management/scheduling packages are also popular.

Chapter 2 is concerned with the characteristics that are important in control interfaces. External memory is the subject of Chapter 3, and input/output control is explained in Chapter 4.

The techniques necessary for successful designs are presented in Chapter 5. These include design planning considerations, design tools, error handling, and testing methods.

Software development costs can exceed hardware costs for some types of control applications. A wide array of software development/cost difficulties are discussed.

High-level application languages for ladder logic or flow charting for control applications which use a CAD-like programming environment are among the newer generation of nonprocedural languages. These can be used in conjunction with artificial intelligence tools. These nonprocedural approaches promise to reduce greatly the time required in writing code.

Software development is explained in detail in Chapter 6, which begins with some basic notions like overlays and advances to programming styles and development aids. Verification methods are also explained along with debugging methods and the art of making performance and timing measurements.

Chapter 7 is concerned with application issues. Some typical applications are discussed along with the use of PLCs with PCs and the necessary interfaces. Workstation trends and environmental issues are also treated in depth in this chapter.

Chapter 8 begins a detailed explanation of interface hardware. It begins with a discussion of coding and error budgets and continues into data converters, multiplexers, sample and holds, timers, and bus standards. This chapter is concerned with PC, XT, and AT interface boards.

PS/2 boards are explained in Chapter 9 as well as MetraBus boards and available drivers.

Chapter 10 considers process control software packages. Packaged software continues to grow in variety and sophistication, providing more relief from the high cost of in-house software development.

In many areas, there is a push for full integration. Complete integration involves a hypercomplexity for the interaction of many unrelated operations. PCs tend to proliferate information that may need to be screened. Communications, data storage, and applications programming can be both strengths and the weaknesses of the PC. They represent strengths in that the PC can perform in these areas, but they are weaknesses since the effort required to get PCs to perform some functions in these areas may be prohibitive.

Users must put in more time to understand automated processes in detail. It takes more effort by people with broader knowledge to get useful results from integrated systems.

A book such as this would not be possible without the help and suggestions of many. I would like to thank William Walvoord of Monsanto, Glenn Vaughn of Celanese, Paul Priba of Conoco, Alvin Iverson of Arco Chemical, Lynn Richard of Setpoint, Raymond Robertson of PPG Industries, Eric Lohry of Nutra-Flow Chemical, David Bishop of Chevron, Bruce Honda of Weyerhauser, Carmen De Vito of Dupont, and Donna Terp of Heuristics for their Views and assistance.

Thanks to Dee at Jablon Computer for doing her usual fine work at assisting me, and a special thanks to Berry Phillips of MetraByte for permission to use specifications, drawings, and programming examples from their product catalogs.

As experience with PCs in data acquisition and engineering calculations grows, it will reduce the concerns users may have regarding PCs in direct control. In the future, there will be more PCs in petroleum refining, oil and gas production, chemicals, foods, and other industries as PCs move into more control applications.

Author's Note: Additional information on products discussed in this book is available from: Jablon Computer, 2250 Monterey Road, Atascadero, CA 93422, (805) 466-3209. There is also a tutorial disk for IBM PCs available from this source.

PCs in Control: An Introduction

This chapter shows you how

- PCs fit into the industrial environment
- PCs evolved from office applications
- Software development costs control applications
- Packaged software fills many basic needs

Applications for the personal computer (PC) and software packages had their initial appearance in office and business automation. Today, there are many applications in engineering analysis, production and quality control, and computer-aided design.

One of the major application areas is measurement and control. This is due to the extension of PCs to the laboratory, collecting data and monitoring the status of processes and equipment. The introduction of industrial software and PC versions allows the user to incorporate microcomputers directly in control applications or indirectly through programmable or process controllers.

Because of the digital interface of PCs buses, analog data acquisition requires the use of an analog-to-digital converter to transform measurement data into a PC bus-compatible format. Once the data has been acquired, the information can be readily transformed, analyzed, stored, or displayed.

The major application of PCs in industrial plants is in configuring control systems. The next largest application is data acquisition, either as a front end to programmable logic controllers (PLCs) or process controllers or in direct connection to a process through input/output (I/O) boards or I/O processors.

Since most PCs lack real-time capabilities, they are primarily used to monitor and control only simple processes. In the future, they can be expected to be used along with and in place of other major types of monitoring and control devices, such as PLCs or process controllers.

Industrial PCs are available in four different configurations:

1. Table or desktop
2. Portable, battery powered
3. Rack mounted
4. National Electrical Manufacturers Association (NEMA) enclosured

A typical configuration for control devices in U.S. plants is rack mounting. NEMA enclosures are generally required by plants with corrosive environments.

Most applications software developers have aimed their products at the IBM-PC family because of its greater market share and its availability in industrial versions capable of surviving the characteristics of plant environments. These computers are provided with cooling removable filters and special cases. Industrial versions of the IBM-PC family are available from several suppliers in different forms. IBM's Model 7552 industrial computer uses a passive backplane and battery backup for protection against transients. IBM compatibility will continue to be a strong consideration for PC selection into the future. Other companies that have introduced industrial PCs include General Electric, Hewlett-Packard, and AT&T.

An important development in industrial PC growth is Intel's 32-bit microprocessor, the 80386. Because of its greater computing power and speed, the 80386 allows real-time and multitasking capabilities. The full potential of the 80386 microprocessor will not be realized under current versions of DOS, but the 25 MHz operating speed that some systems offer will increase throughput considerably. DOS-based programs will run about twice as fast as the highest-speed IBM-AT.

Most processor-intensive chores, such as number and data manipulations, will take about half as much time. Additional hardware and software advances may potentially double this performance again.

1.1 HISTORICAL OVERVIEW

In the late 1970s, a number of companies began marketing PCs, including Apple, Tandy, and Commodore. During this time the use of PCs in data acquisition and industrial control was not an important consideration. Apple started a trend for applications like data acquisition when it began incorporating extra slots into the chassis for adding extra memory or peripheral devices. The IBM-PC was introduced in 1981 and also featured expansion slots that could be used for analog interfaces. Shortly after the introduction of the IBM-PC, several companies offered add-in accessory boards including analog input/output and IEE-488 interfaces. Most of these initial offerings supported Apple personal computers. Today many companies provide analog interfaces for several different PCs; most of these are designed for the IBM-PC family.

There are many competing ways to implement automated data acquisition systems and personal computer–based data acquisition has received the support from many companies, including Hewlett-Packard, Fluke, and Burr-Brown.

Most vendors have adopted the IBM-PC format for their analog interfaces, mostly due to the acceptance of the IBM-PC family in scientific and engineering applications.

There is also a growing ease in the implementation of PC-based data acquisition systems. As new data acquisition hardware and software products appear, they feature higher performance, lower cost, and ease of use. There have been improvements in speed, number of channels, resolution, ruggedness, and processing intelligence. These systems tend to compete with specialized test, measurement, and control systems.

Declining costs and more powerful software are resulting in new applications for PCs, as replacements for oscilloscopes, data loggers, and chart recorders. These stand-alone units have a negative image because of their inflexibility.

1.2 PCS AND INTEGRATION

A major use of PCs is in development work, including the development of control applications for other devices as well as performing calculations in support of engineering. Personal computers are becoming part of a move to construct fully integrated data handling systems. These generally parallel the physical processes being controlled. The PC would be one of the fundamental building blocks in these systems.

PCs are often used as an operator interface for PLC applications. Here, they are used to change set points, start and stop motors, and control valves. The PC with the proper software can be used to replace control and graphic panels as well as annunciators.

PCs have been used to control furnaces in petrochemical operations and generators in acid plants. About half the current applications are for monitoring and off-line development rather than for direct control. Of those applications that use PC units for direct control, fewer than a quarter use them for any type of time-critical operations. The present PCs have been judged too slow for these applications. The majority of PCs used in direct control are laboratory, pilot plant, or other applications where the flexibility of the PC was important. PCs are particularly useful in those parts of processes which are subject to frequent major adjustments, the pilot plant, start-up, and laboratory environment.

Dedicated electronics are still preferred for some control applications because the users do not want to have to program to get the level of control needed or the requirements for speed and reliability are more than an all-purpose machine can offer. Dedicated devices may have already proven these requirements with an installed base.

Due to the limitations of PC-DOS, PCs are more often used for process monitoring. Control applications are usually in nontime-dependent control situations where high-speed response is not critical. PCs have been used in tandem with PLCs for automatic crane control in the manufacture of films and for kiln control in electronics manufacture. This combines the ruggedness and quick scan time of the PLC along with the data storage, manipulation, and reporting capabilities of the PC. PCs are particularly useful in their ability to perform precalculations on data from instruments and controllers in the field. An example from the chemicals industry is a PC used to reconstruct gas chromatograms from data supplied by remote instruments. PCs have also used digitizers pressure waves in explosives testing.

As experience with PCs in data acquisition and engineering calculations grows, it will reduce the concerns users may have regarding PCs in direct control.

In the future, there will be more PCs in petroleum refining, oil and gas production, especially chemicals, foods, and other industries as PCs move into more control applications.

1.3 ENVIRONMENTAL CONSIDERATIONS

Since PCs were designed for the office environment, they are viewed as fragile. The floppy disk is not compatible with industrial environments. Dust or other particulates are a problem. Even control rooms contain materials that can be detrimental to the disks.

Normally, PCs without floppy disks do not have the means for program loading and maintenance. Environmental concerns such as fumes can destroy floppy disk heads over time. Other electronic devices may also be degraded, but the disk drives appear to be the biggest concern. Moisture, dust, and corrosive chemicals are the main causes of problems to disk drives.

Electromagnetic interference (EMI) can also be a problem, even if the power supply is conditioned properly. The plant floor is often electrically noisy. Shock and vibration are also hard on PCs, although these problems are generally easier to solve.

Disk drives can be replaced in some applications by magnetic bubble memory packs. If a network is used, field updates of software can be done using the network. Some industrial PCs employ a cooling system where the air is drawn in through a filter and returned out through the disk openings. The opposite path is used in office machines. This can reduce the exposure of the internal components to corrosive materials and particulates.

Another solution is to keep PCs out of harmful environments. This means installation in control rooms, enclosured offices, or some place remote from the processes they are intended to monitor and/or control. It sometimes becomes a trade-off between getting far enough away to keep the machine operating and being close enough for the machine to be able to get the data it needs, given the distance limitations of some of the communications schemes.

Cathode ray tube (CRT) screens and mechanical keyboards are also weak links in the PCs ability to withstand the industrial environment. A primary limitation of PCs is the standard keyboard, which are difficult to protect. CRTs are now available for washdown and explosive hazards areas.

1.4 HARDWARE STANDARDIZATION

Standardization is critical in engineering, particularly in instrumentation and control. Without standards, there tends to be a greater flexibility, but this can also result in duplicated effort.

The lack of standards can be a serious problem, and most companies struggle to establish some kind of standards for computer hardware, either in their own department or corporatewide. Although there are many PCs available, most firms standardize on either IBM or an IBM compatible. This may not always provide the best PC available, but it does diminish concerns about the proliferation of different brands and models. However, compatible is not the same as identical. Compatibility software can be costly. Metrology software is one example that is dependent on specific machines and is not always transportable. Many problems in compatibility can be minimized by using the same DOS and BIOS.

In some cases, users may already have a mix of different machines and they prefer to apply the extra effort needed to make a variety of brands and models work together. Some of these applications may have been using a particular machine in a particular function and this is judged to be more important than its ability to work well or easily with other machines at that site.

1.5 TRAINING CONSIDERATIONS

In about half the existing installations, the use of PCs has required little or no increase in training. Most training requirements center on the need for increased understanding of programming and of the need to know the process better. PCs are actually excellent training devices, and once users become familiar with the basic methods of using computers, they can quickly learn revised procedures that are to be implemented.

1.6 THE PC IN INTEGRATION

In many areas, there is a push for full integration. While the ultimate value of a fully integrated monitoring and control system is widely believed, how the PC will contribute to this goal is still a question. Their ability to collect data and automate inexpensively helps integration as well as their ability to network with each other. The inability to network efficiently with plantwide computer systems looms as a major problem for integration. The PC networks may become islands of automation. Communications can improve access to data collected by individual PCs, but software can be a large obstacle to accessing this information if it does not work in a manner which will facilitate connectivity. Standard data structures and software architectures are needed which can be added to without a complete rewriting. If the capability is not anticipated in the specification, it may not get implemented later.

Complete integration involves a hypercomplexity for the interaction of many unrelated operations. PCs tend to proliferate information that may need to be screened. Communications, data storage, and applications programming can be both strengths and the weaknesses of the PC. They represent strengths in that the PC can perform in these areas, but they are weaknesses since the effort required to get PCs to perform some functions in these areas may be prohibitive.

Data sharing is basic to integrated systems, but problems facing PCs and other types of computers in this area can be formidable. Data structure standards and communications standards are really two forms of the same problem.

Users must put in more time to understand automated processes in detail. It takes more effort by people with broader knowledge to get useful results from integrated systems.

1.7 SOFTWARE DEVELOPMENT

Software development costs can approach or exceed hardware costs for some types of control and monitoring applications. Software development costs are sometimes more than the cost of hardware and in some automation projects in discrete manufacturing approach 750% of total project costs. In other applications, they may not be a significant factor. The software may have been developed and in place, complete monitoring may require the installation of additional or more accurate instruments.

Lead times for software development can be a problem since it is difficult to estimate the time required to complete a particular program. A wide array of software development/cost difficulties are possible. Some companies stay away from in-house software development altogether. They contract for customized programs from outside, or packaged software for control and monitoring. There is some loss in flexibility, but there may be some gains, for example, the ability to keep the packages maintained and updated.

The other side of this spectrum is improved flexibility and the ability to optimize performance for each application. This is often the case in research or laboratory settings where requirements change frequently.

1.8 LANGUAGES AND PROGRAMMING TECHNIQUES

A critical part of software development costs hinges on the issue of languages. There is a trend toward standardizing on one or two programming languages. Established standards are important and the most popular languages are BASIC or FORTRAN. Once useful code is written and running in a particular language, there is a tendency for more code to be written in that same language. FORTRAN and BASIC are not the fastest, or the most powerful, or the most elegant languages. They have been in use for some time, and much control code has been written in these languages.

Many are familiar with them and feel comfortable writing programs in them. BASIC, in its many versions, is by far the most widely used language. It meets the needs of many applications, but it does have problems.

The most critical problem with BASIC for control or monitoring applications is its speed even in the compiled version (usually BASIC is interpreted) and even when the BASIC programs can call assembly language subroutines. The slow execution is compensated by fast I/O calls.

The BASIC language is a good all around choice due to the number of drivers and compatible I/O systems available for it which far exceeds similar offerings for other languages.

Although the Instrumentation Society of America extensions of FORTRAN have given the language real-time capabilities, it still has the problem of strong hardware dependence. Programs written in FORTRAN for use on one kind of machine generally must be rewritten if they are to run on another type of machine.

Among the newer languages, C, especially in a UNIX or Xenix environment, and Pascal offer considerable improvements in programmer productivity and in their ability, in some versions, to handle real-time multitasking applications.

1.9 SOFTWARE PACKAGES

Packaged software continues to grow in variety and sophistication. They continue to provide more relief from the high cost of in-house software development. Spreadsheets are the most widely used packages. Database packages were also widely used for everything from parts lists and maintenance inventory control to storage and the manipulation of local process data. Graphics packages for the PC are also widely used, although the graphics available for the smaller machines may be limited. Their ability to display data in a readily usable format and to assist in such tasks as the production of diagrams continues to grow. Word processing software is needed wherever text editing is done, such as specification creation and revision. Statistical packages as well as project management and scheduling packages are very useful.

Custom programming may be needed in some applications, but there are many ready-made packages that are easily configurable to specific applications.

There is likely to be more high-level application languages for ladder logic or flow charting for control applications which uses a CAD-like programming environment. These are nonprocedural languages as opposed to languages such as BASIC or Pascal which list the procedure to be followed. Ladder logic has been in use longer than digital computers, but the newer generation of nonprocedural languages asks the user to list the desired result rather than the desired procedure. Used in conjunction with artificial intelligence tools, the nonprocedural approaches to machine instruction hold the promise of greatly reducing the time required in writing code.

1.10 WORD PROCESSING

A word processor can be used to write anything from the shortest, simplest reports to long specification documents complete with table of contents and extensive footnotes. A word processor can insert a standard piece of text and generate the same reports every week with only slight variations. It can be used to customize documents like invoices and generate labels. Programs like OfficeWriter, Executive Writer, PFS:Write, and IBM Writing Assistant provide some advanced functions, yet they are among the easiest word processors to learn. IBM Writing Assistant and PFS:Write are both good for the creation of form documents. Other programs which are generally more powerful, but also more difficult to learn, include DisplayWrite, Leading Edge Word Processor, MultiMate, OfficeWriter, Samna Word, Volkswriter, WordPerfect, and WordStar.

The MultiMate and OfficeWriter packages have a user interface similar to that of the Wang word processing system. MultiMate has more features, but OfficeWriter is faster and less expensive. DisplayWrite 2 and 3 are similar to IBM's Displaywriter. Standard phrases and paragraphs (boilerplate text) are handled well by MultiMate, DisplayWrite, WordStar, WordStar 2000, and Samna Word.

For long documents with complex formatting requirements, there is Microsoft Word. It is somewhat complicated to learn and use, but it has powerful formatting capabilities and can be used with a mouse.

DisplayWrite, MultiMate, OfficeWriter, Samna Word III, Samnat, and WordPerfect are DIA/DCA compatible. This allows documents created with these word processors to exchange information under IBM's Distributed Office Support System (DISOSS).

There are also word processing accessories like Word Plus, which is a spelling checker that works with any word processor that produces an ASCII file. PFS:Proof is a spelling checker that works with PFS:Word and other word processors. ZyINDEX is a retrieval program that creates keyword indexes for files.

Many integrated programs include word processors. In general, these word processors are not as powerful as the ones discussed in this section. An exception to this is Enable, which has a word processor that is competitive with most of the dedicated word processors.

For creating documents based on an outline, Framework or Symphony (with its outline option), are among the best in integrated programs. For jotting down and organizing quick notes Sidekick or other desk organizers are useful.

A simple program has very few commands or codes. Instructions and command choices are displayed at the top of the screen at all times, so reference to the manual is rarely necessary. Before anything drastic is done to the text, the program may ask for confirmation and it may have an undo capability to reverse the last operation.

A simple program does not have the advanced features of bigger word processors (such as multiple formats or advanced cursor movements), so it should not be used for complex documents. It can also be slow and tedious to use.

1.10.1 DisplayWrite 2

DisplayWrite 2 is a text processing system similar to the IBM Displaywriter with Textpack 4. It is a full function word processor that will handle a wide variety of documents. DisplayWrite 2 uses a Get function to retrieve a document or a paragraph and insert it into the document currently being created. This function can be used to retrieve other DisplayWrite 2 documents or a DOS print file, including spreadsheets and graphs. There is also a paragraph assembly feature for creating documents from a library of boilerplate paragraphs.

The program includes a 100,000-word spelling checker with automatic hyphenation. It has a full set of column operations, including layout, revise, delete, move, or copy columns. Full four-function math capability is included, as well as the ability to calculate average and percentages.

Although this is a logical program to learn, its extensive use of menus for formatting operations may prove confusing or annoying for some users. Although documentation is thorough, the program has no tutorial or online help function.

DisplayWrite 2 is one of the fastest of the programs designed to replace a dedicated word processor. It is DIA/DCA compatible.

1.10.2 DisplayWrite 3

DisplayWrite 3 includes all the functions provided by DisplayWrite 2 plus some advanced functions and features. DisplayWrite 3 offers column manipulation and four-function math capability. Automatic outlining can be used to renumber a document by section. Footnotes are also automatic. A draw function allows the user to create line drawings and simple bar charts and graphs.

1.10.3 IBM Writing Assistant

IBM Writing Assistant is a casual word processor designed to be fully integrated with other programs in the IBM Assistant Series. This product is similar to PFS:Write. One difference between the two is that it is possible to remove underlining and boldface from Writing Assistant's text without retyping the words. This product includes Word Proof, a spelling checker with a 125,000-word dictionary.

1.10.4 Leading Edge Word Processor

Many features resemble Wang word processing, but there are differences. For example, the Leading Edge program scrolls through pages instead of jumping from screen to screen. A tutorial is included, and the program is easy to learn and to use. The Spelling Correction version offers a spelling checker with an 80,000-word expandable dictionary.

1.10.5 MultiMate

In this program, the personal computer's function keys substitute for the dedicated keys on a Wang word processing system which it closely resembles. Multi-Mate is a what-you-see-is-what-you-get system. It has a document summary screen that tracks documents by operator, author, date of creation, date of last edit, and keyword. Like most dedicated word processors, it allows editing while printing. The library feature allows pages of text to be entered into the current document with several keystrokes. The program also allows in-document calculations and a spelling checker is included. MultiMate's speed of operation tends to be slow. Since only one page of a document is brought into memory at a time, moving from one page to another is also slow.

1.10.6 PFS:Write

PFS:Write is good for inserting boilerplate text. The program is easy to learn and use, yet it has features found on the more powerful word processors. For boiler-plate applications it can append files from other documents. It is one of the simplest word processors available with boilerplate capability. It allows temporary left margins for indenting a section of text and a maximum document size of 32 pages.

1.10.7 Samna Word III

Samna Word III is a what-you-see-is-what-you-get word processor. It can run on a variety of microcomputers, and it is useful if compatibility is required across different brands such as IBM or DEC. Because of this versatility, the program executes certain functions such as move and reformat more slowly. Samna Word III allows two files on the screen at the same time, scrolling independently. It has all the functions found in a dedicated word processor.

1.10.8 Volkswriter

Volkswriter Deluxe provides advanced word processing features such as true proportional spacing, page orientation, and footnotes. Volkswriter Deluxe comes with a notepad feature and allows the use of foreign language, engineering, and scientific symbols by assigning a single keystroke.

1.10.9 Word

This word processor has versatile formatting capabilities for sophisticated text layouts. Standard formats for contracts, tables, annual reports, and other complex documents can be stored on style sheets. Once a style sheet has been designed for a particular type of document, all documents of that type will automatically be in the standard format.

Word has eight windows which can be used to view different documents or parts of the same document simultaneously. It is especially useful for input to typesetters or to laser or dot-matrix printers producing documents with complete layouts. The simple functions are easy to learn, but the advanced features are not intuitive and not as easily learned. Word includes a spelling correction program that identifies misspelled words and suggests alternatives. The spelling checker can be accessed directly from within a document.

1.10.10 WordPerfect

WordPerfect is a full-function word processing package that includes more features than many dedicted word processors. WordPerfect tries to anticipate mistakes, erased text can be retrieved, major deletions require confirmation before they are performed, and text may be automatically saved to guard against loss in case of a power interruption.

This program includes a color-coded key template listing the commands performed by each key when it is pressed alone or with Shift, Alternate, or Control. Because several keystrokes are required to execute certain basic functions, WordPerfect can be tedious to use.

1.10.11 WordStar

WordStar has been available since 1979 and has a large installed base. The system is difficult to learn, but many users become comfortable with it. The online tutorial that comes with the program is helpful, and there are also supplementary training materials available.

1.10.12 WordStar 2000

WordStar 2000 has some menus and commands that are similar to those of the original WordStar, but a number of features have been added. Among these are automatic paragraph reformatting, imbedded rulers, go to page, undo, proportional spacing, on-screen underlining and bold, automatic hyphenation, windows, predefined format sheets, keystroke glossary, typewriter mode, math function, and a footnote feature that numbers footnotes and locates them at the end of the document. Included with WordStar 2000 is MailMerge and a spelling corrector.

WordStar 2000 uses a two-step menu system similar to WordStar. The commands are more logical, but they require three keystrokes; control plus two letters. Other drawbacks relative to the original WordStar are slower performance and larger memory requirement. WordStar 2000 comes with a file conversion program for WordStar data.

1.11 SPREADSHEETS

Electronic spreadsheets are like flexible electronic calculators. The spreadsheet format lists numbers in rows and columns. A spreadsheet organizes the numerical data so it can be analyzed. It is useful for comparisons since it allows immediate results. The user specifies the relationships between values and the spreadsheet functions as a powerful tool for what-if data analysis.

There are programs like 1-2-3 to produce large spreadsheets or to develop an application system for use by others. They use a programming language to automate spreadsheet preparation. Many programs allow a part of a spreadsheet to be stored and inserted into another spreadsheet. Some support the 8087 and 80287 which allows a faster spreadsheet. Many programs can consolidate data, such as Multiplan, which allows the merging of data from separate worksheets.

Many programs include graphics, text editing, and file manager capabilities, but they are primarily spreadsheets. There are a number of packages that can enhance the graphics produced by these programs into presentation-quality materials.

The Spreadsheet Auditor is useful for locating errors in a spreadsheet, it also prints spreadsheets sideways. SIDEWAYS is another accessory, which rotates wide spreadsheets by ninety degrees and allows them to print without interruption along continuous-form paper.

1.11.1 Lotus 1-2-3

This program is simple enough to encourage a novice yet sophisticated enough to hold the expert user. It has many features, a large capacity, and speed. Lotus 1-2-3 combines a spreadsheet with simple information management and analytical graphics.

The spreadsheet contains 15 arithmetic logical and relational operators, 41 functions, and 66 commands. Including database and graphing, 1-2-3 has 110 commands. In addition to the standard spreadsheet functions of data entry, labeling, manipulation, and calculation, 1-2-3 has other features. A macro capability allows the user to write menu-driven applications. This product has a good tutorial and manual, screen prompts, and context-sensitive help.

1.11.2 Multiplan

Multiplan is useful for building consolidated spreadsheets with data from other files. The consolidated sheet is automatically updated whenever the data changes in any related sheet. Multiplan allows multiple color windows and the naming of cells or blocks for formulas. The program also has row sorting and a good help facility with menus and alternative responses to guide the user.

1.11.3 PFS:Plan

This is an easy-to-use spreadsheet program designed for the first-time spreadsheet user. One helpful feature is the Quick Entry key, which allows automatic entry of a series of headings.

Spreadsheet entries are typed directly into the cell where they will appear rather than entered on a command line and transferred. PFS:Plan is fully integrated with the other products in the PFS series. With a few exceptions, it works the same as the IBM Planning Assistant.

1.11.4 Spreadsheet Auditor

The Spreadsheet Auditor is valuable for locating and correcting errors in spreadsheets. It can be used to verify or document a spreadsheet by printing or displaying the formulas behind the spreadsheet.

Spreadsheets are useful and reliable tools, but they can contain minor errors that can cascade into major problems. In the development of a large model there will be many insertions, deletions, and changes for constants, formulas, and the locations of data. During this process it becomes easy to introduce errors, and a mistake in the early stages of modeling a spreadsheet can be multiplied many times by successive application of formulas that rely on the erroneous cell. Typical spreadsheet errors include specifying the wrong ranges in a formula, entering data on top of a formula, copying a formula incorrectly, and entering an otherwise correct formula with an incorrect reference. One way to prevent these errors is to scan the spreadsheet, keeping track of the formulas. This can be difficult when the spreadsheet is larger than the display. The Spreadsheet Auditor displays formulas in a grid that matches the layout of the spreadsheet. All formulas are shown with column letters and row numbers.

The program includes a utility to allow spreadsheets to be printed sideways. The user interface is like 1-2-3. Besides 1-2-3 the Spreadsheet Auditor can be used with Symphony, VisiCalc, or SuperCalc3. It can handle a spreadsheet of great complexity.

1.11.5 SuperCalc3

SuperCalc3 is an improved version of SuperCalc, one of the original CP/M spreadsheets. Its formatting features are similar to 1-2-3, including sort, data, arithmetic, and macro commands. SuperCalc3 includes integrated presentation-quality graphics. The program can print several graphs on one sheet. Graph styles include pie, line, area, bar, stacked bar, high-low, and X-Y. A form of preview graphics is visible on a monochrome screen without a graphics option. If both a monochrome and a color monitor are used, the spreadsheet and graph can both be viewed.

A feature for faster math speeds up the calculations and a memory management system allow 9999-row and 127-column capacity.

1.12 DATA MANAGERS

Data management programs can act like a simple Rolodex file or maintain a large database of records. They can search for particular records and display them on the computer screen, or they can sort records and print out detailed reports. Data management systems work with information keyed directly into the program or with information furnished by other programs or computers.

Data management products can be divided into two types: file managers and database managers. File managers operate as nonrelational, or flat, systems, while database managers operate as relational systems. A relational system can store data in more than one file and to retrieve information from several of these files simultaneously. A relational system is useful for information that comes from several different sources and is used in a number of different ways, since it allows the database to be reduced to a number of smaller files that may be accessed individually with or without reference to the rest of the database.

A file manager maintains all data in a single file. It is simpler than a relational system but provides less flexibility. No matter where the information comes from or how it is used, it must be entered into a common file and retrieved from that file. A flat system is useful for simple applications such as maintaining a computerized card file.

There are two basic parts in setting up a data management system. The first part concerns how the information is to be entered. If it is to be keyed in by an operator, there must be an input format. If it comes from another program or computer system, there must be a plan to map the data into files. The second part concerns how the information is to be retrieved—it could be displayed online, printed, or stored—and how it is to be formatted.

Most file managers and a few database managers require no programming and are simple to set up. Data entry and retrieval are handled by making selections from menus and responding to prompts. Menus and prompts make the program easy to use, but the limited number of choices limit the program's usefulness.

Most database managers use a built-in programming language that can be used to set up the system to any specifications. Some of the newer database managers include a menu/prompt system to make the programming easier. A programmable system can be used to create a turnkey system which can handle a variety of data entry and retrieval tasks, customized to the needs of those who operate the system.

1.12.1 IBM Reporting Assistant

IBM Reporting Assistant works with Filing Assistant to produce tabular reports from Filing Assistant data. Reporting Assistant is fully integrated with other programs in the IBM Assistant Series. Except for a few differences, this product is identical to PFS:Report.

1.12.2 PFS:File

PFS:File is a popular simple file management program. It allows the user to set up a data entry form on the screen, add data, and then retrieve and summarize information. PFS:File has fast, flexible search capabilities. For reports the program should be used with PFS:report. This product is identical to IBM Filing

Assistant except that it can also do on-screen formula calculations and includes a ditto key for entering data that is the same as that entered in the previous form.

1.12.3 PFS:Report

This program is designed to access information in PFS:File. It will total, average, and count items and includes pagination. To prohibit unauthorized viewing of confidential information, a data field in the report can be invisible. Information from the invisible fields can be included in a derived column formula but will not be included in the printed report.

1.12.4 CLOUT (Conversational Language Option)

CLOUT is a database query facility for retrieving data from software products like 1-2-3, dBASE II, and R:base 4000 and 5000. It uses expert systems theory and natural language techniques to simplify the retrieval of information stored on disk. CLOUT can retrieve up to five files. It automatically converts plain English queries into the proper syntax. CLOUT has a vocabulary of commonly used phrases and will learn new words as they are used. CLOUT accesses files through a FileGateway facility which reformats the files into an R:base 4000 format. CLOUT can be used to combine data into a single database.

1.12.5 dBASE II

dBASE II was the first attempt at a relational database management system for microcomputers. At start-up, only a period appears. English-like commands are used to retrieve information through queries, or a program can be developed to create menus that allow untrained personnel to run complicated applications. The person entering or retrieving the data only needs to follow the menus. A tutorial is included, but there is a lot to learn to make full use of this package.

1.12.6 dBASE III

dBASE III does away with some of the limitations of dBASE II which was originally written for CP/M 8-bit machines. dBASE III was written for the 16-bit microprocessors used in the IBM PC. It is easier to use and has other advantages as well. There can be up to 10 databases open at the same time while dBASE II allows only 2. There can be 128 fields per record instead of 32 and records may store 4000 bytes compared to 1024 for dBASE II.

dBASE III allows up to 1 billion records per database with a computational accuracy of 15.9 digits. It provides better browse and list procedures and better index updating. It includes a built-in word-wrapping word processor for inserting text comments into the database. It uses context-sensitive help and an Assistant package to help the user through procedures. It can be 40 times as fast in sorting compared to dBASE II.

dBASE III is not compatible with dBASE II, but there are utility programs to convert dBASE II files to dBASE III format. The program converter can translate most of the code, but the rest is flagged and must be converted by hand.

1.12.7 dBASE IV

dBASE IV offers some additional capabilities over dBASE III. There are 255 fields per record instead of 128, and there is a 64K-byte memo field in addition to the 4000 bytes per record allowed by dBASE III.

dBASE IV also has extensive password protection and uses disk sector editors and other tools at the DOS level to encrypt files. It also includes a System Query Language facility for data extraction and manipulation.

1.12.8 Quickcode

Quickcode translates code for dBASE II/III programs. It allows users with little programming background to write dBASE programs. The user enters the appropriate data at the prompts, and Quickcode writes the dBASE program. The program includes the Quickscreen facility that allows the user to create forms by drawing directly on the screen rather than building the form as required by dBASE II.

1.12.9 Quickreport

Quickreport is a dBASE report generator. It allows the user to produce reports from information stored in a dBASE II or III database without learning dBASE's programming language. Reports are created by drawing on the screen. A simple word processor is included as well as line drawing characters for drawing lines and boxes.

1.12.10 EntryManager

This program complements a database manager by allowing the user to set up screens for the entry of large amounts of data. The menu interface allows screen development to proceed quickly. EntryManager stores files in standard ASCII format. Records may have fixed or variable lengths. Each file can contain up to 63 record types. EntryManager can perform arithmetic on the input data and handle other operations such as range checking, table lookup, and field type checking.

1.12.11 R:base 4000

This program is similar to IBM's Sequel (SQL). It is similar in power to dBASE II, and it uses many mainframe database concepts and techniques. The program provides step-by-step command prompts to guide the user through each query. The manual and tutorial are well prepared, but screen messages tend to be cryptic.

1.12.12 R:base Extended ReportWriter

This is an optional utility package for use with R:base 4000 to generate complex and detailed reports. It uses menus to help the user create a detailed report. The extensive on-screen help aids in preparing the report formats.

1.12.13 R:base 5000

R:base 5000 is a relational database program. It is designed for creating custom applications without requiring the user to learn a programming language. R:base 5000 includes Application Express, which is a menu-driven application generator. With a few keystrokes, the user can view the program code that was generated. R:base 5000 is designed to grow with the user's experience. Although a complex turnkey system can be designed with Application Express, there are additional commands available to those who wish to write their own programs using the programming language directly.

R:base 5000 has all the features of R:base 4000 and more. It includes report-writing capabilities and a file gateway to access data stored in 1-2-3, Symphony, PFS:File, and dBASE II files as well as ASCII and DIF.

1.13 STATISTICS

These packages help the user make predictions from data. They can be used to point to trends and establish a level of confidence in test results. They provide descriptive statistics such as mean, standard deviation, skewness, frequency distributions, and statistical testing.

ABSTAT is a collection of frequently used statistical routines. It is easy to use but is limited in the type of analysis it can perform. SPSS/PC is a more comprehensive package based on the mainframe package SPSS.

1.13.1 ABSTAT

ABSTAT is a simple package of analysis routines. It is command driven and accepts data from dBASE II or ASCII files. ABSTAT is useful in interpolating missing values. It can be used for the analysis of variance, correlations, and multiple regressions.

1.13.2 SPSS/PC

SPSS mainframe software has been in use since the late 1960s. SPSS/PC incorporates the most popular parts of SPSS. Commands are checked as they are typed, and the user is alerted to errors and given a suggestion for the source of the error. Raw data may come from other files or be entered at the keyboard. The user is limited to 200 variables. The report writer allows calculations and can display the results in custom formats. Graphic displays are available with a set of PLOT procedures.

1.13.3 Systat

Systat provides a number of statistical procedures and is especially appropriate for multivariate analysis. It has similar procedures to SAS, BMDP, or SPSS-X mainframe statistics packages. Both accuracy and speed are good. A data module allows one to merge and join multiple files by one or more variables. The package includes most of the data management capabilities of SAS. The data module may be used as a programming language based on commands such as rank and standardize. The selection and merging of variables allows the manipulation of large data sets. This program uses a set of commands that are simple relative to the power of the program, but the program is not among the easiest to learn. The manual contains useful examples of the commands. Systat is valuable for regular users of statistics. It is not designed for the casual user.

1.13.4 STATA

This package provides descriptive statistics, scatterplots, regression models, and forecasts. It allows other types of analysis including analysis of variance and covariance (ANOVA & ANCOVA), multiple regression, N-way cross-tabulation, and parametric and nonparametric testing.

STATA does its work in random access memory (RAM) (with EMS/EEMS compatibility), which makes it fast even with large data sets. With an 8 Mb expansion card STATA can provide fast analysis of up to 32,000 observations on 254 variables, which is close to a million data elements in memory. STATA has the ability to sort, merge, and append sets. It has an interactive mode which provides a conversational quality. An option allows the user to move data files between programs like 1-2-3 and dBASE while preserving labels, names, and missing value codes.

STATA provides a range of high-resolution analysis and presentation graphics including scatterplot matrices, multiple imaging from single commands, and the ability to overlay images. The data moves seamlessly from the statistical to graphics mode, so it is easy to spot perturbations and trends quickly without having to leave the STATA environment.

Optional menus with pull-down help windows help get the user started, and there is more than 700 pages of documentation along with a complete tutorial.

The Characteristics of Personal Computers

This chapter shows you how

- Microcomputers function internally
- The microprocessor evolved from relatively simple devices
- The 80286 microprocessor used in AT class personal computers operates
- Addressing takes place internally in personal computers
- Microcomputer architecture influenced personal computers

The personal computer contains the required circuit boards, including the microprocessor and other processing elements, as well as the supply source and disk drives needed to store data and programs. Input/output (I/O) lines are required for control and communications, and there must be enough internal memory to operate the programs.

The microprocessor functions as the central processing unit (CPU) for the microcomputer. It usually consists of a single semiconductor chip with several interconnected chips. Microprocessor functions include instruction decoding for the execution of the program as well as the synchronization and control signals needed for the input and output operations. The microprocessor's functional parts may include an arithmetic-logic unit (ALU) for processing instructions and instruction decoder, register banks for temporary storage and timing, and control circuits such as oscillators, frequency dividers, and counters for sequencing operations.

Since all computers have a central processor, some memory, and a way to bring data in and present it to the outside world, what is unique in the personal computer is that the processor is on only one semiconductor chip and some memory and input/output circuits may also be on that same chip, or they are on a limited number of chips on the same circuit board. The personal computer is not only small, but it is low cost relative to larger computers.

Typically, the personal computer has been used where only a few single tasks were to be performed or where the string of instructions known as the program is relatively small. The range of input/output equipment to which the personal computer was connected has also been limited compared to larger computers.

The microprocessor evolution began in the late 1960s when semiconductor manufacturers began defining chips with high gate-to-pin ratios and regular cell structures. This marked the beginning of semiconductor memory market. These early semiconductor RAMs, ROMs (read-only memories), and shift registers were used in many calculator and CRT terminal products.

The Intel 4004 was the first microprocessor. It was actually designed as the processing element of a desk calculator in 1971. It was never designed to be used as a general-purpose computer, but it was the first general-purpose computing device in a chip.

Other chips introduced in this time frame were called "microprocessors," but they were, in fact, only calculator chips, and many of them used serial bit arithmetic. Although not intended to be a general-purpose microprocessor, the introduction of the 4004/8008 series was a success even with its limited performance. This success motivated the conductor manufacturers to produce improved designs.

The 8080 was the first chip designed specifically as a microprocessor. It used all the 8008 instructions and offered improvement in throughput.

Other chips like the 6502 introduced by metal oxide semiconductor (MOS) technology combined memory and I/O systems could be built with fewer chips.

Zilog achieved a major design improvement with the Z-80, which incorporated on a single chip the 8080, its clock, and system controller along with some additional facilities. It was compatible with the 8080 software, and the Z-80 provided two major additions compared to the 8080. It used two banks of registers resulting in a larger number of internal registers as well as faster response to interrupts. The register banks are implemented with both the accumulator and the status word duplicated, and each register bank contained all the 8080 registers as well as a set of X and Y index registers. The Z-80 also used a dynamic memory refresh, which allowed the direct connection of dynamic RAMs to the system. Two of the unused instruction codes of the 8080 were allocated to provide block transfer operations for shorter programs and faster execution times. Higher speeds were also allowed with the larger number of internal registers. The Z-80 had two interrupt levels versus one for the 8080 and required a single power supply instead of three. The Z-80 provided significant improvements in performance.

The 8085 was to be compatible with the 8080 at the machine code level. Architecturally, the 8085 appeared as not much more than a repackaging of the 8080. The added features were an on-chip oscillator, power-on reset, vectored interrupts, serial I/O, and a single power supply. Two new instructions Read Interrupt Mask and Set Interrupt Mask, were used to support the serial port and interrupt mask. The 8085 did not provide additional registers in multiple banks or dynamic refresh, but provided additional interrupt levels which were not provided by the Z-80.

Improved technology made it possible to build 8-bit single-chip microcomputers. The F8 was the first true microcomputer using two chips. Then, all its functions were implemented in a single chip, the 3870. The major use for these chips is embedded in low-cost industrial and consumer applications. Other single-chip devices appeared in the 8048 from Intel and the Z-8 from Zilog. The 8048 architecture is derived from the 8080, but is not compatible with it. The 8048 also has its own instruction set. One version of the 8048, the 8748, uses a UV-erasable programmable read-only memory (EPROM) instead of ROM which can be erased with ultraviolet light and then reprogrammed. The Zilog Z-8 is similar to the 8048 as a one-chip microcomputer but it is based on the Z-80.

The first 16-bit microprocessors appeared in 1974, with the National Pace unit. The Pace used PMOS technology, and it was comparatively slow. During this same period several faster N-type Metal Oxide Semiconductor microprocessors were designed for a variety of minicomputers. The Data General MN601 implemented on a single chip most of the slowest NOVA minicomputer architecture. The minicomputer manufacturers were now implementing some of the slower minicomputers using microprocessors. These implementations reduced the number of components and resulted in a lower-cost product. Most of the early 16-bit microprocessors were targeted at the minicomputer market. The later ones would establish new markets. The first of these was the Texas Instruments 9900. It had a 16-bit multiply and divide in a 64-pin package. The 9900 was used in the Texas Instruments 990 minicomputer/microcomputer. In 1973 Intel introduced a 16-bit processor, the 8086. Throughput increased by an order of magnitude over the 8080 memory space was 16 times greater at 1 megabyte and the number of I/O ports increased from 256 in the 8080 to 64K in the 8086. Other improvements included high-level language addressing, string manipulation, and full decimal arithmetic. The 8086 used 29,000 transistors on a die 27% larger than the 8080.

The Z8000 appeared in 1979, not as an enhancement of the Z-80 but with its own internal structure and unique instruction set. One set of registers controls the system calls and the internal registers allow 32-bit double-word operations. Traps for illegal addresses instructions may be used in debugging.

The Motorola 68000 appeared the following year. It uses an external 16-bit bus which is multiplexed from the internal 32 bits. It has a 32-bit ALU and 16 32-bit registers. The address bus has 23 bits for addressing, providing a memory space of 16M bytes. Still wider bit sizes were introduced later such as the Intel 80286 and 80386.

Many of these latter microprocessors were designed with features to support the operating system software and self-test or system debugging. This can include built-in trace capability for debugging and a user and a supervisor state for supporting operating systems.

2.1 THE 80286 MICROPROCESSOR

The 80286 is a high-performance microprocessor with a 16-bit external data path, up to 16 megabytes of directly addressable physical memory and up to 1 gigabyte of virtual memory space. The operating speed ranges from 6 MHz to 16 MHz. The 80286 operates in two modes: protected virtual address and real address.

2.1.1 Virtual Address Mode

The virtual address mode provides a 1-gigabyte virtual address space mapped onto a 16-megabyte physical address space. Virtual address space is larger than physical address space, and the use of a virtual address that does not map to a physical address location will cause a restartable interrupt.

This mode uses 32-bit pointers that consist of a 16-bit selector and offset components. The selector specifies an index into a memory-resident table, and the 24-bit base address of the desired segment is obtained from the memory table. A 16-bit offset is added to the segment base address to form the physical address. The microprocessor automatically references the tables whenever a segment register is loaded with a selector. Instructions that load a segment register will refer to the memory-based tables without additional program support. The memory-based tables contain 8-byte values called descriptors.

2.1.2 Real Address Mode

In this mode, physical memory is a contiguous array. The selector portion of the pointer is interpreted as the upper 16 bits of a 20-bit address and the remaining 4 bits are set to zero. This mode of operation is compatible with the 8088 and the 8086.

Segments in this mode are 64KB in size and may be read, written, or executed. An interrupt may occur if data operands or instructions attempt to wrap around the end of a segment. In this mode, the information contained in the segment does not use the full 64KB, and the unused end of the segment may be overlayed by another segment to reduce physical memory requirements.

2.1.3 System Timers

The typical AT system has three programmable timer/counters controlled by an Intel 8254-2 timer/counter chip. These can be called channels 0 through 2 and connected as follows:

Channel 0	System Timer
GATE 0	Wired on
CLK IN 0	1.190 MHz OSC
CLK OUT 0	8259A IRQ 0
Channel 1	Refresh Request Generator
GATE 1	Wired on
CLK IN 1	1.190 MHz OSC
CLK OUT 1	Request refresh cycle
Channel 2	Tone Generation for Speaker
GATE 2	Controlled by bit 0 of port hex 61 PPI bit
CLK IN 2	1.190 MHz OSC
CLK OUT 2	Used to drive the speaker

The 8254-2 timer/counter is treated by system programs as an arrangement of four programmable external I/O ports. Three are treated as counters; the fourth is a control register for mode programming.

2.1.4 System Interrupts

Sixteen levels of system interrupts can be provided by the 80286 NMI and two 8259A interrupt controller chips. Table 2-1 shows how the interrupt-level assignments are set in decreasing priority for MS-DOS.

2.1.4.1 ROM subsystem

The ROM subsystem is usually a 32K by 16-bit arrangement consisting of two 32K by 8-bit ROM/EPROM modules. The odd and even address codes reside in separate modules. The top of the first megabyte and the bottom of the last megabyte address space is assigned to ROM (hex 0F0000 and hex FF0000). Parity checking is not done on ROM. BIOS is supported and placed in this subsystem.

2.1.4.2 RAM subsystem

The RAM subsystem starts at hex address zero of the 16M address space. It may consist of 512KB, 640KB, or 1MB of 256K or 64K by 1-bit RAM modules. Memory refresh forces one memory cycle every 15 microseconds through channel 1 of the timer/counter. The following functions are performed by the RAM initialization program:

1. Write operation to any memory location.
2. Initialize channel 1 of the timer/counter to the rate generation mode (15 microseconds).

The memory can be used only after being accessed or refreshed eight times.

TABLE 2-1   80286 INTERRUPT-LEVEL ASSIGNMENTS FOR AT PCs

Level		Function
Microprocessor NMI		Parity or I/O channel check
Interrupt controllers		
CTLR 1	CTLR 2	
IRQ		Timer output 0
IRQ 1		Keyboard (output buffer full)
		INTERRUPT
IRQ 2		FROM CTLR 2
	IRQ 8	Real-time clock interrupt
	IRQ 9	Software redirected to INT OAH
		(IRQ 2)
	IRQ 10	Reserved
	IRQ 11	Reserved
	IRQ 12	Reserved
	IRQ 13	Coprocessor
	IRQ 14	Fixed disk controller
	IRQ 15	Reserved
IRQ 3		Serial port 2
	IRQ 4	Serial port 1
	IRQ 5	Parallel port 2
	IRQ 6	Diskette controller
	IRQ 7	Parallel port 1

2.1.4.3 Direct memory access

Eight DMA channels can be supported by the system. Two Intel 8237-5 DMA controller chips (four channels in each chip) can be used with the DMA channels assigned as follows:

CTLR 1	CTLR 2
Ch. 0, Spare	Ch. 4, Cascade for CTRL 1
Ch. 1, SDLC	Ch. 5, Spare
Ch. 2, Diskette	Ch. 6, Spare
Ch. 3, Spare	Ch. 7, Spare

Channels 0 through 3 are contained in DMA controller 1. Transfers of 8-bit data, 8-bit I/O adapter, and 8-bit or 16-bit system memory are supported by these channels. Each of these channels will transfer data in 64KB blocks throughout the 16-megabyte system address space.

Channels 4 through 7 are contained in DMA controller 2. To cascade channels 0 through 3 to the microprocessor, channel 4 is used. Transfers of 16-bit data between 16-bit adapters and 16-bit system memory are supported by channels 5,6, and 7. DMA channels 5 through 7 can transfer data in 1238K blocks throughout the 16-megabyte system address space. These channels will not transfer data on odd-byte boundaries.

The addresses for the page register are typically set as follows:

Page Register	I/O Hex Address
DMA channel 0	0087
DMA channel 1	0083
DMA channel 2	0081
DMA channel 3	0082
DMA channel 5	008B
DMA channel 6	0089
DMA channel 7	008A
Refresh	008F

Address generation for the DMA channels is typically as follows:
For DMA channels 3 through 0

Source	DMA Page Registers	8237A-5
Address	A23 $\longleftrightarrow$ A16ñ	A15 $\longleftrightarrow$ A0ῗ

To generate the addressing signal "byte high enable" (BHE), address line AO is inverted.
For DMA channels 7 through 5

Source	DMA Page Registers	8237A-5
Address	A23 $\longleftrightarrow$ A17	A16 $\longleftrightarrow$ A1ñ

The BHE and AO addressing signals are forced to a logic 0. DMA channel addresses do not increase or decrease through page boundaries (64 KB for channels 0 through 3 and 128 KB for channels 5 through 7).

2.1.4.4 I/O channel slots

The I/O channel supports

1. Refresh of system memory from channel microprocessors
2. Selection of data accesses, either 8 bit or 16 bit
3. 24-bit memory addresses (16MB)
4. I/O wait-state generation
5. I/O address space hex 100 to hex 3FF

6. Open-bus structure, allowing multiple microprocessors to share the system's resources, including memory
7. DMA channels

Numbering of the I/O slots for the IBM PC follows:

J1–J8 I/O Channels

GND —— B1		A1 ——————	I/O CH CK

+RESET DRV ——		——	+D7
+5V ——		——	+D6
+IRQ2 ——		——	+D5
−5VDC ——		——	+D4
+DRQ2 ——		——	+D3
−12V ——		——	+D2
Reserved ——		——	+D1
+12V ——		——	+D0

GND —— B10		A10 ——————	+I/O CH RDY

−MEMW ——		——	+AEN
−MEMR ——		——	+A19
−10W ——		——	+A18
−10R ——		——	+A17
−DACK3 ——		——	+A16
+DRO3 ——		——	+A15
−DACK1 ——		——	+A14
+DRO1 ——		——	+A13
−DACK0 ——		——	+A12
CLOCK —— B20	A20 ——	+A11
+IRQ7 ——		——	+A10
+IRQ6 ——		——	+A9
+IRQ5 ——		——	+A8
+IRQ4 ——		——	+A7
+IRQ3 ——		——	+A6
−DACK2 ——		——	+A5
+T/C ——		——	+A4
+ALE ——		——	+A3
+5V ——		——	+A2
+OSC ——		——	+A1
+GND —— B31	A31 ——	+AO

J10–J14 and J16 I/O Channels

−MEN CS 15 —— D1		C1 ——————	SBHE
−I/O CS 16 ——			LA23
IRQ 10 ——			LA22
IRQ 11 ——			LA21
IRQ 12 ——			LA20
IRQ 15 ——			LA19
IRQ 14 ——			LA18
−DACK0 ——			LA17

DRQ0 ——			—MEMR
—DACK5 ——	D10	C10	—MEMW
DRQ5 ——			SD08
—DACK6 ——			SD09
DRQ6 ——			SD10
—DACK7 ——			SD11
DRQ7 ——			SD12
+5VDC ——			SD13
—MASTER ——			SD14
GND ——	D18	C18	SD15

2.2 MATH COPROCESSOR CONTROL

The math coprocessor can function as an I/O device through I/O port addresses hex OF8, OFA, and OFC. The microprocessor sends OP codes and operands to the I/O ports. The microprocessor also receives and stores results through the same I/O ports. A "busy" signal sent by the coprocessor forces the microprocessor to wait until the coprocessor is finished executing.

2.3 MICROPROCESSOR GENERATIONS

Like other computer components, microprocessors have gone through several generations. The first generation of microprocessors was ushered in by the Intel 4004 and 8008. These calculator product chips had limited instruction sets and were based on p-channel MOS technology. The second generation began with the 4040 and 8080. These chips used larger instruction sets with up to 80 instructions and employed the faster n-channel MOS technology. The third generation began with the Intel 8086 uses a more sophisticated instruction architecture and improved high-density MOS technology.

2.4 MICROPROCESSOR REGISTERS

Inside, a personal computer's microprocessor registers help to control and keep track of the various operations. Every microprocessor must have the following registers.

2.4.1 Accumulators

The accumulator is the focal point for data manipulation operations. Here, numbers are added to or subtracted. Shift operators and complementing can be done, as well as many Boolean operations. Most of today's microprocessors use more than one register for these functions.

The accumulators function as temporary storage registers during calculations. The accumulator always holds one of the operands in arithmetic operations. Since the computer may also use accumulators in logical operations, shifts, and other instructions, accumulators are generally the most frequently used registers. With a single accumulator, programs spend more time moving data to and from the accumulator. Some chips such as the 8086 family have all eight of the general registers available as accumulators.

2.4.2 Instruction Registers

Instruction registers hold the instruction during the instruction decode and execute phase of microprocessor operation. This register receives the instructions from the program memory. The instruction register (IR) holds the instruction until it can be decoded. The bit length of the instruction register is the bit length of the basic instruction for the computer. Some computers use two instruction registers so they can save one instruction while executing the previous one while using "pipelining." The programmer can seldom access the instruction register.

2.4.3 Program Counters

The program counter or instruction pointer contains the address of the memory location which contains the next instruction. The instruction cycle typically begins with the CPU placing the contents of the program counter on the address bus; then the CPU fetches the first word of the instruction from memory and increments the contents of the program counter. This allows the next instruction cycle to fetch the next instruction in sequence from memory. When the instruction occupies more than one word of memory, the CPU increments the program counter each time it is used. In this way the CPU executes the instructions sequentially unless an instruction like a JUMP or BRANCH changes the program counter. Thus, the program counter keeps track of the processor's progress through the program. Often the processor has other instructions to modify the way the counter behaves such as decrementing instead of incrementing and skipping a count.

2.4.4 Stacks and Stack Pointers

The stack pointer is a register that contains the address of the top of a stack. The stack is the last-in, first-out (LIFO) buffer that is used for memory referencing. In most computer stacks, the stored elements do not actually move, the only change that occurs is in the stack pointer, which contains the address of the top of the stack. The CPU adds data to the stack by placing the data in the memory location addressed by the stack pointer and then incrementing (or decrementing) the stack pointer. It removes data from the stack by decrementing or incrementing the stack pointer and obtaining the data from the memory location addressed by the stack pointer. The elements in the stack do not move. The stack may be composed of read/write memory or a register array.

The major idea behind the use of a stack is that data can be added to it up to the capacity of the stack without disturbing the data that is already there. If this data were stored in a memory location or register, the previous contents would be lost. The stack can be used over and over since its previous contents are automatically saved. Also the CPU can quickly transfer data to or from the stack since the address is in the stack pointer and the stack instructions can be very short.

The major use of the stack is to store subroutine return addresses. Each JUMP TO SUBROUTINE instruction moves a return address from the program counter to the stack and each RETURN instruction fetches a return address from the stack and places it in the program counter. Thus the program can trace its path through the subroutines by using the stack. Some microprocessors use a dedicated stack to save the program counter. These systems have a minimum of status information and are limited in the calling subroutines or serving polled inputs and interrupts.

When the stack is in RAM for saving return address, certain locations of the data memory are assigned as the stack. These bytes provide the locations which will permit stacking. A counter will point initially to the first location. A CALL instruction increments this counter, and a RETURN decrements it. This configuration usually has a fixed depth. The stack register may also be used as conventional data memory.

The 6500 family (Apple II) uses a stack in data memory. A dedicated register of 8 bits in length points to the stack in the zero page of RAM. An instruction loads this stack pointer with a value to establish the location of the stack in RAM. This type of "context-switching" instruction increments or decrements this pointer as required.

Context switching can also be used with registers that are in memory and are pointed to by the contents of a "workspace" pointer. The context switch is initiated by a interrupt to fetch a new workspace pointer and program counter values from the interrupt vector. The current workspace pointer, program counter, and status register value are stored in a new workspace region. This type of stacking into successive workspace regimens can go to any depth in memory.

Another scheme takes the new value for the program counter from an addressed memory location and stores the current value of the program counter into the current workspace region. Return instruction are used to return control and status to the original condition. After the status information is stored, a polling interrupt service routine must restore the contents of the accumulator and working register so that these registers will be available for the service routine.

A major fault of the stack concept is the difficulty in debugging and documenting programs that use them. Since the stack does not use a fixed address, its location and contents can be difficult to determine. Lists of the current of the stack called dumps are useful for documentation purposes. The errors in stack usage can still be difficult to find. Typical errors include removing items from the stack in the wrong order, placing extra items in the stack, and removing extra items from it.

2.4.5 Flags

Condition code or status registers use 1-bit indicators or flags to represent the state of conditions inside the CPU. These flags form the basis for internal decision making. Different microprocessors use different types of flags. Table 2-2 illustrates flags.

Status registers evolved in the development of subroutine calling and interrupt techniques. The architecture proposed by von Neumann in 1946 had no convenient way of determining the return location from a subroutine which could be called from more than one place.

2.4.6 Index Registers

The index registers are used for addressing. The contents of such registers are added to the memory address which an instruction would use. This sum then becomes the actual address for the data or the effective address. When the con-

TABLE 2-2   TYPICAL MICROPROCESSOR FLAGS

Carry	Usually equal to 1 if the last operation generated a carry from the most significant bit. The CARRY flag uses a single bit of information to handle the carry from one word to the next in multiple-precision arithmetic.
Zero	Usually equal to 1 if the result of the last operation was zero, it is useful in loop control and for searching for a particular data value.
Overflow	Usually equal to 1 if the last operation produced a 2's complement overflow. The OVERFLOW bit determines if the result of the arithmetic operation exceeded the capacity of a data location or register.
Sign	Usually equal to 1 if the most significant bit of the result of the last operation was 1. It is sometimes called NEGATIVE, since the 1 indicates a negative 2's complement number. The SIGN bit is used in arithmetic or in examining single bits within a word.
Parity	Usually equal to 1 if the number of 1 bits in the result of the last operation was even for even parity or odd parity. PARITY is used for character manipulation and communications.
Half-Carry	Usually equal to 1 if the last operation generated a carry from the lower half-word.
Interrupt Enable	Usually equal to 1 if an interrupt is allowed or a 0 if not. The CPU can automatically disable interrupts during a start-up or service routine. The programmer can disable interrupts during critical timing loops or multiword operations. Several interrupt enable flags may be used if the CPU has several interrupt inputs or levels.

tents of the index register are changed, the same instruction can be used to handle data from different addresses. Data can also be moved from one location to another using index registers.

Auto indexing allows the index register to be automatically incremented or decremented each time it is used. This is useful in program loops.

Each instruction that uses index registers must contain codes to indicate when indexing is being used. When there is more than one index register, the instruction must also call out which one is to be used.

General-purpose registers can have a variety of functions. These registers can serve as temporary storage for data or addresses. The programmer may even be able to use them as accumulators or program counters.

2.5 ARITHMETIC-LOGIC UNITS

The arithmetic unit of microprocessors has evolved from simple adders to units which can perform several arithmetic and logical functions. If the arithmetic unit cannot perform a function directly, several instructions are required to produce the desired result.

Most of the arithmetic units use binary adders. These adders accept two binary inputs and produce the binary sum and a carry from the most significant bit of the addition. Since operations are usually performed in a 2's complement mode, subtraction is done by taking the 2's complement of one input before sending it to the adder. Multiplication and division may be performed by repeated additions and subtractions. Extra circuits are required to form status outputs, such as a zero or overflow indicator.

A typical ALU can have two data inputs, function inputs, a carry input for performing multiple-precision arithmetic, data outputs, and status outputs to set the various flags described earlier. The function inputs determine which function the ALU performs. A typical set is shown in Table 2-3.

2.6 MICROCOMPUTER ARCHITECTURES

Some modern computer architectures are patterned after the Mark I calculator, developed by Howard Aiken of Harvard University in the 1940s. This machine provided the architecture concepts of what is known as the Harvard machine

TABLE 2-3 ALU FUNCTIONS

Addition	NOT (complement)
Subtraction	Increment (add 1)
Multiplication	Decrement (subtract 1)
Division	Left shift (add input to itself)
AND	Clear (result is 0)
(INCLUSIVE) OR	
EXCLUSIVE OR	

architecture. It accepted programs on punched paper tapes, which controlled the electromechanical calculator. Aiken's work, which started in 1939, still provides the basic architecture in many microcomputers. In the Harvard architecture, the program memory and the data memory are separate. This separation of instruction storage and data storage gives the microcomputer designer flexibility in word size selection.

The major advantage of this architecture is that it permits an overlapping of the instruction and data accesses and tends to increase performance for a given technology, over that of the single-memory von Neumann architecture.

In the von Neumann architecture, both the data and instruction reside in the same memory. Therefore, the data word size sets the instruction word length as well. For example, for a data word size of 16 bits, the instruction word length must be 16 bits or some factor of 16 bits.

The Harvard machine is not restricted in this way. If the computer is to operate on 16-bit quantities, the instruction word length can be of any length, since there is no need to have these instructions reside in the same memory. Also, the various registers of the computer need not be of lengths which are multiples of the data word.

The program counter, for example, must be a length sufficient to address only the memory. The saving of return addresses can be handled by a small stack dedicated to this task or by a stack in the data memory.

The von Neumann architecture uses one address space, and data and instructions can be mixed within that space. Instructions can be used as data and processed by other instructions, and data may be used as instructions. In microprocessors of the von Neumann architecture, the instructions and operands must have lengths which are equal or are factors of each other. If the memory word length is 16 bits, the instruction and operand lengths must be 16 bits or some factor lengths, such as 8 or 24 bits. In practice, all lengths are multiples of the 8-bit byte.

The different types of computer architectures are due to variations such as the number of registers or arithmetic-logic circuits or by specifying the nature of the control exercised between these basic units.

The more sophisticated architectures may also define hierarchical levels of memories and processors and establish system control procedures for optimizing the use of system resources. Such architectures are now becoming implemented using microprocessors, and future applications of personal computer systems will require these features.

Some specific trends of microprocessor architectures in the past are shown in Table 2-4.

The allowable chip size and the need to save registers quickly when interrupts are being serviced tends to put a limit on the number of registers. A short word length forces the register addresses to be short in order to be handled easily. The use of RAM allows for temporary storage of data and addresses. The difficulty of addressing using short instruction words also makes more temporary storage desirable.

Most microprocessors use a stack for saving subroutine return addresses. Some use a limited on-chip stack, while others have their stacks in external read/

TABLE 2-4 MICROPROCESSOR ARCHITECTURE TRENDS

A limited chip size, which forced the chip to have a limited number of narrow registers and buses

The use of read-only program memory, which did not allow saving addresses or data in program memory

A limited read/write memory, which forced simple low-level applications

Short word lengths, which forced memory addresses to occupy several data words

An interrupt-driven operational concept, which services the registers with rapid recognition and servicing of interrupts

Special-purpose structures designed for specific applications, such as calculators, terminals, or control

write memory. These stacks require the proper initialization of the stack pointer and allow the stack to be as long as necessary.

Most microprocessors use special features for their registers in order to handle interrupts. These features can involve the use of a different set of registers during the interrupt service routine. Microprocessors with only a few internal registers can respond to interrupts quickly, since they have less data to save.

2.7 ASSEMBLY INSTRUCTION CHARACTERISTICS

The basic instruction set for most microprocessors fall into four groups. These types are basic to all computer systems and are shown in Table 2-5.

Data transfer or memory reference instructions perform operations on the data or program memory. They may also contain an arithmetic or logic function to complete the memory reference.

Data transfer instructions are used in setting up data addresses, returning from subroutines. They also allow the nesting of subroutines. Typical data transfer instructions take the form shown in Table 2-6.

The first three of these instructions may be used to modify the transfer addresses for the next instruction if required by the program. To replace the contents of an address in RAM, the LDA instruction is followed by an XDA instruction. To exchange the contents of two addresses in RAM, the LDA instruction would be followed by EXA and XDA instruction.

TABLE 2-5 ASSEMBLY INSTRUCTION TYPES

Transfer Instructions. These tell the CPU where in memory to load or access the instructions or data.

Arithmetic and Logic Instructions. These perform the number data manipulation.

Input and Output Instructions. These allow the processor to communicate with the external environment.

Jump and Branch Instructions. These modify the contents of the program counter so that the CPUs modify the flow of the program.

TABLE 2-6 DATA TRANSFER INSTRUCTION EXAMPLES

Three-letter mnemonic	Name	Description
LDA	Load accumulator	The contents of RAM currently addressed are placed in the accumulator
EXA	Exchange accumulator and memory	Same as a LDA except the contents of the accumulator are also placed in the currently addressed RAM location.
XDA	Exchange accumulator and memory and decrement	Same as an EXA except the RAM address in the transfer register is further modified by decrementing this register by 1.
LDA	Load accumulator	The contents of the instruction are placed in accumulator.

Basic arithmetic operations can be performed using the general types of instructions shown in Table 2-7.

ADD and the ADD WITH CARRY-IN instruction are among the most common arithmetic instructions. The ADD instruction may be used to initialize the adding operation for the first word of a multiword number to be added. It also may be used for additions that do not extend the basic word length for the microprocessor.

The DCC instruction adds a fixed constant to the accumulator. Addition of a constant will convert binary arithmetic operations to decimal arithmetic. This instruction is used to correct the sum in the accumulator to a binary-coded deci-

TABLE 2-7 ARITHMETIC INSTRUCTION EXAMPLES

Three-letter mnemonic	Name	Description
ADD	Add	The result of the binary addition of the contents of the accumulator and the contents of RAM currently addressed replace the contents of accumulator. The resulting carry-out is loaded into the carry status register.
ADC	Add with carry-in	Same as ADD except the carry register serves as a carry-in to ALU.
ADD	Add and skip carry-out	Same as ADD except the next ROM word will be skipped if a carry-out is generated.
Three-Letter ACS	Add with carry-in and skip on carry-out	Same as ADS except the carry register serves as a carry-in to the adder.
DCC	Decimal correction	A binary correction is added to contents of accumulator. Result is stored in accumulator. Instruction does not use or change carry register.

mal. Decimal subtraction can be performed when the subtrahend is loaded into the accumulator and complemented. Multiplication and division instructions are available in the 8086 family.

Logical instructions are used for performing Boolean logic operations. A sample of these is shown in Table 2-8.

The AND instruction will cause the contents of the accumulator to be modified depending on the contents of the addressed memory location. If there is a 1 in the corresponding bit positions of both words, then that bit position in the accumulator is retained as a 1. Any other combination in that bit will result in a zero in the corresponding bit position in the accumulator as shown here:

> 11001100 = Contents in the accumulator
>
> 01100110 = Contents in the memory location
> _____
>
> 01000100 = Logical AND result in the accumulator

The OR instruction causes the contents of the addressed memory location to be ORed with the contents of the accumulator. In the corresponding bit positions of the memory location and the accumulator, a 1 and a 0 will result in a 1, two 0's will result in a zero, and two 1's will result in a 1. This is shown here:

> 11001100 = Contents in accumulator
>
> 01100110 = Contents in memory location
> _____
>
> 11101110 = Logical OR result

The use of the EXCLUSIVE OR instruction will cause the appropriate bit in the accumulator to be set to 1 only when the corresponding bit positions in

TABLE 2-8   EXAMPLES OF LOGICAL OPERATIONS

Typical mnemonic	Name	Description
AND	Logical AND	The result of a logical AND of the accumulator and the contents of RAM currently addressed replace the contents of the accumulator.
OR	Logical OR	The result of a logic OR of the accumulator and the contents of RAM currently addressed replace the contents of the accumulator.
XOR	Logical exclusive OR	The result of a logic exclusive OR of the accumulator and the contents or RAM currently addressed replace the contents of the accumulator.
NOT	Complement	Each bit of the accumulator is logically complemented and placed in the accumulator.

memory are different. This is shown here:

$$11001100 = \text{Contents in accumulator}$$

$$01100110 = \text{Contents in memory location}$$

$$\overline{\hphantom{00000000}}$$

$$10101010 = \text{EXCLUSIVE OR result}$$

The logical COMPLEMENT will cause all of the bit positions in the accumulator to be set to their opposite value. If a particular bit position is initially a 0, it is set to 1, and if the bit position is initially 1, it is set to 0. This is shown here:

$$01010101 = \text{Contents in accumulator}$$

$$\overline{\hphantom{00000000}}$$

$$10101010 = \text{COMPLEMENT result}$$

Logical AND instructions are used to test or reset individual bits in RAM. To test an individual bit in RAM, the contents of the accumulator are set to 1 in the desired bit position and to 0 in all other bit positions. To reset a bit to 0, the contents of the accumulator in all bit positions except the desired positions are set to 1. The contents of the memory location are ANDed with the accumulator, and the result is stored in memory. This is known as bit masking.

The logical OR instruction is used to set bits in memory to 1. The desired bit position is set to 1 in the accumulator with all other bit positions set to 0. Then contents of the memory location are ORed with the accumulator and the result transferred to memory. This is sometimes called bit packing.

The EXCLUSIVE OR instruction is used for manipulating individual bit positions. For example, the individual bit positions can be inverted by loading the accumulator with all ones and then performing the EXCLUSIVE OR operation. The value in the accumulator can then be stored in memory. The EXCLUSIVE OR instruction may also be used to test for equality between the contents of the accumulator and the contents of the addressed memory location. Only when all the bits are identical will the contents of the accumulator remain 0.

The input/output instructions handle the transfer of data between the CPU and external devices or peripherals. The transfer can involve status and control signals as well as data. The input/output operations must reconcile any timing differences between the CPU and the peripherals, format the data properly, and handle the status and control signals. Any irregular transfers can be handled with interrupts. These are the control signals that receive the immediate attention of the control section and cause the suspension of normal operation. We consider the use of interrupts on input/output operations in Chapter 4.

The jump and loop instructions allow the microprocessor to move about nonsequentially within the program. A program might contain three tasks, A,B, and C, with each being a complete section or code or a subroutine; then, the microprocessor can be directed to perform them in any order. The program flow is controlled using the jump or branch instructions. This may be done as shown here:

```
0              Jump  to  44  (Program  C)
1
2
3
4              Program  A
  .
  .
  .

24
25
26                  Jump  to  62  (End)
27
28
29
30                  Program  B
  .
  .
  .

38
39
40                  Jump  to  04  (Program  A)
41
42
43
44                  Program  C
  .
  .
  .

57
58
59                  Jump  to  30  (Program  B)
60
61
62                    End  of  program
```

This type of jump or branch instruction is known as an unconditional jump since the jump will occur no matter what the external or internal conditions are. A more powerful jump command is the conditional jump, which will check the internal and external conditions before jumping. After meeting one of the specified conditions, the program changes flow. An example might be, if condition X is true, then jump to instruction X; otherwise, perform the next sequential instruction. Status register bits can serve as the checkpoints for these conditional jumps.

Instruction formats depend on the characteristics of the application environment. The functions more frequently used will tend to have the shortest, most compact format. These short formats are used for the most frequently executed operations to conserve memory.

The ease of decoding and control are also of importance since complication multifield, multistep formats complicate the control logic of the computer. It is better to have a sequence of two or three simple instructions for an operation than to implement a multistep, single-function instruction. The number of instruction bits is not increased while the control complexity is reduced. The multi-instruction functions usually have a longer execution time.

2.8 MICROPROCESSOR ADDRESSING

To get data or instructions into and out of the microprocessor, the information must be addressed and then transferred. The most basic technique used to address memory is direct addressing. No registers are involved.

2.8.1 Direct Addressing

Direct addressing includes the address of the relevant data within the instruction. This mode introduces some limitations to the system, since every time a data address is used, it must be included in the instruction. For example, if you wish to find the average of our numbers stored at addresses, A,B,C, and D, then one would write a program using direct addressing as shown here. This program leaves the result in the accumulator.

    Clear Accumulator
    Add A
    Add B
    Add C
    Add D
    Shift right
    Shift right

Both the number of instructions and the memory space can be reduced by using more complex addressing schemes. Direct addressing tends to be wasteful of bits. A fifth bit added to a 4-bit address adds 16 words to the memory, but a sixteenth bit added to a 15-bit address adds 32,768 words to the memory. Even short addresses can add to the program and memory space.

2.8.2 Indirect Addressing

Other techniques used to deal with addressing are indirect addressing and zero page addressing. The conventional form of indirect addressing uses registers which are pointed to by a field in the instructions. When the address registers are located in data memory, the address length is constrained to the same length as the data word or some multiple of the data word.

Some early computers were designed with short instructions. By reducing the length of the instructions, the available memory was used more effectively. One technique used two fields of 3 bits each which then pointed to two groups of eight registers which contained the addresses of the operands. Instructions were provided to load, index, and test these address registers. This scheme of indirect addressing is different than the more conventional type in which a direct address to memory finds the address of the operand.

Some microprocessors take this indirect addressing scheme one step farther. When there is only one data memory address register, there is no need for special bits in the instruction to select the address register. In those instructions which address the data memory, the use is implied in the instruction.

This is known as implied indirect addressing where the data memory is addressed by a register. Any instruction which references the memory uses the address preestablished in the register. There are instructions to load, increment, and test the address register. In some systems incrementing of the address register occurs automatically and concurrently with some of the instructions. The probability of the next location containing the desired data is high, so these compound instructions can save code space and execution time.

2.8.3 Page Addressing

In page addressing the page memory is small so only a small address is needed. Also, a short address can be used with a base plus displacement addressing scheme.

The high-order address byte can be stored in the processor, while the low-order address byte is specified by a direct addressing instruction. This works well when most of the addresses to be accessed are located near each other (on a same page) so they have the same high-order address byte.

In paging, one register is used to hold the page address and there must be instructions to manipulate the register contents, such as an increment or decrement command. The zero paging technique is used for small memory spaces. Here a single implied base register is assumed to contain the value zero. The address is then a displacement from this zero base.

The number of bits used in the instruction for addressing within the zero page will be small. For example, an 8-bit address will give a zero page of 256 words. Above the zero page size, an additional mode of addressing must be provided which takes the address out of the zero page.

2.8.4 Indexing

Indexing was developed to compress the coding. It allows a program loop to address data by adding a value to the address in the instruction. This value is then incremented or decremented to access the data array.

The indirect or implied indirect address registers can also be incremented, decremented, and tested for zero or some value and no address in the instruction is needed, only the index value in the indirect address register. Some systems address data memory with two registers, an X and a Y register. The address may then be manipulated using the instruction like the following:

```
TRANSFER ACCUMULATOR TO MEMORY AND INCREMENT
TRANSFER CONSTANT TO MEMORY AND INCREMENT
INCREMENT X,  IF CARRY,  1 = STATUS
DECREMENT X,  IF NO BORROW,  1 = STATUS
X / A,  1,  = STATUS
X / C,  1 = STATUS
COMPLEMENT Y
```

These instructions establish a loop which generates the addresses to the data memory. Some systems use implied indirect addressing with an indirect scratch-pad register to address the data memory. This register may have the low-order bits automatically incremented or decremented during the execution of instructions which reference the data memory. The higher-order bits may be modified by a load or add. The lower bits may be tested for all ones and then a branch taken for looping.

Some microprocessors combine the indirect address register scheme with indexing. An instruction such as DECREMENT REGISTER AND JUMP ON REGISTER NOT ZERO provides the dual functions of an indirect address register and the index. These three indexing systems are summarized in Table 2-9.

2.8.5 Base Registers

These registers extend a limited address to a larger address. The base register is used to point to a region of memory where the displacement takes place.

In one simple technique the data memory is divided in half and an instruction is provided which will select bank A or bank B. This in effect provides two base registers with an implied selection.

Base registers also provide a technique for program segment relocation which is the binding of the program segments into an absolute address.

TABLE 2-9 TYPICAL INDEXED INSTRUCTION SEQUENCES

#SEQUENCES		
1. OPERATION	1. OPERATION AND INCREMENT OR DECREMENT	1. OPERATION
2. INCREMENT	2. TEST AND BRANCH	2. DECREMENT, TEST, AND BRANCH
3. TEST AND BRANCH		

Segmented instruction addressing is used in microcomputers where the ROM is subdivided into pages and other segments. The size is determined by the number of bits which can be contained in the instruction word. For example, 6 bits could be reserved for the address within a page of 64 words.

2.8.6 Segment Registers

The addressability of the memory can be extended beyond the instruction word limit by another register which addresses the segments. Extensions beyond the word length are accomplished by adding additional bits to the address. Special instructions may be dedicated to the manipulation of these registers.

A branch from a segment requires that two branch instructions be executed. The first one prepares to branch into a new segment by changing the value in a segment address buffer. The branch instruction may load the immediate value into the program counter and swap the contents of the address register and the buffer. Another procedure for a segmented memory system is to establish a logical address with a short address register implemented hardware. For short branches and calls, an 8-bit displacement can be added to the program counter, using this short relative address to conserve program memory. Some typical forms of these instructions are shown here:

```
BRANCH
(1)  CONDITIONAL,  8-BIT IMMEDIATE,  RELATIVE
(2)  UNCONDITIONAL,  8-BIT IMMEDIATE,  RELATIVE
(3)  UNCONDITIONAL,  16-BIT IMMEDIATE,  ABSOLUTE
CALL
(1)  COMPUTED,  16-BITS ABSOLUTE
(2)  UNCONDITIONAL,  16-BIT IMMEDIATE,  ABSOLUTE
```

TABLE 2-10   8086 ADDRESS CALCULATION TIME

Address type, registers		Clocks
Displacement only		6
Base or index only	(BX, BP, SI, DI)	5
Displacement + base or index	(BX, BP, SI, DI)	9
Base + index	BP + DI, BX + SI	7
	BP + SI, BX + DI	8
Displacement + base + index	BP + DI + DISP. BX + SI + DISP.	11
	BP + SI + DISP. BX + DI + DISP.	12

Note: Add two clocks for segment override.

The use of relative addresses will reduce the average bytes per branch or call while giving the flexibility of a larger address space.

Table lookup in a Harvard-class microcomputer requires that the separate data and instruction memories have a connective path so that a value in the data memory or accumulator can serve as an address to the program memory. The value in the addressed location is then returned to CPU as the desired table entry.

One technique is to use the value in the accumulator as an address for the active or current page of segment. The value in the memory location is returned

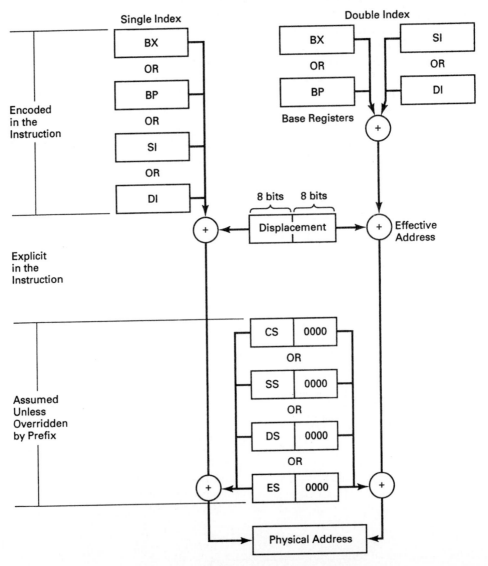

Figure 2-1   8086 Memory Address Computation

to the accumulator as the table entry. Two registers can also be used to address the memory for table lookup. These registers function as data counters. Instructions load and store the counter registers from a memory load with an immediate value and exchange the contents of the two counter registers.

Figure 2-1 shows the 8086 computing a memory address by summing a displacement, a base register, and index register. Table 2-10 shows the clock periods required for address computation.

Segmentation and addressing mechanisms are based on 16 bits. The 8086 has 95 basic instructions, some of which are only 8 bits long. In the 16-bit instructions, only the first 8 bits are used for operation codes and the additional byte specifies the data displacement.

2.9 MICROPROCESSOR CONTROL SIGNALS

Some of the early microprocessors used the PMOS process and 18-pin packages. Eight pins were used for the 8-bit bidirectional data bus along with two clock signals.

Three lines were used to indicate the state of the microprocessor to external circuitry.

1. A SYNC output indicated the beginning of a new machine cycle when information can be sent out.
2. A READY line was used to stop the operation of the microprocessor temporarily.
3. An interrupt input was used to change the execution sequence of the program.

Address information was multiplexed over the 8-bit bidirectional data bus. At the beginning of a machine cycle requiring a read from or write to memory, the address information is put on the data bus, after being saved or latched by external circuitry.

The address word was 14 bits long so the 8 low-order bits were sent out and latched and then the 6 high-order bits were sent out and latched. This multiplexing of address information reduces performance. The next microprocessors used an 8-bit bidirectional data bus for transferring data and an address of 16 bits. Some microprocessors used the data bus to propagate status information during a certain state of each machine cycle by multiplexing the data bus externally. This required system chip is called the system controller.

An INTERRUPT REQUEST line was used to request interrupt sequences. The processor would wait until the current instruction was completed before it recognized the request. Then, if an interrupt mask bit in a condition register was not set, the interrupt sequence began:

1. The contents of the index register, program counter, accumulator, and condition code register were stored in the stack.

2. The CPU set an interrupt mask bit so that no additional interrupts could occur.

3. An address was then loaded which allowed the CPU to branch to the interrupt routine.

A NONMASKABLE INTERRUPT is one that allows the processor to complete the current instruction; then the contents of the index register, program counter, accumulator, and condition code register are stored in the stack; then an address is loaded to allow the CPU to branch to the nonmaskable interrupt which is not affected by the condition code register. A HALT stopped all activity at the end of an instruction. A VALID MEMORY ADDRESS is used to signal to the peripheral devices that there is a valid address on the address bus. A BUS AVAILABLE line is normally in a low state until the microprocessor stops and the address bus becomes available.

A DATA BUS ENABLE line removed the data bus from a high-impedance condition, and a RESET line would reset and start the microprocessor from a power-down condition or during the initial startup of the system. A READ/WRITE line signaled the peripherals and memory devices when the microprocessor is in a read or write state.

In the 8086 the data bus is 16 bits wide and the address bus has 20 bits with the lower 16 multiplexed on the data bus. Since the 20 address lines are latched, address information appears only at the beginning of a machine cycle, during the T1 state. One of the control outputs, BHE, also appears only during T1. When BHE is low, the high byte of the data bus can then be used for a data transfer during the other states of that machine cycle.

The 20-bit address bus allows the direct access of 1 megabyte of memory using addresses OOOOOH to FFFFFH.

Many of the control lines of the 8086 control bus are similar to those of other microprocessors. The clock input (CLK) accepts the clock pulses. The 8086 has a nonmaskable interrupt request input line (NMI) and a maskable interrupt request line (INTR). A READY line is used to stop the processor during a machine cycle.

The RESET line is a little difficult since following a logic "1" reset signal, the 8086 begins its execution at location FFFFOH rather than at location OOOOOH. TEST is a control input which may be tested by the wait for test instruction. If the TEST input is low, excecution continues; otherwise, the processor will wait until this input does go low. The RD output indicates a memory or an input port read operation.

The complete 16-bit data bus may be used for a data transfer in a machine cycle only when both Bus High Enable and Address Lines are low during T1 of that machine cycle. Eight lines of the control bus can serve one of two functions depending on whether the 8086 is in minimum or maximum configuration. The Minimum/Maximum Mode control input line selects one of these two modes. When this line is high, the minimum mode is selected and the eight lines function as follows. INTRA is used to acknowledge interrupts. Address Latch Enable appears during T1 and is used to strobe the address and Bus High Enable latches.

If the 8286 bus driver is connected to the data bus, Data Enable enables the outputs of the drivers while Data Transmit/Receive sets the direction of the bus drivers. Memory/IO control distinguishes a memory cycle from an I/O cycle. WR is used to indicate a write operation to memory or an output port. HOLD and Hold Acknowledgement are used to initiate and acknowledge DMA operations.

When the MN/MX line is low, the 8086 is in the maximum select mode. Now OSO and QS1 are used as status bits used to provide information on the status of the internal instruction queue. Status bits S0, S1, and S2 are used to encode information that, in the minimum mode, appeared on five pins, these status bits are decoded using the 8288 bus controller.

The three remaining signal lines are used for multiprocessor systems. The LOCK output is under the control of the program, and it is used to prevent other processors from controlling the bus. Two request/grant pins are used to force the processor onto a Hold state to give up control of the bus. RQ/GT0 has a higher priority than does RQ/GT1.

The address space of 1 megabyte is implemented through a memory segmentation scheme with 64K segments. Memory segments of up to 64KB are placed on an 8-bit boundary.

Interfacing the PC Memory

This chapter shows you how

- Microprocessor input/output operates
- Mapping memory for input/output functions is accomplished
- Auxiliary storage is used in personal computers

Once the processing inside the PC is complete, the next concern is how to communicate with the peripherals. The information has been gathered and processed; now this information must be stored in memory or sent out to control other devices. This requires the use of input/output techniques.

A 16-bit microprocessor will use 16 pins for the movement of data into and out of the chip. These pins are known as the data bus, and the information can usually flow in both directions along the bus at different times. The directional data bus concept is used by most microprocessors since it reduces the number of pins in the package.

The microprocessor also has a set of pins which carry the binary numbers known as addresses. These pins are called the address bus. The address bus carries the information out from the microprocessor to ROM, RAM, or I/O chips. The signals on the address bus are then used to select a certain memory or I/O chip and to select a particular location inside that chip.

There is also a group of assorted signals that enter and leave the microprocessor. Some of these control signals were discussed in Chapter 1. These signals are sometimes grouped together and called the control bus.

The control bus contains the control logic signals which operate the sequence of operations for the microprocessor. This logic controls the various cycles and data transfers through the internal bus system. It also provides the external signals which indicate to other modules the status of the microprocessor at any particular time.

For example, during an instruction fetch cycle, the microprocessor may generate a status signal which requests an instruction from memory. In an execute cycle the microprocessor may be in a memory-read, a memory-write, or an input/output status. The bidirectional bus buffers are controlled by the status request. When the microprocessor is requesting data from the external environment, the bidirectional bus is placed in an input mode. If it sends data to the external environment, the bus buffers are then placed in the output mode, and the information is placed on the data bus.

If only one external data bus is available to the microprocessor, it must be used alternately for data, addresses, and instructions. A double bus system allows one bus for data and instructions and the other for addresses. The control information usually does not have a special bus. A double bus system allows data and addresses to be transferred back and forth simultaneously in the same cycle without waiting for the sequential use of a common bus; however, a multiple bus requires a larger number of pins.

Bus buffers to control the direction of information flow are usually constructed with tristate gates as shown in Figure 3-1. The control input of each

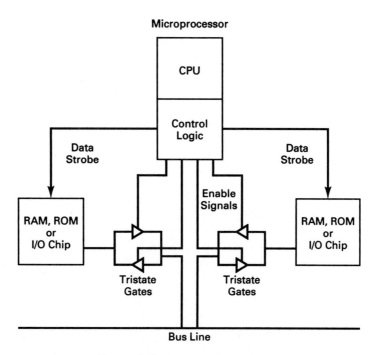

Figure 3-1 Tristate Buffer Operation

tristate gate controls its output, so when this control input is enabled, the output of the gate is equal to the input value. When the control input is disabled, the output of the buffer is disabled regardless of the input condition. Selection lines are used to place the data bus lines in an input or output status. The selection lines may also be used to inform external modules of the status condition in which the data bus is at a particular time.

3.1 MEMORY ADDRESSES

The internal memory of the PC system contains storage units, consisting of array semiconductor cells with two stable states to represent the 0's and the 1's. The memory is organized into bytes or words, which may have the same bit length as the data registers, data buses or arithmetic-logic unit.

The memory is arranged sequentially into bytes or words, with each having a unique address. An address segment is a binary number that can range from 0 to 65,535 (for a 64KB segment).

These binary numbers, since they are 16 bits long, are difficult to work with, and it is also clumsy to think of the addresses in decimal form, since it requires some effort to convert back and forth between the decimal number and the pattern for 16 bits.

To debug the system, it is necessary to work comfortably with these 16-bit or longer addresses. All these external devices are selected by the microprocessor placing addresses on the address bus.

These hex codes are much easier to work with and to remember, and conversion back and forth from the bit patterns is much simpler. To aid in the conversion, try to visualize patterns in the conversion chart of the bits and the letter/number codes as shown in Table 3-1. The usual technique is to work with the

TABLE 3-1 ROM ADDRESS MAP

	—0	1	2	3	4	5	6	7	8	9	A	B	C	D	E	F
—																
A																
Row B	OB00														OBFF	OB
0 C																OC
D																OD
E																OE
F															OFFF	OF
Row 0																
1 1																
2																
3																
4																

addresses in hexadecimal form. Here, the bits are broken up into groups of 4 bits each, with each group represented by a code, consisting of a letter or number. An address that is 16 bits long, then, is given as four of these number codes.

Some memories may contain either data or instructions, both of which may be represented as similar binary numbers. A microcomputer that uses the same format and memory for data instructions is known as a von Neumann machine. These systems must distinguish between an instruction or a piece of data so the microprocessor must know what to expect at a particular time. If the program is in error at any particular time, the microprocessor may interpret data as instructions.

The different devices external to the PC must also be addressed through the I/O chips that allow connection to the outside environment. The first 4-bit patterns begin with 00; the next 4 with 01; the next 4 with 10; and the last 4 with 11. This is the sequence for a 2-bit binary number: 00, 01, 10, 11. Also note that the groups of 4 in going down the table start with 0, 4, 8, and C and the last 2 bits of each pattern go through the same sequence—00, 01, 10, 11—as one goes through the set 4, 5, 6, 7.

The first 2 bits give the starting point which is 0, 4, 8, or C. Use the last 2 bits to sequence within the group. Thus, 1111 is in the group that starts with C, and it is the last one in that group, so it is 11.

In summary, we start with the letter/number code, denoting the group to obtain the first 2 bits and note where it is in the group, to obtain the last 2 bits. For longer words, the conversion from an address as 23F to its binary equivalent is 0010, 0010, 0011, 1111, 1110, and easily done using hex codes.

3.2 MEMORY CYCLE CHARACTERISTICS

In a memory system, access time is the time difference betwen the time a memory unit receives a read signal and the time when the information read from memory is available at its outputs. In a destructive read memory, information read out is destroyed during the reading process. It is automatically restored, but this requires an additional time. The sum of the access time and restoration time is called the cycle time.

In a nondestructive read memory, the cycle time is the same as the access time since no restoration is required. In a random access memory, the access time is always the same, regardless of the word's location in memory. In a sequential memory, the access time depends on the position of the word at the time of the request.

3.3 MEMORY MAPPING

One major reason for using decimal numbers is to verify that there is enough room in memory. There is a way to do this in hex decimal without converting to decimals. A map can be made of the memory as in Table 3-2.

TABLE 3-2   MEMORY MAP FOR A 64K MEMORY

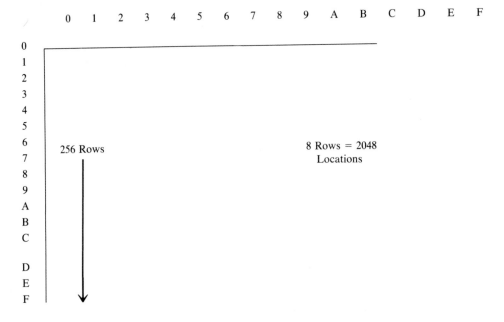

Let the memory space contain 65,536 locations; then divide it up into 256 rows with 256 locations in each row. Then, a 2K memory of 2048 locations is 8 rows on the map, and an 8K memory of 8192 locations is 32 rows.

Let the map be marked on the left side with the hex digits 0 to F as shown. These correspond to the leftmost digits of the address. Note that between each pair of digits there are 16 rows also numbered from 0 to F; this corresponds to the second digit. The digits 0 to F along the top edge of the map correspond to the third digit. Between each pair of digits are 16 locations again numbered 0 to F to produce the fourth digit.

This mapping technique allows the movement about the memory space using hex addresses to set the locations of the various block boundaries. An 8K memory block (8192 locations) would be within 32 rows on the map.

As an example, consider selecting a small section of ROM with addresses that go from 0B00 to 0FFF hex. The first two hex digits indicate the row of the memory map. This memory occupies rows 0B, 0C, 0D, 0E, and 0F. The locations in the first row range from addresses 0B00 to 0BFF, and the others are similar, so that the fifth-row locations range from 0F00 to 0FFF. Since each row contains 256 locations, the ROM section must have 1280 locations.

To address one location out of the 1280, 11 bits are needed for the address, since 10 bits will give only 1024 locations (2^{10} = 1024).

By carefully choosing the addresses in RAMs, the number of address bits required can be minimized. In this example, the 11 least significant address bits are being used. These are the address bits A0 to A10. A11 and A12 can be used to distinguish among the chips. In this case let them be a ROM, a RAM, and two I/O chips.

Let the addresses for bits A11 and A12 be 00 for the RAM, 01 for one I/O, 10 for the other I/O chip, and 11 for the ROM. When A11 and A12 are both 1's, the ROM is selected, and the address of the first or starting location in the ROM is 000 1000 0000 0000. Converting each set of 4 bits to hex, this becomes 1800. If the ROM has 1024 locations, then the addresses in the ROM will go to OFFF, which is 000 1011 1111 1111. Note the 10 least significant bits have all changed from 0's to 1's to include the 1024 locations.

In the addressing of the other chips, we must be careful not to cause the address bits 12 through A0 to use any values that could activate the ROM. Thus, the combinations used for 12 and 11 cannot be used for any other functions or devices. Bits A15, A14, and A13 are not critical in this simple case because we have only used A11 and A12. Since the first 3 bits of the address are not critical, the microprocessor can address one of the chips with any of 12 different first digits, and it will still operate the same.

It is generally convenient to place the RAM addresses in the lower range starting from 0000, while the ROM address space is in the next range. The RAM could start at 0000 since the programs in the ROM will be referring to data stored in the RAM. These programs must include addresses for the data in the RAM, and keeping the addresses short will save ROM memory space. Microprocessors with short instructions can save this space.

The starting address for the ROM depends on several considerations. When an interrupt occurs, the microprocessor should stop what it is doing and immediately begin another operation. The instructions in the ROM for this operation will begin at some other location in the ROM and the microprocessor must be directed to these. In some microprocessors when an interrupt occurs, the microprocessor will always use the same locations to get the address which directs it to where it should begin executing the interrupt operations. In the 6800 this is FFF8 and FFF9, in which we store the address of the start of the new operation and we want to store that address in the ROM, along with the rest of the program.

A basic addressing need in ROM is the program counter which points to the location of the current program step. Incrementing of the program counter is used to change its value. There is also a need for a random address system which will allow a change in the value of the program counter for branching, subroutine calls, and returns.

This section of the microcomputer can have a larger influence on the static program storage efficiency. Branch and subroutine calls may be over 50% of all functional instructions in some systems. These instructions need to have the longest addresses. A basic technique is to keep those addresses short that are used most to select a location within a component. In performing this function, two selections must be performed. First, the device must be selected, and then the location within the device must be selected.

3.4 MICROCOMPUTER DECODING TECHNIQUES

There are two basic techniques which are used to perform the component address-ing functional, although there are a variety of internal decoding techniques which may be implemented on the devices themselves both for the chip select and the location functions. Relative to the address bus connections, these basic tech-niques are linear selection and decoded addressing.

The linear selection technique which we have just discussed uses a line of the address bus to select a component. If a function requires an 8K memory, 13 bits of the address are reserved for this function since $2^{13} = 8K$. The other 3 bits can be used for chip selects.

In medium to large systems, the major limitation of this technique quickly becomes the number of addressable devices; however, it is frequently used in smaller systems that require a smaller amount of memory and few I/O chips.

Another consideration in the use of linear selection is the fragmenting of the address space since each time an address line is used, the addressing space is divided in half. This produces discrete address blocks in the addressing space which may not be fully utilized. Since these blocks are discrete, programming can be a little more difficult because of the caution that must be exercised in address-ing the various blocks. When blocks are not used, they become gaps or disconti-nuities in the memory space which must be considered when working with the program.

In decoded addressing the lines are connected to a decoder which then selects the components. A typical decoder might accept three inputs and select one of eight possible outputs. A small ROM could also be used to implement the decoding function. Combinations of decoder chips and ROMs can also be used for decoding in systems with many memory and I/O chips. The decoder chips can vary in the number of bits fed to the memory chips and in the number of inputs used to generate the select code.

RAMs for data memory are decoded in a similar manner, with extra circuits provided for the read and write functions. The chip select must be true for either a read or write to take place. When both the chip select and write signals are true, the output drivers of the RAM will be in a high-impedance state allowing the data on the data bus to be stored in the RAM's memory cells.

Decoder circuits can also be constructed with logic comparators as shown in Figure 3-2. This technique is used when it is desirable to have flexibility in the address selection. In systems which may require unique address selection fea-tures, combinational logic can be used to implement the addressing function.

Most microprocessor manufacturers have decoding chips which are de-signed to be used with their microprocessors. The lower-order address bits are sent to the memory's address lines while the higher-order bits are used for the decoding as shown in Figure 3-3. The 8205 has been widely used in many Intel-based systems. When a large address space is used, the required decoders be-come complex.

A number of alternatives can be used. This includes a partial decoding which is combined with linear addressing. Another simpler approach is to use

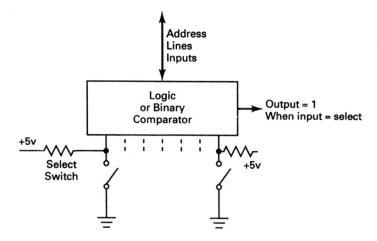

Figure 3-2   Address Decoding with Logic Comparators

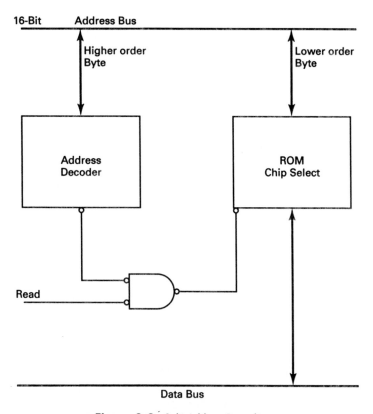

Figure 3-3   Split Address Decoding

components which are equipped with multiple-chip selects or enables. These devices provide the address decoding within the component. If three-chip selects are provided, three lines from the address bus are directly connected to these pins. Provided that all chips connected to the system decode a different combination, then the necessity of external decoding disappears. In the 6800 system each device has three-chip selects or more, and a multiple-chip system can be built without any decoders. Many peripheral interface chips use multiple-chip select inputs. These chips can also be ganged using the decoding technique that we have discussed to construct larger systems.

The need for memory expansion requires the consideration of various technical factors. There will be many cases where the user will want to provide memory expansion capability for the microcomputer. This additional instruction memory and/or data memory must have a planned addressing scheme. This requirement is originally based on the memory needs of a particular application which may exceed the capability of the system in the future.

A memory management system which allows almost unlimited memory can be employed. For instruction memory expansion, a pointer expansion technique may be used. A pointer address register is provided, which can point to one of a number of banks or segments.

Another technique involves instruction memory expansion with the program counter. Here, a bit is set and reset with special instructions or logic. The effective address enable additional bytes of instruction storage. The addresses are then automatically routed by the expansion logic. Other similar techniques that can be used involve the use of additional registers as program counters.

3.5 MODULAR TECHNIQUES

A memory unit can be organized in a number of modules. Each module has its own address register and buffer register. The two most significant bits of the address can be used to distinguish between four modules. A memory controller then routes the address from the bus to the words which match the specified content. This type of search can be done on an entire word or on a field within a word.

An associative memory is more expensive than a random access memory since each cell must contain the storage facilities as well as some logic facilities for matching the content. Associative memories are normally used in only those applications where the search time is critical.

3.6 AUXILIARY STORAGE

Almost all computers run more efficiently if there is additional storage beyond the capacity of the main memory. Many industrial applications tend to accumulate large amounts of information; thus, there may be a continued need for memory expansion since not all the information is needed at the time of installation. It is also cost effective to use lower-cost storage media which serves as a backup for holding the information that is not currently required to be in use.

The memory that communicates directly with the CPU is known as the main memory, and the devices that are used to provide the backup storage form the auxiliary memory. Typical auxiliary memory devices include magnetic disks and tapes. The programs and data currently needed by the processor will reside in the main memory while the other information which is stored in auxiliary memory is transferred to the main memory when needed.

A buffer memory is sometimes used to compensate for the speed differential between the main memory access time and the processor logic. The processor logic may be faster than the main memory access time with the result that the processing speed is limited by the speed of the main memory. To compensate for the mismatch in operating speed a high speed, smaller memory can be used between the processor and main memory with an access time closer to the processor logic delay. This type of memory is also called a cache memory and is used in some 386 PCs.

The total memory capacity of the microcomputer can be viewed as a hierarchy of components as shown in Figure 3-4. This hierarchy consists of all the

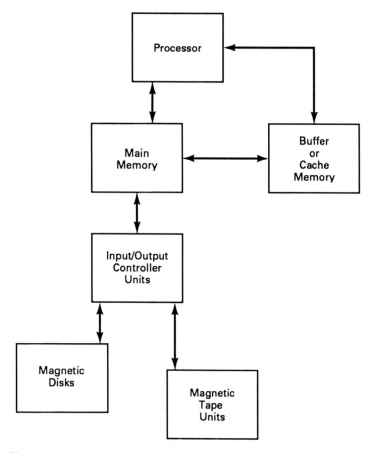

Figure 3-4   The Memory System as Viewed as a Hierarchy of Components

storage devices used by the microcomputer system ranging from the slow, high-capacity auxiliary devices to the faster semiconductor main memory.

The cost per bit of storage is proportional to the storage device's level in this hierarchy. It is not effective to maintain large programs and data in the main memory during the time when they are not required by the processor.

The memory management system, which is a combination of hardware and software, will distribute the programs and data to the various levels in the memory hierarchy according to their demand by the application. The memory management system can be configured to provide the most efficient method of the use of the various levels. The proper management configuration should tend to maximize the utilization of all the components.

The most common mass or auxiliary memory devices used in microcomputer systems are magnetic disks and tape. Although the physical characteristics of these storage devices differ, their system properties can be characterized by a few parameters. The most important characteristics are access time, transfer rate, capacity, and cost. The average time required to reach a location in memory is called the access time. In electromechanical devices such as disks and tapes, the access time consists of a seek time required to position the read/write head and the transfer time to transfer data to or from the device. The seek time is typically much longer than the transfer time.

Auxiliary storage is usually organized in records or blocks to aid the retrieval of data. A record is a specified number of characters or words and usually reading or writing is done on entire records. The device transfer rate is the number of characters or words that the device can transfer per second, after it is positioned at the beginning of a record.

3.6.1 Magnetic Disks

Magnetic disks use a rotating surface coated with a magnetic recording medium. The recording surface rotates at uniform speed. The bits are recorded as magnetic spots on the surface as it passes the write head.

The bits are detected by sensing the change in magnetic field produced by the recorded spots on the surface as it passes the read head. The amount of surface available on a disk is a function of the type of electromechanical assembly used. In some units both sides of the disk are used, and larger units may use several disks stacked on a spindle.

Some units use a single read/write head for each disk and the address bits are used to move the head to the specified track position for a read or write operation. In other systems, separate read/write heads are used for each track on each disk. The address bits then select a particular track with a decoder circuit. This type of unit is more expensive and is used in larger systems.

Timing tracks are used to synchronize the bits and recognize the sectors which form the recording tracks. The disk is then addressed by bits that specify the disk number, disk surface, sector number, and the track using the disk controller. As the read/write heads are positioned on the specified track, the system waits until the rotating disk reaches the specified sector under the head. The information transfer then starts once the beginning of a sector is reached. Some units use multiple heads for the simultaneous transfer of bits from several tracks to improve the transfer rate.

Since a track near the circumference is longer than a track near the center of the disk, if bits are recorded with equal density, some tracks will contain more bits than others. Thus, to make all the records in a sector of equal length, a variable recording density may be used with a higher density on tracks near the center than on tracks near the circumference.

3.6.2 Floppy Disks

A common mass memory for microcomputers is the floppy disk, which is a soft magnetic disk using a movable head. The disk is divided into sectors which resemble slices and tracks of concentric rings.

The flexible disk is plastic coated with a magnet recording medium approximately the size and shape of a 45-rpm record. The disk can be inserted and removed easily. The typical size of a data block in a sector is 128 words and the typical floppy disk can supply 125K bits per second. The drive mechanism uses a disk controller to interface with the microcomputer system.

Typically, the drive motor rotates the spindle at 360 rpm, with the average access time of about 80 ms. A single $5\frac{1}{4}$ inch floppy disk may be divided into 77 tracks with 26 sectors on each track and 128 8-bit words on each sector.

Most microcomputer systems require two disks. The requirement for this is that if the floppy disks are typically used for large files, which are to be sorted, or merged, then one may need access to two files simultaneously. A dual-disk drive is usually only a little more expensive than a single drive, and it operates off the same controller.

The main advantage of the floppy disk system is that it is inexpensive to manufacture since the drives do not need the critical tolerances required for rigid disk to minimize crashing the head and damaging the recording surface. The main advantage of rigid disk systems are the faster access times of up to 50 microseconds and larger capacity.

3.6.3 Hard Disks

A hard disk memory uses 1 to 10 rigid metal disks that are stacked and driven together with a common drive. The popular Winchester drive uses a sealed disk package which also contains the recording head. These units can be made small, and this technology has become the most popular memory system for microcomputers. Removable cartridge drives are available with 9 or 14 inch disks with capacities from 80 Mb to 1.6 Gb.

Removable and replaceable disk files are available in the form of disk packs. These removable groups of disks share a common spindle and offer an alternative to fixed-head disks or magnetic tape.

One type of disk pack design uses six 14 inch diameter disks which are mounted on a common spindle, 0.35 inch apart. The 10 inside disk surfaces are used for recording, while the outer 2 surfaces are not used. The data is recorded on 200 tracks, at bit densities varying from 765 to 1105 bits/inch, using a 2 inch wide band on each surface. Table 3-3 lists the major design characteristics for magnetic disk pack units. Trade-offs between performance (primarily the access times) and costs determine the choice for a particular application.

3.6.4 Magnetic Tape Memories

A magnetic tape transport system contains the electrical, mechanical, and electronic components required to control for magnetic tape reels or cartridges. The tape is a plastic that is coated with magnetic particles to provide a recording medium. The bits are recorded as spots on the tape along several tracks. Usually 7 or 9 bits are recorded simultaneously to form a character along with a parity bit. The read/write heads are mounted side by side with one for each track so the data can be recorded and read as a sequence of characters.

A $10\frac{1}{2}$ inch reel of tape may contain 2400 feet of $\frac{1}{2}$ inch wide tape and store 160 to 200 million bits. Most tapes use a base 1.42 mils thick and a magnetic coating of oxide of about 400 microinches thick.

Magnetic tape units may be stopped, started to move in forward or reverse, or rewound. They cannot be started or stopped fast enough between individual characters. So the information is recorded in blocks known as records.

Gaps of unrecorded tape are inserted between the records where the tape can be stopped. The tape starts moving while in a gap and attains a constant

TABLE 3-3 MAGNETIC DISK SYSTEMS

Floppy drives

$3\frac{1}{2}''$ half-height microfloppy with 1MB (unformatted) capacity, 135 tracks per inch
$5\frac{1}{4}''$ half-height floppy, 500KB (unformatted) capacity, 48 tpi
$5\frac{1}{4}''$ half-height floppy, 1MB (unformatted) capacity, 96 tpi
$5\frac{1}{4}''$ half-height floppy, 1.6MB (unformatted) capacity, 96 tpi (IBM AT compatible)
$8''$ floppy, 1.6MB (unformatted) capacity, 48 tpi

Winchester disk drives

$5\frac{1}{4}''$ 20MB (formatted) half-height Winchester disk drive, average access time of 85 ms
$5\frac{1}{4}''$ 45MB (formatted) half-height Winchester disk drive, average access time of 40 ms
$5\frac{1}{4}''$ 173MB (unformatted) full-height, 23 ms average access time
$8''$ 85MB (unformatted) Winchester disk drive, average access time of 25 ms
$8''$ 82.9MB (unformatted) Winchester disk drive, average access time of 18.5 ms, power supply optional
$8''$ 167.7MB (unformatted) Winchester disk drive, average access time of 20 ms, power supply optional
$8''$ 337MB (unformatted) Winchester disk drive, average access time of 20 ms, power supply optional
$9''$ 520MB (unformatted) Winchester disk drive, average access time of 15 ms
$9''$ 520MB (unformatted), 15 ms average access time
$9''$ 800MB (unformatted), 15 ms average access time

---

speed by the time it reaches the next record. Each record has an identification pattern at the beginning and the end. Reading the bit pattern at the beginning, the tape control identifies the record number, and reading the bit pattern at the end of the record, the control recognizes the beginning of a gap.

Supply and take-up reels have a high inertia and are generally isolated from the mechanism which drives the tape past the heads so that the tape can be quickly accelerated or decelerated. The tape may be laced around sets of tension arms or passed through a vacuum column between the reels in larger units. Start/ stop times are in the order of 1 to 5 milliseconds with tape speeds up to 200 inches per second.

A number of other tape packaging systems besides reels are available for magnetic tape. Most employ some form of cartridge. The tape lengths are usually shorter than those used for reel-to-reel systems, and therefore the average random accessing times are less.

A cartridge system that uses endless 100 foot, $\frac{1}{4}$ inch tapes can operate at a speed of 10 inches per second and have a 7- to 9-bit character transfer rate of about 500 characters per second.

Magnetic tape recording systems are suited for sequentially organized data. When either the data is randomly organized or the processing is done randomly, these applications are inefficiently handled with magnetic tape since the serial nature of the storage medium produces long average access time of seconds. For large-capacity online storage requirements, the magnetic tape is the lowest-cost storage medium. Because of the smaller average access times, disk storage is better suited than magnetic tape for medium-size storage requirements. The basic characteristics of magnetic storage units are shown in Table 3-3.

3.6.5 Bernoulli Box Systems

The Bernoulli box is an external storage subsystem designed to support the IBM PC, XT, AT, and compatibles as well as newer models of the Apple Macintosh Plus. Single- or dual-drive models can provide online data storage ranging from 10 to 120 MB. A high-performance standard in PC mass storage, the Bernoulli box provides average random access times as low as 35 milliseconds and transfer rates exceeding 1 megabyte per second, backup, and organizational flexibility. It can also increase the system's storage capacity using removable Bernoulli disk cartridges.

3.6.6 Optical Disk Drives

Optical disk drives are available with 12 inch, $5\frac{1}{4}$ inch high, 19 inch rack-mountable optical disks. Drives are available with SCSI or ISI interfaces and include an internal power supply.

A standard $5\frac{1}{4}$ inch cartridge tape is full height with 240 MB formatted. It has a 250KB transfer rate and an imbedded SCSI interface and uses an IBM 3480 $\frac{1}{2}$ inch tall cartridge.

3.6.7 Cartridge Tape Drives

A $\frac{1}{4}$ inch streaming cartridge tape drives offers 70MB storage capacity per 600 foot cartridge. The $\frac{1}{2}$ inch streaming tape drives are available in vertical, horizontal, and cabinet mounts. Half-inch streaming tape drives write and read between 1600 and 6250 bpi group-coded recording (GCR) format. The following models are available:

1. Writes and reads 1600 bpi phase encoded (PE) format
2. Writes and reads 1600/3200 bpi double phase encoded (DPE) format
3. Writes and reads 6250 bpi group-coded recording format

3.6.8 CDROM

CDROM (compact disc read-only memory) is a by-product of audio technology that packs 333,000 2048-byte blocks—a total of 682MB of data—onto a single 4.7-inch plastic disc (in the audio industry it is called a disc rather than a disk). Read by a low-power laser beam, the inexpensive polycarbonate platter is immune to magnetic fields, head crashes, and surface contaminates that are the bane of conventional disk and tape storage systems.

Creating a CDROM disc and retrieving its contents is similar to the process of cutting and playing back a high-fidelity LP recording. This two-step process differs from conventional EDP applications where the same system and technique are used for both data recording and playback. Users will find that the substantial cost of converting a database from magnetic disk to CDROM disc is influenced by a variety of factors, including the amount of preprocessing and the software engineering needed for data preparation and mastering, the required turnaround time, and the desired quantity of discs.

CDROM discs, like LP albums, are available in prerecorded form only. Mass-produced CDROM discs are of no value to users who want to archive a corporate database, CAD schematics for a proprietary VLSI microchip, or an extensive collection of text files. A growing number of high-capacity WORM (write once–read mostly) drives do, however, allow users to archive their own data on optical media.

WORM technology offers storage capacity far beyond that provided by CDROM discs and magnetic tape—it would take some 50 reels of 1600 bpi magnetic tape to store the same 2GB of information that can be archived on one dual-sided 12 inch WORM platter. In addition, WORM drives provide faster access times and higher data throughput rates than do CDROM drives. WORM drives have the same 3.8MB per second peak data transfer rate as the relatively slow ST506 disks, with access times that range from 150 to 250 milliseconds.

Like CDROM discs, WORM disks have a single spiral track that is read by a highly focused laser beam. Most WORM drives write data onto the disk using the same laser beam—at about 10 times the read power level (some WORMs use a second independent head for writing). When the higher-power beam creates a hole or a bump in the thin recording layer within the WORM disk, the spot represents a binary one. While information on a WORM disk can be deleted, however, the space it occupies cannot be erased and reused. Although this limitation might seem to be a crippling drawback, a variety of applications are well suited to the permanence of write-once media. Information that must be retained in a static format for protracted periods—yearly system backups, corporate financial records, or the contents of a newspaper's "morgue," for example—lends itself to storage on WORM media.

WORM technology may be short-lived, however, if vendors perfect the erasable optical disk. Erasable WMRA (write mostly–read always) optical disks and drives are being demonstrated as prototypes and engineering test models for both the computer and consumer markets. Although several techniques have been developed to permit repeated erasure and rewriting of optical disk data, the magneto-optical method seems to hold the most promise. In this technique, data are written to a premagnetized grooved platter by a precisely focused high-intensity laser beam. The beam heats a micron-sized spot on the disk to its Curie point, the temperature at which the spot loses its magnetic polarity. As the spot cools, it assumes the polarity of the magnetic field generated by a coil in the optical drive's read/write head.

To read data, the same laser beam is aimed at the surface of the platter after being directed through lenses and prisms that reduce its intensity. The more diffuse reflected beam goes through a beam-splitting prism that diverts it to a detector where it is interpreted as a binary 0 or 1. The angle of polarization of the reflected beam is slightly changed wherever the magnetic polarity of a spot is reversed, and the stream of light's changing polarity is translated into a bit stream for hardware decoding.

Data erasure takes place in a similar fashion. The laser beam is directed at the surface of the platter without any magnetic field from the coil in the read/write head. As the beam heats a spot on the platter to its Curie point, the particles beneath the spot realign themselves and adopt the natural magnetic polarity of the platter.

Input/Output Control

This chapter shows you how

- I/O controllers operate
- The different microcomputer I/O architectures function
- To build an I/O interface
- Interface scheduling is performed

The addition of an input/output device to the microcomputer system usually requires an interface controller. The proper use of a device connected to the microcomputer system will normally require some form of scheduling strategy to be utilized. The required interface may range from a few simple latches or registers to several I/O boards. General-purpose interface chips will be described in this section. The actual interfacing techniques used for most common input/output devices are dependent on the system application. Complex controllers may be required for I/O devices having complex time-dependent operations. Some controllers incorporate an internal microprocessor which receives instructions from the main processor and executes them. These controllers implement the control sequence required by the I/O device. In some cases, it might advance the read/write head linkage for a mass memory device, perhaps using a stepping motor. Controllers are available in LSI form for the more common I/O applications. Three major types of applications exist: input devices, output devices, and mass or bulk memory devices.

The microcomputer's environment is, in general, low speed and bit oriented. Examples are keyboards which must be scanned and read, relays which are turned off and on, and transducers which must be sensed.

4.1 BIT I/O

The emphasis on bit I/O is a consequence of the problems solved by the microcomputer. These problems are dominated by performing BCD arithmetic and logical operations based on binary inputs and/or data comparisons. Thus, the I/O format can relate to 1-bit or 4-bit characters. In other applications the microcomputer may need a high-bandwidth byte or word I/O.

The techniques used for dealing with single microcomputer I/O employ bus or port I/O and bit I/O schemes. The bus or port I/O technique divides the I/O pins onto 8-bit groups called ports. A few bits in the instruction address of these ports give a coarse addressability. Fine addressing within the bits can be accomplished by a logical operation with a mask and the port. For example,

> Output operation
>> Port mask transfer to port
>> The result is latched into the port
> Input operation
>> Port mask transfer to accumulator
>> Or port transfer to accumulator

Many variations of the bus or port architecture may exist. For example, memory locations may be declared to be I/O ports, but bits in these ports are then manipulated with moves and logical instructions.

The major advantage of this is that no additional specific I/O instructions are required. The same instructions which address memory perform the I/O functions.

4.2 MEMORY-MAPPED I/O

The type of I/O architecture is called "memory-mapped I/O." This technique generally requires more bits in the instruction than the bit technique, but the CPU control is simpler. It is more efficient to use this architecture where the use of bit I/O is small.

In those applications where higher-bandwidth, bytewide I/O is required, the microcomputer can transfer data to or from the data memory and a port using a program loop which can transfer the data through the accumulator or other registers.

The traditional computer normally had many more memory instructions than I/O instructions. In the memory-mapped I/O system, arithmetic may be performed directly on an input or output port or register without having to transfer the data in and out of intermediate registers.

The bit I/O architecture provides specific features and instructions for addressing bits or individual output pins. In a typical example of this I/O architecture, each of the output pins is addressed with an implied address, using an instruction like

SET BIT

and

RESET BIT

This technique is useful for output devices like fixed displays using light-emitting diodes (LEDs) or liquid-crystal displays (LCDs). These are the cheapest display devices and may be used in low-cost applications. Many other bit-oriented output devices are available for applications where the system might be connected to some external mechanism such as relays or stepper motors.

In a memory-mapped I/O system, the processor can use the same instructions for memory transfers as it does for input/output transfers. The I/O ports are treated as memory locations.

Instructions that operate on the memory tend to require several bytes to address the location while I/O instructions may need only one byte to specify a port. In I/O dependent applications memory-mapped I/O instructions can take longer to execute than I/O instructions because of the extra bytes. This problem can be minimized by using the shorter addressing modes.

Compare this to an I/O mapped input/output system where the processor uses control signals which indicate when the present cycle is for input or output and not for memory. In this scheme, fewer address lines are required to select the input/output ports, since there will be fewer input/output ports than memory locations.

Another advantage in I/O-mapped input/output is that the separate I/O instructions can be easily distinguished from memory reference instructions during programming. The shorter addressing also requires less hardware for decoding, and the instructions are usually faster.

4.3 BUILDING AN INTERFACE

A basic parallel interface requires latches and bus drivers. The latches hold signals from the microprocessor until the external device requires them. There must also be a selection mechanism and read/write control for the I/O registers or ports. Figure 4-1 shows the basic requirements of an I/O port.

An input latch must hold the external information until the system can read it, and an output latch must hold the data from the system until required. There may also be buffers to receive and drive the data bus and a status register to indicate when data is to be read or if data from the processor can be sent to the device.

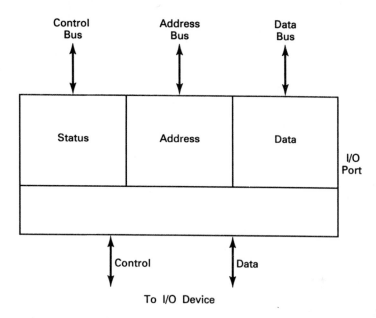

Figure 4-1 Typical I/O Interface

These ports may be built up using separate logic devices, or components with a high level of integration can be used. LSI input/output devices may be used to perform the following functions: address decoding, data input/output buffering, multiplexing, status for handshaking, and other control functions.

The selection of the input/output interface chips for addressing purposes can be done using the same techniques for memory which have already been described. The selection of registers within the chips is accomplished using the address bus, in the same way as addressing a memory location. Chips with up to eight internal registers will use three pins for internal register selection which are internally decoded to select one of the registers. These pins will be connected to the address bus. The internal registers may be read or written into and consist of input or output latches, direction registers, and a status register.

Of the three basic general-purpose I/O interfaces, the nonprogrammable hardware interface is simplest. It will perform the basic bus-interface functions and may include some interrupt-request control logic. It operates basically as a parallel I/O port.

4.3.1 Programmable Interfaces

A hardware programmable interface includes decoding logic, addressable parallel I/O ports, and interrupt control logic. External wiring or switches will determine the address, data direction, and width of each port and control the operations of the interface.

The type of general-purpose interface that we will discuss is software programmable. Here the microcomputer software determines how the interface is structured as it operates from the contents of a control register which is loaded and updated by the program. The interface can also include other control registers for functions such as data direction. This register allows the input or output function of individual I/O lines to be selected by the program.

These programmable input/output (PIO) interface chips are not an industry standard, and different manufacturers may use various names for these devices. PIO is used here to designate the general class of programmable I/O devices. The various differences can be found in referring to the manufacturers' literature.

The PIO programmable interface device provides the basic input and output functions for a parallel data interface. In order to connect an input or output device to a microprocessor data bus we have found that at the minimum, it is necessary to provide latches for the inputs and outputs.

The input latches must hold the data long enough for the microprocessor to read the data; they also function to isolate the signals from the bus. The output latches hold the output data long enough for the output device to make use of it. The data presented on a typical bus may be valid for less than 500 nanoseconds, which is too fast for many input/output devices to react and make use of it.

The status of these latches or registers must also be available to allow handshaking communications between the microprocessor and I/O. Before reading the contents of an input buffer or register, the microprocessor should know if the contents are valid. Thus, a status bit may be supplied, or an interrupt is sent as a signal to the microprocessor. This may signal that the output buffer register is full or empty, and the microprocessor can determine if it should output the next word. The same status signal can also be used by the output device to determine if it can use the contents of the buffer or register.

The basic type of general-purpose parallel I/O interface requires at least one input register, one output register, status bits, and some interrupt control. Most systems will use at least 16 or 24 I/O lines for the general-purpose interface. These channels, which are also called ports, can be configurated as some combination of inputs or outputs.

The use of the data direction register allows a bit-by-bit basis to define these ports as bits configured as inputs and outputs. Each bit of the data direction register specifies if a corresponding bit in the PIO port will be an input or an output. The use of a 0 in the data direction register may specify an input, while a 1 specifies an output. One or more command registers may be used to specify the configuration of the ports and the operation of the control logic.

The typical PIO will multiplex its connections to the microprocessor data bus into two or more of the 8-bit ports. A typical PIO configuration is shown in Figure 4-2. Each port has its own buffer and direction register. A status or mode register is used to indicate the status of each 8 bit port.

The main difference between the PIO concept and a hardware interface is that the PIO unit is programmable. Since the control logic is programmable for each port, the user can specify which line will be used for handshaking and the function or direction in which it will be used. The control logic can also specify when a device's signal will trigger interrupts. The fact that each data line or group of data lines for a port is programmable is foreign to the traditional hardware

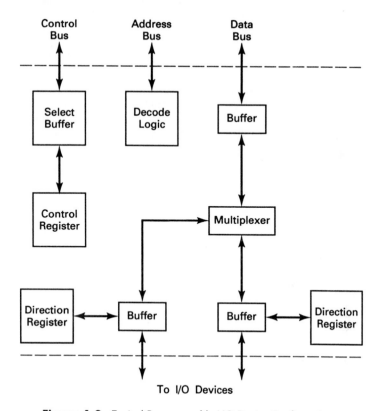

Figure 4-2 Typical Programmable I/O Device Configuration

interface where it is almost never done. This feature allows a general-purpose interface device which can be used in many interface situations. It is possible to connect combinations of input and output lines to the interface for almost any application.

In this type of general interface, the data registers will accumulate the data for the inputs or outputs on each of the I/O lines. The direction registers which configure the lines as an input or an output use zero for an input and one for an output. This is done for safety reasons, since when the system is initialized, the contents of all registers are normally reset to zero. As the system starts up, spurious signals can be generated. If any of these signals are present on the I/O lines, the lines are configured as inputs to the microprocessor rather than as outputs to devices which could cause safety problems.

The control register stores the command bits issued by the microprocessor for controlling the port. For each port, the microprocessor will specify if interrupts are to be generated and which control signals will be used by the port. When a data buffer becomes full or empty, a status bit in the control register is set or reset.

To use this type of interface, the microprocessor must execute the following basic operations:

1. Load the control registers to specify the mode in which the control signals may operate.

2. Load the direction registers to specify the direction in which the lines which make up the ports will be used.

These operations must be done for every port in the interface. The data transfer is then performed using a transfer instruction, such as a MOVE.

The data is transferred to the proper internal PIO registers in the following sequence. The data which is to be loaded in the various PIO registers is placed on the data bus, and then a register select is performed. This is done by providing the correct address on the address bus. Thus, the microprocessor selects one of the internal registers with the appropriate pattern on the address bus and then supplies the 8 data bits to be transferred into one of these registers using the data bus. The multiplexer in the PIO will gate the 8-bit data to the register. The microprocessor must also generate the read or write signal on the control bus. To read the status from the PIO, the contents of the status register are read.

After the PIO has been configured with its control and direction registers loaded, no additional changes are normally necessary and the microprocessor will communicate with the data buffers using a single instruction.

4.3.2 A Programmable Interface Example

Consider a simple programmable interface used to connect three LED display digits. It might use three I/O ports, one for each digit. There are a number of devices that can be used for this simple application and depending on which type is used, it will tend to have certain characteristics that may differ from other devices.

The PIO device designed for use with the 6800 microprocessor is the 6820 peripheral interface adapter called a PIA. Each 6820 is a double port device with two sets of eight output lines. In an application requiring three digits, one and a half PIA chips are needed to service the display. Each device has two data registers which are called peripheral registers. One of these registers is used for each set of input/output lines.

There are also two other type of registers used with each peripheral register. This results in a total of six registers for each chip. One is the data direction register which controls the directions of the input/output lines. Each data direction register has 8 bits, one for each input/output line.

The control register format for the A side is shown in Figure 4-3. Bit 7 indicates the state of the CA1 input to the register. It is used as an interrupt flag. Bit 6 monitors the CA2 input to the register. Bits 5,4, and 3 are used to establish the eight different modes of the device and the function of the CA2 pin. Bit 2 indicates if the direction register or data register is to be selected. Bits 1 and 0 are used as interrupt enable/disable control bits. The PIA has six registers and two register select (RS) pins so the data and data direction registers in each port must share the same address. They differ by the value of bit 2 of the control register. This and other similar quirks can be a possible source of programming errors.

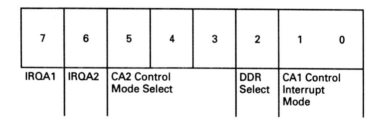

7	6	5	4	3	2	1	0
IRQA1	IRQA2	CA2 Control Mode Select			DDR Select	CA1 Control Interrupt Mode	

Figure 4-3 6820 Control Register Format

Table 4-1 indicates how the registers are selected by use of the RS1 and RS0 pins and the state of the internal bit 2 of the control register. Since the PIA cannot drive a heavily loaded data bus, it is sometimes required to buffer the data to this chip using a tristate buffer as discussed earlier.

Many 16-bit microprocessors have their own family of peripheral control devices. Eight-bit compatible devices may also be used. For example, the 6846 I/O timer and ROM chip may be used by dividing the address and data buses and connecting all other signals in parallel.

When 6800 peripheral devices are connected in this way with the 68000 microprocessor, then the least significant bit is always located at an odd address and the most significant bit is always located at an even address. The data direction and control registers must be configured in a similar manner to the 6820.

If a single 6846 is used, the 68000 could not use any of the ROM capability of the peripheral device because of the difference in the bus width. The use of two devices allows the 68000 to use and execute programs stored in the ROMs.

Along with the two 16-bit timers, this provides a programmable controller that can be used for many real-time control applications. Using these timers a signal can be generated when the desired period of time has elapsed for scheduling purposes. The independent counters can operate in binary or BCD with several programmable modes of operation.

In some applications, it may be necessary to measure the elapsed time for input or output scheduling and using looping techniques is time consuming. The availability of programmable timers frees the microprocessor for other tasks.

In real-time systems using interrupts, software counters cannot usually provide the accuracy required for timing. A software counter could be affected by events which can result in erroneous time measurements.

TABLE 4-1 6820 REGISTER SELECTION

RS1	RS0	Bit 1	Bit 2	
0	0	0	—	Data direction A
0	0	1	—	Data buffer A
0	1	—	—	Control A
1	0	—	0	Data direction B
1	0	—	1	Data buffer B
1	1	—	—	Control B

Other I/O devices are available which are a combination of PIA, a UART for serial interfacing, and other components such as the programmable interval timers. One typical I/O device has a PIO with two 8-bit ports plus an asynchronous serial line, interrupts, and programmable interval timers. It interfaces in a similar manner to the 6846.

To connect the 6846s to the 68000 in the synchronous mode of operation, a low input is provided to the VPA pin of the 68000 when one chip is selected for synchronization and to generate the VMA signal. Asynchronous operation requires the generation of a DTACK signal for the 68000.

The 8086 family has an input/output processor designed to use its own instruction set for I/O operations. It is similar to a microprocessor with two DMA channels. It can service the peripherals directly and is able to match 8- or 16-bit buses to 8- or 16-bit peripheral devices.

Z80 peripheral devices can be used with the Z8000 microprocessor, some decoding circuitry is required, and the required control signals such as $\overline{IORQ}$, $\overline{MI}$, $\overline{RD}$, and $\overline{RETI}$ are obtained by coding an emulation in the Z8000 instruction memory.

Many available interface devices can function as direct peripheral controllers. In the past, this type of controller may have required one or more boards of logic to connect it to any type of processor. Since the mid-1970s it has become possible to implement complete interfaces using these simplified controller devices. There are controllers for printers, disk memories, and CRTs. Typically, these controllers are interfaced directly to one or several PIOs or a UART. There are also a number of functional utility devices available which can supply the hardware facilities which in the past required additional external components and software. These devices tend to keep the interface hardware at a minimum.

4.4 INTERFACE SCHEDULING

Integral to the interface operation is the scheduling method of handling the input/output communications. As the input/output device is connected to the system using the interface, a communication procedure is established between the device and the microprocessor.

The three basic scheduling techniques used for controlling the input/output devices and synchronizing the data transfers are

1. Polling or program control
2. Interrupt control
3. Direct memory access control

The one which is used in the microcomputer system will depend on three factors:

1. The rate at which the data is to be transmitted
2. The time delays between the I/O device and the actual data transfer
3. The feasibility of overlapping or interleaving I/O operations

The polling or programmed I/O technique is the most basic to implement. The I/O devices are connected to the system bus with some connections to the control lines. The principal idea is to implement a procedure in hardware and/or software for determining which input/output device requires service. The polling technique is synchronous in nature as the microprocessor periodically questions each device if it requires service. Each device then answers with a yes or no. If a no is reached, the microprocessor will advance to the next device and question it. In this way the microprocessor checks each I/O device successively to determine if service is required. In practice, a status flag is tested in the device or the interface. When the test is true, an action is initiated. This typically is the transfer of a word or block of data to or from the I/O device. The required polling algorithm often takes the form of a polling loop.

The process of checking the device and receiving an answer in return is a form of handshaking. It sets the communications protocol between one device and the next one in the link.

In a typical polling loop, a status bit is checked in order to test if the device is ready to accept data. Before reading data from the device, a status bit is checked to test if the word is complete. The structure of a typical polling loop is shown in Figure 4-4. Using this program-controlled I/O, the input/output instructions will be used to initiate and control the transfers data.

The two basic types of information transferred are the control data and message data, which are transmitted between the microprocessor and the I/O device. The control data is used to synchronize the I/O device with the program execution before the message data is transmitted.

Typical input control data includes the device-status words, while the output control data form the device-command words. The status words describe what the I/O device is doing. Each status bit will indicate a certain condition such as

```
MESSAGE DATA
READY FOR TRANSMISSION
DEVICE BUSY
TRANSMISSION ERROR
```

The command words control the device operation using command bit, for example, to stop an operation or change a transmission rate.

I/O program instructions can be organized in several ways. A unique instruction may be used for each type of I/O data transfer. This might result in four instructions:

```
READ THE INPUT MESSAGE
WRITE THE OUTPUT MESSAGE
SEND THE OUTPUT COMMAND WORD
ACCEPT THE INPUT STATUS WORD
```

Separate I/O instructions can also be used to transfer the message and control data. Two different device addresses could be used for the message and

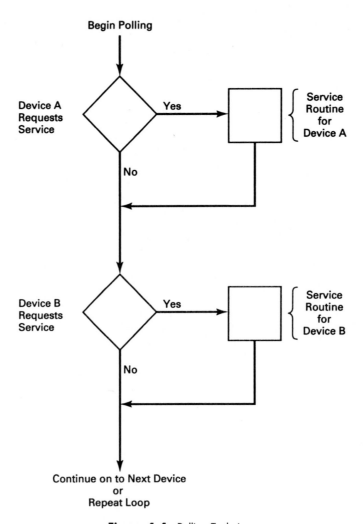

Figure 4-4 Polling Technique

control-data transmissions. These might be a

READ DATA

for the message data or status word and a

WRITE DATA

for either the message data or command word.

Another technique is to use memory data-transfer-instructions for communicating with the I/O devices. Here, a block of unused memory addresses will hold the device addresses.

The memory-mapped I/O approach uses some of the available memory address area, but it can result in reduced program storage requirements and execution times in some applications. Typical memory transfer instructions include

LOAD DATA

for an input message data or status word and

STORE DATA

for an output message data or command word.

The message and control data are usually sent or received through one of the registers. Some microprocessors use special registers for the control data, while others use a status register. When a status register is used, the conditional branch instructions may check the status register's individual bits directly. The control data may synchronize the data transfer using the following steps:

1. A command word is written in the device.
2. A status word is read from the device.
3. The status bits are tested. (This checks if the message data may be transferred to the device.)
4. If the device is not ready for the transfers, repeat the first two steps until it is.
5. The message data is read or written. (This resets the status of the device.)

When the data transfer originates from the I/O device itself, the device signals its need to transfer data by setting the correct status bits.

In a typical polling program, the status check is repeated continuously until the device is ready. This loop tends to slow the program execution and may use too much processing time in some applications. To overcome this, the status check can be interleaved with other operations.

A polling microcomputer will use asynchronous inputs. These will be detected by an instruction which checks to determine if the input has occurred. The sequence of instructions in the polling loop tests the various input lines at a rate which will provide the desired system response time.

This poll of the inputs must be a time which permits the processing task associated with the input to be accomplished. The polled inputs may use a latch or a flip-flop for each input which will recognize and retain the presence of an input. If an input latch is not used, the polling must be fast enough to detect the input change. The instructions will test the conditions of these latches or flip-flops and, if set, branch to the service program. An input can be tested by instructions and jump to a new program if equal to one or jump if equal to zero.

Another technique for detecting the presence of an asynchronous input uses an input bus of several bits which is tested by an instruction. The instruction looks at all input lines, and if any one of these lines is a logical one, the status bit is set to a 1. A second instruction branches if the status is equal to 1.

The main advantage of the polled input system is the simplicity of hardware and software. For industrial applications where the response time is satisfactory, the possibility of programming error is reduced since the input is serviced when the processor can attend it. In a microcomputer system that communicates with several I/O devices, the periodic status checks that must be made on each device, can result in considerable time lags for some devices since it indicates that it is ready to transfer data and the actual transfer. In some microcomputer systems, the time spent checking the device status may be reduced with a common test line, which signals when a device requires attention. The microprocessor can periodically check the status of this line without having to poll the individual devices until one of them signals for service. It then goes into the polling loop to find which device requested service.

Polling offers several other advantages. It adds minimal hardware to the interface since usually no special lines are required. It is also synchronous with the program execution. It is relatively easy to determine when a device is being interrogated and how long it takes to service it. No events may occur that tend to disrupt the scheduled polling sequence.

The main disadvantage of polling is the software overhead, since each time the polling loop is entered, all the devices are checked. Most of them may not require service. But to guarantee that each device is checked within a certain time, the entire loop must be executed, even though it is not always required. This waste of processor time may require the consideration of one of the other techniques.

When this use of microprocessor time is not critical, polling can be the best as well as the simplest technique to implement. The knowledge of the order in which devices are polled can be a major advantage in programming some applications. Polling should be considered for applications that do not require an interrupt-driven design.

4.5 INTERRUPTS

In applications where the polling technique does not provide fast enough response, or uses too much microprocessor time, interrupts can provide a solution. In an interrupt-driven system, the devices have the option of requesting service.

An interrupt line is connected to the microprocessor and each of the devices is connected to this line. Each one of the devices which may be required to get service has the option of using this line to request service. When a device requests service, it generates an interrupt pulse or level on this line. The microprocessor then senses this change on the line.

The use of the interrupt technique requires that the microprocessor accept the interrupt, identify it, and service it. Accepting the interrupt may be implemented using an internal mask bit called either an interrupt mask, interrupt inhibit, or interrupt enable. This bit is normally stored in the flag or status register.

After an interrupt is accepted, the microprocessor must then determine which device originated it. There is also the possibility that several devices might generate interrupts simultaneously. When multiple devices are connected to the same interrupt line, priorities must be assigned.

Once the interrupt has been accepted and the device identified, the service requested by the device can be performed. The microprocessor will suspend the program it was executing and branch to the interrupt routine. If the required branching address is available, the interrupt can be presented to the microprocessor as a vectored interrupt.

4.5.1 Interrupt Routine

The execution of the interrupt routine handler is similar to that of a polling system. The termination of this routine allows the program which has been suspended by the interrupt to continue its execution. This can require several instructions. When the interrupt-controlled I/O device is ready to transfer data, it can break into the main program.

The simplest interrupt system uses a single I/O device connected to a single interrupt-request line. A change in the signal on this line causes the microprocessor to jump from the main program to the location in the program memory which holds the interrupt trap address provided that the following three conditions are met:

1. The current instruction is executed.
2. The current contents of the program counter are stored in the stack.
3. The program counter is loaded with the proper program memory address.

When only one I/O device can generate interrupts, its service routine can be loaded into the memory locations starting at an interrupt trap address as shown in Figure 4-5. At the completion of the routine, the previously stored contents of the program counter will provide the return address back to the main program. Interrupts are inhibited before the service routine starts, to prevent multiple interruptions by the same interrupt request. In some systems, the instruction for the jump back to the main program may also reenable the interrupts.

The interrupts may be inhibited by setting a mask bit in the microprocessor's status register which may be set or reset by the program. The mask bit can also be used to prevent the interruption of sections of program that are to be executed before the next input/output operations can occur.

Indirect addressing links can be used to allow the service program to be located at an arbitrary position in the program memory. Then, if the interrupt trap address is in read/write memory, the program entry point can be changed while the main program is operating to vary the response of the system to the interrupt.

4.5.2 Register Modification

The service program can modify the main program execution if it uses and modifies registers in the microprocessor. The service program must save and restore the contents of these registers. This information needs to be saved so that the complete state can be restored after the interrupt is serviced. The levels of status

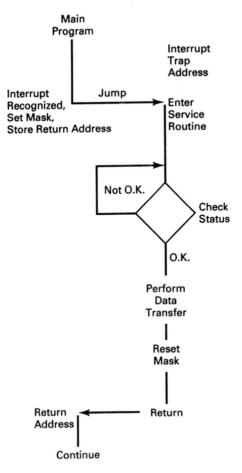

Figure 4-5 Interrupt Controlled Program

that must be saved for a subroutine call or poll is different from that which is saved for an interrupt.

The status consists of two types of information: results from the execution of the program and conditions which are established by the program for use in the future. The first type includes the program counter value, overflow bit, and carry bits. The conditions set by the program include the interrupt enables, internal timer enable, internal counter enable, and internal flags. Some items of status may be saved by the hardware under the conditions of the interrupt. A trade-off occurs between evaluating the space in the CPU for status saving versus the bits required to save status by programming. If there is a heavy use of subroutines, polling, or interrupts, hardware saving of the status information may be used to improve performance.

4.5.3 Multiple Interrupts

The interrupt-servicing procedures discussed apply when a single device is generating interrupts. Many industrial microcomputer systems will have more than one source and more than one type of interrupt. The following types of interrupts may exist:

1. External interrupts which are generated from one or more devices
2. Internal interrupts which are generated by the microcomputer system to indicate error conditions such as a power failure, system malfunction, or transmission break
3. Simulated interrupts which are generated by software techniques for use in frequent testing for debugging purposes

Interrupts from different sources will often have different service requirements. Some require immediate attention, while others can wait until the task underway is completed. The interrupt procedure must be able to

1. Differentiate between the various sources.
2. Determine the order in which the interrupts are serviced when more than one occurs at the same time.
3. Save and restore the contents of registers so the program can continue after the multiple interrupts.

When several interrupt-request lines are used, each can have its own interrupt trap address. If one source of interrupt is assigned to each line, the system may distinguish among internal, external, and simulated interrupts. If several I/O devices use the same interrupt request line, the interrupt can be recognized either by polling using software or by vectored interrupts using hardware. In the polling technique the interrupt produces a jump to the service program using the interrupt trap address. The service program will check the status word of each I/O device to determine which one caused the interrupt. Figure 4-6 shows this operation for two I/O devices The interrupt status bit will indicate if a device has generated an interrupt request as it is checked for each device. The device status word is then read into the status register of the microprocessor, and if the bit is set, a jump is then made to the service program.

The more registers are used, the longer the interrupt response time will be. A more rapid interrupt response can be achieved with several sets of internal registers: the main program can use one set while the service program has the other set.

If locations in data memory are used to replace some of the internal registers, then a pointer register can define the memory locations. The system can store and modify the contents of the pointer before executing the service program, using a workspace that is separate from that used by the main program. When this service is complete, the pointer register is restored.

4.5.4 Real-Time Applications

When the input/output operation is required to occur at a particular period within an interval, the operation of the I/O device and the execution of the program controlling the data transfer must be synchronized in real time. To synchronize

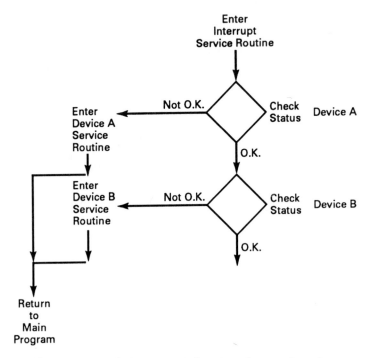

Figure 4-6   Multiple Interrupt Polling Using Separate Status Bits

the I/O device with the program, a real-time clock is tied to the interrupt request line. The program is then interrupted periodically. The microprocessor counts the interrupt requests and controls the data flow as required.

A typical example of a real-time application, which is timer driven, is an online data acquisition system using a processor-controlled multichannel analog-to-digital converter. The flow shown in Figure 4-7 illustrates the program operation during data collection.

A vectored interrupt system allows the microprocessor to recognize the interrupting device since each I/O device is assigned a unique interrupt address. This address then generates an interrupt trap address for the device.

The trap addresses are normally located sequentially in the program memory to form the interrupt vector. Thus, each location contains the starting address of a device-service program. The contents of the interrupt vector can then be loaded into the program counter and program control transferred to the correct device service program.

Some vectored systems, instead of transmitting an address, use an I/O device to transmit an instruction to the microprocessor after the request has been acknowledged. Then, the interrupt control loads the instruction into an instruction register. Normal operation continues after this instruction is executed. The vectoring is achieved by a jump instruction which derives the jump address from part of the instruction. A unique jump address is defined for each I/O device in the system.

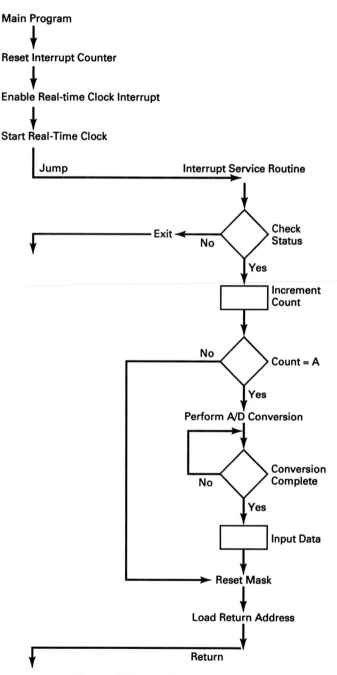

Figure 4-7 A Real-Time Application

Another problem in systems with several sources of interrupt is that one or more interrupt requests can occur during the servicing of an earlier request. In the simplest technique, the interrupt mask bit is set when the first request is recognized and the following requests are placed in a queue, waiting until the service of the first interrupt is complete before they are recognized and serviced. The order in which the queued interrupts are recognized will determine the delay before service. This order, or priority, is set either by software or by hardware. After recognizing the interrupt request, the service program can poll the devices in the desired order. The devices which are polled first will be serviced first.

In systems with hardware priority, interrupt logic sends an external signal to the request logic in each of the I/O devices. This signal reflects the state of the interrupt mask bit and is passed to each device according to its priority. When the mask is set, the signal prevents any devices from generating an interrupt request. When the mask is reset and if a device has no interrupt request pending, the signal is passed on to the next device.

The interrupt logic will generate the interrupt request and prevent the signal from passing on. When more than one device requires interrupt service, the device receiving the control signal first will be serviced first.

Priority logic can be used to resolve conflicts and issue a hold request to the CPU. The controller keeps a count of the cycles used and notifies the peripheral when the programmed number of cycles used for the data transfer is complete. The operation of these controllers is considered next.

4.6 INTERFACE SCHEDULING

Supplying the input or output facility for a microcomputer requires, at the minimum, a latch. It is usually more economical to provide the minimal facilities using an I/O interface device like a PIO. In the typical microcomputer system, PIOs or other I/O devices are connected to the microprocessor buses. This involves connections to the data bus and connections to the address bus.

The last section has examined the essential operational characteristics of the three input/output scheduling techniques: polling, interrupts, and direct memory access (DMA). There are various interface devices for implementing these techniques. The required input/output facilities can be provided with three basic kinds of devices: the PIO type of interface device, device controllers, and scheduling devices.

Two different types of devices are available for the scheduling of input/output operations. There are the priority interrupt controllers (PIC) and the direct memory access controllers (DMAC).

When it is required to service the I/O devices, two problems may occur which have already been discussed:

1. Simultaneous interrupts may require the use of a priority scheme.
2. The use of a single interrupt line requires identifying the device which first requested the interrupt.

The interrupt identification problem is a result of the pin limitation of the package.

In a software implementation of priority interrupts, the priorities do not have to be fixed, and some controllers allow the user to modify the priorities using software. Some priority interrupt controllers use a mask which allows the programmer to mask out any interrupt level.

The interrupts are managed by a mask register. When the contents of a bit in the mask are 0, the propagation of the interrupt signal stops and the interrupt level is masked. A 1 in the mask register allows the interrupt to propagate. When all interrupt lines are allowed, the mask register contains all 1's. The interrupt levels which are not masked set a bit in the interrupt register. The contents of this register may be read by the data bus.

In normal operation, the mask register is loaded with the desired bit pattern to enable the selected interrupt lines. As the enable interrupts are requested, they propagate to the interrupt register. The microprocessor may then read the contents of the interrupt register. To implement a priority scheme, the microprocessor tests the bits of the interrupt register, starting with the highest priority, until it finds a 1. The corresponding interrupt line is serviced, which is the highest level of interrupt that requested service. After service to this interrupt is completed, the microprocessor can again read the contents of the interrupt register and service any other waiting interrupts.

The mask register allows the program to mask out interrupt levels selectively, and it is possible to mask levels at certain times in the program. The level of the interrupts is compared to the contents of a priority register which can be set by the user.

Some devices will prevent interruptions by an interrupt line of level higher than a desired priority. This acts as a global masking process for interrupts for any higher-level interrupts. A comparator in the chip may determine if the level of the interrupt is acceptable. If it is, then it is allowed to generate an interrupt request. Some devices may supply the branching address. This is accomplished with RAM or a set of 16-bit registers. A level vector is used to select the contents of one of the registers; then the contents of the register are placed on the data or address bus to allow a branch to the desired address. A complete controller will have the form of Figure 4-8.

A priority interrupt controller like the 8259 can provide interrupt management facilities including priorities, interrupt mask, and automatic vectoring. It may be cascaded with up to 8 other controller chips to manage 64 separate interrupt levels.

Interrupt management operates as follows. In response to an interrupt signal, the microprocessor accepts the interrupt and returns an interrupt acknowledge signal. The microprocessor then waits for the instruction to appear on the data bus. The 8259 places the instruction on the data bus and provides automatic vectoring. The program must preserve the data which existed prior to the interrupt.

The 8259 uses an interrupt mask and for a priority facility, the priority level is loaded into a register and compared using a comparator.

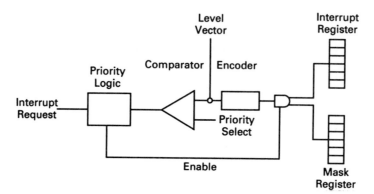

Figure 4-8   Interrupt Controller

Some microprocessors like the 6800 supply an external bit in a mask register which can then be set by the program. The microprocessor saves its register automatically and branches to a reserved memory location. This can result in a faster response to interrupts, but it does not allow the use of automatic vectoring. It operates as follows. The interrupt signal forces a bit to be checked in one of the control registers, then if the bit is set, an input to the register is stored. If the bit is not set, or after the branch to memory is made, a bit check is made of the other register which produces an output if the bit is set and produces a return from the interrupt if it is not set.

This type of polling approach tends to be a low-cost method for identifying interrupts, but for some applications it may be too slow. In these cases hardware may be used for priority encoding. The output of this encoder may be used as an address to transfer control to the correct routine. Then, when the interrupt occurs, the program will branch to the address that has been stored at FFF8 and FFF9. A software routine will then determine which interrupt service routine should be activated.

The 6800 programmable interrupt controller can manage eight interrupt levels. To provide automatic vectoring, it monitors the address bus for FFF8 and FFF9. When it detects these addresses, it assumes control of the data bus, and instead of the memory supplying the contents of FFF8-FFF9, the controller supplies the branching address.

The controller uses eight 16-bit registers. Depending on the interrupt level that is activated, it provides the correct branching address for that level. It substitutes the correct 16-bit address for one of the interrupt levels, instead of the 16-bit address that was contained in the memory location at FFF8-FFF9. It automatically preserves the registers. In some controllers this must be accomplished using a short software routine. In some applications, it may not be necessary to store all the internal registers. In systems with many internal registers saving all the internal registers all the time could be inefficient.

The interrupt technique may not be fast enough for devices which require fast word transfers, since when the interrupt is received, the microprocessor suspends the program under execution and switches to another routine. It then usually transfers at least one word using software. Some instructions will be executed before the word is completed, and a number of machine cycles may elapse. This can be too slow for devices such as CRT display terminals which must be refreshed. To speed up the transfer process, a hardware implementation of the software which produced the slow-down will result in the use of the DMA technique.

4.7 DMA CONTROLLERS

A direct memory access controller acts as a block-transfer processor. The controller implements in hardware the process which normally would be executed by the flow diagram of Figure 4-9. The basics of DMA operation are illustrated in Figure 4-10.

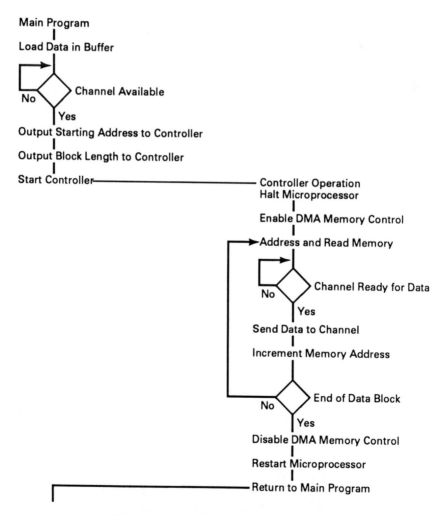

Figure 4-9 Detailed DMA Operational Flow

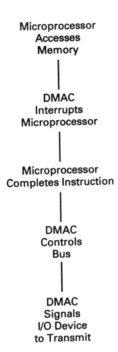

Figure 4-10 Basic DMA Operation

Instead of sending the interrupt to the microprocessor, the I/O device sends the interrupt to the DMA controller. The DMA controller then stops the microprocessor putting it in a HOLD mode. It may then take over operation of the system and transfer the data between the I/O device and the memory.

The complexity of a DMA controller approaches the complexity of a small microprocessor. It is the most expensive of the interrupt techniques and is used when the application requires high-speed word or block transfers between device and memory for the faster I/O devices such as CRTs.

Several methods may be used to allow the peripheral to communicate directly with the memory. The microprocessor can either be halted by the DMAC to suspend or stop operation or the DMAC may steal memory cycles from the microprocessor, or a combination of these techniques can be used. The simplest technique and most common is to suspend the microprocessor operation.

In the operation of a typical DMA controller, the following sequence of operations is performed:

1. The PIO requests service from the DMA controller.
2. The DMA controller forwards the request to the microprocessor.
3. The microprocessor completes the instruction it was executing and returns an acknowledge signal to the DMA controller.
4. The microprocessor enters a WAIT state and places the data and address buses in a high-impedance or floating state.
5. The DMA controller forwards an acknowledge signal to the PIO stating that the transfer may proceed.
6. The DMA controller loads the transfer address on the address bus. (The

DMA controller's registers are used for the beginning address for the transfer to memory. Other registers may be used such as a counter register which specifies how many words are to be transferred. The contents of these registers are preloaded by the program prior to their use.)

7. The DMA controller supplies the read or write signal.
8. The I/O device may now input or output the data via the PIO.
9. Each word transferred causes the DMA controller to increment an internal address register and update the word counter.

The block transfer operation will normally continue until one of the following conditions occur:

1. A command in the block transfer itself stops the DMA request.
2. The word counter reaches zero to signal the end of the block of words.

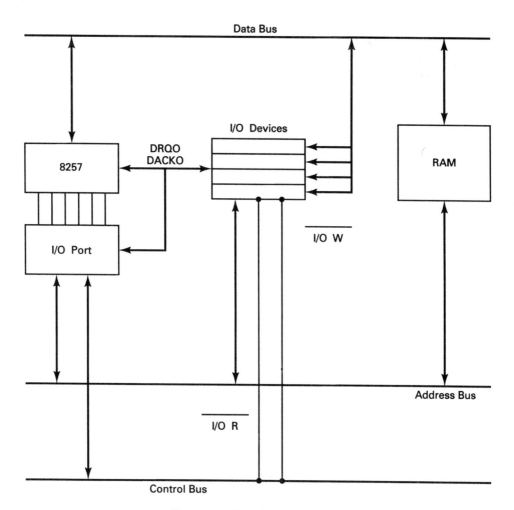

Figure 4-11 8257 DMA Application

3. An interrupt of the highest priority level occurs. (This level is normally reserved for power failure on most systems. Some cycles of processing time will still be available to preserve some of the system state. This time is used to preserve the contents of the most critical registers and then to shut down the system in an orderly way. The DMA transfer, as well as any other I/O operations, will be stopped and a branch to a power failure routine is used.)

4. An interrupt request at a higher priority level occurs. (Any request of higher priority levels will result in a suspension of DMA. The highest priority level will always be honored. When the block transfer at the higher priority level is completed, then the transfer for the lower level will resume.)

Each manufacturer has its own version of a DMA controller for its microprocessor family. The Intel 8257 requires an external latch in which to preserve the address bits. A typical application for the 8257 is shown in Figure 4-11.

Four DMA levels are shown for controlling four different I/O units each with its own DMA level. The 8257's priority logic is used to resolve the I/O unit's requests. An internal counting circuit maintains the cycle count and sends a control signal when the programmed number of cycles is complete. Blocks of 16,384 bytes may be transferred at a rate of 500KB per second using a 2 MHz clock.

Design and Development

This chapter shows you how

- The interface design must be planned
- An initial feasibility study is performed
- Proper documentation is generated
- The interface is flow diagrammed
- Decision tables are used in planning the design
- Human factors are included in the design
- Errors are handled using fail-soft and self-test techniques

There are a number of stages involved in the development of a microcomputer interface, and specific aids and techniques can be applied to check the desired results at each stage. In developing a microcomputer interface the major areas are

1. *The initial task definition.* This represents the initial definition of the task and includes the specification of inputs and outputs, processing requirements, response times, and possible error checking. In this early stage, flowcharting is often used to structure the sequence of steps involved in a typical task.
2. *Software/hardware design and/or selection.* In this stage the major concern is the methods that will allow a software package to meet the specified

requirements of the task. The available methods include top-down design or combination of structured or modular programming. The hardware criteria will also be evaluated based on the initial product definition. The process may consider the use of hardware/software partitioning.

3. *Program development*. This stage is concerned with the actual coding of algorithms that were developed in the initial task definition. The use of assembly and higher-level languages and the situations where one or the other is most appropriate can be critical in this stage. The proper use of the software techniques which were chosen in stage 2 can speed up the completion of this stage.

4. *Program verification and system debugging*. After the completion of the initial program, the major concern is seeking and correcting the programming errors. Various tools may be used and some types of errors are most likely to occur and there are some techniques that can be used to reduce their occurrence.

5. *System test*. The major concern is the selection of the test criteria and the proper test methods.

6. *Evaluation and redesign*. In this stage the testing of an interface which operates properly is complete, now the system performance is evaluated and it is determined if the result is adequate. The importance of documentation can emerge as a key factor in improving the system performance.

Efficient planning is always required for developing a working system. The detailed use of software and hardware design techniques is critical to this planning.

5.1 INTERFACE DESIGN PLANNING

The planning of an interface project is not always a simple task because of the different disciplines that may be involved and the level of technology required to achieve technical success.

A typical interface design involves not only the development of the specifications for the equipment used in the system, but also the interactions and mechanics of the process and instrumentation. This includes the available methods of processing the information and transmitting signals between the hardware.

The planning of any design project can be broken down into six separate phases.

1. Feasibility or product definition
2. Equipment specification or selection
3. System or program development
4. Equipment assembly or installation

5. Test

6. Operational evaluation

During the feasibility phase the initial scope and goals are specified. This can involve management from production, engineering, research, quality control, and personnel. Such topics as development costs along with space requirements can be worked out in this initial phase and weighed with such considerations as system flexibility or expansion and other basic requirements. Usually during this phase the various options are tested to determine feasibility, and opinions are voiced and recorded for further investigation when required. Also, the criteria for success such as the economic payoff, improved yields, and other benefits are investigated, formulated, and refined. The feasibility phase also sets the composition of the group which will administer the project to its final phase. The following disciplines may be required:

1. Process knowledge, familiar with the operations, problems, equipment management, economics, and the relation of these within the process plant structure.
2. Knowledge of the task or problem from the standpoint of its processing requirements, the ability to define the problem or processing in mathematical terms.
3. Ability to evaluate and select components and subassemblies and to specify the installation and calibration procedures for a variety of equipment.
4. Knowledge of applications. This includes the acquisition and the processing of data and the techniques for the optimization of cost.
5. Programming knowledge for the digital manipulation of data and the ability to plan the programming and convert equations into programs.
6. Industrial engineering and personnel specialists may be required if extensive procedures and work operation systems need to be developed as a result of the new system. Most systems are designed to minimize the work operation procedures to be the most cost effective, but there are still many types of industrial applications that can best be done with a mixture of labor and automation.

After the project is defined the initial technical investigation can begin, the boundaries and objectives of the proposed system are defined, typical processing flows can be studied and diagrammed, and the data requirements are studied and diagrammed.

During this phase it is useful to adapt a set of guidelines which may be unique to the application; this can prevent much misunderstanding if such items are left with only a vague understanding. Initially it is very difficult to determine if a project is feasible because the costs cannot be defined until the system is decided. Once the major system objectives are decided from the initial technical investigation, a preliminary cost analysis can be made.

5.2 FEASIBILITY STUDIES

At the beginning of a project it is possible to have a reasonably clear idea of what the objective appears to be without really having any understanding of how much money may be spent in getting the new system going. It is sound business practice for a detailed estimate of costs and time scales to be made before the go-ahead is given to anything but the most trivial of projects. Many times it will be found that a much more exact definition of the problem must be provided before any estimate can be made of the costs involved. The definition of the problem and a properly organized initial study can be the foundation of a successful project. This initial study is usually called a feasibility study. The study can be designed to answer the following questions about the potential application.

1. Where can the boundaries of this application be drawn?
2. What are the current costs? Does it seem probable that these costs can be reduced?
3. What are the volumes involved—data, likely processing time, frequency of processing?
4. Are the existing procedures and methods satisfactory?
5. If the application is not currently carried out by some means, what benefits can be expected from doing it on a microcomputer?

Once answered, these questions can be the basis of a feasibility report.

It will not always be possible to estimate the costs accurately at the feasibility stage, but even more difficult will be the assessment of the value of those benefits which cannot be directly quantified. These are generally grouped under the heading of savings.

In the preliminary planning stages, before any detailed feasibility study, it is unlikely that there will be any clear indication of costs involved and potential savings, although other desired benefits may be identified by this stage.

The difficulty in estimating cost benefits becomes apparent when attempts must be made to give a value to such items as the efficient utilization of resources or better information leading to better management decisions or more efficient control. By the time the final documentation is prepared any original estimates are likely to have undergone modification.

In the preliminary stage it may be possible to include overall estimates of current costs and the hoped for savings and benefits. Each document used will have considered the costs under the following general headings:

1. The cost of the present equipment, installation, and its accommodation values
2. The cost of the proposed equipment, installation and its accommodation values
3. The cost of running the present system

4. The cost of running the proposed system, including items like supplies and data transmission

The costs and incentives for the new system should be evaluated by a set of standards which are determined systematically and realistically for both equipment and labor costs.

An initial screening may be made with estimates and rationale for all factors in a checklist format to simplify the screening task. The estimates will represent the payouts and the equipment costs. Actual operating data can then be used to adjust the estimates. The operating records can be analyzed to improve the product throughput and quality.

Improved inventory control if achieved can result in lower costs. The improvement possible may have to be an estimate based on judgment. Sometimes it is possible to test the estimate using a small sample.

Computer simulation can also be used to estimate the payoffs for a new process. Figure 5-1 shows the typical factors and interactions involved in estimating the return. This figure is useful for both computer simulations and manual methods of estimation, a thorough effort may have many iterations between the blocks before a satisfactory resolution is achieved.

Besides the economic benefits, there may be intangible incentives which cannot be accounted for directly in terms of costs and payoffs. An analysis or survey can be conducted to point out areas which offer the greatest payoff for improved control mechanization. Basic data such as the costs of raw materials, energy, and labor may have to be predicted and judged against the value and demand in the future. Processing costs may have to be defined and weighed against the costs predicted for the proposed system.

The feasibility phase can result in a report which can be developed into detailed specifications and drawings if the project is approved. The report should consider the possible methods of solution and recommendations for a choice of methods based upon the costs and benefits as analyzed.

The feasibility report can provide the basis for deciding to shelve the project or to authorize additional costs for development. Authorization for the costs of purchasing equipment can be done after a more detailed analysis. Equipment specification is usually carried out in parallel with system development and im-

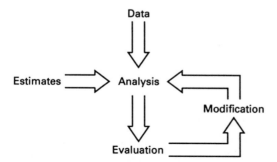

Figure 5-1 Estimating Flow

plies a strong interaction betwen these two phases. Specification can start from an approximate configuration of the system recommended in the feasibility report.

The number and type of input devices can be estimated along with the number and type of control output devices. Besides performance and cost, the preliminary specifications should consider such topics as manufacturers available, maintenance required, and possible additional training required.

Preliminary specifications may include such basic factors as the environmental requirements such as temperature, dust, and vibration. Power and emergency power requirements can also be specified. If expansion is planned in the future, this can be specified on the drawings.

Modifications in the basic processing may also be considered. These might involve a different way of segregating data handling or flow. It is possible that some of these have been considered earlier, but were discarded as too expensive a modification to the existing system. These costs can now be analyzed as a part of the new system and many times can show a different return on investment. The locations of the system components can be specified on the drawings and cable layout diagrams prepared. The use of preassembled hardware and cable racks can be used to reduce costs as these can be labor intensive.

The diagrams should consider the problem of signal noise, and the isolation of sensitive devices and noise sources should be an integral part of the design. Any unusual requirements for maintenance such as periodic cleaning should be identified and located so there is minimum interference during system operation.

As these sections of the system are defined, the product configuration can be updated toward its final form. When sufficient detail is achieved, the cost analysis performed for the feasibility phase can be updated.

5.2.1 Cost Savings and Estimation Considerations

The costs per unit of finished product tend to follow industry demand. Considerable savings can be achieved when supplier contracts are closely monitored and controlled, with alternate sources being available to avoid penalties from undersupply. Balancing suppliers can also reduce costs. Supplies can also be reduced by more efficient utilization of stocks and fewer losses through closer operating tolerances. By careful monitoring of overstress conditions, damage to expensive components can be prevented.

Automated lines can cause labor costs to decline, but while the number of operating personnel are reduced, those that are left must be better qualified to monitor the system and react to emergency situations. Also, the support services for some computerized systems can be large enough to offset any reductions in labor costs.

If operations can be completely automatic, savings may be realized, while in situations which may already have some automated processing, costs may increase. Increased costs can usually be expected because improvements may require more highly skilled maintenance personnel, but an improved product or system can also produce better maintenance procedures resulting in less down-time due to failures.

Training costs will also be incurred as the new system goes on line, but this is usually a small part of the total cost. Depreciation costs will tend to rise as a function of the cost of the system equipment; these expenses will usually be treated as normal capital investment for tax purposes. Selling expenses will be increased with a new product, but improved inventory control can be implemented to reduce costs due to the better allocation of materials and improved scheduling of material and product flow.

Administrative costs can also be expected to increase, but improved controls may result in a better safety record, which can lead to lower insurance costs. Increased staffs in both clerical and technical support can be used to achieve improvements in safety and quality control.

Net sales may be increased if the sales price or the quantity sold can be improved upon the new product or system. Better quality control can lead to a high-quality product or new product grades or classifications which can produce higher profits. Sales volume may be improved with quicker production cycles, and faster delivery can improve service and attract more orders.

Fixed investment costs can be reduced by a more efficient utilization of equipment, but if the market is limited, improved production will not result in higher sales volume. In these cases improved control systems can sometimes result in some modernization to improve efficiency, and with the improved efficiency older lines which are no longer needed may be retired.

A smoother flow of product can reduce the peak capacity requirements of the overall system and in turn lower the fixed investment costs. Also, less space is required for storage and production. A properly designed system causes less wear and tear on equipment resulting in a longer life and a saving of funds required for replacement.

To evaluate the incentives for a new process or system, it is necessary to examine the factors that have been discussed up to now and apply these cost considerations to the specific problem and develop payout versus return figures. An initial screening can be made of the various methods of improving the process and system estimates, and rationale can be made for all factors by using a checklist which simplifies the screening task. These estimates may represent savings in costs, production, materials, or labor.

In some systems full capacity is not achieved since maintenance or loading must be performed frequently, in these cases improved production can be achieved from better utilization of labor and equipment. Operating records can be analyzed to improve throughput, yields, waste, cycle time, and quality.

The improvement possible may have to be a theoretical estimate based on engineering judgment, but sometimes it is possible to test the estimate using some form of simulation. A small-scale test may be devised, for example, to test an improvement for data handling or processing. A system may also be operated around the clock for a few days to determine yields from the improvements. Operating records may also show the higher production possible due to exceptional circumstances if good records are kept. These production rates can then be extrapolated upward for the proposed modifications.

These records can also be analyzed statistically to improve yields. By determining the standard deviation of the distribution of the parameter under study it may be possible to predict the frequency of the improvement in yields due to the change in process variable.

Simulation techniques can also be used to model systems and estimate advantages. Figure 5-2 shows some typical factors and interactions involved in developing a model for a proposed new product or system.

Besides the economic benefits, intangible incentives can occur from a new process or system. At times these intangibles can be an overriding consideration, for example, an improved process or system may be the only way to achieve the desired safety or quality required. Intangible benefits may be found in improved plant management, more efficient coordination of production and facilities, and improved scheduling. These considerations are all based on real economic benefits, but these benefits may be difficult to measure in dollars and cents.

5.2.2 Cost Trade-offs

The advent of the microcomputer has brought a new philosophy to computer applications. Because processor memory and input/output logic are now contained on a few chips of silicon, the cost trade-offs differ from those used in the past for the use of computers and minicomputers.

There are two characteristics of a program which are of some interest. The static characteristic of a program refers to the occurrence of the use of the instructions. The dynamic characteristic refers to the frequency of execution of those instructions.

The dynamic characteristics primarily affect the performance of the system. In terms of space occupied in the program memory, there is no difference between instructions that execute only once and those that execute hundreds or thousands of times. All instructions occupy a portion of the memory space.

The microcomputer's performance capability is to be determined by the dynamic characteristics of the program. The number of times a feature is executed will help determine if the use of CPU resources is worthwhile.

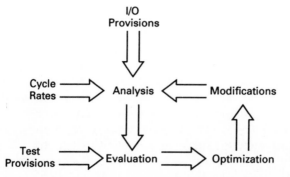

Figure 5-2 System Development

A feature may be included if it is needed to achieve a higher performance level. A low frequency of execution suggests that the feature should not be included but should be programmed as a part of the software. An example might be the inclusion of floating point arithmetic.

5.3 DEFINING THE INTERFACE

Many microcomputer system applications involve several operations rather than single tasks which can require additional definition efforts. For example, the use of a microcomputer to control an electrical or mechanical system such as a CRT terminal or card reader requires a variety of calculations, and the device may generate a variety of outputs.

The user may wish to solve a particular set of equations, find data records, or perform some other tasks. The initial stage of development must define the tasks to be performed and the requirements to be met. A major consideration is the form of the inputs and outputs required. There is the need to determine what devices will be attached to the microcomputer and in what form they will send and receive data.

Other important considerations include the required data rates, error-checking procedures and the control signals which the input/output devices might use to indicate the availability of data or the readiness to accept data. The formatting requirements and protocols must also be decided.

In many tasks the input/output requirements tend to be major factors during the definition phase. There are also the questions involving the processing requirements, the sequence of operations for the input data, and the order in which other tasks are to be performed.

The order of operations in many applications may be critical and the input/output signals must be sent or received in a particular time sequence. The system may also have timing requirements such as minimum data rates, mechanical and electrical delays, holding and settling times, recovery times, and enable and disable rates. The use of latches and timing circuits may be used to satisfy many of these requirements. Memory limitations may control the amount of program and data memory or the size of buffers.

5.4 PAPER CHECKS

Paper checking involves the checkout of the design using calculations for the logic design and the program timing. In a paper-checking exercise, the program is executed by hand, filling out entries in a table corresponding to the expected values and calculating the critical timing parameters using the specified instructions and cycles. This permits a check gross of the result of the program.

This technique requires no hardware; however, it can be long and tedious. Paper checking can also be accomplished at the flowchart level to verify the overall design. It may not always result in a reasonable evaluation of performance. To truly evaluate performance, one normally has to use actual test results. In many cases, however, paper checks can be used to evaluate a number of different approaches using a common benchmark for the application.

5.5 DOCUMENTATION REQUIREMENTS

The total engineering concept embodies the creation, implementation, and documentation of a design. The documentation discipline is an important part of this concept since it allows the interface design to be initially produced and then maintained and reproduced with the same initial characteristics.

In systems using instrumentation and test equipment with conventional electronic or electromechanical components the documentation may specify only the electrical and mechanical characteristics of the components used. The electronic components sense the outside world through the inputs and cause events to happen by driving the outputs.

The input signals may come from switch contacts or other devices. The outputs can control devices relays such as motors and displays.

The way the system functions when power is turned on is determined by the circuits used in it and the interconnects between the circuits. These internal circuits can include input and output drivers, timing, logic, arithmetic, and memory. If the circuits are standard modules used in other systems, they are fully specified, documented, and tested apart from the system itself.

The principal documents are the specification, the schematic, and the assembly print. The specification tells what the circuit does when it stands alone. The schematic is vital for describing how a circuit works. It is a conceptual document. The assembly print will be used to put the hardware together. The three documents must be related by common labels and descriptions, and each has a distinct purpose.

The design cycle tests the accuracy of the documents. The final documents are the product of the design cycle. Breadboard and prototype hardware are vehicles to prove that the hardware can be built from these documents since a specification may be written for field servicing for each component or module.

5.6 DESIGN TOOLS

Some circuits and interconnect wiring may be used just for this system; in this case, the documentation will be developed as the system evolves. The use of a microcomputer in these systems introduces a new element: operating the software programs. The microcomputer and its software program replace many of the conventional circuits used in the past and their interconnects. This results in reduced hardware costs and increased system flexibility.

In conventional logic systems, the basic tools are the block diagrams, schematics, assembly drawings, and the parts and wire lists. For systems that use microcomputers it is necessary to use some of these old tools along with additional tools and disciplines due to the abstract nature of the software program design.

These additional tools have their origins in the computer industry. Some basic tools are flowcharts, memory maps, and program listings.

5.7 BLOCK DIAGRAMMING

The block diagram can be an essential tool in most microcomputer designs, it acts as the key link between the program and the hardware and allows the partitioning of the problem to take place. The block diagram serves several purposes. Its major purpose is to condense overall concepts into a single drawing. In general, it should provide maximum communication with as little detail as possible. In the initial design stages, the block diagram provides the foundation for collecting and communicating the design idea.

In this early phase the block diagram can be used to show the interconnection of the microcomputer to all the input/output elements. From the block diagram it is also possible to partition the I/O program modules. Input/output modules may then be programmed independently. For example, I/O modules could be written to scan and read the keyboard and output to the display. Systems can be well represented in the form of a number of block diagrams. These can help in the understanding of a system and recording of it for future use.

The main fault is that the relevant actions cannot be immediately detected by looking at the chart, and it may be possible to work out what is happening only by a reference through each detailed step. If the number of steps followed is large, then much will be forgotten on how a particular sequence began by the time the end is reached. If this is the case, then the flowchart will not have fulfilled its function of informing—only that of recording. Consider the main points of the system and then take some time to plan the best method of grouping the activities of the system so that these main points are easily seen. Sometimes this can best be done by a more narrative description, with a number of blocks each describing an operation in the system. The block diagram allows each statement a greater power and each step in the system is drawn in an appropriately sized box. This technique allows one to show how the various steps interlink, and how each step might be repeated as a result of other actions.

The block diagram technique should generally follow these rules:

1. The use of few words
2. The use of as much space as possible
3. The liberal use of cross-reference

The requirement for space helps to make the diagram more visually and therefore more easily understood. It also allows changes to be made when further areas are uncovered later.

In the later stages the block diagram can be used as a training tool for educating test and service personnel. The block diagram is also useful as a reference for allocating system resources. It can be used to show how the elements of the system are required for interfacing details such as port assignments and memory allocation.

5.8 FLOWCHARTS

Flowcharts provide a visual statement of the problem solution using sequentially interconnected symbols to illustrate the program sequence. The flowchart thus serves to complement the block diagram. The block diagram illustrates the interconnection of the hardware, while the flowchart shows the interconnections for the program flow.

Flowcharts can be a major tool for program partitioning, reduction, and simplification. To avoid addressing conflicts, it is necessary to chart or map out the resources available to the CPU and then to make the allocation assignments as required. All the resources such as memory or I/O can be allocated in this way. As an aid to keep track of the resource, allocation is very useful. These visual aids or maps can be modified to allow memory or I/O space assignments as they are required.

The design of the programming task is greatly dependent on block diagram techniques in real-life applications. In a typical application, problem partitioning, program reduction and simplification, resource allocation, and program assembly will use these basic tools and techniques.

The program listing is a step-by-step list of the program operation. The listing can be made up of the machine language bit patterns, their numerical representations or verbal assembly, or high-level language statements.

The listing should always include comments or other descriptive notations that are easily recognized, since changes may occur frequently in the program. If hardware changes require the use of another device and address, the programmer may need to find each instruction and change it. If the programmer has used a proper name or definition, then it can be easy to correct what name needs to be changed, if the original definition and the typical use are easily recognized.

Flowcharts have some advantages over program listings in that they can

1. Show not only the order of operations but the relationships between the various sections of the program.
2. Be independent of a particular microcomputer or language.
3. Use a standard set of symbols as typically shown in Figure 5-3.

In beginning an interface design, think first of the tasks to be done. After these task requirements have been established, consider the details of how the program carries it out. Here, the flowchart is used as a tool for simplification and reduction. Approach the problem solution in a straight-away manner and develop the decisions.

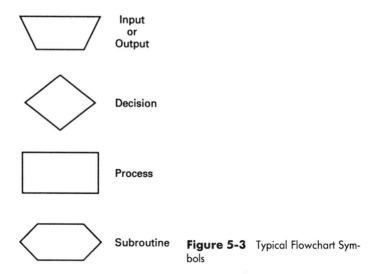

Figure 5-3 Typical Flowchart Symbols

The solution can be reworked until it has been simplified and reduced. The simplification and reduction using the flowcharts are accomplished by moving the repeated functions into common paths.

Flowcharts have similar advantages of pictures over words. They provide a way for nonprogrammers and programmers to communicate. Several levels of flowcharts may be used: one can show the general flow of the program while others provide the details.

In many cases flowcharts may have little connection to the actual structure of the system or even the data. These flowcharts tend to describe only the program flow. They normally will not show the relationships of the data structure or the system elements.

Too much detail can make a flowchart difficult to understand. A very detailed flowchart has only a small advantage over a program listing. Flowcharts are usually more helpful when they are more general.

In many of the programming stages, a flowchart can be prepared to show diagrammatically the logical relationship between the successive steps in the program. The steps represented in the flowchart may vary in the level of detail from almost a one-to-one correspondence to each individual program instruction to sections of large numbers of instructions.

5.8.1 General and Detailed Flowcharts

The levels of flowcharts normally prepared for a program may range from an outline or general flowchart to detailed flowcharts. The general flowchart will identify the main functions to be performed, relating them to the requirements of the specifications. It will relate the input and output functions, the main loops, and any entry and terminal points.

If the program is made up of segments, the general flowchart may indicate the relationship between these segments and the control routines. In some cases a separate segmentation flowchart may be prepared as a higher level, this is particularly true for a lengthy or complex program. The general flowchart acts as a link between the requirements of the specifications and the coding. The flowcharts should be cross-referenced to the sections of the specification in such a way that they can be checked for completeness and consistency.

For any flowchart to be useful, the individual steps should be noted, not with the operation code of the instruction, or even a direct interpretation for the code, but with the logical purpose of the step.

A detailed flowchart is more of a working document from which the instructions of the program can be prepared. The steps of this flowchart may be related to groups of instructions. Techniques such as loops, subroutines of switches, should be indicated symbolically on the flowchart so as to provide consistent directions for coding.

The use of cross-references from the detailed flowchart to both the general and to the resulting coding allows the program to be easier to understand. It also establishes a direct link from the specifications to the code.

The representation of the different types of steps in a flowchart uses a generally accepted set of symbols. Several sets are in use, one such set has been shown in Figure 5-3.

Flowcharts can be an essential part of the documentation of the program. By cross-referencing or indexing, the listing of the instructions may be linked through the flowcharts to the specifications and ultimately to the overall system definitions. In this way the effects of modifications can be checked. Since flowcharting is used to represent the logic of a program symbolically as a series of successive steps, it can be used in the preparation of all programs which are coded as a series of instructions performed in sequence.

Alternative techniques for planning programs may be used. Another technique that may be used for linking the requirements of specifications is the use of decision tables.

5.8.2 Vertical Flowcharts

In the planning of larger systems, a vertical sectional chart may be used. Here, as in the block diagram, we represent each step in the system in chronological order. This is used when it is required to record each action of the system and show how it interacts with other activities. The vertical sectional chart follows the same general pattern of plotting out the movements, but it shows them in streams or channels of actions carried out by separate tasks or groups.

This technique is useful when different groups or parts are required to check out their tasks in what may be a complex interactive system. If these are presented with a conventional block diagram, with all the activities carried out in a mass of detail, it is easy to overlook an incorrectly recorded task or not notice when one has been omitted.

The vertical organization allows each section of the system to be followed in one stream, and yet allow the whole system to be plotted as a block diagram. The chart can also be drawn horizontally, but it is still known as a vertical chart to avoid confusion with the type of horizontal chart described next.

5.8.3 Horizontal Flowcharts

The horizontal flowchart is used to describe a complex program or system in terms of all the documents. Each document is considered separately in the system, from its inception to the time when it is destroyed. The technique illustrates the life of each document and uses a limited number of symbols to indicate the operations involving each document. This allows each document's lifetime to be plotted on a separate line so the relationships between the documents can be shown. Each line begins with an origin symbol and ends with a destroy symbol so that each document is likely to be thoroughly plotted without omissions. This technique has the advantage of being understood by various individuals who may have to confirm the documentation. These charts may tend to be unwieldy and it may not always be possible to detect problem areas from an analysis of the chart. Its main use is to ensure that details of documents are completed.

A related form of chart is the procedures flowchart. Here, existing or proposed procedures are illustrated by means of standard symbols which may represent data gathered on different types of devices, or the processes through which the data must pass. A single symbol in a procedure flowchart might be a complete program or processing step.

5.9 DECISION TABLES

Decision tables may be used along with flowcharting as a method for representing the logical structure. Decision tables are based on the use of tables for recording information. This technique is similar to everyday life in timetables, price lists, interest rates, and tax tables. Decision tables are an extension of this technique. They allow alternative conditions to be related to the required actions using a simple structure.

The decision table structure uses a number of blocks to reference the conditions and actions. The structure can be illustrated by an example. Suppose a traveler at station A wishes to find the correct waiting platform for the destination, D: from a list of destinations, A to B, A to C, A to D, and so on, it is possible to find the entry which satisfies a requirement from A to D. For each entry in the list, there is an appropriate platform, finding A to D locates the proper platform.

The process of decision uses a tabular format where each condition is shown, together with the appropriate action necessary. The decision table is always divided up into an arrangement of four blocks or sections. Each block or section is reserved for specific entries.

Block 1 is called the condition stub. It contains a list of the conditions to be examined.

Block 2 is the condition entry. For each entry in the condition stub list, it contains a list of values that the condition can have.

Block 3 is the action stub. It contains a list of the actions that must be taken when a condition is fulfilled.

Block 4 is the action entry. For each entry in the action stub, it contains the value which the action has for the equivalent condition entry. Common modules can appear in the flowcharted system solution either directly or implied. Additional modules may be used with statements which can be further partitioned into additional flowcharts.

These statements may be used to build the subsystem modules. These subsystem modules can be composed of existing modules.

Now, consider a typical application from the specifications, relevant facts are gleaned about the application and these facts are used to achieve the design. First, consider those application characteristics which will provide the design foundation.

5.9.1 Functional Requirements

The use of microcomputers for conveyor control will be used as an example of a typical control environment. Some of the typical functions that may be required from the logic are

1. Different timing cycles including separate cycles for normal day conditions, night hours, rush hours, or special conditions depending on the product or batch, the time of day, or the monitored physical characteristics.
2. The initialization sequence which occurs after the power is applied.
3. Special facilities such as the preemption by policy or emergency situations.
4. Inputs by operators.
5. Computation of required parameters such as specified density, weight, or volume.
6. The capability for linking the controller to a central site or to other controllers in a network.

There are several limitations using the more traditional electronic logic controllers. A major problem is cost since a change in any of the functions may require expensive rewiring and redesign. There are major limitations in the complexity of the algorithms which can be implemented, both in the design and hardware costs involved. An adaption scheme using switches or jumper wires may be required for different situations which would require different algorithms. The limited switch or jumper wire pattern can limit the flexibility of the system.

The various modules are combined into the design. These may include volume, density, or weight counters; time-of-day counters; and other control modules. The microcomputer implements these modules into the system using software programs or subroutines contained in the program memory. The main variables are the number of inputs and outputs. The external loads are connected to the system based on general electrical and mechanical guidelines. The program is designed and documented using the required combination of tools and programs to accomplish the specified functions. Customization occurs at the software level. Software features such as status monitoring can be implemented which can result in a higher system reliability using fault detection.

Three basic modes of operation can exist with variations and combinations for various conditions:

1. A restart mode assumes that no information is available. This is used in the power-up stage until the other system parameters are available. These basic input parameters include the time of the day and the physical measurements.
2. Time-of-day programs are based on conditions during segments of the day such as rush hour or late night.
3. A parameter actuated mode can be used after the system has been in operation long enough to accumulate sufficient data.

It may use parameters such as the temperature, weight, or density.

5.10 HUMAN FACTORS

The human interface includes the controls as well as the display format. The control system in this example may be used to specify a number of physical parameters and the selection of the various modes of operation.

The system should have some manual actuation or capabilities for emergency situations. These facilities are to be used by operators when an accident occurs. The system can then be placed into a special emergency mode. It is important that this facility be easily and quickly operated in emergency conditions.

As microcomputer equipment becomes more automated, the role of the human operator becomes more important for effective utilization of these machines. Such factors as loading the machines, the physical location of controls and displays, the types of controls and displays or output devices, and the amount and nature of the data generated are critical for an efficient operator station.

Controls and keyboards should be located at angles and heights that allows comfortable arm positions and permit straight postures. Labeling should be sharp with high contrast images to reduce eye fatigue. Despite the advances made in keyboard design, problems still occur from multiple depressions of the same key and high-speed typing. Optimum positioning of the keyboard can do much to minimize the problems.

Displays should not be deeply indented as this tends to reduce the effective viewing angle. Maximum viewing angles and viewing distance should be considered for the display. Devices that require manual as well as visual attention should be mounted so that they are not difficult to monitor and operate.

Control devices should have sufficient clearance so that they can be manipulated without interference from other devices or surfaces. The clearance required should be a function of the control device, the frequency with which the device is likely to be manipulated, and the size of the operator's hand.

Control devices should also be located in the same general sequence that the operator uses them during normal operation of the equipment. When the equipment is large enough, one can control devices in the same relative positions as the locations of the various functions of the equipment. Devices which are related should always be grouped together and separated using a different color or a colored barrier.

Consistent criteria should be used to identify specific locations for all status light or other critical labeling. Guarded or protected controls may be used for critical applications such as emergency shutdown to minimize inadvertent actuations.

The standardization of control functions can do much to provide increased operator efficiency, especially if the functions are similar and are likely to be used with similar frequencies. For the display of data, a consistent system of pattern recognition can aid in the detection of variables when scanned by the operator. Pointers should move from the bottom to the top or from the left to the right as the variable increases.

Displays should consider the range of the human operator, which without any head movement approximates a solid cone with an angle of 60°. Although some head movement is usually done when scanning a large panel, adherence to the 60° figure can reduce fatigue over the long term.

Displays should be positioned such that they are perpendicular to the normal line of sight of the operator. For displays positioned below eye level the angle from horizontal should be greater than 30° for a standing operator. For a seated operator, displays below eye level should not vary from vertical more than 30°.

Display devices should always be mounted above the controls so that no part of the display is blocked when the operator is manipulating the controls. Hinged doors used in equipment should not block displays or controls when these doorways are opened.

Displays should be assessed based on the light intensity of the phosphor, the lighting levels of a typical installation, and the degradation of phosphor brightness with age.

Glare is sometimes a problem due to lighting levels and can be treated by one or more of the following techniques:

1. Antiglare window devices
2. Hoods which cover the tops of screens
3. Optimization of the angle of the viewing screen in relation to the operator and the source of the reflected light
4. Reducing the light level directly above the equipment

In color displays, a consistent color-coding system can aid in the identification of functions and grouping. Each color should designate specific groups or status. Contrasting colors for lettering and pointer backgrounds can aid readability and reduce eye strain.

Flashing displays should be used to call the operator's attention to off-limit or other error conditions. Flash rates may be varied to show the importance of the condition.

Visual input provides about 90% of the information to the operator with audible input providing the remainder. Because of the distracting nature of audible methods, it is usually delegated to alarms or to indicate error conditions.

Audible signals should have a distinct sound compared with others in the area that may occur. A different tone or frequency should be used. Another problem with audible devices is volume. Changing background noise conditions and variations in individual operator's hearing abilities make the proper volume difficult to achieve.

5.11 RETENTION FACTORS

The sensing of visual or audio information begins a chain of events that leads to some form of reaction. The amount of time needed by an operator to react to various amounts of information is shown in Figure 5-4. This type of data can be useful when estimating the time required for scanning an array of data and making a response.

Even if there is no information, a reaction time of about a quarter of a second is required. The minimum time is typically 0.25 to 0.33 seconds per bit of information, so 3 bits would require about 1 to 1.25 seconds of reaction time and this quickly increases for larger amounts of information.

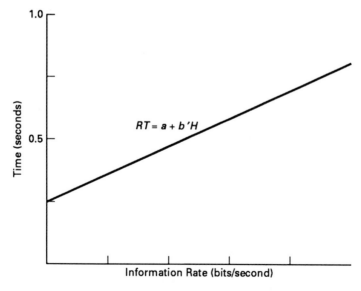

Figure 5-4 Typical Operator Reaction Time

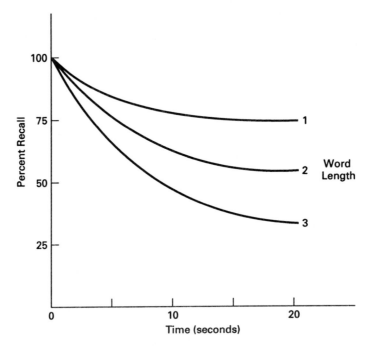

Figure 5-5 Memory Retention

The human memory provides an information storage unit to allow the integration of previous data into present activity. Job performance will be a function of how well the data can be retained in memory.

The thought process can be easily overloaded with information resulting in inefficiency and critical errors. The low capacity of the average memory to recall simple words and syllables when observed with others for a short time is shown in Figure 5-5. One word can be retained with about 80% recall, while three words can reduce the recall to about 20%. The proper operator training can improve these retention factors.

5.12 GRAPH PATTERNS

Pattern recognition techniques can also be used to overcome some of the recall problems. CRT displays are useful in this area, but at the same time, their flexibility can allow such a wide latitude of information to be displayed that the operator can be easily swamped. For a complex process or sequence, the structure of display parameters should carefully be designed.

Part of the display can contain an overview of what data is being scanned at that particular time, while other areas of the screen are broken into sections related to more detailed displays of the system. The proper structure can allow visual access to a great deal of data, while allowing little recall of previous information.

One technique for displaying related parameters uses each spoke inside a circle or a wheel to represent a parameter. In the normal state a circle is formed. A change in parameter is easily recognized since the circle will become distorted. A maximum or minimum circle can be used in this type of display.

Another method is the familiar vector concept where the parameters are plotted using a grid to show time or comparison trends. This technique is popular since it requires little computer memory and screen space and compacts a large amount of information in a small area. This type of display also does not require a large amount of recall once the operator has a few hours of practice in sensing trends.

An even greater amount of data can be compacted into a small area using the bar graph technique, and a dual bar system can be used to show trend data. This system may be a little harder for the operator to sense and slight trends may go unnoticed.

The bull's-eye concept is a form of motivational display which was designed to improve operator performance. The bull's-eye display of circles is divided into a number of segments, each with parameters. The ideal situation is to have all parameters within the inner circle or bull's-eye; thus it is easy to sense deviations. The concept is similar to the spoked wheel. Both techniques are a departure from conventional methods of displaying data. They attempt to stimulate operator awareness in order to reduce fatigue and improve performance.

If the common bar graph is expanded, it becomes a histogram. Other graphic displays that may be used include shmoo plots, scatter plots, and log curves. Histograms in three dimensions can be useful to show trends of multiple parameters.

Studies have shown that a majority of operators could absorb more information than they are given. Most of the more sophisticated display techniques have been developed from an engineer's point of view. One of the first requirements of a design project should be the definition of the role to be played by the operator. The objectives of the mission of the operator should be clear. A means to evaluate the operator and equipment interface can be established and periodically reviewed. This will allow the human interface to be incorporated into the interface hardware and software system.

5.13 ERROR-HANDLING CONSIDERATIONS

Many systems need to interface with the electrical or mechanical equipment without direct human interaction. The software must not only provide the proper interface but must also be able to handle errors. The task is to keep the system operating if possible and ensure that the occurrence of the error is recognized. This is another part of problem definition.

In error handling, the recovery method from incorrect sequences or erroneous signals must be specified. The most common errors can be handled specifically in the program. Some errors may be handled by restarting the operating procedure.

The most likely errors should always be carefully considered and described in the design documentation. The interactions with other programs must also be considered.

Assume, for example, an application in which a microcomputer is used to control a scale. The operator places a quantity on the weighing table and enters the desired parameter (weight or density) on the keyboard. The scale displays the weight or density of the quantity on a display. There are two inputs in this system. One input is the scale which may come from an analog-to-digital converter to the weighing mechanism.

The microcomputer starts a conversion cycle, determines when it is completed, and collects the data. The sequence of operations will depend on the particular type of converter being used. The microcomputer may perform some of the conversion tasks, and a part of the converter may consist of software.

The other input is from the keyboard which consists of a matrix of switches connected in rows and columns. The microcomputer will identify which key has been pressed by determining the row and column that are connected. The microcomputer may debounce the keys by waiting for a clean contact to be made since the key closure will initially bounce up and down. The microcomputer may also scan the keyboard and separate any multiple key closures by distinguishing a single longer closure from separate shorter closures.

The program must encode the keyboard results and send the digits to the display and multiply the weight by the cost per pound of the item. The weight is usually specified to the nearest hundredth of a pound.

The time requirements will be based on a reasonable human reaction time. The total system time includes the conversion time of the A/D converter, the time required for the keys to be pressed and bounce, the time required to process the display, and the frequency needed for viewing the display. The overall speed of this system is not a critical factor, since the calculations are minimal. The operator prepares the input and examines the output. The program must observe the limitations of the I/O devices and be coordinated with them using interrupts or some other means. The memory requirements are small since the program will not be large.

A number of erroneous inputs may occur. These may be human or electrically induced. Errors may exist due to

1. Improper keyboard inputs such as too many or too few digits or two or more keys pressed at once
2. Display malfunctions
3. Processor malfunctions
4. Keyboard malfunctions
5. Converter malfunctions

The most frequent errors will be improper data from the keyboard. The program may automatically recover from some errors by ignoring extra digits or multiple keys that are depressed simultaneously.

The operator will discover other input errors by checking the display. The program will need to continue the processing in a reasonable manner while the operator will attempt to correct the error.

Errors in the weighing mechanism or converter may not be apparent. The CPU might check the converter by providing it with a known input. A standard weight input could be used to check the weighing system. The program could also provide special displays to warn the operator of these errors.

Some errors may not be easy to detect. Calculation results may cause overflows. The program should provide a warning, a special display, or audible warning to ensure that the operator is aware of this condition. A conflict flasher may also be provided for the same reasons.

5.14 FAIL-SOFT METHODS

Fail-soft facilities may be desirable in case of hardware or software malfunctions. This can be done in the case of a conveyor controller with a conflict monitor and flasher message. A conflict monitor may monitor the system status continually. If two conflicting conditions should ever be on simultaneously, the conflict monitor detects this, disconnects the microcomputer controller, and turns on the flasher message. This may remove a dangerous situation which can result in damage. In critical applications such as this, if a software or hardware malfunction should occur which would result in a conflict, the system should detect this condition and take action. The complete system should not be disabled if possible.

5.15 SELF-TEST TECHNIQUES

Techniques can be used by the microcomputer itself to diagnose and correct the possible error conditions; these are self-test techniques. When a malfunction occurs, another microcomputer could take over the functions if the system is equipped with additional software and connecting lines.

When a significant flow of information may occur between a local controller and a control center, time division multiplexing (TDM) may be used to encode the data. The microcomputer may provide some TDM facilities in software, reducing the need for additional hardware.

In general, in operated applications, electrical and mechanical failures will be less frequent than operator keyboard errors. Keyboard failures, such as keys that are stuck or fail to make contact, will usually be apparent to the operator. Usually processor failure will also be apparent. It can, however, be difficult to diagnose and so some mechanisms may be required.

In a completely dynamic self-optimizing process control system, the microcomputer may start in the time-of-day mode, then it may switch to a parameter actuated mode as the parameters become available and then into a self-optimizing mode.

Process control can become very complex, requiring the simultaneous measurement of a variety of parameters. There is no simple formula which allows the direct optimization of the timing of the network. Heuristic techniques are often used.

It is also possible to experiment with new control strategies, and to implement them on the microcomputer using adequate safeguards. The microcomputer can implement a new strategy and then measure the resulting performance. This can be measured as an improvement over the performance obtained in similar situations.

5.16 SOFTWARE/HARDWARE DESIGN

Consider now the design of the software package to meet the requirements of the problem definition. The techniques available include top-down design, structured programming, modular programming, and flowcharting. The initial phase of this part of the development is a design and evaluation phase, where solutions to the problem are proposed and evaluated. The total design will involve the selection and the assembly of the hardware and the design of the software functions to be implemented on it. The essential consideration at this point is the selection of the hardware and software for the application.

The hardware design can be relatively simple when one uses standard microcomputer hardware. It tends to be more complex when nonstandard interfaces are required.

A more significant task is usually the software design. However, a number of tools and systems are available which allow the software to be designed more efficiently.

A major decision to be made is how many functions to implement in the form of devices and how many to implement in the form of software. This is the hardware/software partitioning.

After the overall product definition task has been defined, the development of the software/hardware design can begin. Traditionally, system design is closely linked with flowcharting. The techniques of flowcharting are helpful in describing the program structure and in explaining the program flow. Flowcharts are also useful in documenting the software. Programs can result from a detailed flowchart which is used to write the code. But drawing a detailed flowchart is almost as difficult as writing code and can be less useful since the program must then be derived from it.

A number of formal design techniques or concepts are available for writing programs for microcomputers. These include

1. *Modular programming.* Here, the programs are divided into small parts or modules which are designed, coded, and debugged separately and then linked together.
2. *Top-down design.* Here the overall task is first defined by generalized subtasks that, in turn, are more fully defined. This process continues on down

until all the subtasks are defined in a form suitable for coding. (The opposite of this technique is bottom-up design in which subtasks are first defined and coded and these are then integrated into the overall system design.)

3. *Structured design.* Here, the programs are written according to defined formats. Only certain types of program logic are allowed, but the routines can be nested within each other to handle the more complex program flow situations. Structured programming tends to use sections with a single entry and single exit.

Software Development

This chapter shows you how

- Programs are designed and developed
- Overlays or segmenting are used
- Programming styles are utilized
- Execution time and memory size may be minimized
- Modular design techniques may be utilized
- Top-down design techniques may be utilized
- Defensive programming may be utilized
- Software development tools may be utilized
- Testing and debugging time may be shortened

It is involved with the concept of programming, the means of which micro-computers achieve their flexibility. The program is the set of instructions to be obeyed by the microcomputer. As each instruction is obeyed, the sequence of operations determines the overall task. Since the programs are infinitely variable, the number of possible tasks is limited only by the ingenuity of those doing the programming.

This chapter describes methods that can be used in developing the program. There is also the task of translating the program into a format which can be accepted by the microcomputer. This is the programming language. The methods by which programs are checked and corrected will also be discussed.

Developing the program involves coding the algorithms into a programming language. Coding involves the translation of the program specifications into instructions. These instructions form the actual program or software product. The coding may be done using the assembly language for the particular microprocessor or alternative higher-level language.

6.1 SOME BASIC TECHNIQUES OF SOFTWARE DEVELOPMENT

Good program design requires the precise formulation of the program logic and timing. Flowcharting, modular and structured programming, and top-down techniques are all methods for formulating the types of programs that can be easily coded, debugged, and tested. The use of good design practices at the earlier stages greatly simplifies the later stages. The basic emphasis in developing the program should be on clarity and comprehensibility. A simple program structure along with thorough documentation can make the program easy to debug and test later.

The choice of language will determine the organization of the program, both at the flowcharting stage and at the coding stage. Programming in machine assembly code will require a greater degree of detail in the flowchart, since the programmer has to code more instructions. The use of high-level languages enables the programmer to use single instructions which contain a number of assembly code instructions.

The rules of writing the program in different languages requires the programmer to set the coding in certain standard formats, and to organize the arrangement of data and instructions according to the requirements of the language chosen. However, certain basic principles of coding apply regardless of the language chosen.

6.1.1 Simplicity

An overriding principle should be simplicity. Programs are likely to be used by someone other than the original programmer. Since there is no single programming solution to any particular problem, any program tends to be (at least in part) an original creation of the individual, and it displays some idiosyncrasies of that individual.

Simplicity is achieved by the program organization. The program can be divided into logical related parts, such as initialization, inputs, processing, outputs, and exceptions. This organization should be reflected in the flowchart and adhered to at the coding stage. The programmer should not use complicated and obscure methods for performing an operation, even at the cost of storage or speed. The saving of several microseconds is not as important as completing a working program.

There is usually a trade-off between simplicity and the requirements of speed and memory space. The program should operate as fast as possible and take up as little storage as possible, but the two requirements are not always mutually compatible. Memory may be saved by avoiding repetitive sequences by using subroutines and loops to perform sequences of instructions occurring repeatedly through the program. Improved storage of data can be achieved by sharing, for example, input and output areas. But these can require the setting up of parameters, and the loops can require counting and instruction modifications resulting in an increase in time.

The task of explaining how the program works can be simplified to a great extent by a good flowchart. The sequence of instructions chosen to perform the steps on the flowchart should not only be correct, but should be the simplest sequence possible.

Speeding up a program by buffering and the avoidance of instruction modifications can mean an increase in storage. In applications where one of these factors may be critical, one or the other must be sacrificed.

Since the advent of larger memory chips and faster processors, the former memory and hardware constraints are not as critical in microcomputer software development as they have been in the development of software for larger computers.

A major emphasis should be on how to write reliable programs in a reasonable time and how to document them. To begin with, there must be criteria for evaluating programs. These criteria should help to determine the aims, methods, and relative importance of the various stages of software development.

The following factors can be considered in writing programs. The most important criterion for a program is whether it works reliably. The structure, the efficient use of time and memory, the short design time, and documentation are all meaningless if the program does not work. The program must be checked to see that it works correctly under test conditions which reflect the actual application conditions. The selection and execution of the test conditions are not always simple tasks. The problem definition and program design stages can greatly aid in producing test plans and a program that can be easily and thoroughly tested.

A program that executes tasks more quickly will do more work than will a slower one. Speed may determine if the program works at all, if critical timing requirements exist. When the speed of the system depends on external factors, such as operator response time or data rates of displays or converters, the program speed is not as important.

Each chip needed for the system memory adds to the system cost. The additional memory requires additional interconnections, board space, decoding circuitry, and increased power. As larger semiconductor memories have become available, the critical importance of memory size has decreased. But memory must still be considered, particularly in the smaller applications.

A program that is easier to work with is more valuable than is one that is relatively hard to use. Complicated data formats and unclear error messages can make a program difficult and expensive to debug, use, and maintain.

The program design and documentation are important factors in determining if a program is easy to use. Human factors are important if the program requires human interactions.

Programs that tolerate errors are easier to maintain. This usually requires that the program be designed to react in some way to errors whose occurrence may be foreseen. Error tolerance is important in situations where human operators are involved. The program should make the operator aware of erroneous inputs or malfunctions without shutting the system down.

Since reliability and programming costs are among the most important objectives in software development, a primary objective is to develop a program that works using a reasonable expenditure of time and money.

Improvements can always be made later if required. A major item in many projects is programming time so methods that can minimize the time required to complete a program are always desirable.

6.1.2 The Use of Overlays

For a program to be run with a minimum of storage, the program may be divided into modules which are also known as segments or overlays. Each module can be considered as an independent program, which performs a part of a longer routine. When a module's task is over, it calls in the next section, which replaces the previous section in storage. Certain parts of the program or data areas may remain common to all modules so that communication can take place between different parts of the program.

The technique of considering the program in sections or modules is useful even if actual overlaying is not required. Each part of the program may be written and tested separately as an independent routine and the completed parts brought together when all are tested and debugged separately. The decision on how to segment the program and if overlaying is necessary will depend on the amount of storage available to the completed program and the amount of coding necessary to complete the program. These are estimated before the programming starts, so that the modules can be planned at the outset.

If a program is written as one segment and finally proves too large, it can be difficult to split. If it is split before coding starts, the modules can be turned into overlays if necessary or combined into a single program.

6.1.3 Programming Style

There are several specific guidelines on programming style that are useful regardless of the particular language or microcomputer involved.

1. The use of names or labels is always preferred instead of specific memory addresses, constants, or numerical factors.
2. These names should always suggest the actual purpose or meaning of the particular address or data.
3. Repetitive operations should be done outside loops.
4. The use of short forms of addressing is preferred when possible. This can require that the data be reorganized.

5. Limit the use of jump statements, since they tend to use up much time and memory.

6. Take advantage of the addresses that are multiples of 8-bit quantities. This includes addresses such as the even multiples of 100 in hexadecimal.

Some techniques can minimize both the execution time and memory size, since longer programs require more memory accesses and more execution time. Subroutines present a memory savings to the program at the cost of the time required for the call and return execution. Loops require a similar trade-off. When minimum execution time is desired, the subroutines and loops may be replaced by repeated copies of the same instructions; minimum memory requires the opposite. Typical gains from program optimization can result in speed increases or memory reductions of about 25–30%.

Programs tend to obey a 80/20 rule; 80% of the time is spent executing 20% of the code. To speed up a program, find that 20% and recode it. Often significant improvements in performance will result.

This 20% can usually be found in the inner-loop portions of the program. The recoding of selected subroutines can cut the running time approximately in half.

If larger gains are required, the following methods may be used:

1. The implementation of new algorithms can provide larger increases in speed or decreases in memory.

2. The increasing of the clock speed can improve performance provided that the processor and memory can be adapted to the higher speeds.

3. The use of hardware such as high-speed arithmetic processors can increase the throughput by relieving some of the processing burden from the microprocessor.

Find the loops that are executed most frequently by hand checking or testing the program. Then, try to minimize the number of instructions in these loops. The instructions that are used only a few times will have little impact on program execution time.

Use register operations when possible since these operations are faster than any others; however, they may require additional initialization software.

While obtaining simplicity and comprehensibility, the main objective of programming is still to write a program that works. The initial saving of a few microseconds or a few memory locations is seldom critical since the coding can be optimized later. The initial program should always be obvious rather than clever. Practices to avoid are

1. Performing operations out of order.

2. Using leftover results to initialize variables or for calculations.

3. Using parameters as fixed data.

6.2 SOFTWARE DESIGN TECHNIQUES

The more recent interest in software design resulted in the evolution of a number of new approaches. This growth in software design methods has been partly due to the increasing complexity of the problems involved. Software designers must relate to problems both intuitively and procedurally at the same time during the design effort. But, as the effort progresses, the emphasis shifts. At the start, one initiates the ideas which set the design into motion. The designer may have an intuitive feel for the solution but suspects that it may be wrong. So one must scrutinize the ideas and develop some conclusions. This process has been characterized as divergence, transformation, and convergency.

6.2.1 Modular Design

When a bigger problem is broken down into small problems, the basis of modular design emerges. In a similar fashion to a modular hardware design, the modules tend to isolate and separate the functions, making designing, troubleshooting, and debugging easier. The advantages of using program modules are many. The programming efforts can be distributed among several individuals or groups. Program modules can be designed and tested separately before they are linked together. The linking program and the modules may be designed with separating open locations which allow for changes without affecting the other parts of the program.

A first step in program partitioning for modular design is the division of the working memory space and the program storage space. The division is accomplished conceptually with the aid of mapping. The available memory space is visually presented as an array of identifiable address partitions. The partition size is selected as a portion of memory that is easy to handle both physically and conceptually, a memory module. The use of multilevel modules allows the designer to partition the problem. Figure 6-1 shows how the problem can be partitioned into system, subsystem, and hardware levels. The lower level is designated to control the individual hardware elements.

A hardware-level module might perform the port selection for the input or output of control signals or data. The hardware-level module can relieve the designer of port assignments once the module is written. Another advantage of the hardware-level modules is that port assignments can be changed without causing changes throughout the program. The hardware changes are isolated to the hardware-level modules. In a similar manner the system- and subsystem-level modules are to be used to partition the problem solution. In complex systems, additional levels may be required.

A program module can be executed using jumps as shown in Figure 6-2. A jump instruction may be used to go to the module, and another jump instruction is used to return to the control program. The module may also be linked into the main program using relocatable addresses.

As the I/O modules are developed, small test programs can be written in memory in place of the control program. After all the I/O modules are developed,

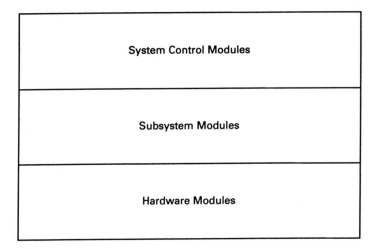

Figure 6-1 Modular Partitioning of the Program

the subsystem modules are developed to tie together any interacting I/O modules. Then the control program may be assembled by tying together the subsystem and I/O modules according to the operational specification.

Data memory allocation also takes place during the process of module development. The data memory resources are allocated using the mapping technique. The data memory will consist of various dedicated storage areas.

As the program modules are developed, they can be allocated to program memory. Assignments can be made on a program memory map.

6.2.2 Segmentation

Since each area has a set of modules or processes that may access it, depending on the items stored in it, it has a particular length. The architectural structure requires segmentation. Using segmentation, the memory areas can be separated,

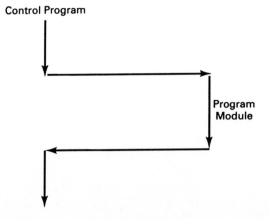

Figure 6-2 Linking Program Modules with Jumps

accessed, and shared. Without any segmentation, the memory areas appear as unstructured arrays with no apparent mechanism for the dynamic sharing or position independence needed. The larger the address space, the more important is the structure and the control access.

The major benefit from segmentation is the decomposition of the memory areas. Segments allow the system area to be divided into system communication areas that may hold messages or data that may be passed among processes. The process area might contain data segments that are private to the process and global to its modules. The module area could contain a code segment and a data segment for each module.

As an example, the 8086 uses a segment selector to reference segments. The current module code segment, module data segment, and process stack segment are selected according to the type of access. Outside the immediate environment, access is made to process data segments or system communication segments using an explicit segment selector.

Intermodule transfers are accomplished by changing the segment selectors. Interprocess transfers also alter the segment selectors and a stack selector to establish a new segment environment. This scheme defaults to the localized references of modular programs.

Modular programs can be used to support higher-level applications which require systems that execute multiple processes. A three-process system might consist of a job process that performs useful work, such as controlling a group of output units, an input process that provides the necessary data to the job process by sampling and queueing the outputs of the units, and an output process that delivers the results of the computation to the output devices.

A command module may accept the job process for execution. All commands to initialize or calibrate are directed to a calibration module, while commands for data are directed to a data module. This module deals with data in the proper representation and units on command. The data module obtains this data, and the command module queues it for the job process.

Sampling conversion and other computations on raw data may be required, and these operations are performed by an input module. The calibration module has access to the input module for calibration purposes. In general, any changes in the queueing scheme between the command module and the job process should not affect either the data or the input modules.

The partitioning of the functions into modules and the defining of the module interfaces is a part of structured design.

The system is composed of processes, which are divided into modules, which implement the functions. Table 6-1 illustrates this approach.

TABLE 6-1   SYSTEM MODEL

System	
Process	Process
Module	Module
Function	Function

The module is a collection of related functions and data whose internal structure may not be known by the users of the module. Programming languages such as Ada support this type of system mode, while others such as FORTRAN, BASIC, COBOL, C, and Pascal require nonstandard language extensions to group functions and data into modules. Ada was specifically designed to overcome Pascal's lack of support modularity.

Continuing this approach produces the system memory structure of Figure 6-3. The modular approach produces a system/process/module layering. The innermost section is the system communication area, where the processes send and receive messages which coordinate their activity and pass data and results. The sections are divided into individual areas for each process. They may be private or local to a single process.

The outer layer is divided into different areas for each module, and each area contains instructions and data that is private to its module. The area for a process is public, or global, to each of the modules in the process.

The modules are usually divided along functional lines. In many computer applications, this type of division has much utility because the modules can be used to form a library of programs that can be easily modified for other design tasks or products.

Modular programming techniques allow programs to be written, tested, and debugged in smaller units that are then combined. Top-down design requires

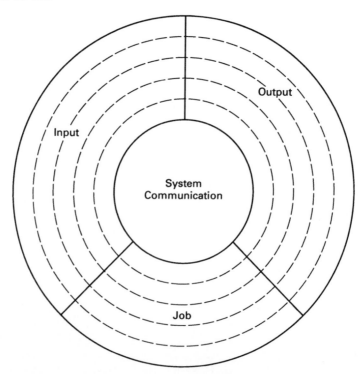

Figure 6-3 System Layers

modular programming, but modular programming is older and is often used independently of other techniques.

Another advantage is that the modular technique tends to limit the size of the program that needs to be debugged and tested. It can also provide a library of programs to be reused and the division of tasks can result in shorter design cycles.

The disadvantages include the additional program interfacing that may be required and the extra memory needed to transfer control to and from the modules, along with the need for separate testing of modules. Modular programming can also be hard to apply if the structure of the data is critical. Modular programming techniques can be used for developing the software in concert with other design techniques. Examples of typical modules are

1. A converter control program that signals a converter to begin conversion, waits for the conversion to be completed, and then places the results in a memory location.
2. A multiplication program that multiplies two decimal numbers.

A combination of techniques may be used since structured and modular methods are not mutually exclusive. The actual task is to produce a working system and one that does not follow the restrictions of any particular design method to achieve this end.

6.2.3 Top-Down Design

In the top-down design method the testing and integration can occur along the way rather than at the end, and problems may be discovered early. The testing can occur in the actual system environment instead of requiring the driver programs needed in the bottom-up concept.

Top-down design tends to combine the design, coding, debugging, and testing tasks during the software development. A problem with top-down design is that it sometimes forces the overall system design to not fully utilize the hardware. It can also require the system hardware to perform tasks that it does not do well. Top-down design can also be difficult to apply when the same task occurs in several different places in the program. The routine that performs the task must interface properly at each of these places, and the proper stub can sometimes be difficult to write. A program may not have the simple tree type of structures that tend to mesh easily with the top-down approach. A program that incorporates the sharing of data by different routines may also present difficulties. Design errors at the top level can also have major effects on the entire project. In some applications, top-down design has resulted in improved programmer productivity.

Considerable effort is often needed so the top-down approach does not interfere with the development of reliable programs. The efficient use of top-down design implies that it be used in unison with other design techniques.

An example of a top-down design for A/D conversion could include the following steps:

1. The overall flowchart is written (Figure 6-4). The program calls A/D input routine which is a program stub and calls the other routines or program stubs if the input data is not 0 and then returns to reading the A/D input.
2. The input routine stub is expanded to perform the following tasks:
   a. Send a signal to the A/D converter to start the conversion.
   b. Check the CONVERSION COMPLETE line and wait if the conversion is not complete.
   c. Fetch a digit.
   d. Check the digit for 0.
   e. Repeat 2c and 2d for each digit to be converted.
   f. If all digits are 0, repeat the sequence starting with step 2a.
   g. Check for a final value for the conversion by waiting a period of time and then repeating steps 2a through 2f.
   h. If the inputs are not equal, repeat step 2g until they are equal to within the accuracy of the converter.
   i. Save the final input value.

A flowchart of the partially expanded program stub appears in Figure 6-5. Steps 2g through 2i would also be expanded and the procedure would continue to expand each block until there is enough detail for coding.

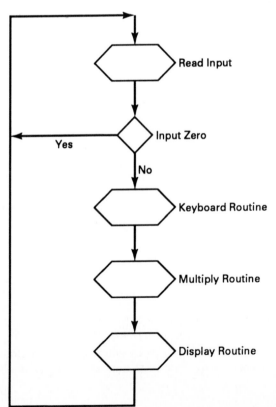

Figure 6-4 Typical Top-Down Design Flow

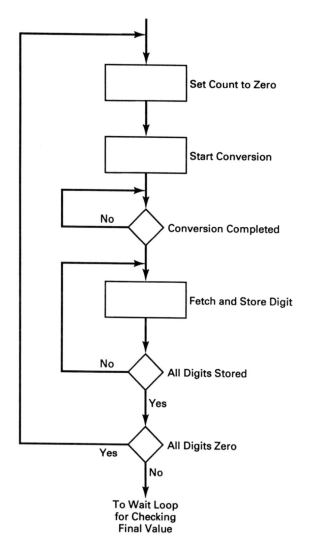

Figure 6-5 Top-Down Design Detail

     Consider now basic tasks for system development at the hardware level, the software level, and at the systems level. The major choices that must be made are

1. Choosing a microcomputer.
2. Performing the hardware/software partitioning.
3. Choosing a programming language.

6.3 THE BASIC TASKS IN HARDWARE/SOFTWARE DESIGN

Selecting the microcomputer involves the selection of a product which has the proper performance for the application. Other important considerations include product availability and the availability of support equipment and trained personnel.

The hardware/software partitioning task should be based on an evaluation of the various cost/performance aspects of the design task to be undertaken. The techniques used to assemble the various components of the microprocessor system, as well as the software techniques used to implement the program, will facilitate this choice.

The hardware/software partitioning task is one of the more delicate phases of the system design. The partitioning will have a major impact on the software design task. It may become desirable to change from a polling scheme to the use of interrupts, or even add hardware encoders as the initial design evolves.

In the past many designers tried to minimize memory usage and external hardware, since hardware and memory were much more expensive than additional software. But, today, the cost of memory and external hardware has been reduced while the labor costs to develop software have increased.

The tasks that once had to be done in hardware can now be done in software with reduced costs of both processors and memory. Additional hardware which can substantially reduce the complexity of programming is also available at relatively low cost.

Software costs remain the same regardless of the number of units produced, but hardware costs are proportional to the number of units. The trade-offs between hardware and software differ today from the days of expensive hardware, and new types of functional devices are becoming available all the time.

The proper design, debugging, testing, and documentation methods can do much to reduce the overall development costs. Writing programs in high-level languages can increase programmer productivity, and it makes many of the stages of development much simpler.

An important characteristic of the design is that it should be modular. The typical procedure is first designed on paper; then it can be built from the documents for testing.

Software development is primarily concerned with development of a mathematical model of the process or task of the microcomputer and the interpretation of the model into a set of control programs. There should be a strong interplay between this development and the product definition phase, since the model must eventually be based on available hardware and not theoretical paper hardware.

Development of the process or control model should attempt to explain such topics as

1. The sequence and frequency of all calculations.
2. Priority ranking of system interrupts and other processing functions.
3. Control optimization techniques.
4. Interface control provisions.
5. System failure provisions.
6. Backup and manual override features.

From the specific operating requirements, signal characteristics, and control system configuration, the operating strategy and detail flowcharting can be developed. Cycling loops can be specified during this period. These loops will be a function of the processing cycles and the amount of data involved. The loops used should depend upon what is taking place at that time for maximum utilization of the system.

Logging and alarm functions and message formats must be planned for content, format, and frequency to fit the recipient of the information. Flexibility should always be incorporated into these areas, so that changes in emphasis can be accommodated along with any shortcomings which are uncovered during the later test and operational phases. The flowchart documentation of these tasks should be extensive enough to allow its understanding by other personnel besides the programmer.

The software tests which will be used to check out the system can also be devised now. The procedures to be developed for the analysis of the test data and the criteria for success should be outlined at this stage.

When the overall program and model has been flowcharted and the interrupts and servicing requirements specified, more detailed flowcharts can be prepared. Program development should also consider provisions for training operators.

All procedures and operating instructions will have to be documented. Early document coordination of the project will allow for a smooth transition to the end of the test and operation phase. Also, this is necessary so that the system configuration does not cause critical operator errors through lack of document utilization. This can easily happen in computer-controlled systems where the computer is in control for more than 99% of the operating time. As long as a system is not completely automatic, an operator will be required to cope with emergencies and make decisions to minimize the loss of materials and damage to hardware in an efficient manner.

As the specifications, drawings, and flow diagrams, along with the cost estimates are completed, this material can be used to build a specification and development package and report any problem areas which need attention. A concise technical and cost estimate will provide the visibility required for approval prior to actual hardware expenditures.

After approval of the project, specifications can be transmitted to suppliers and subcontractors in order to confirm delivery dates as quickly as possible. It is usually better to check each component before installation for such basic parameters as continuity and output. This checking step usually allows the system checkout phase to proceed more rapidly with fewer problems. In systems with CRT displays units, many parts of the system cannot be checked until the computer is online, but some time may be saved by a thorough briefing and demonstration of the hardware, for example, at the vendor's plants or demonstration facility.

A significant proportion of any computer design program will be concerned with events which will probably not happen but which may happen. The system designer needs to be aware not only of the regular pattern of events but of the unlikely exception. For most systems, it is fairly straightforward to design methods of coping with the ordinary events, and most manual systems are designed only for the usual, relying on human intervention and ingenuity to deal with the unusual. Computer systems do not take kindly to unforeseen events and must be prepared to recognize the unusual and take appropriate action. This means that the designer of a new system must be aware of all the exceptions to the general activity. But, in designing a new system which is not going to replace or extend an existing system, it is not easy to determine the likely exceptions since there is no past history or experience to draw on. Where there is already an existing system, no opportunity should be lost in examining its characteristics in detail. Before the start of the design of a new system, the designer should be thoroughly familiar in all the theory on which the existing system or product is founded.

The problem solving aspects of design tend to be a fundamental, personnel issue. In many cases, design methods may be resisted when forced or imposed. The adoption of a particular method may require fundamental changes in both personnel and management attitudes.

The successful application of any method can occur only in a supporting environment. The elements of planning, scheduling, and control must be supportive to be effective. The balance between structured methods and creative environments is critical in problem solving, and a merging of these may be the next evolution in future software design techniques.

As in any new development, one should be sure to establish a timetable, which allows for modifications and training. Check that specifications and all other documentation are properly allocated. Spell out those differences from the actual user's point of view. Make sure that everyone fully understands how one is to use the software. Documentation should include flowcharts with descriptions and program listings. A user's manual with application examples may also be required. Make sure the schedule provides adequate time to develop the documentation and to give the software a thorough checking.

6.3.1 Documentation

Documentation is an important part of development. It is not only required for debugging and testing, but it is essential for maintenance and redesign. The properly documented program can be used again when required, but the undocumented program normally requires so much extra work to use that one might just as well start from the beginning.

The coded program is itself an important document. Proper cross-referencing to the flowchart and specifications can be a great aid to the understanding of the program.

Documentation may include lists of program switches, entry points, halts, and messages produced by the program. Operating instructions can also be an essential part of the documentation.

To achieve generality, use names instead of specific addresses or data along with the collection of definitions at the start of the routine and use names that suggest the purpose or identities of the item. These documentation techniques tend to produce a program that can be used frequently and can be easily modified.

The common techniques used for documentation are flowcharts, program listings with comments, memory maps, and parameter and definition lists. Structured programming and some of the other design techniques have developed some of their own documentation forms; these are different in format but not in substance.

A good program is not just one that works correctly. It must be clearly documented so that it can be readily understood by other than the original programmer. Good flowcharts can provide a clear link between the program and the specification. The coded program must provide links to the flowcharts and should contain explanatory notes. Most languages allow the programmer to insert these comments or narratives in the coding. The narrative has no effect on the code, but only allows the programmer to use notes and other references on the listings of the program.

Communication between programs and flowcharts can be achieved by reference numbers appearing on the flowchart symbols. Each section of coding can also be accompanied by the description of the function of the coding. In the same way the flowchart boxes can contain narratives. This narrative should not just repeat the coded instruction.

Flowcharts tend to act as a visual aid for program documentation. The general flowchart serves as a pictorial description of the program while the more detailed flowcharts are valuable to others who must use or maintain the program.

The proper comments can do much to explain the purpose of the instructions.

Commenting is a tool that must be used properly. It should be the minimum explanation that is needed to understand the program. If comments are provided in a systematic manner, they can be helpful in all stages of the software development.

The following general rules apply to comments:

1. The comments should explain the purpose of the instructions or instruction sequences, not just define the instruction codes.
2. The comments should be clear and brief, but avoid shorthand and obscure abbreviations. A complete sentence structure is not required, but phrases should be complete enough to be well understood.
3. The comments should be limited to the more important sections of the program flow. Too many comments can make the program difficult to follow. Common sequences do not need to be explained unless they are used in an uncommon way.
4. The comments should always be placed close to the statements to which they apply.
5. The comments should be kept up-to-date, and comments that refer to previous versions of a program should be deleted.

Memory maps list the memory assignments for the program. These maps prevent the different routines from interfering with each other and help in determining the amount of memory needed since they act as an aid in finding the locations of subroutines and tables.

The fact that addresses are assigned as part of the hardware design, the need to conserve memory and the need to know the precise locations of parameters that may have to be changed are all important reasons for memory mapping. Parameter and definition lists are also a useful part of the documentation. These lists explain the function of each parameter and its meaning.

Program forms are a convenient tool for the program listings. The program form can provide for several levels of communication between the designer and the hardware. The highest level is found in the comments and notation section where the designer communicates in sequential form using a human language. This section is much like the flowchart and is essentially independent of the machine language. The program forms should describe the subroutines. These can also provide the purpose of the program, the form of the input and output data, the requirements for memory of the program, and a description of the parameters.

Software documentation should combine all or most of the methods discussed. The total documentation package may include

1. General flowcharts.
2. Detailed flowcharts.
3. A list of all parameters and definitions.
4. A written description of the program which is referenced to the flowcharts.
5. A listing for each program module and its function.
6. A description of the test plan.
7. Memory maps.

The documentation is best performed simultaneously during the design, coding, debugging, and testing stages of software development. Good design and coding techniques can make the program easier to document, and good documentation, in turn, will simplify the maintenance and any redesign required.

The use of names can reduce confusion between addresses and data during the redesign. The redesign could involve the adding of new features or meeting changed specification requirements. The redesign should normally proceed through the same design stages of software development.

The redesign process may involve making a program meet critical time or memory requirements. When increases of 20% or less in speed or similar reductions in memory are desired, the program can be reorganized, but the program structure may be sacrificed. This kind of task could require a large amount of time and generally should be avoided if other techniques are possible.

6.3.2 Defensive Programming

Defensive programming tends to take extra time. The programmer can never anticipate all the problems that might occur, but defensive programming can result in fewer errors as well as programs that are easier to use and maintain. It is not always easy to follow the suggestions discussed here, but the use of these techniques can make the software development task much easier.

The required interpretation activity may sometimes seem an unnecessary and tedious task, and it may be felt that the system is good enough and that no benefit will accrue from the process of redrawing facts already familiar. It has been proved many times, however, that a simple restatement in a new form can reveal areas of redundant instructions opportunities for combination and possibilities of reduction—areas that would not be noticed if the system had remained in the context of something that has been done this way and probably always will be done this way.

When the investigation is completed, the designer should have a well-organized file containing the details of the program which gives a clear picture of how the system works and where some of its weaknesses lie.

It is often useful to reshape the facts into a form that allows them to be viewed in a new light. For example, a flowchart of the system could be examined in terms of the data requirements. Tables can be made showing all the data elements used in the system. Another table can show the number of movements from one place to another made by each data type and how many alterations or additions have to be made to the data as a result of these movements. Comparative lists can show how long the data and instructions take to reach their destinations. These can be analyzed to reduce effects due to the organization which result in excess time taken by the information. All these activities consist of a redrawing of existing information and a gathering of data into a new order for improved efficiency.

Program design tends to be a dynamic process. The design starts by breaking the problem or task down into functional modules using flowcharts which act as a tool for describing the sequence of events. The number of levels in the flowcharts are a function of the complexity of the program.

Once the flowchart defines a module, the program can be started for this module. As the program module or subroutine is designed and documented, it is integrated with the other modules into the program. The integration process is similar to the connecting of circuits together to form systems.

6.3.3 Language Considerations

The three basic types of programming languages are

1. Direct binary or hexadecimal.
2. Assembly language.
3. High-level language.

Programming in direct binary code or in the hexadecimal equivalent requires the least amount of supporting hardware and software. This method is often used on simple systems where the user communicates with the system using a hexadecimal keyboard and LED display. Instructions and data are put into the system via the keys in hexadecimal format.

Assembly-level languages use a mnemonic or symbolic representation of the binary code for the particular microprocessor. In terms of efficiency of the user program, it can be the most efficient method.

But the proper use of assembly language requires manipulating the registers to achieve program optimization in terms of code and memory usage. A good understanding of the structure of the computer system is required for the optimization of the program.

The assembler converts the mnemonic terms into an executable binary format. The assembler may also detect gross syntactical errors and flag them for the user. The major disadvantage is the tediousness of the programming in assembly language and the resulting programming effort compared to high-level languages.

Assemblers can produce either absolute or relocatable code. Absolute code must be loaded into a fixed location in memory, but relocatable code can be loaded in any point in the program. Relocatability allows flexibility in both designing the program modules and bringing them together into an executable program.

These block structured assembly languages are part of a software system that contains a relocating/linking loader, text editor, and disk operating system.

Macro techniques can allow improved efficiencies over straight assembly-level language. A macroinstruction, or macro, is a collection of assembly-language mnemonics. Some assemblers contain predefined macroinstructions.

To aid the programmer, the language replaces the mnemonics statements that are more obvious for the respective operation.

Combining assembly-language mnemonics into easier-to-remember statements, incrementing the accumulator can be replaced by

$$++ A$$

which is similar to the C language.

When a register pair is used as a pointer, its address can be enclosed in parentheses and preceded by an "M." For example,

"load the accumulator from memory
using the H-L register pair as address"

could be written

$$A=M(HL)$$

whereas it is

$$MOV A, M$$

in assembly language.

The use of parametric macros allows specific functions in the macro not to be defined until the macro is invoked. Constants can be defined, and addresses of variable and program labels may be preceded with an operator to indicate the address.

Any technique that combines several statements is an advantage because program modules can be developed faster. Macroinstructions yield programs that are almost as condensed and fast as those coded in assembly language but quicker and easier to write. A library of well-defined macros can sometimes be more valuable than a high-level language.

High-level languages such as BASIC or FORTRAN allow the programmer to use more powerful instructions to specify the algorithm. The high-level programming language is closer to the algebraic conventions used in the specification of algorithm. With this facility it is possible to code the algorithm in a shorter time. Programming in a high-level language may be as much as 10 times faster than programming in assembly-level language. This is especially true for longer, more complex programs.

The disadvantage of using high-level languages is that most compilers used to produce the object code tend to be inefficient in terms of the code produced. When they compile the high-level instructions into the machine-level binary instructions, they do not optimize the use of registers which results in many unnecessary register transfers. A compiler may generate two to five times more instructions than would be generated using assembly language. This results in additional memory requirements and in execution times two to five times slower. This may not be an objection in some applications. When programs are very complex, they might never get implemented correctly if programmed in assembly-level language. By programming in a high-level language, most medium to long programs can be written and debugged faster.

6.4 COMPILERS AND INTERPRETERS

The tools used to translate a high-level language into a particular computer's machine code include compilers and interpreters. A compiler translates a program written in a high-level language into machine code, assembly language, or some intermediate language. If the compiler generates assembly language, an assembler must be used for the final translation into machine language. Compilation may take several passes to perform required functions such as

1. Lexical analysis to identify keywords and operators.
2. Syntactic analysis to identify each statement's type and correctness.
3. Flow analysis to find relationships between statements as an aid to error in checking, register assignment, and optimization.
4. Optimization in order to reduce the total number of instructions.
5. Code generation to produce assembly or machine language.
6. Generation of the program listings.

Interpreters tend to be linked with the machine that executes them. They become a part of a host and act to transform it into a new machine having as its native language the high-level language. Interpreters provide fast, interactive programming and debugging, since each instruction is translated before the next; errors show up immediately.

Some high-level languages use compilers, but BASIC mostly employs inter-preters. Since the interpreter converts the statements or source code into machine language one by one, it is suited for interactive use. For highly repetitive tasks, the need to translate over again makes execution times go slowly.

A compiler usually does not interact until the program starts to execute. There may be an error message for a line, but there is no chance to fix the problem until all the statements have been completed.

6.5 SOFTWARE DEVELOPMENT AIDS

In most microcomputer systems there are considerable interactions between the hardware and the software. In these systems, the software development can be aided by means of tools which act as an umbilical to the hardware system.

To aid the task of program development there are a number of software development aids which are available:

1. Assemblers and cross-assemblers
2. Editors
3. Debuggers
4. Loaders
5. Simulators
6. PROM programmers
7. Emulators

6.5.1 Assemblers and Cross-assemblers

The assembler program converts the symbolic assembly instructions written by the programmer into machine-language instructions which can then be executed by the microprocessor. Using the machine's assembly language, there is access to facilities like interrupt control and the I/O ports. To generate the machine code, the assembler takes instructions such as ADD, SUB, and MULT and converts these into machine bit patterns. It also converts the labeled machine addresses designated by the programmer into real machine memory locations.

The assembler translates the source code program into the binary object program, which can then be directly executed by the machine. An assembler program will substitute the actual addresses instead of symbolic ones. The assembly process substitutes the actual binary encoding of data instead of the symbolic names and the suitable binary format for the instructions instead of their mnemonics. The object program is the result of this assembly process. The object program is a sequence of binary words, which can then be directly executed by the processor. The object program can be executed on the actual processor or a simulated processor.

After a program has been typed into the system, it is desirable to print it in order to verify that it is complete. A source program is then printed which appears as a listing.

It was not necessary to use the target microprocessor to develop the object program. The functions that are required could be provided by any processor. The use of a larger processor can allow improved development capabilities through more powerful peripherals and more sophisticated software facilities available in larger systems. In this case, the assembler acts as a cross-assembler. A cross-assembler is a program for one machine which resides on another machine. A cross-assembler for an 80286 is an assembler which will produce 80286 code, but it executes on another machine. The cross-assembler converts the symbolic code written by the programmer into machine-language instructions that are executable not by the target microprocessor, but another computer.

Assemblers may have a conditional assembly capability, list control pseudo-ops, and produce an alphabetized symbol or cross-reference table listing. Assemblers come in two versions, relocatable and absolute. The relocatable assemblers have a linking capability for developing modular programs.

The use of relocatable assemblers facilitates modular program development. A program can be broken up into several independent modules and assembled and tested separately. A linking loader is then used to combine the relocatable modules into a single absolute object module. When an error is discovered in a program module, then only that module need be reassembled.

Some assemblers have a macro capability, which allows an identifier to be associated with a block of text, which is then substituted every time the macro is invoked. Parametric macros can allow a different parameter value to be used each time the macro is invoked, so the text can be varied.

Some assemblers use two passes to produce an object module file and an output listing. Critical variables can have parameters assigned enabling the modification of table size, length of symbols, I/O device assignments, and character definitions.

6.5.2 Editors

To modify a program in work easily, an editor should be available. The editor program allows for the convenient manipulation of text. It allows the user to make textual changes in the program without reloading or reworking the complete text. The editor performs the functions required to add or delete a line or a character automatically. A simple typing error in a program might need to be corrected by retyping the entire program without an editing capability. With an editor, it is possible to issue commands such as

GO TO LINE 8 AND INSERT THE FOLLOWING LETTER, WORD OR PHRASE

or

FIND B2 IN THE TEXT AND REPLACE IT BY B8.

A good editor is a great aid for improving the speed with which a program can be typed and modified when errors are being located. Single commands may manipulate whole blocks of source lines.

6.5.3 Debuggers

A debugger is a diagnostic tool which allows the user to analyze the program. It permits the user to insert breakpoints in the program at critical points and obtain such information as register and memory dumps at desired points of the program execution. If the program detects an error, some debugger programs allow the user to make a modification and let the program continue to run. This feature allows the examination of the contents of registers, and the capability to change them is accomplished by the debugger either executing instructions on the microprocessor or by executing them under the control of a simulator or an emulator, which then stores a copy of the value of the registers in memory.

6.5.4 Loaders

A loader is a program which initializes the processor to allow the user program to begin execution. The loader is often used with a hardware facility for performing a reset. If the processor is halted, the user restarts the program by setting a reset signal. The reset circuit then interrupts the processor so that control is taken away from the program formally being executed, and the processing of the loader program begins.

Some loaders allow separate groups of machine-language code to be linked together and executed by the processor. These more sophisticated loaders tend to act as linking utility programs. Loaders are often included as part of an assembly package.

6.5.5 Simulators

Simulators are programs for performing analysis of user programs. A simulator can model or simulate the timing characteristics of hardware, such as peripheral devices, which may not be available for testing at the time the software is ready. Simulators may perform interpretive execution of the microprocessor object module in both an interactive or batch mode. They can also simulate the RAM/ROM environment, I/O operations, and interrupts, as well as the operand and instruction breakpoints, memory dumps, patching, register setting, and program tracing.

Timing information may be displayed in cumulative cycle counts, allowing the actual routine execution times to be determined. Error messages may be generated for such conditions as illegal op codes or attempts to write into protected memory sections.

Some programs can simulate all aspects of a microcomputer by implementing, in software, the registers and logic control functions of the microprocessor.

Most simulators are used in an interactive mode with a set of simulator commands. To allow flexibility, the simulator commands may be entered one at a time or read from a file.

Registers and status bits are initialized with the simulator commands. The contents of the simulated memory can be displayed and altered. Simulation may be initiated through the use of execute and trace commands. An execute command causes the simulated program execution to continue until the number of instructions specified is executed or a breakpoint is reached. The user may be allowed to set the instruction and operand breakpoints. A trace command operates like an execute command, except the contents of the registers and status bits are displayed after each instruction execution. A cumulative cycle count of microprocessor instructions that have been executed can be kept to calculate subroutine execution times.

A simulator can also provide extensive I/O simulation. The input data can be read interactively from a port, buffer, or a disk file. Output data can also be written to a port, buffer, or a disk file. The user can specify the source and destination of I/O data for each port or memory location. Interrupts can also be simulated. The interrupt may be initiated either after a certain number of cycles or at a particular address.

Another use of simulators is symbolic debugging. The symbols or labels from the assembly program can be read into the simulator and then used as command arguments when performing the simulation. This reduces the requirement to refer to absolute addresses.

6.5.6 PROM Programmers

Hexadecimal code is written into a PROM using a PROM programmer. The PROM can be used as part of a personality module in the system. The operator keys in the hexadecimal code from the keyboard of the PROM programmer. Corrections are made in the PROM by removing it from the prototype, installing back in the PROM programmer along with a second blank PROM, and creating a second corrected PROM from both the original PROM and the manually entered corrections. During this time the PROM programmer acts as a duplicator with the capability of verification of the programmed code.

In addition to a hexadecimal keyboard to allow the manual input of data, some PROM programmers provide additional interfaces such as an RS232 connector so that the device can be connected to the microcomputer system for programming.

6.5.7 Emulators

Another tool which is useful in software development is the emulator. An emulator can greatly assist in the debugging required when the software is first integrated with the hardware. In these early stages of debugging, an emulator device with symbolic debugging capability can greatly reduce the hardware/software checkout time.

One of the most useful facilities in emulation is the trace capability. This is a recording capability that can record events during the previous machine cycles before the events are over. It is analogous to a film of the events within the previous cycles of the system. Normally, when an error is diagnosed at a breakpoint, it is usually too late, since the error may have been caused by a previous instruction. The problem is to identify the instruction which has caused a wrong value at the point where it was first diagnosed. In many programs, a number of branching points will exist, and it can be difficult to determine which branch was being executed prior to the detection of the error. But if the path is recorded which was followed up to the breakpoint, then the problem instruction can be identified or another breakpoint can be set. The other machine cycles may then be recorded until the error is traced to the erroneous instruction. The instruction may be modified and the process repeated until a working program is obtained.

6.6 SOFTWARE VERIFICATION

One of the more critical events in system development is the verification of the initial software. This involves testing the program and determining its adequacy as well as that of the algorithms. Later the program can be made more efficient using optimization techniques. The program verification and debugging stage involves the discovery and correction of programming errors. Only very simple programs generally run correctly the first time, so debugging is a critical and sometimes time-consuming task system development. Editors, debugging software packages, simulators, emulators, logic analyzers, and other tools are useful during debugging. The types of errors that are most common as well as some techniques to reduce their occurrence will be considered.

System testing and program debugging are closely related. System testing is a later stage in which the developed program may be validated for the application by trying it for a number of test cases. Testing ensures that the program performs the required tasks in conjunction with the hardware. Important factors include the selection of the test criteria, the specification, and the development of the testing methods. Later an evaluation and redesign stage may be used as an extension of the design for requirements beyond those described in the initial problem definition.

6.6.1 Hand Checking

The checking of the program should be thorough. The first check can take place at the flowchart level. Have all the requirements of the system specification been covered? The logic of the flowchart should also be checked to make certain that it follows the specification requirements. This includes all the input and output conditions, exceptions, and any special features or requirements. There should be no open ends in any of the flowcharts. If the program has been cross-referenced to the flowcharts, this facilitates the checking of the program logic.

A useful technique is to list each condition that the program is likely to encounter. The effects of these conditions are then listed for each step of the flowchart. In this way the more obvious errors can sometimes be quickly detected and corrected.

Hand checking may also be used to find syntax errors which are easily spotted. Others may go unnoticed during the hand checking, but they will be detected by the compiler. Compilers can generally detect certain types of format errors, or if an incorrect operation code has been used. Compilers can also detect violations of the rules for a particular language, such as the omission of required directives and data labels. Much of this can be done, at least for smaller programs by hand checking. A check can be made for the proper syntax in the op codes, labels that may be missing as well as any initial conditions that may be required.

The major problem with hand checking is the time involved, and there is always the chance that many or most errors will be undetected at this stage. But it is still useful for finding some of the more obvious problems quickly, even if there are development tools available. Once the program has been hand checked and installed in the system along with supporting utilities and other system programs, the program is ready for the initial test and debugging phase. During this shake-down period, modifications and improvements will be made as shortcomings surface. Changes may be made in data formats, computation frequency, and system-operator interchanges to improve operation. Attention to test procedures specified earlier tend to pay off now, the earlier errors can be identified the quicker they can be corrected.

The following questions may be helpful:

1. Are the outputs of the system satisfactory? If not, how can they be improved?
2. Is the data being collected satisfactorily? What changes would be permissible? What improvements could be made?
3. What existing resources could be used more profitably in the system as it is?
4. Are existing processes maintained in the best sequence? Is there any duplication in the processes?
5. Is there an opportunity to improve the design within the system?

6.6.2 Testing and Debugging

In the design of conventional electronic circuits the breadboard hardware is built up from assembly prints and tested to verify the operation as described in the specification. The circuit schematics and the layouts may both be defined in the assembly prints. The debugging phase usually follows this approach: the schematic and assembler print are used to develop the hardware. Testing begins and the discovery of an error results in this following sequence: the schematic is first corrected by redlining the circuits involved with the change. The assembly print may also be redlined, and then the breadboard is reworked to reflect the change. This debugging cycle may be repeated many times during a typical design. The process requires no computer assistance and can be started and stopped at any point. The design and debugging cycle is employed first at the circuit module level, then at the subsystem level, and finally at the system level.

At each level a limited number of items is checked. At the circuit level it is the interactions of the components which perform the circuit function, and at the subsystem level it is the interaction of the modules. At the system level the interaction of the subsystems is checked.

For most electronic systems field trials become another part of the design cycle. They can be used to test the design in a real environment to the product specification. If the equipment can be modified in the field, then the field trials can proceed quickly.

A microcomputer system is most easily tested using the system in which it was developed. The software testing should identify and correct many of the program bugs before the software is introduced into the complete hardware environment.

A checkout of the peripherals can be conducted later. These may be sensors, storage facilities, or actuators that provide the data or transmit the operator response. The timing and synchronization between fast and slow peripherals and the processor are major factors to be resolved. The provision for field maintenance is important for continued reliability.

The testing of software can be a difficult and involved task. The testing can be carried out with the aid of a number of software debugging tools. Some general rules that can aid in program testing and debugging include

1. Plan and document the software testing. The test plan should be a part of the program design, and the testing philosophy should be a major consideration during the definition and design stages.
2. Check for trivial and special cases. These include zero inputs with no data, warning and alarm inputs, and other special situations. These simple cases can sometimes be the source of many annoying and mysterious problems.
3. Select test data on a random basis to eliminate bias. Random number tables or generator programs can be adapted.
4. The use of maximum and minimum values for variables as the test data can quickly isolate many potential sources of errors. These extreme values can be the source of many special errors in programs.
5. Use statistical methods for more complex tests. Optimization techniques can be used to set system parameters.

6.7 DEBUGGING TOOLS

The debugging process may proceed slowly because of the inability to observe the register contents directly, the close interactions between hardware and software, the dependence of programs on timing, and the difficulty of obtaining adequate in real-time applications. Some of the tools that can be used to speed the process are

1. Simulator programs.
2. Logic and state analyzers.
3. Breakpoints.
4. Traces.
5. Memory dumps.
6. Interrupts and trap instructions.
7. Checklists.

6.7.1 Simulator Programs

A simulator program simulates the execution of the programs on another computer. It can act as an aid to trace the effects of the instructions. The simulator usually runs on a larger computer since a smaller computer may lack the facilities needed for convenient testing. Typically simulators are large programs. These programs can allow the programmer to change data, examine the registers, and use other debugging facilities. Many simulators cannot fully model the I/O completely or provide much aid with timing programs.

6.7.2 Logic and State Analyzers

Logic and state analyzers are electronic test instruments that act as the digital bus-oriented version of an oscilloscope. When the logic or state analyzer detects the states of the digital signals, it displays them either as strings or words in binary or assembly code, or it shows them as real-time traces. Most analyzers also have a trace capability.

Most logic analyzers use a menu approach. Some analyzers have a general-purpose interface, which connects the logic analyzer and any dedicated interfaces. Interchangeable interconnection boards with space for integrated circuits are available for user-designed circuits.

There is no universal logic analyzer for all analysis problems, but there is usually a logic analyzer for a particular application. Selecting the best logic analyzer requires matching the features needed to the features available. If the features required are well defined, selection can be done directly. If the required features are not known, the overall measurement problem should be reviewed. The measurement environment and system architecture determine what problems are likely to be encountered. When these are defined, the required measurements become set.

When the analyzer detects the states of the digital signals during a program cycle and stores them in a memory, it displays the information in the selected format on its CRT screen. Several events can be monitored and displayed at once, triggered events can be defined, and thresholds can be set. Logic analyzers provide a convenient display for changing parallel digital signals during debugging. Analyzers have the ability to trigger on a particular instruction or sequence of instruction, recall previous data, and can capture short noise spikes. Logic analyzers can act as a complement to software simulators, since they may be used in solving timing problems.

6.7.3 Breakpoints

A breakpoint is a convenient place in the program at which the execution is halted to examine the current contents of registers, memory locations, or I/O ports. Most microcomputer development systems and many simulator programs have facilities for setting breakpoints. Breakpoints can be created with a TRAP instruction or a conditional jump instruction which is dependent on an external input controlled by the programmer. As an example, the instruction

JUMP ON TEST

causes a jump to occur when the

TEST

input is on. The contents of registers or memory locations may then be examined.

Some microprocessors can place special-purpose status information on the buses while in the halt state. This information can include the current contents of the accumulator, program counter, or other registers.

6.7.4 Traces

The trace is a program which prints information concerning the status of the processor at specified times. Many simulator and development programs employ trace facilities for debugging purposes.

A trace capability is usually necessary for the real-time analysis of any digital system. Because of the quantity of data that may be present in the system, the monitoring instrument should be able to select the desired portions of the activity, and display only the activity of interest. To achieve this, state analyzers must contain extensive triggering capabilities.

6.7.4.1 Selective traces

Selective tracing records only the desired system activity in memory. Without selective tracing, a practical memory is not deep enough to solve all the possible state analysis problems. Data may be selectively traced in two ways. Clock qualification allows the data to be strobed into the analyzer only if additional inputs or qualifiers are true at the clock edge. The qualifiers may be valid memory address lines, read/write lines, or other signals. This type of qualification is required to decipher data on multiplexed buses.

Another method used to qualify recorded data is to program the analyzer to trace only specified states.

The analyzer will then record only data that meets the trigger specifications. The trace selectivity can be controlled by varying the trigger specifications.

In a selective trace mode, a state analyzer's time and count events capability can be used to resolve functional problems. The number of low-order states occurring between successive high-order states is often a clue to an anomaly.

It may be required to trace a specified state only when this state is reached via some infrequent path or other sequence of events. The analyzer must ignore any entry via the other paths.

The selective traces can provide a more detailed pictorial display for a quick global view of the system activity. Each map can be a dot matrix with each dot corresponding to a word with the most significant portion plotted vertically, the least significant portion plotted horizontally. These graphs plot the state magnitude as a function of sequence. Each system activity generates a unique display and after a period of familiarization, one can recognize improper patterns, discontinuities, or other deviations from proper program operation.

The most common use of the trace is to view the status of registers and flags after the execution of an instruction. One can also use tracing for particular registers or memory locations only when the contents change. Traces can result in large amounts of data unless one selects the variables and formats carefully.

6.7.5 Memory Dumps

A memory dump refers to a listing of the current contents of some section of memory. Simulator and development programs can produce memory dumps. A complete or even partial memory dump may be long and may be difficult to interpret.

A memory dump is not always the most effective technique for debugging, but sometimes it may be the only tool available. A complete memory dump is normally only used when all other methods fail.

6.7.6 Interrupt and Trap Instructions

These instructions are useful for debugging purposes since they normally save the current value of the stack registers or program counter and then branch to some specified memory location. This memory location may be the starting point of a debugging program that lists or displays status information.

Normally, the programmer enters a TRAP instruction into the program and provides the debugging routine if it is not part of the package. A monitor program which can place TRAP instructions at specified addresses can also be used. The monitor program can also be used to obtain a listing of the conditions which exist when an error which stops the program occurs.

6.7.7 Checklists

Checklists can be a helpful tool that may be used with flowcharts for debugging. Here, the programmer checks that each variable has been initialized, that each flowchart element has been coded, that definitions are correct, and that all paths are connected properly.

Loops and small sections of programs can easily be hand checked to ensure that the flow of program is correct. In the case of loops, the programmer can check if the loop performs the first and last iterations correctly. These are normally the sources of most loop errors. The program can also be hand checked for the trivial cases, such as tables with no elements.

6.8 ERROR CHECKING

Checking and debugging should proceed in a systematic manner. Some of the more common errors that can occur include

1. A failure to initialize variables, especially in counters and pointers. Registers, flags, and memory locations may not always contain zero at the start of the program.
2. The incrementing of counters and pointers at the wrong time or failure to increment them at all.
3. The failure of the program to handle trivial cases, such as arrays or tables that have no elements.
4. Inverting instruction conditions, such as a jump on 0 instead of not on 0.
5. The reversing the order of operands, such as move B to A instead of A to B.
6. Jumps on conditions that are subject to change after they are set. One problem is the use of flags as jump conditions when they may be changed by intermediate instructions.
7. A lack of follow-through conditions, such as a data item that will never be found in a table or a condition that cannot be met. These may cause an endless loop.
8. Inverting addresses and data. This can occur with immediate addresses where the data is part of the instruction and with direct addressing in which the address of the data is part of the instruction.
9. The failure to save the contents of an accumulator or other register before using the register again.
10. An exchange of registers or memory locations without using an intermediate storage place. For example,

$$H = B$$
$$B = H$$

sets both H and B to the previous contents of B, since the first statement destroys the previous contents of H. The following sequence will exchange the registers:

$$A = H$$
$$H = B$$
$$B = A$$

11. Ignoring the effects of subroutines which could change the state of flags, registers, or memory locations.
12. Confusing the direction of noncommutative operations as can occur in the assembly language command SUB B which subtracts the contents of register B from the contents of the accumulator.

13. Confusing numbers and characters, for example, ASCII zero or EDCDIC zero is not the number zero.

14. Confusing numerical codes like BCD 60 and binary 60.

15. Counting the length of a data block incorrectly, for example, locations 10 through 18 have nine and not eight words.

16. Confusing two's complement and sign magnitude notations.

17. Ignoring the overflow in signed arithmetic operations. Other errors may exist, but this list of simple errors can be helpful.

6.9 OPERATING SYSTEMS

The operating system (OS) is generally independent of the application. A microcomputer without an operating system can be used in controller applications, but an OS can allow it to perform a much greater scope of tasks. Operating systems can be small enough to fit in a single ROM, but for the flexibility needed for program development a floppy disk is normally required.

Operating systems act as managers for the system's resources such as memory, terminals, communications links, and other peripherals. The operating system will usually contain a program or routine for each task. It then links these programs together using other routines to perform the various housekeeping operations as shown in Figure 6-6. The two basic types of systems are the disk operating system (DOS) and the multitasking operating systems (MTOS).

Many disk operating systems are designed to support users in preparing, debugging, testing, and running programs. If the operating system supports several peripherals, it can require a relatively large program in memory at all times. As more services are required, additional programs are loaded into overlayed or common areas.

The services provided by a typical DOS are accessed either from a CRT display or from user programs. The available services which can aid in program preparation are

1. Text editing.
2. Assembling.
3. Compiling.
4. Linking and loading.
5. File manipulation including copying, merging, deleting, and reformatting functions.
6. Debugging aids such as inspecting and changing memory, setting breakpoints, and single stepping.

A DOS program usually starts with an initialization section. Variables such as pointers and flags are set to the appropriate starting values. The initialization usually involves some interaction between the user and the DOS program. After

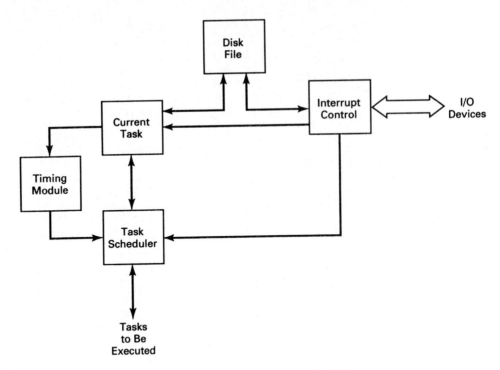

Figure 6-6   Typical Operation of a DOS

the initialization, the typical DOS program enters a loop to read, analyze, and write data. It might read information from a disk file requested by a keyboard input.

The user enters a command into the keyboard and receives a response from the system. Some typical input commands are shown here:

LOGON	Sets up the disk system for the referencing of files.
NEW FILE	Creates new file
DIRECTORY	Lists the user's directory file.
RENAME	Changes the name of a file.
ERASE/DELETE	Deletes a file.
RUN	Loads a program file and executes it.
EDLIN	Runs the line editor.
LINK	Runs the relocating/linking loader.
DATE/TIME	Displays or writes the current data and time on a file.
ABORT	Terminates the program.
RESUME	Resumes execution of program.

SUBMIT

> Changes the input from the keyboard to another device such as a printer.

QUIT

> Terminates the editing of the file.

The time between a command entry and a reply is proportional to the difficulty of the task and the activity of the system at the time of request.

Another type of operating system, the executive, is a real-time system which is reconfigured for each application. Some use relocatable program modules. After the software is developed, it can be linked with the desired system modules and stored in ROM, PROM, or RAM. A disk driver module may be used to give the system a file management capability.

To manage the information storage and retrieval, the OS uses a file system. Some systems treat all the peripheral devices, including printers, display, and disk drives, as files. Here the programs may treat all the I/O in a similar fashion with no special treatment for the particular characteristics of a device. For example, to print on a printer, a system routine to open the file is called for the printer file. This allocates the printer to the user if no other program is controlling it. A file write command may be used to transfer the data. Then the user program calls a file close routine to deallocate the printer.

A list of some of the typical routines a user program might call follows:

FILE

> This routine controls the access to a particular file. Files may be opened for read only, write only, or read and write. The program may also specify a choice of a shared or exclusive access as well as the physical device on which the file exists.

READ/WRITE

> This routine allows the read or write of a file. The application program uses this interface for all I/O functions. Access can be either sequential or random.

CLOSE

> This routine releases access to a file. The file can be either kept or deleted. If the file is a disk file, any unused disk sectors may be released.

TERMINATE

> This indicates to the operating system that the execution of the program is terminated.

CURRENT/DATE/TIME

> The current date and time are displayed.

| FILE DESIGNATOR | This command builds the block needed by the FILE OPEN routine for specifying the file to be opened. |

6.9.1 DOS Applications

Most microcomputer systems will use a variety of applications programs that may be under control of a DOS. These can include editors, assemblers, language compilers, linkers, loaders, debuggers, and utilities. Some may be written as subroutines that can be linked with the application program. Others are used as separate programs handling the user programs as input.

An interactive editor can simplify the software development greatly. The developed programs are typically put into the system through the keyboard and stored in a disk file. The file is then modified using editor commands such as the ones listed here:

ADD	This command adds lines entered from the keyboard into the text file.
DELETE	This command deletes lines from the text file.
LIST	This lists lines on the display or printer.
FIND	This command finds a character string or line.
REPLACE	This is used to replace a character string or line with a new character string or line.
MODIFY	This is used to modify character strings with subcommands.
COPY	This will copy lines or a block of lines.
SAVE	This will store a block of text on disk or tape.

The editor will assign line numbers to the stored text so individual lines can be identified and accessed. Some editors renumber the lines each time new ones are added or deleted. Others use incremental line numbers. In this case, a line added between lines 102 and 103 could be numbered 102.1.

6.10 DEBUGGERS

The debugging of programs can be made easier with a debugger. This is a program which is designed for the debugging of the developed program. It may offer such facilities as

1. Stop at an instruction.
2. Execute instructions one at a time; single-stepping.
3. Change and display the contents of registers.
4. Display the contents of memory in binary, hexadecimal, or symbolic form.

The program may also be started and stopped by the user. This single-step technique removes the processor from its normal operating routine of sequencing through the program memory at a rate determined by the clock. As the instructions are executed, the debugger must have the ability to control the program activity. The READY line can often be used to single step the processor at a controlled rate. This allows a pace to check the basic operation of the system and the interaction with the peripherals. The program evaluation is independent of the clock rate.

The single-step technique requires that the debugger have access to a READY or WAIT line. The wait line allows an input or output to accommodate the slower I/O devices.

The debugger essentially acts as the program memory. It applies data or instructions to the data bus while activating the READY line and placing the processor in a WAIT mode between these applications. It also inserts data at the points where the processor would normally make requests. The debugger controls the write access to the data bus along with the read access to check the test results.

The debugger is also able to write onto the data bus to perform functions during the single-stepping process. When the debugger drives the data bus, the processor reads it during program memory accesses.

Single-stepping can reveal most functional problems. While the program is being debugged under the control of the debugger, the diagnostics are normally printed on a printer or displayed on a CRT. Some corrections at this point may be possible. Otherwise, one must return to the beginning of the process, type in the corrections, and reassemble the program.

Another essential facility of a debugger is to provide breakpoints. These addresses are specified by the user to cause the program to stop automatically at a desired point. The user is then able to examine the value of variables in memory or the contents of registers. The program execution is in a state of temporary suspension at these points.

6.10.1 Hardware-Assisted Software Debugging Tools

These debugging tools provide more capability compared to the software-only debugging tools. The hardware-assisted tools may add the following capabilities.

Hardware-assisted breakpoints can trap events in real time like overwriting a memory location or overwriting a range of memory. This is a common bug when calculated or indirect pointers are used. Hardware-assisted breakpoints can also trap events like reading or writing to I/O or interrupt vectors. A software only debugger could only simulate this by single-stepping and checking. This typically slows down the program 300 to 1000 times.

Real-time trace instructions cause the breakpoints to be traced in real time using a high-speed memory in the hardware debugging tools. This is useful for testing how a pointer was calculated, how interrupts affect the program execution, and how the program got to the point where it is now.

A hidden and write-protected memory keeps the software protected on the hardware board. This prevents an undebugged program from wiping out the debugger. In addition, the symbol table for the program can be stored in this write-protected memory. Any symbol table overflow can be directed back to the system memory. Having this memory on the hardware board also frees up system memory for the program.

6.10.2 Software Debugging Tools

Software debugging tools do not have the real-time trace, hardware breakpoints, or protected memory capabilities. The remainder of the debugging features are common between the hardware-assisted and software-only debugging tools. This allows the lower-cost software tools as well as the more powerful hardware-assisted tools to be used on the same project.

One feature useful in both hardware-assisted and software-only tools is a STOP/RESET switch. This switch allows the programmer to regain control of the system when the program has gone out of control.

6.10.3 Symbolic versus Level Debugging

A symbolic debugging capability allows the programmer access to the variables which have been passed by the compiler or assembler to the linker and symbol table. This capability allows the display and changing of variables symbolically.

It is possible to have source-level debugging capabilities in addition to symbolic debugging capabilities. Source-level debugging can show what is happening with high-level source code instead of only assembly-language code.

6.10.4 Performance and Timing Analysis Tools

Doing performance and timing measurements on the code is another form of debugging. These tools can provide the answers to the following questions:

1. Where is the program spending its time?
2. How much performance improvement is being made from software rewrites?
3. How long does a procedure execute?
4. How much time is spent in going between procedures?
5. How many times did a procedure execute?

There are tools to help find and solve problems which are timing and performance related. These are available in both hardware-assisted and software-only versions.

Breakpoints are a mechanism for stopping program execution because of specified events. Hardware is often used to assist in the detection of breakpoints. The following are examples of breakpoint capabilities:

1. Instruction execution at an address
2. Instruction fetch from an address or range of addresses
3. Reading or writing to I/O ports
4. Reading or writing to memory or I/O locations with specific data values

Software debuggers have real-time breakpoints of only the first type and are limited in debug capabilities. A hardware debugger will have a more complete capability as shown in these examples:

1. Jumping to the wrong place and executing data
2. Overwriting a memory location from point miscalculations
3. Writing characters anywhere in the screen memory
4. Reading data from the system I/O devices
5. Parity errors
6. Unserviced interrupts

Hardware logic allows real-time execution up until the break condition occurs. Up to 20 breakpoints can be active at one time. Conditional breakpoints may be implemented using loop commands and If/Then/Else commands.

The execution of the program is traced and stored while running at full speed. A trace feature implemented in software single steps the program. With a real-time trace, the history of program execution can be displayed after reaching a breakpoint. The previous memory cycles are stored.

A real-time trace answers questions such as

How did the program get here?

or

How did this pointer miscalculation occur?

After a breakpoint has been reached, a display of the real-time trace data will usually answer these questions. Many of the problems which only occur while running in real time such as those due to interrupts can be found in the real-time trace data.

Software can be patched online in order to try out changes before reediting and recompiling. Patches can be inserted into the program using a symbolic line assembler.

The symbolic debugging capabilities allow symbol names, function calls, procedure names, and line numbers in the user's program to be used in place of absolute values. This eliminates references to absolute numbers which are subject to change as program development progresses. For example, referring to a memory location which has been labeled

TEMP

in the program is easier than determining the address of TEMP for each debugging session.

A set of debug commands can be tailored to the type of debugging being pursued. Macro commands can be used to

1. Load programs and perform initialization for a debug session.
2. Display system data structures with labels.
3. Perform commonly used sequences of commands.
4. Display stack-based variables with labels.

The macros can be saved and used in future debugging sessions. Each macro may accept up to 10 parameters in its definition and can be nested in several levels within other macros. Macros can have a conditional and/or iterative execution using loop and If/Then/Else constructions.

A write-protected memory can be used for storing the symbol table and macro tables. This eliminates the chance that a program bug will change critical memory locations during the debugging process. If an AT is running the 80286 in unprotected mode (DOS), this memory can be hidden from the DOS operating system. When the AT is running the 80286 in protected mode, then the memory can be located anywhere in the 16MB address range of the 80286.

Sometimes a program will crash to a level that system control cannot be regained without turning the system off and then on again. The debugger software can provide for a return to the debugger or a system reset no matter what state the system is in. Recoverability is provided with storage in write-protected memory.

Floating point support for the 80287 numeric processor is available. This allows the debugger to display and change the 80287 registers and flags as well as memory in all of the floating point data types. Floating point instructions are included in the assembler, disassembler, and trace data to distinguish 80287 from 80286 operations.

The ability to print system data structures using the data type defined in the source code saves mental conversions. Data includes ASCII, hex, decimal, integer, or string formats. Using print statements within macro commands allows complex structures to be printed with a single command.

6.10.5 User Considerations

Some applications can be intensive in their use of the screen. The following alternatives can provide more utility and ease of use for different debugging requirements.

1. By executing a command which sets a screen switch flag, the contents of the screen are saved before the debugger uses the screen during single-stepping or returning from a breakpoint. The contents of the screen are replaced before the applications program starts to execute.

2. A separate video controller board can be used for the debugging screen which keeps the applications screen driven by the system's video controller board undisturbed.

3. An RS-232 serial interface can be used for the keyboard and screen for the debugger which is isolated from the resident keyboard and screen.

A good debugger should have an easy-to-use human interface similar to a spreadsheet interface. The interface should be designed to be transparent to the user.

When the first unique characters of a command are typed, the syntax for the command is displayed in the menu window as follows:

```
              SAMPLE COMMAND PROMPT SYNTAX
DISPLAY BYTES: BY range  (range is <addr1> <addr2>,  or
<start addr> L)
CHANGE BYTES: BY start address = value, value, value, ...
```

A window can be defined which contains the information desired on the screen. This window is updated each time this information is changed such as during single-stepping or after a breakpoint. The window can be used to monitor registers, the stack, or data structures.

The debugging of a system which uses interrupts to control program flow normally requires each of the following debugging strategies during the debugging process.

1. Debug one interrupt-driven process while other processes which service other interrupts are running in the background.

2. Lock out other selected interrupts while debugging code in a specific interrupt routine.

The first approach is needed when routines such as the real-time clock, disk service interrupts, or communications channel interrupts are processing and need to keep running while debugging another interrupt service routine. The second case is needed when a system crash is caused by other interrupts preempting the routine being debugged.

6.10.6 Command Examples

This section describes some typical commands and gives examples.

6.10.6.1 The GO command

This command starts the program execution and sets the breakpoints. The syntax for the Go command is

```
G[=START ADDRESS,] [BREAKPOINT 1], ..., [BREAKPOINT X]
```

[=START ADDRESS] indicates the location to resume program execution and defaults to the current program counter location if not specified. One form of a breakpoint is

```
[IO] ADDRESS [VERB] [DATA DATAVALUE]
```

ADDRESS is a memory address for the breakpoint unless preceded by [IO] which indicates breaking on an IO address [VERB] can be

    R for reading a location or range of locations
    W for write to a location or range of locations
    F for fetching an instruction from a location or range
    A for all (read, write, fetch)

If no verb is specified, then the default case is instruction execution, [DATA] indicates that the data portion of the operation must also match [DATA VALUE] to cause the break at ADDRESS. If not included, then data is ignored in the breakpoint. A range of addresses may be specified instead of a single address for the breakpoint. Breaks are also generated when a parity error occurs. Breakpoints can be removed or remain activated after the breakpoint is detected. Breakpoints can also be defined in advance.

The following GO command example begins execution at the address defined by the symbol "START" and breaks when the I/O port defined by the symbol "PORTA" is read and has a data value of ASCII "Q."

```
G =.START, IO .PORTA R DATA 'Q'
```

6.10.6.2 Breakpoint command

This command example defines a breakpoint which is activated permanently until deleted.

```
BP 1 = B000:0 TO B000:FFF W DATA "^"
```

The following example sets a breakpoint for a write to the variable FOO with a data value of a5. This overwrite could have been caused by a runtime pointer miscalculation.

```
BP 2 = .FOO WData a5
```

In the next example, program execution starts at location START, and breakpoints are set at reading TEST, reading port KEY, writing a 1 to TEMP, and executing instructions at LOOP or LOOP+5.

```
G =.START, .TEST R, IO .KEY R, .TEMP W DATA 1, .LOOP,
.LOOP+5
```

6.10.6.3 Trace command

This command displays the previous N cycles of real-time program execution before the break condition was achieved. The trace shows assembled op codes and operands, data transferred during execution cycles, stack operations, I/O operations, bus operations, and interrupt cycles. Program symbols in the trace data make the identification of program operation easier to understand. The address of the instruction executed is shown, and when the address matches a symbol or label, it is also shown as well as the op codes and operand fields of the instructions. When an operand matches a symbol, it is shown.

The address of the memory reference cycle which is used during the execution cycle of an instruction is shown. This is the current real-time value of the effective address used to address memory.

The trace also shows if the memory reference cycle is reading, writing, or interrupting as well as the data on the data bus during the memory reference cycle. A typical trace display is shown here:

```
ADDR CODE OPERAND(S)
    0059C RET 0002
        00F2A READ — SS — 01AF
    005AF POP AX
        00F2E READ — SS — 0020
    005B0 POP BP
        00F30 READ — SS — 0854
    000B1 RET
        00F32 READ — SS — 0094
FCMAIN#52:
    00494 JMP $+FFB0                ;..FCMAIN#46+0008
    00444 MOV AX, WORD PTR [0016]   ;..FCMAIN.CELSIU+0004
        006F6 READ — DS — 000A
    00447 ADD WORD PTR [0010],AX    ;..FCMAIN.FAHR
        006F0 READ — DS — 0050
        006F0 WRITE — DS — 005A
```

6.10.6.4 Single-step command

Single-stepping program execution can be accomplished with the STEP command. Each step displays the instruction to be executed as well as the next several instructions. A window can be defined which will display user-defined data after each single step. An option in the STEP command allows stepping over subroutine procedures or software interrupts.

The contents of the operands can be viewed during single-stepping, and conditional branches can be simulated to check if the branch will occur. This is shown in the example display at the end of the sixth line.

A window appears in the lower four lines of the display. This window is due to a macro which contains the following commands:

```
R
pr "Contents of the stack"
Wo ss:sp
pr "Lower=",%@w.lower,"Upper=",%i@w.upper,"Step=",%i@w.step
pr "Fahr=",%%w.fahr,"Celsius= ", %i@w.celsius
```

These commands are executed after each single step. They display registers, dump the top of the stack, and display system variables. Following is an example of the single-step display:

```
FTOCIO - CODE #48
0671:0010 MOV SI, WORD PTR [BP+0114] —,00E6 ;CONSOLEPTR
0671:0014 MOV AL,BYTE PTR [AI]        —,8A
0671:0016 XOR AH,AH
0671:0018 TEST AX,AX
0671:00Aa JNZ 001F <--          —FTOCIO—CODE#57+09—will jump
0671:001C JMP 0117               —FTOCIO—CODE#57+0A
AX=1234 CS= 0000 SS=1000 DS=0011 ES=0100
BX=0104 IP=1000 SP=5000 SI=0000 DI=0000
CX= 0002                BP= 4000
DX= ABAB              FL=00 D1 E1 S0 Z1 A1 P0 C0
CONTENTS OF THE STACK
1000:5000 1234, 12AE, 89FF, FFFF, FE44, F567, E654, ABB6,
CDEF,
9192, 2EFD, 4567
Lower =0        Upper = 100        Step =100
Fahr  = 20      Celsius = —12
```

6.10.7 Symbol Manipulation

A command loads the symbol table into the symbol table space. The symbol table file is the link map file produced at link time. The following example display shows some examples of some symbol commands:

```
SY
VALUE           SYMBOL NAME
10000:00AE    BUFFER
1000:00D0     PRINCIPLE
1000:0102     LOOP
MODULE MAIN
15= 0634:003c  16= 0634:0045  17=0634:005b  19=0634:0075
20= 0634:0089  22= 0634:0692  23=00A3  24=0634:00B5
SYM .PORTS = 5
SYM .PORTS = 5
PORT .PORTS = AA
MOD = MAIN
```

Once the symbol table is loaded, it may be displayed with the symbol command. This command (SY) displays symbols, module names, and line numbers with the corresponding segment:offset values.

The command starting with SYM defines a new symbol called PORT5 and assigns it a value of 5. Then an IO port command writes values of AA to the port described by the symbol PORT5.

Line numbers are associated with module names. Module names can be specified whenever a line number is referenced or the default module name can be used. The command starting with MOD defines the default module name to be MAIN.

6.10.8 Unassemble and Assemble Commands

The assembler and disassembler for an AT will use the standard 80286 assembly language mnemonics. The program symbols used during assembly can be displayed during disassembly. Here are some notes which describe the example on the next screen.

When the disassembly takes place, the symbols which match address fields are shown as labels. An operand which matches a symbol is shown to the right of the code.

The following example display starts with a command that unassembles locations from LOOP to LOOP+5. An ASSEMBLY command starts assembling instructions at the address represented by the symbol PATCH.

```
U .LOOP .LOOP+5
LOOP
1000:0000 MOV AL,byte ptr [BP+SI+008]      ; TEMP_POINTER
1000:0003 MOV BL,AL
10000:0005 JMP $+8                         ; LOOPTOP+56
ASSEMBLE .PATCH
0642:0000 MOV AX,CS:[.LOOPSTART]
0642:00005 JNBE .LOOPREADY
0642:0007 DEC WORD PTR [SI]
```

6.10.9 Macro Commands

Following are several examples of macro commands:

```
MAC  S =
M–LOAD %0.EXE
M–LOAD S %60.map
M– U CS:IP CS:IP+F
M–END
EM S MYPROG,MP1
SAVE MAC B: INIT.MAC
```

The first line is the start of defining the macro named S. When a %# is put in a command, then a parameter is created which will pass to the macro when executed.

The line starting with EM is the command that executes the macro S. It passes the parameter MYPROG which is the name of the program to be loaded to the LOAD commands.

The SAVE command saves all currently defined macros to a file called INIT.MAC on drive B. These macros can then be loaded from here. Macros can also be used to start program execution and set breakpoints as shown here:

```
MAC  D =
M– GO %0
PR "The buffer is:", %s .%1
M– END
EM D #38,.BUFFER
Execution begun:
Breakpoint detected at line number 38
The buffer is: Now is the time.
```

This macro is named D. It sets a breakpoint which will be a parameter (@0) passed to the macro when it is executed. The macro prints a message using the print command (PR). The message is printed as a 0 terminated string starting at the address passed as the parameter %1. The breakpoint is set at line number 38. When the breakpoint is reached, program execution will terminate, and control will be transferred back to the macro. The remainder of the macro will execute which prints the string starting at BUFFER.

6.10.10 Loop Commands

Loop commands provide a method of executing command loops for a specified number of iterations or terminations upon user specified conditions. Using Loop commands, spurious events can be trapped.

Following is a Loop command that stops on the 10th breakpoint at Temp. Then a Loop While command is used to detect the successive execution of breakpoint A followed by breakpoint B. It also stops when A is followed by B with no intervening multiple occurrences of either A or B. In this example, the symbols IPA and IPB represent the breakpoint addresses:

```
LOOP 10
G .TEMP
ELO
Mac AB=
Loop While ip <> .IPB
            Loop While ip <> .IPA
            G
            ELO
G
ELO
END
```

6.10.11 Evaluate Command

An Evaluate command can be used for HEX calculation, expression processing, pointer tabulations, and base conversion. Using Evaluate, a variable can be viewed in Hex, ASCII, Decimal, Integer, or Binary. A segment offset can be viewed as a Hex character number. Complex expressions involving pointers can also be viewed:

```
Ev 'a'
61H 97T 110000Y 'A'
Ev .LOOP__POINTER
70CFE
```

The first EV command displays ASCII 'a' in all bases. The next EV command displays the segment offset Loop__pointer as 5 hex char.

6.10.12 If/Then/Else Commands

Debugger commands can be executed conditionally with the If/Then/Else command. With this command, the user can print messages for certain events or change the flow of a program as shown here:

```
MAC ALARM=
M- G .PROCEDURE__START
M- IF QW .TEMP >%0
M- PRint "TEMP IS OUT OF RANGE! TEMP = ",QW .TEMP
M- EIF
M-END
EM ALARM 1000
TEMP IS OUT OF RANGE! TEMP = 1010
```

The first command prints a message for an out-of-range parameter. Then when ALARM is executed if TEMP ever becomes > 1000, the warning message is issued.

6.10.13 Searching, Filling, Comparing, and Moving Memory

Several commands may allow the manipulation of memory in blocks. These commands are illustrated in the example shown here:

```
SEA. TEMP. TEMP+100"ZERO"
FIL .TEMP L 100 00, "ZERO", 00
COM 0:0 L 100 .TEMP
MOV .LOOP L FFFF .TEMP
```

In the first line the 100H locations starting at TEMP are searched for the ASCII string "ZERO." A report is made for every successful match within this block. Then, the 100H locations starting at .TEMP are filled with the string 00ZERO000. A read after write is performed, and errors are reported when a mismatch occurs.

In the third line, a memory block at 0 of 100H bytes in length is compared with memory starting at TEMP. Any mismatches are displayed. Then a memory block 64KB in length starting at LOOP is moved to a location called TEMP.

6.10.14 Source-Level Debugging

The online interactive debugging of software written in high-level languages is a task which is made more efficient if the debugging utility has the capability of translating between the source code and the runtime machine language environment of the computer. Without this bridge, the programmer must spend time making the translations during the debugging process. These translations involve matching the assembly language to the source code, viewing data in hex which the program interprets in many other bases, and stepping and tracing through code at a low level which is controlled through high-level source code. The process is tedious and can be simplified by letting the debugger do the low-level work.

If the debugger stores the real-time execution of the program in trace RAM, this information can be matched to the source code and displayed as real-time execution of the source code. Since the results of a program bug are usually caused by previous program execution, the real-time trace displays bugs as they happened in real time. The following trace display shows the source code which was executed followed by the assembly language which implements the source code. Then the execution cycles of the assembly language are shown.

```
OP
ADDR CODE OPERAND(S)
----------
112. *C_temp = f_temp - 32;                    (source code)
```

```
0652D MOV AX,WORD PTR [BP+0008]
   0ACE5 READ − SS − 0014
   06530 SUB AX,0020
06533 MOV SAI,WORD PTR [BP+000A]
   0ACE7 READ − SS − 00
06536 MOV WORD PTR [S],AX
   09CA8 WRITE − DS − FFF4
113.  *C_temp =*c_temp* 5;
06538 MOV AX,0005
065B imul word ptr [SI]
09CA8 READ − DS − FFF4
0653D MOV WORD PTR [SI],AX
   09CA8 WRITE − DS − FFC4
114.  *C_TEMP =*C_TEMP/9;
0653F MOV BX,0009
06542 CWD
06543 IDIV BX
06545 MOV WORD PTR [SI],AX
   90cA8 WRITE − DS − FFFA
```

The program can be single-stepped via source statement steps as well as assembly-language steps. The source code for a specified module can be displayed while executing all code outside the module in real time. A window to display user-defined data structures may also be opened and will be automatically updated each time a single step is executed. An example execution of the single-step command for source code is shown here:

```
*c_temp=f_temp − 32;
*c_temp = *c_temp* 5;
*c_temp =*c_temp / 9;
return; }
printf("%5d%5d\n", fahr, celsius); <--
/*-----------------------------------
Go to next line of table.
------------------------------------*/
fahr = fahr + step;
Fahr=20
  Celsius− −12
  Upper=100
  Step− 10
```

First, the source code that is being stepped is shown. The line starting with print indicates the source statement currently being stepped. In the last four lines, a macro has been assigned to show this window which prints system variables with labels.

The process of debugging is iterative and involves finding the program problems at runtime, noting changes to the source code on printed listings of the program, editing the source code, and regenerating the object code. An online text editor allows the user to make changes in any source file and log those changes in a log file. After the debugging session, the user moves the source code changes from the log file into the source files using a standard text editor. This approach gives a log file history of program changes. By noting the changes in a log file instead of the actual source file, source files are not exposed to damage during the debugging session if DOS is not totally functional. The text editor usually contains commands like the following:

Display filename	Opens the filename for text display.
Page up/dn	Shows previous/next page of file.
Ctrl Page up/dn	Shows top/bottom page of file.
Search string	Searches file for a text string.
Line number	Goes to specified line number in file.
Change line	Uses DOS edit keys to make changes to specified lines.
Insert line	Inserts text starting at line.

Multiple file pointers allow the user to switch between different files with automatic repositioning of the displayed portion of the file to its previously displayed position. This allows the user to scroll through multiple files without having to adjust the displayed portion of each new file displayed.

In addition to editing source files, the debugger can also be used to edit the real-time trace data. This capability is useful when searching the real-time trace for specific events. An example of a trace file under edit is shown:

```
Compute (f__temp, &c__temp);
-------------------------------*/
Compute (f__temp, c__temp)
temp f__temp, *c__temp;
*c__temp=f__temp - 32;
*c__temp=*c__temp*5;
*c__temp =*temp /9;
return; }
```

```
Change [linenumer]    DIR [filespec c]    DISplay
[filespec.TRACE]
Insert [linenumber]    Line [linenumber]    Exit
Search [startline] string
```

6.10.15 Performance and Timing Measurements

A timing analyzer is a software enhancement to the debugger which provides a set of timing and performance measurement tools. A macro capability is available for defining, setting up, and saving user-defined measurements.

A program activity measurement determines the relative amount of program execution time spent in user-defined address ranges. This measurement provides the user with a determination of where to start tuning a program and can give an indication of how much progress is being made in the process. Software engineering time can be optimized if it is known where to start tuning a procedure and when the point of diminishing returns has been reached.

A section of the program is sampled at a user-specified sample rate and stored in memory. The result of this measurement is a histogram display of the time spent in the user-defined address ranges. These address ranges can be defined symbolically. An example is shown here:

```
PROGRAM ACTIVITY MEASUREMENT
Terminated by:   Executed ..Memory__Tester#105
Sample Rate:     0.100 MS
```

Min Address	Max Address	#	%	0	20	40	60	80	100
0000:0000	Initialize	0	0						
Memory__TE#75	Memory__TE#79	1	<1						
Memory__TE#80	Memory__TE#84	2515	55	**********					
Memory__TE#85	Memory__TE#90	1101	24	*****					
Memory__TE#91	Memory__TE#98	51	16	**					
Memory__TE#99	Memory__TE#102	1	<1						
F0000:0000	F0000:FFFF	80	3	*					

The ranges can be changed and new histograms displayed without retaking the measurement. This allows the user to zoom in or pan out on memory areas to display new histograms.

A procedure duration measurement determines the execution time of specified procedures. A timer is turned on and off at multiple points in the procedure. The measurement generates a histogram of the collected time samples in the user-specified time ranges over all time samples collected. Time distribution measurements allow the characterization and verification of best and worst case execution times. By highlighting the procedures consuming large amounts of processing time, the sources of overall system degradation are identified. Spurious execution times, as a result of faulty procedure execution or outside procedure influences, become visible. This is especially useful for procedures which disable interrupts, and the maximum interrupt off time must be known. An example of this measurement is shown:

```
PROCEDURE DURATION MEASUREMENT
Terminated by:   Executed ..Memory__Tester#105
```

Min Time	Max Time	#	%	0	20	40	60	80	100
69.5 ms	69.700 ms	0	0						
69.8 ms	69.900 ms	25	65	******************					
70.0 ms	70.200 ms	0	0						
70.3 ms	70.600 ms	1	2						
70.7 ms	70.900 ms	11	28	*******					
71.0 ms	Infinity								

The measurement of program events allows the user to specify executable instructions as events. These events are counted, and a histogram of the number of counts of each event as a percentage of all other events in the measurement is displayed. This measurement can verify the various inner-loop counts of large complex nested loops or can determine the number of times a procedure is called from other procedures. This is especially useful for determining which procedures to put into overlays. An example of this measurement is illustrated here:

```
PROGRAM EVENT COUNTER
Terminated by:   Executed ..Memory__Tester#105
```

ADDRESS	COUNT	%	0	20	40	60	80	100
Memory__TE#76	6	<1						
Memory__TE#80	5125	50	**************					
Memory__TE#89	0	0						
Memory__TE#91	5120	49	**************					
Memory__TE#102	5	<1						

To measure the sequence and time difference between events, the debugger stores the timer value each time a user-specified instruction (the event) is detected. The measurement produces a linear display of the sequence of these events and the relative time between them or the absolute time of each event. Relative time is the time from the previous event to the current event. Absolute time is the time from the first event to the current event.

By specifying only one event, repeat occurrences of the same event are measured. This will allow problems such as interrupt saturation to be found by showing the maximum time delays between events. An example of the output display is shown here:

```
PROGRAM TIMING ANALYSIS
Terminated by:   Executed ..Memory__Tester#105
            Time Base is:   Relative
            Last Sample is:   5
```

Sample No.	Address	Time
0	Memory__TE#76	0.0000 ms
1	Memory__T#103	70.200 ms
2	Memory__TE#76	0.100 ms
3	Memory__T#103	70.700 ms
4	Memory__TE#76	0.100 ms
5	Memory__T#103	70.100 ms

Industrial Control Applications

This chapter shows you how

- Microcomputers can be used to improve industrial processes
- Fail-soft techniques can be used for progressive shutdowns
- Microcomputers can be used in intelligent instrumentation
- Microcomputers may be used for advanced control techniques
- Microcomputers can be used in typical process applications
- The evolution of microcomputers drives an expanding array of process control applications
- Microcomputers can be used with programmable logic controllers
- Microcomputers can be used in hostile environments

7.1 INTRODUCTION

Microcomputers make it possible to use standardized hardware products for a longer period of time. This can result in lower overall costs in plant and facility operations.

A distinct advantage is the availability of low-cost software. The programs available now provide a flexibility for many applications that could not be considered before microcomputers. This software allows the implementation of functions with a complexity that could not be achieved with hard-wired logic. The changes are more simple to implement, and algorithms can be improved or changed with little or no hardware changes.

Many industrial control applications may use analog inputs and outputs. This results in a system which is the equivalent of an analog controller with a number of control loops. The control loop is the implementation of the algorithm which will regulate the output as a function of the inputs.

Some industrial applications use costly sensors and control mechanisms. The cost of the sensors required and the cost of the control devices required for the process output may be greater than the cost of the microcomputer system required for the control function. In view of the overall cost of the control hardware, the low cost of the microcomputer system itself is not the major advantage.

Microcomputers are used to control many processors or flows in manufacturing. These may be discrete or continuous and range from the traffic control of assemblies to the distribution of liquids or mixtures. They are capable of regulating any control process that can be measured.

An example of process control application is the regulation of a fermentation reactor. The system is equipped with sensors for the measurement of temperature, pressure, and other critical parameters, such as PH or flow. The information supplied by the sensors allows the microcomputer system to monitor the reactor and regulate the input parameters to optimize the reaction. The control of the temperature, pressure, and flow of the process can result in optimum reactor performance. There can also be improvements in the reliability of detecting or correcting any system malfunctions. The superior data collection capability also allows improvements in the processing strategy.

Microcomputer hardware and software now offer the flexibility and capability to perform data processing, variable gain control, and communications for many auxiliary purposes.

The microcomputer system can automatically monitor the state of the system and record critical parameter variations in bulk memory for analysis. It can also use this information for instant analysis. These techniques have been used in those industrial process control applications which could afford to use a minicomputer.

Dynamic optimization techniques can now be used in microcomputer systems to improve the performance of the process system. This optimization uses the microcomputer to look up previous values of the control parameters which were judged to be successful in improving the operation of the system. These parameters are interpolated in such a way to improve the system further by trying additional alternatives in the control scheme.

Many industrial applications are characterized by specific control techniques which tend to be almost universal. Most systems use a form of status feedback for more reliable operation. As the microcomputer controls some output device, it must verify that the operation of this device is correct. When a command is given to control an output device, such as to close a valve, the microcomputer must verify that the valve has been closed. Every output device may be monitored in this way to provide the status information needed. The status can be sent back to the microcomputer which will then verify it to complete the status-feedback loop.

In a typical system implementation the microcomputer gives the command to close the valve, and after a predetermined time it reads the status of the valve sensor. If correct, the status bit is true, and the microcomputer determines that the command has been correctly carried out.

If the status is not true, this indicates a malfunction. The microcomputer can then give the order a second and even a third time to try to free the valve. If the valve then closes, the status information indicates that the order has been finally executed.

The initial malfunction might be regarded as a random event and execution could proceed. If this malfunction is critical or occurs repeatedly, the microcomputer could issue an alarm and request maintenance.

If the valve refuses to move, a number of alternatives are possible. Fail-soft techniques can promote a progressive shutdown or idling mode of the system, rather than a complete loss when one of the components fails. The microcomputer could also activate an alternative flow path or execute another algorithm ignoring this device.

As the values of the input sensors are read by the microcomputer, it can determine if they are correct. Reasonable tests based on previous information can be used. A range is determined and checked for each input parameter at any given time.

For example, a parts control system controlling an assembly line might sense metal parts such as engine blocks through magnetic loop detectors. It can use the information from the loop detectors to control the speed of the line. An unreasonable speed may indicate a failure of the speed-sensing system.

In a similar way, a process controller measuring temperatures or pressures can use unreasonable values to detect failures. If there is a single occurrence of an unreasonable input value, it can be ignored as noise. This acts as a filter for random indications.

If the failure is repeated, it is classed as a malfunction. A diagnostic can then be generated to have the problem device disconnected or repaired.

Since there might be a temporary malfunction that can be tolerated, the microcomputer can keep checking the device. If the device then gives within-range indications for the required period of time, it can be reconnected to the system. Connecting and disconnecting the device need not be done physically in hardware. This can be accomplished by software.

A weighing technique can also be used where each sensor has a specific confidence ratio or weight. Measurements are made based on data from several sensors which are then multiplied by the individual weights to compute a final averaged value. The average can also be compared with each individual sensor reading.

In the case of two pressure sensors, one might have a 60% weight, and the other one a 40% weight. The average pressure is the value of the first measurement multiplied by 0.6 plus the value of the second sensor multiplied by 0.4. If the second sensor fails, its weight is set to 0 and its value ignored. The input pressure is then derived from the first sensor, which is given a weight of 1. The second sensor has been effectively disconnected by reducing its weight to 0. If the second sensor recovers and gives in-range values, it can be reconnected by setting its weight to 0.6 again.

In the assembly-line controller, an example of an unreasonable input would be a continuous speed indication of 0 feet minute by one of the part detectors. This could be the result of a line malfunction or a part lodged directly on top of the detector. The microcomputer can determine if a sensor is giving an unreasonable value since the other loops may be indicating 0 also or an actual speed. The faulty sensor can be disconnected and a diagnostic generated.

At a later time the microcomputer can still be monitoring this sensor even though it may not use its results. If the speed indicated is again within the range of the other detectors over a period of time, it can be reconnected to the system. The fault may have been due to a part stalled on top of the detector which was later moved away.

The microcomputer makes it possible to replace most logic hardware modules with their software equivalents. A typical control system uses a standard microcomputer plus the required interfaces. The system functions are accomplished by the programs.

A single desktop unit with plug-in boards may provide the memory, I/O and CPU facilities. Functions include a real-time clock, for the precise timing of external events and a power-fail restart circuit for restarting the system after a power failure and for preserving data when a power failure is detected. A data acquisition board is required to provide the information from the sensors or transducers.

7.2 COMPOSITION ANALYZERS

Microcomputers can be employed as processors in many intelligent instrumentation systems. Among these are systems used for composition analysis.

In a mass spectrometer as shown in Figure 7-1, charged particles of different atoms are separated by their mass to charge ratios. The separation normally takes place in a high vacuum to eliminate collision with other molecules. A sample is taken and ionized under reduced pressure by an electron beam. The charged particles then pass through a magnetic field to determine the mass to charge ratios. Spaced collectors then pass the charges to an electrometer where they are amplified into voltages proportional to the compositions. A closed-loop control system is used to compensate for any variations in sensitivity.

The use of a microcomputer allows the system to be self-calibrating and able to operate automatically. To provide a unit capable of continuous operation, a dual-filament, nonmagnetic ion source is used. Electrons emitted from the filament are focused on the gas sample input area, ionizing the particles to an energy of about 500 electron-volts.

This type of mass spectrometer may use one of the following inlet schemes. A capillary bypass system will use a sample of about 1 cm/sec. The sample does not need to be pressurized since the flow is maintained by a pump.

A flow-by inlet system requires the sample to have enough pressure to flow by the inlet and return back to the process at a lower pressure point. The sample is pulled into the analyzer by an internal pump.

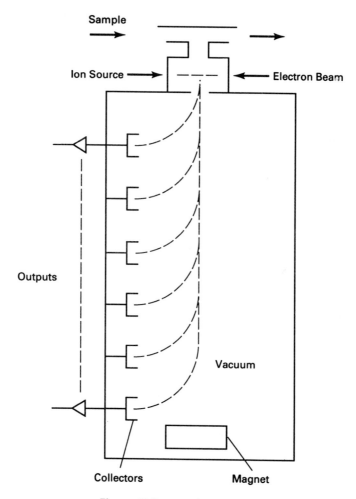

Figure 7-1 Mass Spectrometer

   In the mass spectrometer, a process microcomputer acts as an optimizing controller for the fractionation towers. The use of a high-speed mass spectrometer for analyzing the feed, overhead, and bottom streams provides the means for a feedforward control scheme. This can improve tower efficiencies by up to 20%. Appreciable energy savings can also be achieved.

   The mass spectrometer can take the place of a system composed of a gas chromatograph and oxygen and infrared analyzers in such processes as ethylene cracking furnaces, enthylene oxide production, vinyl chloride production, natural gas production, and gasification control. In this last application, the yield is maximized by controlling the amount of oxygen for the fire. Gases such as nitrogen, oxygen, and carbon dioxide can be readily measured. Carbon balances can be held between 99.7% and 100.3%. Typically, the use of a gas chromatograph and oxygen analyzer for this type of application provides a range of 98% to 102%, with three calibrations per month required for the chromatograph and weekly calibrations for the oxygen analyzer.

Other instruments may use a light source for stack emission measurements. One technique is to use a reference beam along with a measuring beam which is projected across the stack to a reflector unit. The beam is reflected back to the detector, and both beams are chopped alternately and directed to a single photocell. They are forced to match by moving a variable optical density disk in the reference beam. The required movement of the optical disk indicates the relative transmittence of the sample.

A similar detection technique for continuous analysis in process plants is used by the process chromatograph. A process chromatograph can be used to measure many components in the same stream. It can also be programmed to measure many streams, each with different concentrations. By the selection of different columns and detectors, the process chromatograph may be used to measure the parts per million concentrations of impurities in gases. The process chromatograph is limited to the analysis of gases or liquids which can be easily vaporized in the instrument. It is also called a gas chromatograph. Figure 7-2 shows a diagram of a gas chromatograph.

The sampling system can be complex when several streams are cycled to the analyzer. Some of these may drop out liquid components if they are allowed to cool or drop too rapidly in pressure. Heated sample lines may be used along with recycling lines from which a small side stream can be taken to the analyzer. The side stream continuously passes through the loop of a sample injection valve. A measured sample of the stream is injected into a chromatographic column. The sample is carried through the column by a carried gas which is usually helium. The chromatographic column has 3 to 10 feet of stainless steel tubing, $\frac{1}{4}$ inch in diameter, holding a porous solid on the surface of which a liquid has been absorbed. Passing through the column, the sample is dissolved and then evaporated into the column space thousands of times. This action is similar to a distillation column operating with thousands of plates. The components of the sample are separated according to their affinity for the liquid-separating agent, and they emerge from the column separated in time. An optical detector is then used to define the concentrations of the separated components.

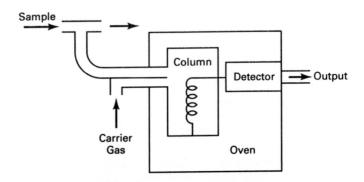

Figure 7-2 Gas Chromatograph

The microcomputer can be used to program the gas chromatograph to use the outputs of the detectors efficiently. Besides recording the height of a peak as the composition of an ingredient, the microcomputer can integrate the area under each curve, multiply it by its calibration factor (which it also calculates), and sum the areas under the curve to determine the total. Then, dividing each area by this total, it can calculate a calibrated value for each component which is corrected for that component and the present state of the instrument, thus calibrating itself. It can also be used to determine the area under those peaks which are not separated, detect the areas over any shifting baselines, and detect the baselines themselves.

Alarms may be set for an unexpected change in concentration and for any undesirable conditions which might occur. Some typical alarms might include the following:

1. Out of calibration conditions
2. Baseline drifts
3. Malfunction condition
4. Power failure
5. Limit checks for components
6. No data transfer to processor
7. Expected peak does not appear

During the time when the process chromatograph was being perfected in the 1960s, various groups in the process industries were trying to convert the mass spectrometer into a continuous process monitor. At that time, mass spectrometers had been used to measure the separation of uranium isotopes, and it was hoped a similar instrument could be used in process streams. But when used in a process stream the fine capillary required for the process sample quickly became obstructed by dust and dirt. By 1978 a number of continuous process mass spectrometers were available. Their success in industry depended not only on the use of microcomputers, but also a very high vacuum and fine capillary were no longer needed due to the newer inlet techniques used. The mass spectrometer has gone on to replace the older process chromatograph in many installations.

7.3 COMPRESSOR AND PUMP CONTROLLERS

In large compressor and pump installations, high-surge conditions can exist which, if not limited or acted upon quickly, can destroy the equipment. Various control techniques can be implemented using a microcomputer.

The greatest benefit for the use of microcomputers in compressor control is the flexibility and adaptability of using advanced control techniques in such systems. A stable mode of operation normally requires the use of some form of adaptive control to compensate for the changing characteristics of the process and compressor. This cannot be accomplished with conventional analog control equipment, but digital control systems using microcomputers can use adaptive control algorithms to perform these functions. The microcomputer system can also provide the facility for preprocessing data related to the detection of surge. The microcomputer can perform a spectrum analysis of the noise generated as the compressor approaches the critical surge point. Then the microcomputer can take corrective action.

When the compressor plays a role in energy conservation, the microcomputer can integrate the compressor as a part of an optimization system. Many installations use compressors at both upstream and downstream locations. The flow is then a function of all the units and their overall operating efficiency. A typical strategy in a multiple-unit installation that uses compressors of different capacities and characteristics is to distribute the load on each compressor. This can be done in such a way so the total demand is satisfied using the least possible energy. This is similar to a utilities distribution strategy where the individual power-generating units contribute power to the system such that the total energy consumed in the generation of power is a minimum. This strategy does not require that each unit be at its lowest energy consumption level or at its greatest efficiency, but that all units operate in such a way that total energy consumption is kept at a minimum.

In some installations it may not be feasible to optimize a single compressor because of a close interaction with the process parameters. It may be possible to optimize the total process with the compressor integrated into the control program.

A major advantage in the application of a microcomputer in a compressor installation is the ability of the computer to perform the mathematical computations required for signal analysis and conditioning purposes. These computations can be used to produce a narrow-band adjustable filter for the frequency analysis of the compressor signal.

A microcomputer programmed with fast Fourier transform algorithms (FFT) could perform a spectral analysis of the frequency character of the compressor. The comparison with a frequency signature of the compressor at an incipient surge condition allows the microprocessor to determine the likelihood of a surge condition occurrence. When the computer determines that surge is about to occur, a corrective action can be initiated.

Surge in single- and multiple-compressor installations stems from variations in process demand and the interaction between compressors due to the capacitive coupling effects of connecting piping.

The surge characteristic is a physical phenomenon and a severe limitation to the operation of a compressor installation. Since mechanical limitations prevents the elimination of surge conditions, control depends on its detection and control. The detection of surge conditions can generally be accomplished by establishing a surge-control line.

Methods of surge detection include

1. The measurement of a fluidic pressure pattern as the compressor approaches surge.
2. A frequency analysis which exhibits amplitude spectrums related to incipient surge conditions.

The use of a surge-control line allows a safety margin, which tends to reduce movements into the surge condition during transient upsets.

Another possible solution is the use of variable gain controllers to compensate for the changes in system gain as the compressor characteristics change with the load. The variable gain control compensates for the pressure-flow rate which is a nonlinear function. At high flow rates, the gain of the compressor is high. At lower flow rates it is low.

The loop gain needed varies as the compressor characteristic. The gain of the loop should be characterized according to the process demand. Variable gain control is difficult to achieve with conventional analog control, but it can be implemented with microcomputer hardware and software. The advantage of the digital implementation is the flexibility and adaptability of the software for a variable gain control. The computer software provides the capability of decision making for the selection of a control strategy based on the process demand, safety, or approaching surge conditions.

7.4 PROCESS-CONTROL SYSTEMS

A wide range of microcomputer control applications are available for local and distributed control tasks. These exist in process control systems at all levels, ranging from simple data acquisition display functions to actual local control.

Many process-control applications use a hierarchical architecture. A major issue in this type of system is the distribution of intelligence within the hierarchy for a particular application. In some cases, it is best to centralize the decision-making and control functions within a master or main processor. This places the local control units under complete control of the master and increases the communications and computation demands for the master. In other applications, a decentralization of the control and monitoring functions may be better. The local control units then operate as independent agents performing local control.

The trade-offs between the centralization and decentralization of intelligence in these systems is a key issue which affects the hardware and software. These trade-offs will depend on the identification of the user needs and system requirements. In such a hierarchical system architecture, the responsibility for the integration of the functions lies with the overall software-control system, the operating system.

The user interface may be required to provide a wide range of capabilities, including active reports, logging, alarms and interactive message communications, and a database for later analysis and record keeping. The system software should be able to execute control and monitoring tasks such as traditional control by event and by time, process-control algorithms, and other applications software as required by the system tasks.

A typical process industry application for microcomputers is fractionating column control.

A typical binary column can include a steam reboiler, water-cooled condenser, and reflux drum. In a conventional single-loop control of this type of column, there are key variables which greatly affect the operation of the column. Some can be manipulated while others cannot.

Among the allowable manipulated variables are the column pressure, feed flow rate, feed temperature, energy input, energy removal, and product flow rate. The variables which cannot be changed are the ambient barometric pressure, ambient temperature, feed composition, cooling water temperature, and inert vapor generation.

The single-loop type of feedback control of the binary distillation column uses a single-input and single-output philosophy. Each loop is independently operated as a feedback device with no provisions made to compensate for any interaction among the controlled variables. When the retuning of a controller is required, the variable on which this controller operates can interact with other process variables. This requires a retuning of these other variables.

Digital control can be applied with a microcomputer and to perform all the functions on the column. A microcomputer implementation can allow advanced control schemes.

Feedback control is the process of maintaining a controlled variable by using a device which compares the deviation between a set point and the measurement of the controlled variable. This comparison tends to force that deviation to 0. A major characteristic of feedback is that the error or deviation must exist before any corrective action takes place.

Feed-forward control is a technique where the magnitude of the error is anticipated and the corrective action is taken prior to the occurrence of an error. Feed-forward/feedback control uses a combination of both. This combination results in an error anticipation and corrective action followed by a readjustment. The feed-forward/feedback control concept is shown in Figure 7-3.

In a column the feed-forward components of control could consist of a feed analyzer and feed flow transmitter. These components will analyze and sense the disturbances due to feed changes and composition. As the feed composition changes, the output changes the produce draw and bottom drain-off to perform the correction.

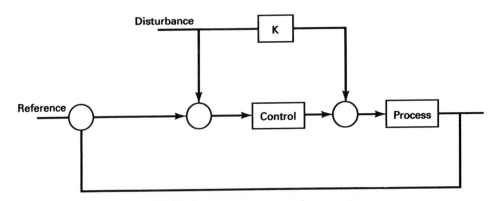

Figure 7-3 Feedforward/Feedback Control

The basic feedback or feed-forward/feedback type of control applies to a single variable using a single-input/single-output control scheme.

Modern process control brings the requirements of closer control, smaller downtimes, and higher throughput. Add these to the energy-saving requirements and the typical interactions become complex. This problem, combined with the realization that the control of one variable can affect others, leads to the use of multivariable systems as shown in Figure 7-4. A multivariable control system will simultaneously monitor many variables and then choose, based on the particular situation at the time, the optimum of several programmed control strategies. The control of a column may be a result of varying the steam flow, differential pressure across the column, feed rate, bottom flow rate, and other variables such as product composition. Each of these variables will usually affect the others. These effects are interactive.

The requirements for control and operation, along with the interactive nature of the system, require that a number of guidelines be established in order to use microcomputers in column control. Some typical variables which may interact in this application include steam flow, differential pressure, pressure, feed rate, feed composition, and temperature.

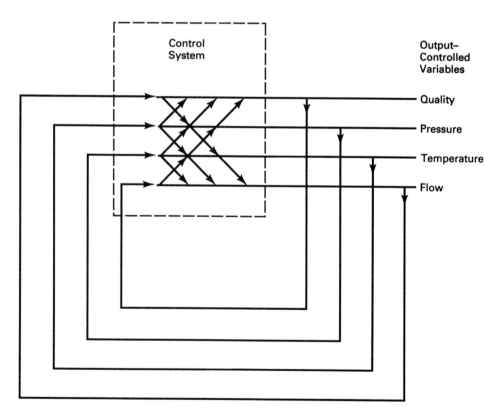

Figure 7-4 Interactive Multivariable Control

1. Identify the variables which may interact with one another.
2. Identify as many of the static and dynamic interactions of the variables as possible.
3. Develop a control philosophy that is not limited to the single-input/single-output type.

Improvements are possible in product quality, product flow rate or throughput, energy requirements, and the dynamic response and recovery from disturbances. The microcomputer system should consider the following factors:

1. Heat and material balance requirements
2. Feedforward and feedback control
3. Compensation of parameter interactions
4. Product, flow rate, and quality controls
5. Safety control

7.5 PC GROWTH IN PROCESS CONTROL

The microcomputer can take on many tasks in process control, it can collect data, generate reports, help design process layouts, model and analyze control parameters, help monitor and control process quality, and even perform plant management functions. The basic personal computer (PC) has undergone a radical transformation in process-control applications, due to low-cost software, powerful plug-in boards, and a growing list of compatible peripherals and communications devices. Just 10 years ago, PCs or microcomputers were restricted to machines that had an 8-bit bus. Minicomputers used 16 bits. And only mainframes used architectures of 32 bits and up.

Those definitions are no longer valid. Even micros are now beginning to use 32-bit chips. Because of this and related developments, the power that was once available only in minicomputers and superminis is now available in many of the new personal computer offerings.

Advanced graphics, multitasking windowing environments, and networking capabilities have become standard features in the latest PC products. A few years ago Intel introduced its 80386 microprocessor. This raised the level of available IBM-compatible PCs to that of 32-bit workstations. Other 32-bit microprocessors include the Motorola 68000 processor (the 68020 is used in the Macintosh II).

The operating system mainly serves to distinguish between networked PCs and full-featured workstations. Workstations normally use UNIX or a similar multiuser operating system, while PCs most often use MSDOS or a similar single-user system. Within the last few years, several companies have introduced products with the capability to run programs written under UNIX or MS-DOS concurrently. AT&T exemplifies this trend with its 6300 Plus PCs. VAXmate from Digital Equipment is another example. It allows users to run programs written for either the MS-DOS or VMS environment. Concurrent UNIX/DOS-type systems can be expected to become more popular in the future.

Many factors have contributed to the increasing acceptance and use of PCs. Besides the rapid increases in computing power has been the advances in graphics technology. Improved graphics chips and display processors have not only enhanced quality but reduced costs. Combined with multitasking, windowing, and artificial intelligent techniques, the improved graphics boards have made PCs easier to use. Features such as pull-down menus and special function keys minimize the operator skills that are required. Some software uses techniques that offer different levels of complexity and adjust to varying operator skill levels.

These features allow PCs to be used for an ever-expanding array of industrial applications. The functions frequently overlap in applications areas due to the PCs versatility. PCs are used as operator consoles, engineering consoles, data acquisition and storage devices, monitoring and control devices, plant (process) management consoles, and programmable controllers and motion controllers.

Improved graphics technology has stimulated the use of PCs as cost-effective operator consoles. They are used as replacements for the traditional operator consoles sold by control companies with their systems. Low cost, versatility, and the enhanced graphics interfaces have led to their acceptance.

The trend to industrially harden and protect PCs from the plant environment has accelerated their use for many applications. Developments in rack mounting, NEMA enclosures, and other environmental protection measures have increased greatly.

Control companies use consoles to configure the system for specific uses. Instead of designing, producing, and selling dedicated consoles, these suppliers are now providing some form of microcomputer or PC as a part of the package. PCs offer the computing power, storage, capacity, and flexibility needed for the application.

PCs are used for control system design, creating plant graphics, programming, building databases, documentation, and report generation. Since it involves no real process monitoring or control, data acquisition became one of the earliest process uses for microcomputers. The PC is connected directly to the process through I/O boards or I/O processors. Several may be interfaced to data highways to extract data from programmable controllers and distributed process control devices. Plug-in cards for PCs offer independent data paths for simultaneous analog input, analog output, and digital I/O.

Plant management is an area in which PCs are beginning to assume a greater role. The growth of applications software for PCs has stimulated their use on the plant floor as well as in offices. Manufacturing resources planning (MRP) software is available in modules covering such functions as scheduling, inventory control, maintenance management, energy management, production control, and forecasting. These systems are often interfaced with process controls through communications networks. This allows automatic updating of production data for use in the plant management functions.

Statistical process control/quality control (SPC/SQC) software packages for PCs are also available. Programs for computing standard deviations and other statistical measures for production trends have become a major application area for PCs in overall plant management.

PC software features can include multitasking, online editing, long-term trending, and real-time displays such as alarming and process monitoring. Many PC-based software packages offer a variety of advanced features, such as PID, batch, cascade, feed forward, and other process-control functions. These packages are usually menu based with programming capabilities. They can include operator interfaces, data logging and trending, and report generation. There is also software for CNC, energy analysis, environmental management, material handling, safety and fire protection, data acquisition, maintenance management, and other applications.

The IBM and compatibles have dominated industrial-control applications, but there are other options due to the availability of the open-architecture Macintosh II, and with the high-speed SCSI (small computer systems interface) built into the Macintosh SE. These computers are readily finding acceptance in many engineering and scientific applications.

The Macintosh II is a 68020 version of its predecessor, with six available expansion slots. The "Nubus" architecture used by Apple offers a 32-bit data path and 32-bit address space. This is larger than those of the IBM PC/XT/AT or compatible computers as shown here:

Microcomputer	Address lines	Data lines
PC/XT and compatibles	20	8
AT and PS/2 Models 50 and 60	24	16
386 and PS/2 Model 80	32	32
Macintosh II	32	32

A significant difference between the Nubus and the AT bus is in the DMA (direct memory access) capabilities. DMA allows the data to flow into or out of the computer's memory without having to go through the microprocessor. This allows the microprocessor to perform other tasks while DMA transfers are occurring. Since the DMA transfers require no intervention by the microprocessor, they can occur at higher speeds.

The PC/AT bus has a built-in DMA capability that is accessible from any expansion slot, while the Nubus has no built-in DMA capability. Expansion board space must be provided for this capability. Nubus expansion boards with DMA will be denser and/or more expensive than IBM boards or require two boards instead of one.

The Mac II has six expansion slots and excellent graphics. An SCSI port is built into the Mac Plus, Mac SE, and Mac II. Although it is used almost exclusively for external disk drive I/O, the SCSI port can also be used for data acquisition and instrumentation. The port allows a speed of over 700 KB/sec with the ability to drive up to 7 SCSI peripherals.

Although the Apple Macintosh personal computer uses a multitasking operating system, it does not have any real-time capabilities. IBM's latest line, the PS/2 with its OS/2 operating system, is also multitasking with no real-time capabilities.

In the PC/AT world, software such as ASYST and Labtech Notebook have emerged as standards for scientific and engineering applications. These packages integrate data acquisition, analysis, and graphics and are capable of supporting I/O boards from a wide variety of manufacturers.

PCs are also being modified to function as programmable controllers (also known as programmable logic controllers or PLCs), motion controllers, and other control devices. Most of these applications are accomplished with the addition of plug-in boards that allow the PC to assume the required functions. The motion control software may provide control of several stepper motors. One module permits the user to create motion profiles which can easily be viewed and edited.

Software like Labtech Notebook can perform process functions such as data monitoring and logging, alarming, and control (including PID loops and cascade control). Some packages offer real-time tuning of control loops so the operator can adjust control limits, gain, reset rate, and PID setpoints. Animated process diagrams also can be created using the graphics capabilities.

PCs are also used for configuring PLCs, distributed control systems, single-loop microprocessor-based controllers and other process-control systems. Through the use of I/O boards and separate I/O processors, PCs can be adapted to perform a variety of data acquisition, monitoring, and control functions. These I/O devices help relieve the PCs of time-consuming tasks and provide a greater capability for real-time data capture and control.

When connected with plantwide information systems, PCs make plant operating data available to a variety of operating personnel. This allows timely, informed decisions to be made. A PC connected to a distributed control system or plant data highway allows process engineers and supervisors to access data from a variety of controllers, processes, and operating workstations. Parameters such as operating efficiency, quality control, energy consumption, and other parameters can be accessed and even graphically presented in real time without interrupting normal work routines. PCs are becoming widely dispersed in many work areas as part of a comprehensive, integrated process communications and control network.

7.6 PCs AND PLCs

As personal computers find their way into more industrial applications in factories and process plants, they are often viewed as a replacement for programmable logic controllers (PLCs). Even though PCs continue to increase in popularity, programmable controller sales continue to expand as well. PLC sales increased by about 35% from 1985 to 1986 and show an annual growth rate of about 15% from that period up to the present.

There has also been an increase in the number of control and instrumentation applications that use PCs and PLCs. In these applications, the best features of each are used to solve specific application problems. The combination is popular in many small to midsized automation and control projects.

Real-time control is an important consideration in applications like machine control where the responses must be in milliseconds. In process control, some digital inputs such as emergency stop and pump failure indications must be answered quickly. Personal computers are impeded by the delays due to their operating system. The standard IBM PC/DOS or generic MS/DOS are single-task operating systems. The majority of PC manufacturing applications continue to be in the areas of data acquisition and operator interface. The PC's value as a control device tends to be limited since there is no universal real-time operating system and most software is written for MS-DOS. This limitation of real-time operating systems is the major reason why PCs have not displaced PLCs in basic machine control applications.

Programmable controllers can handle high-speed I/O. They are able to interpret a large number of input signals, use the information to control a large number of outputs, and repeat the process many times per second. Most PLC vendors provide analog, digital, and special-purpose I/O that meet the needs found in automation and process control applications.

PLCs offer relatively low cost and ease of maintenance compared to PC-based systems. PLCs are capable of handling 50 inputs/outputs. They also use relay-ladder programming, which can easily be maintained and updated.

7.6.1 PC-PLC Applications

In addition to providing the timing, sequencing, and logic functions for basic machine control, a PLC can be used to collect data from a production process and send it to a PC. A typical PC-PLC combination is for data acquisition and analysis. Other applications include process monitoring, operator interfaces, and cell control. In a typical PC-PLC application for online statistical process control (SPC) or statistical quality control (SQC) testing, the PLC gathers the operational data in real time and transmits it periodically to a PC, which then does a statistical analysis on the data. In a textile mill, for example, the PLCs would monitor hundreds of sewing, knitting, and winding machines. The PLCs send data to a PC, which then analyzes the data to identify machines that are not operating at peak efficiency. When it finds such a machine, the PC flags it for maintenance.

In this way, PCs and PLCs can be combined to provide a real-time view into the production process to allow greater supervision and control. In the past, an operator may have monitored a process by using one or more control panels which may have contained annunciators, lights, meters, and readouts. Today, CRT displays and PCs are taking the place of these control panels. Using data sent from the PLC, the CRT display can show the critical values of the production processes graphically and accept operator inputs to control or modify the process. The PC adds versatility; with graphics programs, it can display production data, summaries, and other supervisory information.

Manufacturing cell control is another application for PC-PLC combinations. The cell controller must be able to gather and send production information to the operator or a higher-level device. It should also be able to coordinate and supervise at least one other independent production device and have the capability to store and retrieve production data.

About 20% of cell controllers use personal computers. Typically, the PC retrieves and sends information to the PLCs, which control the individual machines. In addition to collecting, displaying, and storing information, the PC performs supervisory functions to coordinate the individual PLCs.

7.6.2 PC-PLC Interfaces

Connecting a PC to a PLC is usually done with RS-232C or RS-422. The connection is made with a cable from the PC's RS-232C/RS-422 port to the PLC, which may have either a built-in port or interface module. Some PLCs offer a linking module which allows a computer to communicate to PLCs using simple ASCII commands. The host link modules accept data from RS-232C, RS-422, or fiber optic links and offer selectable transmission rates. Multiple PLCs usually can be networked with one PC.

Software is available for the communications link, and if the PC-PLC is to be used for data collection, manipulation and analysis, or process variables, a short BASIC program is usually all that is required.

Graphic options can include trending displays, "cut-and-paste" capabilities, zoom or pan features, and use of a keyboard or mouse for display generation. Program capacity can be reviewed for I/O point monitoring capacity, discrete versus PID control loop capabilities, and page or screen limitations.

Programmable controllers will continue to advance toward higher performance at lower cost, and the PC-PLC connection will continue to be as an effective solution for many small and medium-size control applications.

7.7 INDUSTRIAL WORKSTATION TRENDS

In the late 1960s, operator interfaces for the process or manufacturing industries consisted mainly of push buttons, pilot lights, thumb wheels, and single-loop controllers. Then, message displays, dumb terminals, and programmable controllers began to be used along with limited but dedicated operator interface graphics systems.

The advent of the IBM personal computer, in the early 1980s ushered in a new low-cost means of establishing an operator interface. By the mid-1980s, a number of software packages were available for the IBM PC and compatibles that allowed users to develop a graphical representation of a process; configure the operator interface screens; and provide capabilities for historical trending, statistical process control, and report generation. As advanced versions of the PC became available, these capabilities extended beyond simple interfacing and monitoring to the actual control of a process through the use of interrupts.

The desktop computers are often bundled with a color monitor and keyboard. Others are sold in rack or panel configurations, with monitors and keyboards sold separately. Industrial versions of these computers are designed to withstand the environment found in a process or manufacturing application.

Another approach is to use nonindustrialized, commercial-grade PCs along with equipment to protect the computers on the plant floor. This usually means the use of some form of enclosure for the PCs as well as monitors and keyboards.

These industrial workstations serve as platforms for a user's PC on the plant floor and typically have a built-in industrial keyboard and monitor. They are

TABLE 7-1 OUTLINE OF NEMA CLASSIFICATIONS FOR ENCLOSURES

Enclosure class	Intended for
1	Indoor use, protects against contact with the enclosed equipment.
2	Indoor use, protects against limited amounts of falling water and dirt.
3	Outdoor use, protects against windblown dust, rain, sleet, and external ice formation.
3R	Outdoor use, protects against falling rain, sleet, and external ice formation.
3S	Outdoor use, protects against windblown dust, rain, and sleet and provides for operation of external mechanisms when ice laden.
4	Indoor or outdoor use, protects against windblown dust and rain, splashing water, and hose-directed water.
4X	Indoor or outdoor use, protects against corrosion, windblown dust and rain, splashing water, and hose-directed water.
5	Indoor use, protects against dust and falling dirt.
6	Indoor or outdoor use, protects against the entry of water during occasional temporary submersion.
6P	Indoor or outdoor use, protects against the entry of water during prolonged submersions.
7	Indoor use in locations classified as Class I; Groups A, B, C, or D as defined in the National Electrical Code.
8	Indoor or outdoor use in locations classified as Class I; Groups A, B, C, or D as defined in the National Electrical Code.
9	Indoor use in locations classified as Class II; Groups E, F, or G as defined in the National Electrical Code.
10	Meet the requirements of the Mine Safety and Health Administration.
11	Indoor use, provides by oil immersion, protection against the corrosive effects of liquids and gases.
12	Indoor use, protects against dust, falling dirt, and dripping noncorrosive liquids.
12K	With knockouts, indoor use, protects against dust, falling dirt, and dripping noncorrosive liquids other than at knockouts.
13	Indoor use, protects against dust, spraying of water, oil, and noncorrosive coolant.

* ANSI/NEMA 250-1985, *Enclosures for Electrical Equipment (1000 Volts Maximum)*, National Electrical Manufacturers Association.

designed to provide various levels of protection. An industrial workstation can have the capability to withstand high temperatures, shock and vibration, and other conditions. The cost of an industrial workstation will depend on the degree of protection required and the types of components and peripherals needed. Airborne particulates, dust, dirt, and splashing or hose-directed water are common problems on the plant floor. The environmental classifications established by the National Electrical Manufacturers Association (NEMA) is shown in Table 7-1.

7.8 ENVIRONMENTAL CONSIDERATIONS

A high-temperature application requires that a calculation be made of both the high ambient temperature and the internal heat generation of the PC, monitor, and other peripherals. Industrial computers are usually rated at 0–55° or 0–60°C, while commercial-grade computers have 0–37° or 0–40°C ratings. The maximum operating temperature of the monitor must also be considered. Auxiliary cooling can be in the form of internal fans, external heat exchangers, or air conditioners.

The mounting provided by the industrial workstation must isolate the computer, monitor, and other components from shock and vibration. Rubber shock mounts and special mounting hardware typically are used to prevent the loosening effect of constant vibration.

Installation and seviceability of the internal equipment can be important considerations. Installation can be costly and interrupt normal plant operations. The mounting surfaces can be preconfigured to accept the computer and other equipment, and the enclosure should be designed to allow the computer, monitor, keyboard, and other equipment to be quickly and easily repaired or replaced without causing excessive downtime.

PCs and peripherals will often require protection against the effects of radio frequency interference (RFI) and electromagnetic interference (EMI), as well as noise on the incoming electrical power supply. Surge suppression and isolation transformers are usually employed, and shielded cabinets can provide extra protection in high-RFI/EMI environments.

The standard commercial-grade keyboard may not survive in an industrial environment. A keyboard should be selected with shock, vibration and temperatures in mind and should be sealed as desired to NEMA requirements.

Two basic types of keyboards are available. One is a full-travel keyboard with a NEMA 12 seal. These provide tactile feedback which is desirable when the amount of programming or operator interfacing is great. The other type uses membrane keys with a NEMA 4 seal.

The display monitor should be selected with the actual operator conditions in mind. A minimum size of 12 or 13 inches is recommended because operators are often moving and observing operations. They need to be able to read information on the screen from a distance and a 19-inch monitor may allow more freedom. A color display can permit operators to see problems developing from a distance more clearly than a monochrome display.

7.9 BUBBLE MEMORIES

The weakest link in a microcomputer on the plant floor can be the mechanical disk drive. For PCs used in hostile plant environments, mass memory storage is available in the form of nonvolatile bubble memory disks or cartridges. Reliability and ruggedness are the primary advantages, with some units a mean time to failure in excess of 20 years is possible. Bubble memories offer a high tolerance to dust and dirt, shock, vibration, temperature, and humidity. The disadvantage is that bubble memory costs more on a unit storage basis than mechanical disk systems, but this is offset by less downtime and fewer hardware problems.

In the early years of bubble memories, it was believed that they would be less expensive per bit than semiconductor random access memory (RAM). The popularity of PCs dropped the cost of RAM faster than expected, and bubbles were used only in military and industrial applications where the levels of heat, dust, humidity, shock, and vibration would damage floppy or hard disk drives. Bubble memory applications include chemical, food and pharmaceutical, nuclear power, and steel plants.

The magnetic bubble memory stores data in the form of cylindrical magnetic domains, called bubbles, in a thin film of magnetic material. The presence or absence of bubbles indicates a binary 1 and 0. The bubbles are created by a bubble generator in the memory and converted to electrical signals by an internal detector as the data is read. An external rotating magnetic field propels the bubbles through the film. No mechanical motion is required. Metallic patterns, or chevrons, are deposited on the film to move bubbles in the desired direction. Transfer rates average about 20,000 bits per second.

The bubbles are circulated past a pickup point where they become available to external connections and in this way the operation can be compared to a tape recorder. However, in a tape the stored bits are stationary on a moving medium while in a bubble memory, the medium is stationary and the bits are dynamic.

If power fails, the bubbles and the data they represent are maintained in the film. When power is restored, the data is still accessible.

Bubble memories are available in the form of expansion boards or cartridges that emulate a disk drive in an IBM PC or compatible. Bubble chips can hold up to 4 million bits, and chips holding up to a billion bits of information on a half-inch square chip are possible in the future. Price drops could allow bubbles in a wide range of uses.

IBM PC Interface Boards

This chapter shows you how

- The basic components of data acquisition systems operate
- Available interface boards for the IBM PC family function
- Commercial interface boards for the IBM PC family can be connected and programmed for data acquisition and control

In the next two chapters we seek to help the user in choosing a data acquisition board by providing

1. Relevant questions in making the choice
2. Definitions of specifications
3. Features of selection and evaluation

First, some considerations on what must be done to make the system perform as expected are in order.

A key factor in choosing the right board is to define the design objectives completely. Consider all known objectives and try to anticipate the unknowns. Try to include factors as signal and noise levels, desired accuracy, throughput rate, characteristics of the interfaces, environmental conditions, and size and budgetary limitations that may force performance compromises or a different approach.

General considerations for a control system include the following:

1. Input and output signal ranges
2. Data throughput rate
3. Error allowed for each functional block
4. Environmental conditions
5. Supply voltage, recalibration interval, and other operating requirements
6. Special environmental conditions: RF fields, shock, and vibration

Multiplexer considerations are the following:

1. Number and type of input channels needed, single ended or differential, high or low level, dynamic range
2. Type of hierarchy used for a large amount of channels, addressing scheme
3. Settling time when switching from one channel to another, maximum switching rate
4. Allowable cross-talk error between channels; frequencies involved
5. Errors due to leakage
6. Multiplexer transfer errors due to the voltage divider formed by the on resistance of the multiplexer and the input resistance of the sample-hold
7. Channel-switching rate, fixed or flexible; continuous, interruptible; capable of stopping on one channel during test purposes

Sample-hold considerations may include

1. Input signal range
2. Slewing rate of the signal, multiplexer's channel-switching rate, sample-hold acquisition time
3. Accuracy, gain, linearity, and offset errors
4. Aperture delay, jitter*
5. Amount of droop allowable in hold
6. The effects of time, temperature, and power supply variations
7. Offset errors due to the sample-hold's input bias current through the multiplex switch and sources

It is essential to have an understanding of what the manufacturer means by the specifications. Product information must be interpreted in terms meaningful to the user's requirements, which requires a knowledge of how the terms are defined.

---

* The delay component of aperture time may be correctible, since switching can be advanced in time to compensate. The uncertainty or jitter cannot be compensated. A random jitter of 5 nanoseconds applied to a signal slewing at 1 volt per microsecond results in an uncertainty of 5 millivolts. In systems with a constant sampling rate, using data that is not correlated to the sampling rate, the aperture delay is not important, but jitter can modulate the sampling rate.

8.1 SPECIFICATIONS DEFINED

8.1.1.1 Absolute accuracy.   As the converter's full-scale range is adjusted, it will be set with respect to the reference voltage which can be traced to some recognized voltage standard. The absolute accuracy error is the tolerance of the full-scale point referred to this absolute voltage standard.

8.1.1.2 Acquisition time.   The acquisition time of a sample-hold circuit is the time it takes to acquire the input signal to within the stated accuracy. It may include the settling time of the output amplifier. Since it is possible for the signal to be acquired and the circuit switched to hold before the output is settled, one should be sure of what is meant by this term, since the output may not be meaningful until it is settled.

8.1.1.3 Common-Mode range.   The common-mode rejection usually varies with the magnitude of the input signal swing, which is determined by the sum of the common-mode and the differential voltages. Common-mode range is the range of input voltage over which the specified common-mode rejection is maintained. When the common-mode signal is ± 5 V and the differential signal is ± 5 V, the common mode range is ± 10 V.

8.1.1.4 Common-Mode rejection.   This is the ability to reject the effects of voltages applied to both input terminals simultaneously. It is usually expressed either as a ratio (CMRR = 10^5) or as $20 \log_{10}$.

8.1.1.5 Droop.   A drifting of the output at an approximately constant rate, droop may be caused by the leakage of current out of a storage capacitor.

8.1.1.6 Feed through.   This is the fraction of the input signal that appears at the output in the hold or off mode, caused primarily by capacitance across the switch. It can be measured by applying a full-scale sinusoidal input at a fixed frequency and observing the output.

8.1.1.7 Offset.   For a zero input, it is the extent to which the output deviates from zero, usually a function of time and temperature.

8.1.1.8 Nonlinearity monotonicity.   This is the ability to include all required code numbers in actual operation (the amount by which the plot of output versus input deviates from a straight line).

8.1.1.9 Settling time.   This is the time required for the input to attain a final value within a specified fraction of full scale, usually $\pm\frac{1}{2}$ LSB.

8.1.1.10 Slew rate.   Slew rate, the maximum rate at which the output voltage can change, usually is an indication of settling time.

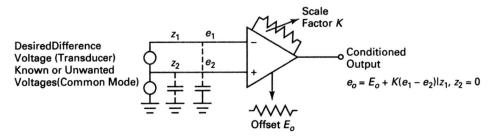

Figure 8-1   Differential Amplifier Used as a Signal Conditioner

When considering the problem of determining performance requirements, it is useful to divide the specifications into three groups. Those that determine accuracy under optimum conditions. Those that are time dependent. Those that are affected by the environment.

The first group includes resolution, relative accuracy, differential linearity, noise, quantization uncertainty, and monotonicity.

Time-dependent specifications include the conversion time, bandwidth, and settling time. Environment-related specifications include the gain or scale factor, temperature coefficients, and operating temperature range.

A relaxation of the specifications of the first type can be done through the use of signal conditioners. The specific form of signal conditioning must be based on knowledge of the input signals and the information to be extracted from them. Unwanted signal components can be extracted from the input signals. A differential instrumentation amplifier may be used to reject common-mode signals, bias out the dc offsets, and scale the input as shown in Figure 8-1.

Logarithmic compression can be used in applications which require a wide dynamic signal range. If the system is capable of tolerating a constant fractional error of 1% or less, a logarithmic amplifier for data compression can be used as shown in Figure 8-2. Modest accuracy in a fixed ratio is substituted for extreme accuracy over the entire full-scale range. For many applications, this is acceptable. The data can be handled easily since it is to be processed digitally.

The most common signal-conditioning device is the filter. Low-pass filters can extract carrier, signal, and noise components above the signal frequencies. These components will appear as noise if the A/D converter cannot follow them. A/D converters often contain follower circuits for impedance buffering. With a

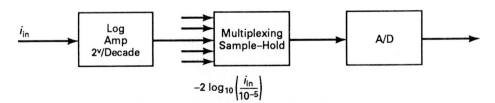

Figure 8-2   Logarithmic Range Compression

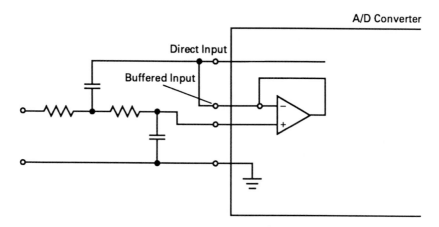

Figure 8-3 A/D Input Amplifier Connected as a Low-Pass Filter

minimum of external wiring, these are connected as active low-pass filters as shown in Figure 8-3.

A relaxation of this type of specifications can be achieved by adding a sample-hold amplifier to the system as shown in Figure 8-4. The use of a sample-hold amplifier will increase the system throughput rate and increase the highest-frequency signal that can be encoded within the converter resolution. System throughput rate, without the sample-hold, is determined mainly by the multiplexer's settling time and the A/D conversion time.

Multiplexer settling time is the time required for the analog signal to settle to within its error budget, as measured at the input to the converter. In a 12-bit system, with a ± 10 V range, the multiplexer units typically settle within 1 μs.

A sample-hold can be used to hold the last channel's signal level for conversion, while the next channel is selected and settles. The throughput time can be reduced to approach the conversion time. Pairs of sample-holds and A/D con-

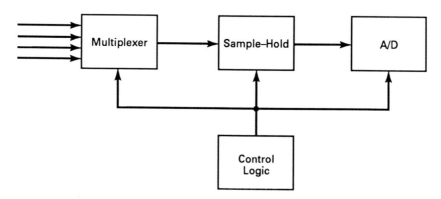

Figure 8-4 Data Acquisition System with Sample-Hold

verters may be used for alternate conversions to increase the throughput rate further.

A relaxation of the errors due to environment-related specifications can be achieved by allotting one multiplexer channel to carry a ground-level signal, and the other to carry a precision reference-voltage level that is close to full scale.

The data from these channels is used to correct gain and offset variations common to all the channels. These could be generated in the sample-hold, A/D converter, or wiring.

8.2 ERROR BUDGETS

Errors may be due to the physical interconnections, grounding, power supplies, and protection circuitry. To evaluate the performance trade-offs, an error budget can be useful. Three types of errors may be considered: those due to the nonideal nature of components, the physical interconnections, and the interaction of components.

The first type of errors is determined from the specifications of the components. The second type results from the parasitic interactions that are a function of the interconnections, grounding and shielding methods, and contact resistance. The third group results from interactions between components in the system. These result from analysis of the specifications of the devices, or how they are designed. An example of this type of error source might be the offsets created by series impedances in the signal path from signal sources or multiplexer-switch impedances. The bias and leakage currents of the stages following these impedances will also be affected. Another example might be the disturbances caused at the source, as the multiplexer switches to its terminal.

The error budget can be used as a tool for establishing the performance requirements of the system. The error budget is useful for predicting the overall expected error. A worst case summation or root-sum-of-the-squares summation or combinations may be used.

The popularity of modular interface boards requires that we consider some elements of their design. Many types are programmable; this allows the user to select one of several voltage ranges by choosing the appropriate jumper connection. Many boards permit modifications by the connection of external resistors. The gain and offset temperature coefficients of these resistors can be a source of error.

To reduce common-mode errors, a differential amplifier can be used to eliminate ground-potential differences as shown in Figure 8-5. The signal source may be a remote transducer. The common-mode signal is the potential difference between the ground signal at the interface board and the ground signal at the transducer, plus any common-mode noise produced at the transducer and voltages developed by the unbalanced impedances of the two lines.

The amount of dc common-mode offset that is rejected will depend on the CMRR of the amplifier. Bias currents flowing through the signal source leads may cause offsets if either the bias currents or the source impedances are unbalanced.

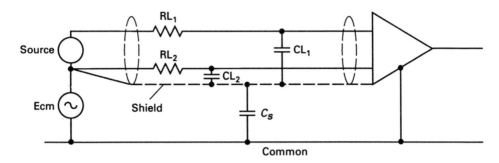

Figure 8-5   High-Frequency Common-Mode Rejection Using a Shield

CMRR specifications may include a specified amount of source unbalance. The specifications may also indicate an upper frequency for which CMRR is valid. At higher frequencies, unbalanced conditions, series resistance, shunt capacitance, and the amplifier's internal unbalances reduce the common-mode rejection, by producing a quadrature normal-mode signal. This error can be reduced by the use of a shield, as shown in Figure 8-5. In this circuit, no part of the common-mode signal appears across the line capacitors since the shield is driven by the common-mode source. The shield also provides some electrostatic shielding to limit coupling to other lines in close proximity. It is important that the shield be connected only at one point to the common-mode source signal and that the shields be continuous, through all connectors. The shield is carrying the common-mode signal so it should be insulated to prevent it from shorting to other shields or ground. A return path must exist for the bias and leakage currents of the differential amplifier unless it has transformer or optically coupled inputs.

In this section we have discussed some of the system aspects of applying interface boards. Considering the different types of boards on the market and the complex manner in which some specifications may relate to a system applications, selecting the best board for an application is not always a simple task. To make the most appropriate choice, we must consider a number of issues:

1. The objectives of the system and how they relate to the board's specifications.
2. How the system may be configured to relax the performance requirements.
3. How the system components limit and degrade performance.

8.3 CODING

Digital numbers are represented by the presence or absence of fixed voltage levels. These digital numbers are binary. Each bit or unit of information will have one of two possible states. In a binary code, the first bit is called the most significant bit or MSB. The last bit is called the least significant bit. The resolution of an analog-to-digital converter is determined by the number of bits. The

TABLE 8-1 NATURAL BINARY CODE

Decimal fraction	Binary fraction	MSB $(x \frac{1}{2})$	Bit 2 $(x \frac{1}{4})$	Bit 3 $(x \frac{1}{8})$	Bit 4 $(x \frac{1}{16})$
0	0.0000	0	0	0	0
$\frac{1}{16} = 2^{-4}$ (LSB)	0.0001	0	0	0	1
$\frac{2}{16} = \frac{1}{8}$	0.0010	0	0	1	0
$\frac{3}{16} = \frac{1}{8} + \frac{1}{16}$	0.0011	0	0	1	1
$\frac{4}{16} = \frac{1}{4}$	0.0100	0	1	0	0
$\frac{5}{16} = \frac{1}{4} + \frac{1}{16}$	0.0101	0	1	0	1

coding used is the set of coefficients representing a fractional part of full scale. The MSB is always positioned on the left and the LSB on the right of the digital code.

The most common digital code is natural binary. In a natural binary code of n bits, the MSB has a weight of $\frac{1}{2}$, or (2^{-1}); the second bit has a weight of $\frac{1}{4}$, or (2^{-2}); and so on to the LSB, which has a weight of 2^{-n}. The value of the binary number represented is obtained by adding up the weights of the nonzero bits. A 4-bit representation is shown in Table 8-1 with the binary weights and the equivalent numbers shown as both decimal and binary fractions.

Table 8-2 shows the bit weights in binary for numbers up to 12 bits, the range for many data acquisition boards (for larger numbers of bits continue to divide by 2).

The weight assigned to the LSB.R is the resolution. The dB column is the logarithm (base 10) of the ratio of the LSB value to unity multiplied by 20. Each

TABLE 8-2 BINARY WEIGHTS

Bit	2^{-n}	$\frac{1}{2}^n$ (fraction)	dB	$\frac{1}{2}^n$ (decimal)	%	ppm
FS	2^0	1	0	1.0	100	1,000,000
MSB	2^{-1}	$\frac{1}{2}$	−6	0.5	50	500,000
2	2^{-2}	$\frac{1}{4}$	−12	0.25	25	250,000
3	2^{-3}	$\frac{1}{8}$	−18.1	0.125	12.5	125,000
4	2^{-4}	$\frac{1}{16}$	−24.1	0.0625	6.2	62,500
5	2^{-5}	$\frac{1}{32}$	−30.1	0.03125	3.1	31,250
6	2^{-6}	$\frac{1}{64}$	−36.1	0.015625	1.6	15,625
7	2^{-7}	$\frac{1}{128}$	−42.1	0.007812	0.8	7,812
8	2^{-8}	$\frac{1}{256}$	−48.2	0.003906	0.4	3,906
9	2^{-9}	$\frac{1}{512}$	−54.2	0.001953	0.2	1,953
10	2^{-10}	$\frac{1}{1024}$	−60.2	0.0009766	0.1	977
11	2^{-11}	$\frac{1}{2048}$	−66.2	0.00048828	0.05	488
12	2^{-12}	$\frac{1}{4096}$	−72.2	0.00024414	0.024	244

successive power of 2 represents a change of 6.02dB ($20 \log_{10} (2)$) or approximately 6dB/octave.

In the A/D conversion process, a quantization uncertainty of $\pm\frac{1}{2}$ LSB exists in addition to conversion errors existing in the converter. To reduce this quantization uncertainty, it is necessary to increase the number of bits.

Statistical interpolation techniques can be performed in processing or in filtering following the conversion. This will fill in missing analog values for rapidly varying signals, but will do nothing to improve the variations within $\pm\frac{1}{2}$ LSB.

Since it is usually easier to determine the location of a transition than to determine a midrange value, errors, and settings of A/D converters are normally defined in terms of the analog values when transitions occur, in relation to the ideal transition values. Both D/A and A/D converters will have offset errors since the first transition may not occur at exactly $\frac{1}{2}$ LSB. Scale factor or gain errors will cause a difference between the values at which the first transition and the last transition occur since this is not always equal to full-scale $-\frac{1}{2}$ LSB. A linearity error may exist since the differences between transition values are not equal or uniform in changing. If the differential linearity error is large enough, it is possible for codes to be missed.

An important factor is the choice of full scale if full scale is (or the bit values are expressed as negative powers of 2) multiplied by 10.

In some codes, the bits are represented by their complements. Unipolar converters use analog signals of one polarity while bipolar converters use an extra bit for the sign.

When the sign digit doubles both the range and the number of levels, the LSB's ratio to full scale in either polarity is $2 - (n - 1)$, not 2^{-n}.

The most common binary codes for bipolar conversion are sign-magnitude (magnitude plus sign), offset binary, 2's complement, and 1's complement. Each of these codes in 4 bits (3 bits plus sign) are shown in Table 8-3.

The analog signal now has a choice of polarity and the relationship between the code and the polarity of the signal must be defined. Positive reference indicates that the analog signal increases positively as the digit number increases. Negative reference indicates that the analog signal decreases toward negative full scale as the digital number increases.

Sign-Magnitude is a way of expressing signed analog quantities. It is used in converters that operate near zero, where the application calls for a smooth and linear transition from a small positive voltage to a small negative voltage. It is the only code in which the three magnitude bits do not have a major transition such as all 1's to all 0's, at the 0.

Sign-Magnitude has several disadvantages compared to other codes. One problem is the two codes for 0. This makes sign-magnitude harder to use since it requires either software or additional hardware and software. The circuits for sign-magnitude conversion also tend to be more complicated and costly than for some of the other codes.

The 2's complement code consists of a binary code for positive magnitudes with a 0 sign bit. The 2's complement is formed by complementing the number and adding one LSB. The 2's complement of $\frac{3}{8}$ (binary 0011) is the complement

TABLE 8-3 BINARY CODES

Decimal number	Decimal fraction		Sign + magnitude	2's complement	Offset binary	1's complement
	Positive reference	Negative reference				
+7	$+\frac{7}{8}$	$-\frac{7}{8}$	0111	0111	1111	0111
+6	$+\frac{6}{8}$	$-\frac{6}{8}$	0110	0110	1110	0110
+5	$+\frac{5}{8}$	$-\frac{5}{8}$	0101	0101	1101	0101
+4	$+\frac{4}{8}$	$-\frac{4}{8}$	0100	0100	1100	0100
+3	$+\frac{3}{8}$	$-\frac{3}{8}$	0011	0011	1011	0011
+2	$+\frac{2}{8}$	$-\frac{2}{8}$	0010	0010	1010	0010
+1	$+\frac{1}{8}$	$-\frac{1}{8}$	0001	0001	1001	0001
0	0+	0−	0000	0000	1000	0000
0	0−	0+	1000	(0000)	(1000)	1111
−1	$-\frac{1}{8}$	$+\frac{1}{8}$	1001	1111	0111	1110
−2	$-\frac{2}{8}$	$+\frac{2}{8}$	1010	1110	0110	1101
−3	$-\frac{3}{8}$	$+\frac{3}{8}$	1011	1101	0101	1100
−4	$-\frac{4}{8}$	$+\frac{4}{8}$	1100	1100	0100	1011
−5	$-\frac{5}{8}$	$+\frac{5}{8}$	1101	1011	0011	1010
−6	$-\frac{6}{8}$	$+\frac{6}{8}$	1110	1010	0010	1001
−7	$-\frac{7}{8}$	$+\frac{7}{8}$	1111	1001	0001	1000
−8	$-\frac{8}{8}$	$+\frac{8}{8}$		(1000)	(0000)	

plus the LSB

$$1100 + 0001 = 1101$$

The 2's complement is easy to work with since it may be thought of as a set of negative numbers. To subtract $\frac{3}{8}$ from $\frac{4}{8}$, one adds $\frac{4}{8}$ to $-\frac{3}{8}$, or 0100 to 1101. The result is 0001, neglecting the extra carry, or $\frac{1}{8}$.

Comparing the 2's complement code and the offset binary code, the only difference between them is that the MSB of one is replaced by its complement in the other. An offset-binary-coded converter can be used for 2's complement by using the MSB's complement at the output of an A/D converter or at the output of a D/A converter's input register.

Offset binary is the easiest code to implement with converter circuits. The offset binary code for 3 bits plus sign is the same as natural binary for 4 bits, except that zero is at negative full scale, the LSB is $\frac{1}{16}$ of the total bipolar range, and the MSB is on at 0.

An offset binary 3-bits-plus sign converter can be made from a 4-bit D/A converter with a 0 to 10 V full-scale range. The scale factor is doubled to 20 V and then offset the zero by half of the full range to −10 V. For an A/D converter, reduce the input by half and increment a bias of half the range.

Offset binary is more compatible with microcomputer inputs and outputs since it is easily changed to the more common 2's complement (by complementing the MSB). It also has a single unambiguous code for 0.

The principal disadvantage of offset binary is the bit transition which occurs at 0 when bits may change, from 0111 to 1000. The difference in speeds between circuits turning on and off can lead to spikes and linearity problems since linearity errors are likely to occur at major transitions, such as the transition is a difference between two large numbers.

Zero errors can be greater than sign magnitude, since the zero level is usually obtained by taking the difference between the MSB ($\frac{1}{2}$ full scale) and a bias ($\frac{1}{2}$ full scale), usually two large numbers. The 2's complement has the same disadvantages as offset binary, since the conversion process is the same.

The 1's complement code is a technique of representing negative numbers. The 1's complement is obtained by complementing all bits. The 1's complement of $\frac{3}{8}$ (0011) is (1100). A number is subtracted by adding its 1's complement, and the extra carry that is disregarded in the 2's complement code causes one LSB to be added to the total in the end-around carry. Subtracting $\frac{3}{8}$ from $\frac{4}{8}$ we get

$$0100 + 1100 = 0001$$

(or $\frac{1}{8}$).

The 1's complement is formed by complementing each positive value to obtain its corresponding negative value, including 0, which is represented by two codes, 0000 and 1111. Along with the ambiguous 0, another disadvantage is that it is not as readily implemented as is 2's complement in converter circuits.

In sign-magnitude and 1's complement converters, the ambiguous 0 must be considered. One of the codes may be forbidden or the $\pm\frac{1}{2}$ LSB zero region can be divided into two regions, 0 to $+\frac{1}{2}$ LSB and 0 to $-\frac{1}{2}$ LSB, one that produces one code, the other the other code.

8.4 D/A CONVERTERS

The R-2R ladder is a convenient and popular form of D/A conversion. It is illustrated in Figure 8-6, which shows its use with an inverting operational amplifier. If all bits but the MSB are off, therefore grounded, the output is $(-R/2R)V_{REF}$. If all bits except bit 2 are off, the output voltage will be $\frac{1}{2}(-R/2R)V_{REF} = \frac{1}{4}V_{REF}$: the lumped resistance of the LSB circuit to the left of bit 2 is 2R.

The equivalent circuit looking back from the MSB toward bit 2 is $V_{REF}/2$, and the series resistance is 2R. The grounded MSB series resistance which is also 2R has no influence since the amplifier is at ground. The output voltage is therefore $-V_{REF}/4$. The same type of reasoning can be used to show that the nth bit produces an output increment equal to $2^{-n} V_{REF}$.

The R-2R network may be used to give an unattenuated noninverting output by connecting the output to a high-impedance load, such as the input of a follower amplifier as shown in Figure 8-6. The entire network may be considered as an equivalent generator having an output voltage NV_{REF} (where N is the fractional digital input) and an internal resistance R. Because of its symmetry and duality qualities, the R-2R network is used in other configurations also. Figure 8-7 shows

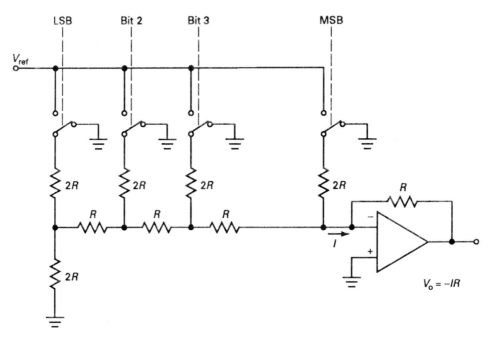

Figure 8-6 R-2R Resistance Ladder

that when the input and output leads are interchanged, it can be used for current switching.

The most common reference is the temperature-compensated zener diode. It is often used with an operational amplifier for operating-point stabilization.

In bipolar current-switching D/A conversion with offset binary or 2's complement codes, an offset current equal and opposite to the MSB current is added

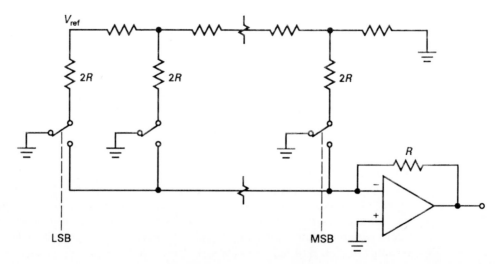

Figure 8-7 Inverted R-2R Ladder

to the converter output. This can be a resistor and a separate offset reference, but usually, it is derived from the converter's basic reference voltage, to minimize drift with temperature. The gain of the output inverting amplifier is doubled to double the output range, from 0–10 V to ±10 V.

When the amplifier is connected for sign inversion, the conversion relationship is negative reference, F.S. for all 0's −F.S. for all 1's. In a noninverting application, the same values of offset voltage and resistance are used, but the value of the output voltage scale factor depends on the load.

Bipolar D/A converters with voltage switches and R-2R ladder networks and offset binary or 2's complement coding, may use terminals that are normally grounded for unipolar operation (one side of the switches and the LSB termination) and use the reference signal in the opposite polarity. If the LSB termination is grounded, the output will be symmetrical. For sign-magnitude conversion, the converter's current output can be inverted.

In the basic parallel-input D/A converter circuit the analog output continually follows the state of the logic inputs. If the conversion circuit is preceded by a register, the converter will respond only when the inputs are gated into it.

This property is used in data distribution, in which the data is continually appearing, but it is desired that a D/A converter respond at certain times and then hold the analog output constant until the next update.

The D/A converter with buffer storage acts as a sample-hold with digital input and analog output with an infinite hold time. The register is controlled by a strobe which causes the converter to update. The rate at which the strobe may update is determined by the settling time of the converter and the response time of the logic.

The inputs to A/D converters are usually in the form of voltages. The outputs from D/A converters are often voltages at low impedance from an operational amplifier. Many converters provide an output current instead of a voltage. The basic conversion process can result in a current output that is fast, linear, and free from offsets. An operational amplifier may be used to convert the current to voltage.

Converters that use current outputs or voltage outputs directly from resistive ladders can be considered as voltage generators with series resistance or current generators with parallel resistance. They can be used with operational amplifiers in either an inverting or the noninverting mode as shown in Figure 8-8. Some types use internal feedback resistors for output voltage scaling which track the ladder resistors, to minimize temperature variations. The gain-determining feedback resistances (R_1, R_2) do not track the converter's internal resistors, only one another.

The inverting current-output connection has several advantages: the internal impedance of the D/I converter is usually high and the loop gain will be close to unity, essentially independent of the feedback resistance, minimizing any amplifier errors, such as voltage drift.

The conversion relationship of D/I converters is usually positive reference. As the current flowing out of the converter increases, the value represented by the digital code increases. It does not depend on the actual polarity of the converter's

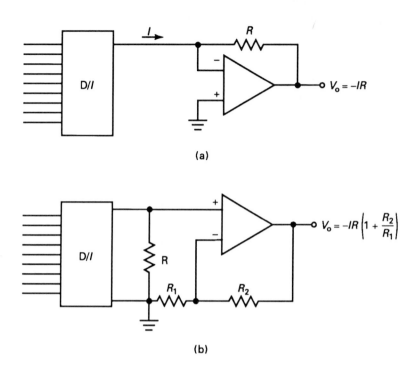

(a)

(b)

Figure 8-8   Current to Voltage Conversion
a. Inverting
b. Noninverting

reference. If current flowing toward the converter increases as the number represented by the digital code increases, the relationship is negative reference.

8.5 SUCCESSIVE APPROXIMATION CONVERSION

At the heart of a successive approximation A/D converter is a D/A converter.
When a conversion command is applied, the D/A converter's MSB output ($\frac{1}{2}$ full
scale) is compared with the input. If the input is greater than the MSB, it remains
ON and the next bit is tested. If the input is less than the MSB, it is turned OFF,
and the next bit tested. If the second bit does not have enough weight to exceed
the input, it is left ON and the third bit is tested. If the second bit exceeds the
input, it is turned OFF and the third bit is tested.

    This process continues until the last bit has been tested. When the process is
completed, a status line indicates a valid conversion. An output register now
holds the digital code corresponding to the input signal. Figure 8-9 is a block
diagram of a successive-approximation A/D converter. The basic idea of successive approximation is simple. When the logic signal is applied to the command
terminal, the D/A switches are set to their off state, except for the most significant
bit, which is set to logic 1. This turns on the corresponding D/A switch, to apply

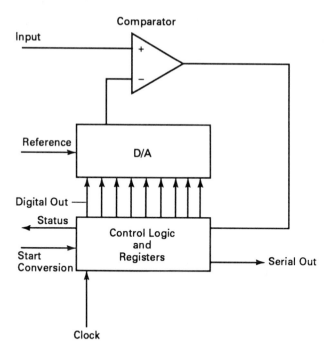

Figure 8-9 Successive-Approximation A/O Converter

the analog equivalent of the MSB to the comparator. If the analog input voltage is less than the MSB weight, the MSB is switched off at the first edge of the clock pulse; if the analog input is greater than the MSB, the 1 will remain in the register.

During the second pulse, the sum of the first result and the second bit is compared with the analog input voltage. The comparator is gated by the next clock pulse. It will cause the register to either accept or reject that bit. Successive clock pulses cause all the bits, in order of decreasing significance, to be tried, until the LSB is accepted or rejected.

Using a wide variety of components are the state-of-the-art data conversion and digital interface boards, they are designed to offer high data throughput, accuracy, and low noise. Multilayer board construction with integral ground planes and the use of board DC/DC power supplies assures low-noise analog measurements and analog outputs even at high data transfer rates.

8.6 ANALOG AND DIGITAL I/O BOARDS FOR IBM-COMPATIBLE COMPUTERS

These boards plug directly into an expansion slot within the computer. All connections are made through a 50-pin connector that extends out the rear of the computer. Field wiring can be connected to a mating 50-pin connector or a screw terminal board that brings all connections out.

8.6.1 Analog Inputs

Boards are available with 16-channel single-ended or 8-channel differential input modes (selected by an on-board switch). There are software selectable input ranges including unipolar (0 to 10 V) and bipolar (± 10 V) configurations. Gains range from 0.5 to 100 with input resolutions ranging from 3 mV down to 2 μV. The addition of user-installed resistors allows the input range to be set to the requirements of the industrial application.

A typical board uses a successive approximation A/D converter with an 8.5 μs conversion rate. This conversion rate, combined with an 800 ns sample and hold time allows the unit to perform conversions at over 100,000 per second. In the DMA data transfer mode on a standard PC or XT compatible, this data can be written to memory at the full 100,000 samples per second analog sample rate. On the PC/AT and some other AT compatible machines, the data transfer rate may be lower (60,000 samples), depending on the system clock speed, and the number of wait states used by the computer and other software tasks being performed.

The A/D converter may be triggered three ways: by a software command, by the on-board counter/pacer clock, or by an external pulse. The transfer of the data can also be performed in three ways: software/program control, interrupt, or direct memory access. The following list details the data throughput rates of the various transfer types.

Operating mode	Throughput (conversions/sec)
Program transfer to simple variable	Up to 200
Program transfer to array variable	Up to 4,000
Interrupt-driven transfer	Up to 4,000
DMA transfer of scan channels	Up to 100,000
DMA transfer on single channel	Up to 100,000

An on-board channel/gain queuing RAM allows a list of channel/gains to be created. The board will then follow the desired sequence. A typical sequence follows:

Sample no.	Channel no.	Gain
0	0	$\times$ 1
1	5	$\times$ 100
2	1	$\times$ 10
3	5	$\times$ 100
4	2	$\times$ 1
5	5	$\times$ 100
6	10	$\times$ 10
N	Return to Sample 0	

where N will be in the range 2 to 2047.

This list allows different channels to be sampled at different rates, under hardware control. The timing of the system can be completely tied to the clock (and not software which can be interrupted by other system functions). The data points will be sampled at jitterless intervals. This is crucial if any type of frequency analysis is to be performed. Since this RAM queueing list can be set to run completely under hardware control, the computer can be performing other software tasks in the foreground with the board acquiring data in the background.

Several channels of analog output may be included. Digital-to-analog (D/A) converters can have 12-bit (1 part in 4096) resolution and switch selectable for 0–10 V, ±5 V, or ±10 V output ranges. D/A converters are double buffered, assuring that no intermediate glitches occur during output updates. The D/As can be operated under software control in applications where the output update rate is low, or in a DMA mode when a high-frequency output is required. The maximum update rate is 130,000 samples per second.

On-board five-channel counter timers include the AMD-9513. Three of the counters are connected to a 5 MHz crystal-controlled oscillator and are used to control A/D and D/A converter sample timing. The remaining two counters can be connected to external signals and used as frequency or pulse generators, measure frequency, pulse widths, or count events.

Digital I/O of 16 TTL compatible lines can be divided into one 8-bit output port and one 8-bit input port. These digital I/O lines are useful in a wide variety of external triggering, switch sensing, and instrument control applications. The digital outputs can be used as controls by the accessory boards.

8.6.1.1 Software and programming

Utility software may include machine-language drivers to simplify programming. Functions can be accessed by simple "call" functions. The drivers are compatible with interpreted and compiled BASIC programs. "C," FORTRAN, Pascal, and Turbo-Pascal drivers are available also.

A wide variety of programs is available including

1. Installation and setup routines.
2. Calibration and test routines.
3. Graphics and X-Y display programs.
4. Thermocouple and other sensor linearization subroutines.

A BASICA-compatible machine-level driver (DAS) is loaded into memory at the start of the program. It can then be accessed via the BASICA "CALL" statement. A typical call statement is

```
200 CALL DAS (MD%, DIO% (0), FLAG%)
```

where

MD% is the mode of operation to use.

DIO% is the data to send to the DAS (or the data which will be returned), and FLAG% will return any errors encountered.

A list of the available software modes is shown here:

Mode	Description of function
0	Initialize the DAS (base address, interrupt level, and DMA level).
1	Load the channel/gain queuing RAM.
2	View the current channel/gain queueing RAM.
3	Perform a single A/D conversion and load the data into a BASICA variable.
4	Perform an N conversion scan and store the data in a BASICA array. Sample rate is set by pacer clock or external trigger, and maximum sample rate is about 4000 samples per second.
5	Perform an N conversion scan, and store the data in memory under interrupt control. Maximum conversion rate = 4000 samples/sec.
6	Perform an N conversion scan under DMA control. Conversion rate is set by on-board pacer clock or by external trigger. Maximum conversion rate = 100,000 KHz.
7	Command a single D/A conversion.
8	Perform N D/A conversions under program control. An array is consecutively written out by one of the D/As based on the pacer clock or an external trigger.
9	Perform N D/A conversions under interrupt control.
10	Perform N D/A conversions, DMA data transfers. Conversion timing from pacer clock or external trigger. Up to 260,000 conversions per second.
11	Cancel DMA or interrupt-driven operations. Return control completely to program software.
12	Return current status of DMA or interrupt-driven data transfers.
13	Transfer data from memory into BASICA arrays. This mode is necessary since interrupt- and DMA-driven conversions write and read directly from memory locations without regard to BASICA variables.
14	Read the 8 digital input bits.
15	Write to the 8 digital output bits.
16	Set analog trigger mode. This mode can cause any other mode to wait until a certain specified input condition is met before proceeding.
17	Initialize the counter/timer chip.
18	Set the 9513 counter's master mode register.
19	Set counter N mode register.
20	Set multiple counter control register.
21	Set counter load register.
22	Read counter N hold register.
23	Measure frequency with counter/timer.

8.6.1.2 Accessories

Accessory products are available. For example,

1. A screw terminal board allows each of the output connections to be brought out to screw terminals.

2. A 16-channel expansion multiplexer allows expansion boards to be connected allowing up to 128 analog input channels. A cold junction temperature-sensing device allows accurate thermocouple measurements.

3. Up to 4 channels of analog input data to be sampled simultaneously (within 30 nS). Boards can be added allowing up to 16 channels of simultaneously sampled input.

8.6.1.3 Typical specifications

Analog Input	
Channels	8 differential or 16 single-ended switch selectable with software-readable status
Resolution	12 bits
Accuracy	0.01% of reading $\pm$ LSB
Input ranges	0 to +10 V, $\pm$10 V, $\pm$5 V, 0 to +1 V, $\pm$0.5 V, 0 to 100 mV, $\pm$50 mV
Coding	Left-justified 2's complement (bipolar)
	Left-justified true binary (unipolar)
Overvoltage	Continuous single channel to $\pm$35 V
Input current	1 nA max at 25°C
A/D Converter	
Type	Successive approximation
Resolution	12 bits
Conversion Time	8.5 μs (typ), 9.0 max
Linearity	$\pm$1 LSB
Zero drift	5 ppm/°C
Gain drift	45 ppm/°C
Trigger	Software command, timer generated, or external with programmable edge
Gate	Internal or external with programmable level
Sample and Hold Amp	
Acquisition time	0.8 to 1.2 μs to 0.1% accuracy
Aperture	0.3 ns (typ)
Analog Outputs	
Channels	2 independent
Type	12-bit nonmultiplying double buffered
Linearity	$\pm$1/4 LSB (typ), $\pm$1/2 (max)
Output ranges	0 to 10 V, $\pm$5 V, $\pm$10 V
Coding	Right-justified true binary (unipolar)
	Right-justified 2's complement (bipolar)
Output drive	$\pm$5 mA
Output resistance	0.2 ohms
Reference	Built-in 6.3 V, 10 ppm/°C
Range select	Switch selectable/software readable
Settling time	10 V range 3 μs (type), 4 μs (max), 20 V range 2 μs (typ), 3 μs (max)
Data transfer	Single write or DMA to either or both modes
Interrupt Capabilities	
Levels	IRQ2–IRQ7 software programmable
Enable	Software programmable
Sources	ACD end of conversion, end of ADC Que, timer 2 terminal count, external or DMA terminal count
DMA Capabilities	
Levels	1 or 3, software programmable
Enable	Software programmable
Termination	By interrupt on terminal count or autoinitialize
Transfer modes	ADC data to host, from host to either or both DACs paced by timer 2
Transfer rate	100 Kwords/sec (ADC)
	130 Kwords/sec (DACs)
Digital I/O	
Output port	8-bit latched with readback
	low = 0.5 V max, sink = 8.0 mA
	high = 2.4 V min, source = -0.4 mA

Input port   8-bit transparent latch
                          low = 0.8 V max, −0.4 mA max
                          high = 2.0 V min, 20 μA max
Counter/timer   (5) 16-bit multimode programmable counter; counters 3, 4, 5 used to
                             delay or pace ADC start of conversion; counter 2 used to pace
                             DACs during DMA or real-time clock interrupt; counters 1 and 2
                             also usable externally
Internal time base   5 MHz
Output drive   IO L = 3.2 mA, IO H = −200 μA
Inputs, gate, and CMOS, DTL, CMOS-compatible source
Max input freq.   5 MHz
Active gate   User-definable software, level, or edge
Minimum   70 ns clock pulse width
Timer range   5 MHz to real time (24 hr)
Power Consumption
  +5 V   1.6 amp (typ), 1.8 amp (max)
Environmental
  Operating temp.   0 to 50°C
  Storage temp.   −20 to +70°C

8.6.2 Multiplexer Boards

A multiplexer offers an inexpensive way to expand the input capabilities of boards. Differential inputs can be multiplexed into a single A/D board input channel. Daisy chaining allows up to 256 analog input to be monitored; 256-channel operation is possible when the A/D board is set for 16-channel, single-ended operation. The channel to be enabled is determined by a 4-bit digital input (generated by the A/D board's digital output port). An on-board instrumentation amplifier provides 9-switch selectable input gains that range between 1 and 800. A

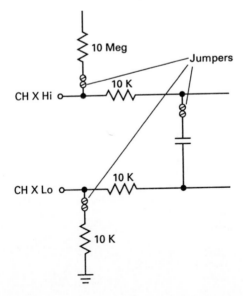

Figure 8-10   Input Filter

temperature sensor allows the monitoring of the cold junction temperature for measuring thermocouple inputs. Cold junction outputs of 20 mV and 200 mV/°C are selected by a jumper. Jumpers are also available to connect an open thermocouple detection and a low-pass filter circuit to each input channel.

Each input channel includes three corresponding jumper blocks. A jumper connects a 100 megohm resistor from the channel input to −15 volts. This allows open thermocouple detection. A second jumper connects a 10 Kohm resistor from ground to the low terminal. When connecting the unit to an isolated voltage source (one that does not share a common ground with the PC system), the 10K resistor should be connected as it keeps the instrumentation amplifier inputs from floating outside the available common mode range. A third jumper installs a 60 Hz low-pass filter. An input circuit is shown in schematic form in Figure 8-10.

8.6.3 Thermocouple Gain Settings

The following list illustrates typical gain settings for thermocouples over their operating range.

Thermocouple type	Maximum output	Maximum °C	Suitable gain*
J	43 mV	760	100
K	55 mV	1370	50
T	21 mV	400	200
E	76 mV	1000	50
S	19 mV	1760	200
R	21 mV	1760	200
B	14 mV	1760	200

* Higher gains may be used for less than full-scale span. Gains are based on ±5 V output.

8.6.3.1 Typical specifications

Input channels	16 fully differential
Input gains	× 1, 10, 100, 200, 300, 500, 600, 700, 800 switch selectable
Maximum input Voltage	± 30 VRMS continuous
Input bias	100 pA Typ, 200 pA max
Input impedance	Over 500 megohm
Offset voltage	Zeroed by potentiometer trim
Offset voltage Temperature drift	× 1 20 μV/°C (typ), × 1004 μV/°C, × 500 2.5 μV/°C

Gain error		(typ)	(max)
	× 1	0.002%	0.04%
	× 10	0.01%	0.1%
	× 100	0.02%	0.2%
	× 200	0.04%	0.4%
	× 500	0.1%	1.0%

Nonlinearity		(typ) % F.S.	(max) % F.S.
	× 1	±0.001	±0.01
	× 10	±0.002	±0.01
	× 100	±0.004	±0.02
	× 200	±0.006	±0.02
	× 500	±0.01	±0.04
Typ settling time*		0.1%	0.01%
	× 1	4 μs	5 μs
	× 10	2 μs	3 μs
	× 100	3 μs	4 μs
	× 200	5 μs	7 μs
	× 500	11 μs	16 μs
	* Without input filter		
Common-mode rejection ratio			
	× 1	90 dB	
	× 10	104 dB	
	× 100	110 dB	
	× 200	110 dB	
	× 500	110 dB	
Cold-junction reference			
	+200 mV/°C or 20 mV/°C		
	Jumper selectable		
Power requirements			
	+5 V at 100 mA (max)		
Environmental			
Operating temp.	0 to 60°C		
Storage temp.	−20 to +80°C		

8.6.4 Simultaneous Sample and Hold Accessory Boards

A 4-channel, simultaneous sample and hold accessory board allows analog input data to be acquired from 2, 3, or 4 inputs with less than 30 ns of channel-to-channel sample time uncertainty. Additional boards can be daisy chained into the system, allowing up to 16 channels to be sampled simultaneously. Applications include digitization, transient analysis, frequency analysis, and transfer function/phase angle analysis.

Suppose the sample acquisition time of the sample and hold is less than 10 μs. To calculate the maximum sample rate, this 10 μs is added to the length of time the A/D converter board requires for its samples. For example, if three input channels were to be sampled, the sample time would be 10 μs for the acquisition, plus 30 μs (three channels times the 10 μs conversion time) for a total of 40 μs or a 25 KHz sample rate. The maximum sample rate for two channels will be 33.3 KHz, and for four channels it will be 20 KHz.

The inputs are differential, and each channel has its own gain select control. The available input gains are switch selectable and range from 1 to 800.

The board has an on-board channel/gain queueing RAM. This RAM allows a list of channel/gains to be sampled to be created while the board follows a sequence. A typical sequence is shown here:

Sample	Channel no.	Gain
0	0	× 1
1	5	× 100
2	1	× 10
3	5	× 100
4	2	× 1
5	5	× 100
⋮	⋮	⋮
N	Return to sample 0	

N will be in the range 2 to 2047.

Each time the process is return to sample 0, it samples the inputs, and then holds the data. Samples 1 through N are then performed while in the hold mode. An example sample list for a 4-channel simultaneous sample and hold function is shown next:

Sample	Channel	Gain	Functions
0	Any*	Any*	Command unit to sample and then hold the inputs
1	0	X 1	Read channel A
2	1	X 1	Read channel B
3	2	X 1	Read channel C
4	3	X 10	Read channel D
5	Returned to sample 0.		

A single bit in a control register on the board controls the S-H bit. The sample-hold bit is then controlled by a software routine. The software should operate according to the following flow list:

1. Set in sample mode.
2. Wait 10 microseconds (acquisition time).
3. Set in hold mode.
4. Read the desired channels.

8.6.4.1 Typical specifications

Input type	Differential
Acquisition time	<10 μs
Aperture time	<20 ns
Output droop rate	<10 μV/ms
Input gains	1, 10, 100, 200, 300, 500, 600 700, 800 switch selectable

Gain errors	× 1 ±0.001% typ
	× 10 ±0.01% typ
	× 100 ±0.02% typ
	× 500 ±0.1% typ
Nonlinearity	× 1 ±0.001% typ
	× 10 ±0.002% typ
	× 100 ±0.004% typ
	× 500 ±0.01% typ
Common-mode rejection	Greater than 90 dB
Power supply	±5 V 400 mA max
Temp. range	0 to 60°C

8.6.5 DMA Boards

DMA is used in high-speed analog and digital interface boards for IBM PC/XT/AT-compatible computers. These are full-length boards that install in an expansion slot inside the personal computer. They turn the computer into a high-speed, high-precision data acquisition and signal analysis instrument. These boards use a multilayer construction with integral ground plane to minimize noise and cross-talk even at high sample rates.

A typical board will use an AD674 successive approximation A/D converter or a faster AD774 12-bit converter with slightly faster input circuitry. The board can be operated with 8 differential or 16 single-ended inputs and can be set in unipolar or bipolar modes. The input configuration is set by switches on the boards. The maximum A/D throughput for a variety of operating modes is described as follows:

Operating mode	Throughput (conversions/sec)
Program transfer to simple variable	Up to 200
Program transfer to array variable	Up to 4,000
Interrupt-driven transfer	Up to 4,000
DMA transfer DAS-16F	Up to 100,000 (PC/XT)

A/D conversion may be triggered three ways: by software command, by an on-board programmable timer, or by an external trigger pulse. The transfer of the data can also be accomplished in three ways: by program control, by interrupt service routine, or by DMA. All modes are selectable in software.

Input ranges are selected by DIP switch on the board. Selectable ranges include +0.5 V, +1 V, +2 V, ±2.5 V, ±5 V, and ±10 V. Other user-selectable input ranges can be obtained by installing a single gain-setting resistor.

A three-channel programmable interface timer (Intel 8254) is used to provide trigger pulses for the A/D or for external frequency generation at any rate from 2.5 MHz to 1 pulse/hr. An on-board 10 MHz crystal controller oscillator provides the time base. The counter timers can also be used to measure frequency, period, and pulse width.

Two channels of multiplying 12-bit D/A converter are also provided. An on-board -5 V reference can be used to provide analog outputs in the 0 to $+5$ V range, or external references can be used for other output ranges.

Eight bits of digital I/O (4 input and 4 output) allow an interface to a variety of digital signals. These digital bits can be used to control multiplexers, read external status, or gate the counter/timer.

Utility software includes

1. A machine-language driver for control of the A/D, D/A, and digital interfaces. The program is accessed via "calls" from basic.
2. Initial installation, setup, and calibration routines.
3. Simple graphics utilities.

8.6.5.1 Programming

All I/O is accessed via a CALL statement:

```
CALL  DAS  (MD%,  DIO%(0),FLAG%)
           MD% = MODE
           DIO%(0) = DATA
           FLAG% = ERRORS
```

There are 18 modes of operation available to the programmer and are represented by the integer variable MD%. The following lists the capabilities:

Mode	Function
0	Initialize; input base address, interrupt level, and DMA level.
1	Set multiplexer low and high scan limits.
2	Read multiplexer current channel and scan limit setting.
3	Perform a single A/D conversion. Return data and increment multiplexer address (programmed conversion): speed, slow; operation, foreground.
4	Perform an N conversion scan after trigger. Scan rate set by programmable timer (Mode 17). Data is transferred to an integer array: speed, medium; operation, foreground.
5	Perform an N conversion scan after trigger into memory buffer area. Scan rate set by programmable timer. Data is transferred by interrupt.
6	Perform an N conversion scan after trigger into memory buffer area. Scan rate set by programmable timer. Data is transferred by DMA.
7	Disable DMA/interrupt operation of modes 5 or 6.
8	Report status of DMA/interrupt operation initiated by mode 5 or 6.
9	Transfer data from buffer memory area to BASIC integer array.
10	Set counter 0 operating configuration.
11	Load counter 0 data.
12	Read counter 0.
13	Output to digital outputs.
14	Read digital inputs.
15	Output data to single D/A channel.
16	Output data to both D/A channels.
17	Set programmable timer rate.

8.6.5.2 Example program

For the purposes of an example, assume we want to perform 1000 conversions, scanning channels 2–6 at a 10 KHz rate, transferring the data to memory starting at segment &H2000.

First, perform the initialization:

```
10 MD%  = 0                   'initialize mode #
20 DIM DIO%(5)
30 DIO%(0) = &H300            'base I/O address of DAS
40 DIO%(1) = 2               'selected interrupt level = 2
50 DIO%(2) = 3               'selected DMA level = 3
60 DAS 16 = 0                'CALL offset
70 FLAG% = 0                 'declare error variable
80 CALL DAS (MD%, DIO%(0), FLAG%) 'execute initialization
90 IF FLAG% <0 THEN PRINT "ERROR #"; FLAG% : STOP '? all o.k.
```

Now set the scanning limits:

```
100 MD% = 1                  'Mode 1 – set scan limits
110 DIO%(0) = 2              'lower limit
120 DIO%(1) = 6             'upper limit
130 CALL DAS (MD%, DIO%(0), FLAG%) 'set limits
140 IF FLAG%<0 THEN PRINT "ERROR #";FLAG%: STOP '? all o.k.
```

Next, set the scan rate. The 1 MHz internal xtal clock is divided by 100 (= DIO%(0)*DIO%(1)) to output 10 KHz:

```
150 MD% = 17                 'Mode 17 – set programmable timer
160 DIO%(0) = 2             'Counter 2 divide by 2
170 Dio%(1) = 50            'Counter 1 divide by 50
180 CALL DAS (MD%, DIO%(0), FLAG%) 'set sample rate
190 if FLAG% < > THEN PRINT "ERROR #" ;FLAG%: STOP '? all o.k.
```

Now do a conversion using DMA to memory segment &H2000:

```
200 MD% = 6                  'Mode 6 –DMA conversions
210 DIO%(0) = 1000          'Number of conversions
220 DIO%(1) = &H2000        'Starting segment of memory
230 DIO%(2) = 1             'Trigger source = timer 0 =
                             external trigger
240 DIO%(3) = 0             'Nonrecycle = 1 shot mode 1 =
                             auto-initialize recycle
```

```
250 CALL DAS (MD%, DIO%(0), FLAG%) 'start DMA on IPO high
260 IF FLAG% < > 0 THEN PRINT "ERROR #";FLAG%: STOP "? all o.k.
```

8.6.5.3 Base address

The board requires 16 consecutive address locations in I/O space. Some I/O locations will be occupied by internal I/O and other peripheral cards, so to provide flexibility in avoiding conflict with these devices, I/O addresses can be set by a base address DIP switch to be anywhere in the PC decoded I/O space.

8.6.5.4 Software

The machine-language I/O driver provides control of D/A, A/D, timer, and digital I/O channel functions via a BASIC CALL. The I/O driver can select multiplexer channels; set scan limits; perform software command A/D conversions, interrupt-driven conversions, and scans; set and read the timer/counter; and measure frequency and pulse width.

Using state-of-the-art data conversion components, these boards are designed to provide a powerful and inexpensive analog/digital interface in a full-sized slot. They are suited to applications requiring high-speed 12-bit data acquisition at low cost. The I/O mapped control makes programming straightforward.

8.6.5.5 Typical specifications

Power consumption	
+5 V power	@ 800 mA typ, 1 A max
+12 V power	@ 2 mA typ, 5 mA max
−12 V power	@ 20 mA typ, 30 mA max
Instrumentation amplifier	
Switch selectable gains	0.5, 1, 2, 5, 10
Resolution range	0.244 mV to 4.88 mV/bit
Analog inputs	
Switch-selectable	16 single ended or 8 differential
Converter type	12-bit successive approximation
Conversion time	10 μs
Accuracy	0.01% of reading ±1 bit
Full scale	±10 V
Coding	Offset binary
Maximum overvoltage	to ±30 V
Input current	100 μA max at 25°C
Temp. coef. F.S.	±25 ppm/°C
Analog outputs	12-bit multiplying D/A (unipolar)
Voltage ranges	0 to +5 V with reference supply
	(+10 V with external reference)
Maximum load current	5 mA
Environmental	
Operating temp.	0 to 50°C (32 to 122°F)
Storage temp.	−20 to +70°C (−4 to 158°F)

8.6.6 Programmable A/D Boards

There are also multifunction high-speed programmable gain analog/digital I/O expansion boards for the IBM Personal Computer. They are full-length boards that install internally in an expansion slot of an IBM PC; IBM PC/XT, PC/AT, or RT-PC; or PS/2 Model 30 and turn the computer into a fast, high-precision data acquisition and signal analysis instrument. They can also be used in bus-compatible computers such as Compaq, Tandy, AT&T 6300, Olivetti M24, Zenith, Leading Edge, Televideo, and Epson Equity. The board is of a multilayer construction with integral ground plane to minimize noise and cross-talk at high frequencies. A register at a I/O address location sets the gain. The following functions may be implemented.

A/D conversion is done using a 12-bit successive approximation converter with a 12 μs conversion time giving a maximum throughput rate of 70 KHz in DMA mode. The throughput varies with the gain selected as follows:

Gain	Unipolar	Bipolar	Throughput
1	0 to +10 V	±10 V	70 KHz
10	0 to +1 V	±1 V	60 KHz
100	0 to +100 mV	±100 mV	50 KHz
500	0 to +20 mV	±20 mV	30 KHz

The programmable gain amplifier has a fixed gain-bandwidth product so that its settling time increases at higher gain. This causes the maximum throughput rate to decrease as the gain increases.

Slide switches control the channel configuration. The user can select unipolar (zero to + full scale) or bipolar (−full scale to + full scale) operation and 16 single-ended channels or 8 differential channels. In differential mode, the maximum common-mode input voltage of all channels at any gain is ±10 V.

A/D conversions may be initiated in one of three ways: by software command, by internal programmable interval timer, or by direct external trigger to the A/D. At the end of the A/D conversion, it is possible to transfer the data by polling a status register and reading data when ready, by generation of a hardware interrupt and an interrupt service routine, or by hardware through DMA. Operating modes are selected by a control register and supported by utility software.

The programmable gain amplifier is a full differential design, and the gain is selected by a 2-bit gain code through a read/write register at (base I/O address + 11). The gain setting is global, it affects all channels until changed. In non-DMA modes, the software driver can select different gains for each channel prior to conversion so it is possible to perform scans with a variety of channel gains at speeds up to a few thousand conversions/second. Operation in the high-speed DMA mode precludes any intervention from the software, so in this case the gain setting is global and affects all channels.

A three-channel programmable interval timer (Intel 8254) provides trigger pulses for the A/D at any rate from 250 KHz to 1 pulse/hr. Two channels are operated in fixed divider configurations from an internal 1 or 10 MHz xtal clock. The third channel is uncommitted. It provides a gated 16-bit binary counter that can be used for pulse counting, for frequency or pulse generation, or for delayed triggering, and in conjunction with the other channels for frequency and period measurement.

D/A converters are available in two channels of multiplying 12-bit D/A output. The D/A converters may be operated with a fixed -5 V reference available from the board to give a 0 ± 5 V output. Alternatively an external DC or AC reference may be used to give different output ranges or programmable attenuator action on an AC signal. D/As are often double buffered to provide instantaneous single-stepping updates. Arbitrary or periodic waveform generation using interrupts may be supported by the utility software.

A -5 V (± 0.05 V) precision reference voltage output is derived from the A/D converter reference. This is typically used for providing a DC reference input for the D/A converters, offsets, or bridge excitation to user-supplied input circuits.

Digital I/O usually consists of 4 bits of TTL/DTL-compatible digital output and 4 bits of digital input. These are addressed as individual I/O ports in some modes as they function as A/D trigger and counter gate control inputs.

8.6.6.1 Typical specifications

Channels	8 differential (HL/LO/GND) or 16 single-ended (HI/GND) switch selectable
Resolution	12 bits
Accuracy	0.01% of reading ± 1 bit
Coding	Offset binary (bipolar $\pm$ inputs)
	True binary (unipolar $0 \pm$ inputs)
Overvoltage	Continuous single channel to $\pm$ 35 V
Input current	250 nA max (125 nA typ) at 25°C
Input impedance	Greater than 50 megohms
Temperature	Gain or F.S., ± 25 ppm/°C max
Coefficient	Zero + 12 ppm/°C max
A/D Specification	
Type	Successive approximation
Resolution	12 bits
Conversion	15 μs max (12 typ)
Monotonicity guaranteed over operating temperature	
Linearity	± 1 bit
Zero drift	± 10 ppm/°C max
Gain drift	± 30 ppm/°C max
Sample-Hold Amplifier	
Acquisition time	1μs for full-scale step input
Aperture uncertainty	0.3 nS typ
Reference Voltage Output	
Reference voltage	-5.0 V ± 0.05 V
Temperature coef.	± 30 ppm/°C max
Load current	+5 mA max

D/A Converters	
Type	12 bit multiplying double buffered
Linearity	$\pm\frac{1}{2}$ bit
Monotonicity	$\pm\frac{1}{2}$ bit
Output range	0 ± 5 V with fixed -5 V
Output resistance	<0.1 ohm
Reference input range	+10 V
Gain	−1.000 adjustable 1%
Setting time	30 μs for full-scale step
Digital I/O	
Output port	4 bits
Input port and trigger	4 bits
Compatibility	TTL/CMOS
Interrupt Channel	
Level 2–7 software selectable	
Enable via INTE of CONTROL register	
Programmable Timer	
Type	8254-2 programmable interval
Counters	3 down counters, 16 bit; 2 connected to $\frac{1}{10}$ MHz clock as programmable timer; 1 counter free
Output drive	2.2 mA @ 0.45 V
Capability	5 LSTTL loads
Input, gate	TTL/DTL/CMOS compatible
Clock input	dc to 10 MHz
Active count edge	Negative
Minimum clock	30 nS high, 50 nS low
Pulse width	
Power Supplies	
+5 V supply	800 mA typ/1A max
+12 V supply	2 mA typ/5mA max
−12 V supply	20 mA typ/30mA max
General	
Operating temp.	0 to 50°C
Storage temp.	−20 to +70°C

8.6.7 A/D Converter and Timer/Counter Interface Boards

An 8-channel 12-bit high-speed A/D converter and timer/counter board for the IBM PC can be fitted in a half slot. Connections are made through a standard 37-pin D male connector that projects through the rear of the computer. The following functions are implemented.

An 8-channel, 12-bit successive approximation A/D converter with sample-hold has a full-scale input for each channel of ±5 V with a resolution of 0.00244 V (2.44 mV). Inputs are single ended with a common ground and can withstand a continuous overload of ±30 V and brief transients of several hundred volts. All inputs are fail safe open circuit when the computer power is off. A/D conversion time is typically 25 μs (35 μs max) throughputs of up to 4000 samples/sec are attainable operating under BASIC.

An 8254 programmable counter/timer provides periodic interrupts for the A/D converter and can additionally be used for event counting, pulse and waveform generation, frequency period, and pulse width measurements. Applications include data logging, process control, signal analysis, robotics, energy management, product testing, and chromatography.

An external interrupt input is provided that is jumper selectable for any of the IBM PC interrupt levels 2–7 and allows interrupt routines to provide background data acquisition or interrupt-driven control, The $\frac{1}{2}$ slot board includes status and control registers for interrupt handshaking. The interrupt input may be externally connected to the timer/counter or any other trigger source.

There are three separate 16-bit down counters in the 8254. One of these is connected to a submultiple of the system clock, and all I/O functions of the remaining two are accessible to the user. Input frequencies up to 2.5 MHz can be handled by the 8254. Seven bits of TTL digital I/O are provided. These are composed of one output port of 4 bits and one input port of 3 bits. Each output will handle five standard TTL loads.

8.6.7.1 Programming

I/O is accessed via a call statement:

CALL DA (MD%, DIO%, FLAG%)

There are 18 modes of operation available to the programmer which are represented by the integer variable MD%. The following list shows the capabilities:

Mode	Function
0	Initialize; input base address.
1	Set multiplexer channel low and high scan limits.
2	Set multiplexer (channel) address.
3	Read multiplexer (channel) address.
4	Perform a single A/D conversion; return data and increment multiplexer address.
5	Perform an N conversion scan after trigger; scan rate set by counter 2 or external strobe.
6	Enable interrupt operation.
7	Disable interrupt operation.
8	Perform conversions on N interrupts and dump data in segment S of memory (background operation).
9	Unload data from segment S and transfer to BASIC array variable.
10	Set timer/counter configuration.
11	Load timer/counter.
12	Read timer/counter.
13	Read digital inputs IP1-3.
14	Output to digital outputs OP1-4.
15	Measure frequency with timer/counter.
16	Measure pulse width with timer/counter.
17	Tag lower nibble of data with channel number.

The integer variable DIO% represents input or output data. FLAG%, the third integer variable, contains the error codes. If FLAG% is returned nonzero, then an error has occurred. There are 13 error codes available to the programmer for error diagnosis.

After initializing the unit the following example program illustrates how 4000 samples/sec can be obtained.

xxx10 MD%=1	Set mux scan limits
xxxLT%(0)=2	Start scan on channel 2
xxx30 LT%(1)=5	End scan on channel 5
xxx40 CALL DA (MD%, LT%(0), FLAG%)	Setup
xxx50 IF FLAG% < > 0 THEN PRINT "ERROR"	Checks for errors
xxx60 DIM A% (100)	Dimension array of 100
xxx70 MD%=5	Mode 5
xxx80 TR%(0)−VARPTR (A%(1))	Start as element 1
xxx90 TR%(1)=100	100 conversions
xx100 CALL DA (MD%, TR%(0), FLAG%)	Do conversions, load array
xx110 IF FLAG% < > 0 THEN PRINT "ERROR"	Checks for errors

8.6.7.2 Software

In addition to an assembly-level driver utility software also includes

- Thermocouple linearization routines.
- A simple graphics and plotting package for display of data.
- A simple data logger program.
- A simple strip-chart recorder emulator program.

8.6.7.3 Typical specifications

Power Consumption	
+5 V	107 mA typ/180 mA max
+12 V	6 mA typ/10 mA max
−12 V	10 mA type/16 mA max
Analog Input Channels	
Resolution	12 bits (2.4 mV/bit)
Accuracy	0.01% of reading ± 1 bit
Full scale	±5 volts
Coding	Offset binary
Overvoltage	To ±30 volts
Configuration	Single ended
Input current	100 nA max at 25°C
Temp. coef.	Gain of F.S.,
	±25 ppm/°C max 0
	±10 mV/°C max
Environmental	
Operating temp.	0 to 50°C
Storage temp.	−20 to +70°C

8.6.8 Analog and Digital I/O Interface Boards—Low Speed

A typical low-speed multifunction analog/digital I/O expansion board for the IBM Personal Computer is designed to allow use of the IBM PC/XT/AT in low-speed, high-precision data acquisition and control.

It combines in a single board most of the features needed for acquisition systems. Applications include data logging, process control, robotics, meteorology, energy management, product testing, laboratory, and medical.

Features include

Graphics plotting and storing graphs (real-time and later analysis)

Transducer and RTD linearization

CRT-assisted board calibration/setup procedures

Strip-chart recorder and data logger programs

1 CALL statement accessing all analog and digital I/O

12 bits of digital I/O

12-bit resolution of analog I/O

4 analog input channels with overvoltage protection to 120 volts rms

4 analog input 30 dB (60 Hz) switchable filters

2 switch selectable RTD interfaces

2 precision-adjustable voltage references

2 precision 1 mA constant current sources

2-, 3-, 4-wire RTD bridge operation

Battery backed-up clock/calendar

External interrupt capabilities

30 channels per second throughput

Some channels of the A/D converter may be equipped with instrumentation amplifiers by plugging them into the sockets provided and selecting the appropriate gains by switches. The instrumentation amplifiers provide gain scaling for thermocouples and resistance bridge transducers such as load cells and strain gauges. They extend the F.S. range down to ± 2.0475 mV with a resolution to 0.5 μV/bit. System noise at this level is approximately ± 1 μV and drift typically 1 μV/$°$C. Other inputs are switch selectable for direct input for use with interfaces for 2-, 3-, or 4-wire RTDs for temperature measurement.

If the input signals are noisy, an additional 30 dB of attenuation at 60 Hz can be switched into each channel filter. This engages a single-pole passive RC filter with 20 dB/decade attenuation slope. The filter time constant introduces a 0.9 sec settling time penalty for 0.01% settling to a full-scale step input.

There are channels of 12-bit D/A output available. Output range of ± 10 V, ± 5 V, $+2.5$ V, ± 10 V, and $+5$ V are DIP switch selectable and digital inputs are double buffered.

The board requires 16 consecutive address locations in I/O space. Some I/O address locations will be occupied by internal I/O and other peripheral cards. I/O address can be set by the base address DIP switch to be anywhere in the PC decoded I/O space.

A good choice is to put base address at hex 300, 310, or 320 (decimal 768, 784, 800). If you are using an IBM prototype board, it uses the Hex 300-31F address space, and there would be a conflict.

Precision-adjustable voltage reference outputs include each output, which can be adjusted between +/−6.8 volts at 5 mA. These references are useful for exciting strain gauge bridges. Precision 1 mA constant current sources (−10 to +2.5 Volts compliance) can be used for exciting RTDs, semiconductor temperature sensors measuring resistance, or providing selected offsets.

Digital I/O includes 12 bits on the main connector, which are composed of one port of 8 bits and another 4 bits. Each port may be independently programmed as an input or output and is TTL/CMOS compatible. Electromechanical relay boards and solid-state I/O module boards utilize these ports as a means to monitor and control various AC and DC loads.

External interrupt control is provided so that the user can select any of the IBM PC interrupt levels (2–5) for programmed interrupt routines. This will then allow background data acquisition and interrupt control.

RTD interfaces include two built-in RTD (platinum resistance thermometer) interfaces. These provide temperature measurement capability from −200°C to +650°C with 0.2°C resolution using industry standard 100 ohm platinum RTD probes (alpha = 0.00385). Lead resistance compensation is included for 3- and 4-wire probes.

The board also contains a battery–backed-up real-time clock/calendar. This clock is used to update the PC's time and date functions automatically, thus eliminating DOS prompts for manual entry upon power up. It is accurate to 2 seconds per month. Under normal use the batteries will keep the module's time and date for 2 months without recharging on the system's power. The clock also provides reference pulses of 1 second, 1 minute, or 1 hour intervals or outputs a frequency of 1024 Hz, which can be used as a source for processor interrupts or to initiate external timing.

Instrumentation amplifier gains are shown here:

CHANNEL 0 or

CHANNEL1	
Instrumentation amplifier gains	Input voltage range
Gain = 1	±0.5 mV to ±2.0475 V
Gain = 10	±50 V to ±0.20475 V
Gain = 100	±5 V to ±20.475 mV
Gain = 1000	±0.5 V to ±2.0475 mV

8.6.8.1 Software

Software includes an I/O driver subroutine accessed by a single BASIC "CALL" statement. Also included are utility programs for installation graphics, a polynomial approximation to linearize most transducers (RTDs, strain gauges, thermistors, thermocouples), and step-by-step CRT-assisted calibration/setup procedures.

The single CALL statement is used to access all analog and digital I/O on the board. The INp and OUT commands standard with BASIC can also be used to access all I/O.

The graphics package includes a provision which lets the user plot predicted versus actual measured data from an experiment in real time and store the entire graph for retrieval at a later date.

The following list illustrates the 11 modes of CALL statements available.

CALL (MD%, CH, DIO% (0), DIO% (1), BASADR%

The values contained within the parentheses are integers.

$$MD\% = \text{Mode} \qquad CH = \text{channel number}$$

$$DIO\%(B) = \text{a data I/O integer array}$$

$$BASADR\% = \text{the base address currently accessed}$$

Mode	Function	Channel	Data I/O integer array
0	Free scan of all analog inputs	Does not matter	DIO% (0–3), channel 0–3 data DIO% (4–7), channel 0–3 error flags DIO% (8) mode, channel error flags
1	Conversion on one analog input, data transferred when finished	0–3	DIO% (CH%), channel data DIO% (CH%+4), channel error flag DIO% (8) mode, channel error flag
2	Conversion on all analog input, data transferred when finished	Does not matter	DIO% (0–3), channel 0–3 data DIO% (4–7), channel 0–3 error flags DIO% (8) mode, channel error flags
3	Conversion on all analog inputs, initiated by data transferred when finished	Interrupt level (2–5)	Use mode 6 to obtain data after interrupt DIO% (8) mode, interrupt-level error flag
4	Terminates interrupt processing initiated by modes 3 and 5	Does not matter	DIO% (8) mode, error flag

Mode	Function	Channel	Data I/O integer array
5	Free scan of all analog inputs, data collected on interrupt	Interrupt level (2–5)	Use mode 6 to obtain data after interrupt DIO% (8) mode, interrupt level error flag
6	Collect data after an interrupt using modes 3 or 5	Does not matter	DIO% (0–3), channel 0–3 data DIO% (4–7), channel 0–3 error flags DIO% (8), new-old data flag
7	Single-channel analog output	0 or 1	DIO% (0), channel 0 or 1 output DIO% (1), not used DIO% (8) mode, channel error flag
8	Output data to both analog output channels	Does not matter	DIO% (0), channel 0 output data DIO% (1), channel 1 output data DIO% (8) mode, error flag
9	Digital I/O on 8-bit port PB and 4-bit port PC	0–PB output PC input 1–PB output, PC output 2–PB input PC input 3–PB input, PC output 4–PB strobed output, PCD–2 handshake, PC3 input 5–PB strobed input, PCD–2 handshake, PC3 input	DIO% (0) If PB output, data (0–255) If PB input, data (0–255) DIO% (1) 1 PC output, data (0–15) IF PC input, data (0–15) DIO% (8) data range, mode, channel error flag
10	Enables/ disables clock output	Enabled; CH% = 1; disabled; CH% = 0	DIO% (8) mode, error flag

Following is a programming example for energy management:

```
 10  CLEAR 32768!
 20  DEF SEG=0
 30  SG=256*PEEK (&H511) +PEEK (&H510)
 40  DASCON=0
 50  SG=(32768!/16)+SG
 60  DEF SEG=SG
 70  BLOAD "DASCON.BIN", 0
 80  DIM DIO% (8)
 90  DIM REL% (8)
100  BASADR%=&H300
110  MD%=0
120  RD%=9
130  RH%=0
140  CLS
150  FOR J=1 TO 100
```

```
160 FOR I-1 TO 1000
170 NEXT I
180 CALL DA (MD%, CH%, DIO% (0), DID% (1), BASADR%)
190 IF DIO% (2)/5>20 THEN RIO%(0)=1.GOTO 220 'TURN ON Air
    Conditioner
200 IF DIO% (2)/5<19 THEN RIO% (0)=2.GOTO 220 "Turn on
    Heater
210 RIO% (0)=0
220 CALL DASCON (RD%, RH%, RIO% (0), RIO% (1), BASADR%)
230 NEXT J
240 END
```

This program example illustrates how the board can be utilized in the controlling of temperature. Each bit is equivalent to 0.2°C. Therefore, 5 bits is equivalent to 1°C. Program line 190 examines the value of the temperature read from the RTD (resistive temperature detector) on channel 2's analog input. If the temperature in degrees C is greater than 20 (68°F), then it turns on the air conditioner or chiller. If (on line 200) the temperature is less than 19°C (66.2°F), then it turns on the heater. If the temperature is between 19 and 20°C, then it writes a "zero" onto the port connected to the relays controlling the environment and deenergizes both units.

8.6.8.2 Typical specifications

Analog Input	
Resolution	12 bits plus sign (0.5 mV/bit)
Accuracy	0.01% of reading ±1 bit
Full scale	±2.0475 V
Overvoltage	Continuous single channel to 120 V RMS, 5 sec all channels to 120 V RMS
Common-mode range	±2 V min
Common-mode rejection	60 dB min, 70 dB typ
Input current	1 nA max at 25°C
Input filter	Switchable, 30 dB attenuation at 60 Hz, 0.9 sec settling time to 0.01% for F.S. step
Temperature coefficient	
Gain or F.S.	±25 ppm/°C max
Zero	±10 μV/°C max
A/D	
Type	Integrating dual slope
Resolution	12 bits plus sign
Conversion rate	30 conversions/sec min
Linearity	±1 bit
Zero drift	1 μV/°C max
Gain drift	5 ppm/°C max
Instrumentation Amplifiers	
Switchable gain	10, 100, or 1000
Gain error	Gain = 10, error 1.5% max, 0.6% typ
	Gain = 100, error 0.5% max, 0.1% typ
	Gain = 1000, error 1.5% max, 0.4% typ
Gain nonlinearity	0.01% typ, 0.05% max

Drift	Gain = 10, 10 μV/°C typ, 100 μV/°C max
	Gain = 100, 2 μV/°C typ, 10 μV/°C max
	Gain = 1000, 1 μV/°C typ, 5 μV/°C, max
Gain temperature coefficient	Gain = 10 or 100, 5 ppm/°C typ
	Gain = 1000, 15 ppm/°C typ
Input current	10 nA max, 2 nA typ at 25°C
Common-mode range	−2.7 V to +3.8 V min
Common-mode rejection	Gain = 10, 105 dB typ, 90 dB min
	Gain = 100, 120 dB typ, 94 dB min
	Gain = 1000, 130 dB typ, 114 dB min
Overload capacity	120 VRMS continuous single channel

RTD Interfaces

RTD type	100 ohm, alpha = 0.00385 (DIN or European) platinum 2/3/4 wire
Temperature range	−200 to +650°C with 0.2°C resolution
Excitation current	1.000 mA
Lead resistance compensation	Included for 3- and 4-wire RTD types

D/A Output Channels

Switch	0 to +10 V (unipolar)
Selectable	0 to +5 V (unipolar)
Output	−2.5 to +2.5 V (bipolar)
Ranges	−5 to +5 V (bipolar)
	−10 to +10 V (bipolar)
Output current	±5 mA min
dc output impedance	0.05 ohm typ
Coding	Complimentary binary or offset binary
Resolution	12 bits (1 part in 4095)
Differential linearity	$\frac{1}{2}$ LSB typ, $\frac{3}{4}$ LSB max
Linearity	$\frac{1}{4}$ LSB typ, $\frac{1}{2}$ LSB max
Buffering	Double buffered, single-step update
Zero drift	±3 ppM of F.S./°C max
Gain drift	±30 ppM of F.S./°C max
Setting time	5 μs to 0.01% for FS step

Digital I/O

Main digital I/O is via the PB and PC ports of an 8255-5 programmable peripheral interface.

Output low voltage	0.45 V max at sink = −1.7 mA (1 standard TTL load)
Output high voltage	2.4 V min at source = 200 μA
Darlington drive	4 mA max 1 mA min with Rext = 750 ohm
Input low voltage	0.8 V max, −0.5 V min
Input high voltage	2.0 V min, 5 V max
Input current	±10 μA max

Voltage and Current Sources

Voltage sources	±6.8 V at 5 mA max (user adjustable)
Current sources	1.000 mA with 1000 megohm output impedance @ DC
Compliance of current sources	−10 V to +2.5 V min
Temperature coefficient	±30 ppm/°C max

Environmental

Operating temp.	0 to 50°C
Storage temp.	−20 to +70°C

Power Supplies

+5 V	450 mA typ/600 mA max
−5 V	8 mA typ/15 mA max
+12 V	70 mA typ/100 mA max
−12 V	60 mA typ/100 mA max

8.6.8.3 Chromatograph boards

These boards are used with software to form an integrated chromatography data acquisition and analysis system. A voltage-to-frequency (V/F) conversion technique is used to provide 1 part in 20,000 linearity. The boards are also useful for nonchromatography low-level, high-accuracy voltage measurements. They provide high-precision integrations with optically isolated inputs and outputs and offer a simple, inexpensive way to acquire chromatography or other high-precision analog input data with a personal computer.

The boards plug directly into one of the I/O expansion slots inside the PC. A 25 pin "D" connector extends out the rear of the PC and can be connected directly to the application.

The V/F converter allows high resolution and integral accuracy. Typical linearity achieved is 0.005% (1 part in 20,000). The V/F can be connected to two inputs as well as ground (for zeroing) and a +1.000 V calibration reference. The input ranges are software selectable to +1 V, +2 V, +5 V, or +10 V, and all inputs are optically isolated from the computer's ground.

The board along with a software package form an integrated chromatography data acquisition and analysis sytem. The package sets up sample rate, duration of test, type of data storage to be utilized, and input range. For applications which require a specialized routine, an assembly driver is provided. The assembly driver allows the user to interface using Calls from BASIC.

To facilitate starting and stopping the chromatograph or another external process the board includes opto-isolated digital input points and relay outputs.

8.6.8.4 Programming

Most applications can be implemented using the menu-driven software routine provided with the board. The driver allows the user to select input channel, scan rate, test duration, relay states, and type of disk file to write. For those applications which cannot be implemented using the menu driver, an assembly driver is supplied which allows the user to interface to the board using CALLs statements in BASIC.

The board uses four consecutive addresses in the computer's I/O space. The actual base address used is determined by a DIP switch on the board. Typical addresses which are available for use are 76B (hex 300), 784 (hex 310), and others in the 768 to 816 range.

Each of the four addresses used by the board has a different function. These are listed here:

I/O address	Function	
	Read	Write
Base address + 0	Counter data	Counter data
+ 1	Counter status	Counter control
+ 2	Main control	Main control
+ 3	Aux. inputs	Relay outputs

The counter/data/control/status lines interface to an AMD 9513 counter. The 9513's five channels are used for measuring V/F outputs and setting up scan rates.

The main control register controls the selection of V/F input source, input range, interrupt level, and the interrupt enable/disable. The control register functions are shown here:

BITS

	D7 D6	D5 D4	D3 D2	D1 D0
	Int. enable	Int. level	Source	Range
F	0—disabled	000—inactive	00—In 0	00—10 V
U	1—disabled	001—inactive	01—In 1	01—5 V
N		010—2	10—1 V cal	10—2 V
C		011—3	11—zero	11—1 V
T		100—4		
I		100—5		
O		110—6		
N		111—7		

The base address + 3 register reads the digital inputs in the read mode and controls the output relays in the write mode. This is shown here:

BITS

	D7	D6	D5	D4	D3	D2	D1	D0
Read	0	0	0	0	IP2	IP1	IP1	IP0
Write	X	X	X	X	X	X	REL1	REL2

An energized input will return as a logic 1 and writing a logic 1 to a relay will energize the coil. An "X" signifies a don't care state.

Typical specifications are as follows:

Number of channels	2
Linearity	0.005% (1 part in 20,000)
Maximum sample rate	350 Hz
Maximum test run	11.93 hours (at max of input range)
Input ranges	+1 V, +2 V, +5 V, or +10 V
Input isolation	500 V min
Output relay rating	1A at 28 V dc or 0.5A at 120 V ac
Environmental	
Operating temp.	0 to 60°C
Storage temp.	−40 to +100°C
Power Supplies	
+5 V	700 mA typ/900 mA max
+15 V	20 mA typ/25 mA max
−15 V	25 mA typ/30 mA max

8.6.9 Resistance Sensor Input Boards

There are analog input boards for a variety of variable resistance sensors. They are suited for the measurements of devices which are operated in a current excitation mode or in standard bridge configurations. Sensors included in these categories include 2-, 3-, or 4-wire RTDs, thermistors, strain gauges, variable potentiometer devices, and other sensors. Some are designed with all cold-junction compensation circuit boards for thermocouple measurements.

A typical board accepts up to eight input sensors and multiplexes the inputs into a single A/D board channel. The channel is selected by digital control lines which are provided as outputs from the host A/D board. Each input channel includes a differential input amplifier with jumper selectable input gains from 1 to 500. Also included for each input channel is a precision current source for current excited measurements and a 0.50 to 4.00 V (jumper selectable) precision reference voltage for voltage excited sensors.

These boards may provide thermocouple cold-junction compensation circuitry that measures the actual input terminal temperature and allows the linearization software to subtract out the CJ error.

When used for bridge measurements, the board allows the bridge completion resistors to be mounted on or off the board. Two user-installed resistors can be set to form one half the bridge. A relay and calibration resistor allow shunt calibration.

8.6.9.1 Typical specifications

Instrumentation amplifier gains
  Jumper selectable 1, 10, 100, and 200 or 2.5, 25, 250, and 500.

Gain	Input offset drift	Common-mode rejection	Gain non-linearity
250	5.1 μV/°C	100 db	0.075%
100	5.1 μV/°C	100 db	0.075%
25	6 μV/°C	100 db	0.045%
10	6 μV/°C	100 db	0.045%
2.5	15 μV/°C	94 db	0.045%
1	15 μV/°C	94 db	0.045%

Gain	Settling time	Gain temperature coefficient
250	350 μs	20 ppm max
100	350 μs	20 ppm max
25	35 μs	15 ppm max
10	35 μs	15 ppm max
2.5	3.5 μs	10 ppm max
1	3.5 μs	10 ppm max

Thermocouple types	J, K, T, E, S, R, B
Cold-junction compensation	+24.4 mV/°C (0.1°C/bit)
Input bias current	5 nA typ, 20 nA max
Analog output voltage	±5 V max
Analog output current	10 mA max
Excitation Current Sources	
Number	8
Excitation current	1 mA
Accuracy	Better than 0.1%
Compliance	0 to 2 V
Voltage Excitation	
Range	0 to 10 V dc
Current	350 mA (current limited)
Power Requirements	+5VDC/1 amp typ, 1.4 amp max
Environmental	
Operating Temp.:	0 to 60°C
Storage Temp.:	−40 to +100°C

8.6.10 Isolated Expansion Multiplexers

These boards allow the expansion of any analog input to four channels. They can supply cold-junction compensation for thermocouple inputs and shunt terminals are provided for current measurements.

An expansion multiplexer allows isolated inputs to be connected to an analog input board. The board uses digital output bits from the A/D converter board to select which board is to be monitored, and which channel is to be enabled. Each input is isolated from all other inputs and from the A/D converter board. Each input includes an instrumentation amplifier that can be set for input gains with a user-installed resistor.

Thermocouple measurements can be handled with a cold-junction temperature measurement device which provides an input signal of 24.4 mV/°C. With a 12-bit A/D converter and a 10 V full scale, this corresponds to 10 bits/°C. The temperature measurement feature allows the CJ error to be subtracted out in software. Thermocouple linearization routines written in BASICA are available for J-, K-, T-, E-, S-, R-, and B-type thermocouples.

The multiplexer is controlled by four digital output bits from the master A/D board. Each multiplexer has an address selection switch. To allow expansion capability, the most significant two bits of the digital control lines are used as an enable control. This allows up to four boards to be connected to the same A/D input channel (one will be enabled while the other three will be disabled). The two least significant bits are used to control which channel is enabled.

A complication arises when monitoring thermocouples. For accurate thermocouple measurement, it is necessary to know the temperature of the connection of the thermocouple wire to the input terminal. This cold-junction temperature error is then compensated for in the software. However, each CJ temperature measurement device requires an A/D input channel. If each MUX is also monitoring CJ temperature, then some of the available input channels are taken, and the maximum number of thermocouples that can be monitored is reduced. If all boards are at approximately the same temperature, then the CJ monitoring device can be connected on one bank with only a slight loss of accuracy.

8.6.10.1 Thermocouple gain settings

The following list illustrates the gain settings for thermocouples over their entire operating range.

Thermocouple type	Maximum output	Maximum °C	Suitable gain*
J	43 mV	760	100
K	55 mV	1370	50
T	21 mV	400	200
E	76 mV	10000	50
S	19 mV	1760	200
R	21 mV	1760	200
B	14 mV	1760	200

* Higher gains may be used for less than full-scale span.
Gains are based on ±5 V output.

8.6.10.2 Typical specifications

Available input gains	X1, 2, 10, 50, 100, 200, 1000
Isolation	500 V dc min
Input offset voltage	150 μV max
Input offset current	6 nA max
Input bias current	±12 nA max
Input impedance	8 megohms min
	33 megohms typ
Temperature drift	20 ppm/°C typ
Nonlinearity	±0.025% typ
Input bandwidth	5 KHz min
Cold-Junction Compensation	
+24.4 mV°C	0.1°C/bit for 10 V FS, 12-bit A/D
Environmental	
Operating temp.	0 to 60°C
Storage temp.	−40 to +100°C

8.6.11 Digital-to-Analog Converter Boards

A typical DAC board (Figure 8-11) consists of two separate doubled buffered 12-bit multiplying D/A channels plus interface circuitry. The D/A converters can be used with a fixed DC reference as conventional D/As. On-board references of −5 V and −10 V provide output ranges of 0–5 V, 0–10 V, ±5 V and ±10 V and 4–20 mA for process control current loops.

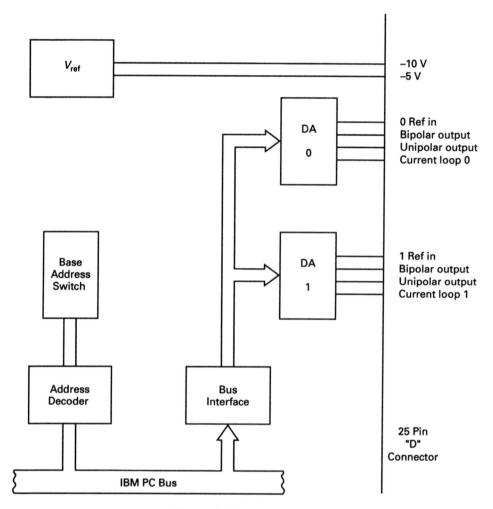

Figure 8-11 DAC Board

The D/As may also be operated with a variable or AC reference signal as multiplying D/As, the output is the product of reference and digital inputs. With an AC reference, the unipolar outputs can provide two quadrant multiplication and the bipolar outputs provide four quadrant operation. A 12-bit accuracy can be maintained up to 1 KHz.

Since the data is 12 bits, data is written to each D/A in two consecutive bytes. The first byte is the least significant and contains the 4 least significant bits of data. The second byte is the most significant and contains the most significant 8 bits of data. The least significant byte is usually written first and is stored in an intermediate register in the D/A, having no effect on the output. When the most significant byte is written, its data is added to the stored least significant data and presented in broadside fashion to the D/A converter, thus assuring a single-step update. This process is known as double buffering.

The board is addressed as an I/O device using eight I/O locations and may have its I/O address set by a DIP switch to any 8-bit boundary in the 255–1023 (decimal) I/O address space. The board uses the internal +5 V, +12 V and −12 V computer supplies and consumes 850 mW of power.

8.6.11.1 Programming

The following example shows how to output data in BASIC. Since the D/As have 12-bit resolution, data D should be in the range of 0–4095 decimal. First split the data into 2 bytes DL% (low) and DH% (high):

```
xxx00 DH% = INT(D/16)      'generate high byte
xxx10 DL% = D - 16*DH%     'derive remainder in low byte
xxx20 DL% = 16 * DL%       'shift low nybble 4 places left
```

Next write the data to the D/A. The example assumes D/A #0 with a board-based address of hex 300:

```
xxx30 OUT &H300, DL%       'low byte
xxx40 OUT %H301, DH%       'high byte and load
```

An assembly-language routine is even simpler. Assume AX contains the data and DX has the board I/O address. To write to D/A #0

```
MOPV CL,4                  ;set up for 4 left shifts
SAL AX, CL                 ;left justify data
OUT DX, AX                 ;write to D/A #0
```

The following program in BASIC shows how the board can output a voltage or current sink depending on the value of "D."

```
10 INPUT "Enter the data from 0 to 4095" ;D
20 DH% = INT(D/16)
30 DL% = D - 16*DH%
40 DL% = 16*DL%              BASE ADDRESS
50 OUT &H330, DL%            OF BOARD IS
60 OUT &H331,DH%             &H330
70 GOTO 10
```

8.6.11.2 I/O mapping

The board requires eight consecutive addresses in I/O address space. The locations of the D/A registers are as follows:

Base address +0	D/A #0	low byte
" " +1	D/A #0	high byte
" " +2	D/A #1	low byte
" " +3	D/A #31	high byte

The next four addresses are redundant and repeat the pattern just given.

Base address +4	D/A #0 low byte
" " +5	D/A #0 high byte
" " +6	D/A #1 low byte
" " +7	D/A #1 high byte

8.6.11.3 Output ranges

The operating range is selected by jumpering pins. The various ranges that can be selected follow. For unipolar outputs 0–5 V, 0–10 V, and 4–20 mA, data coding is true binary. Due to the analog inversion in the bipolar output ranges, ± 5 V and ± 10 V, data coding is complementary offset binary, zero digital corresponds to + full-scale analog, and 4905 digital corresponds to − full-scale analog.

For example,

Unipolar	Decimal	Volts
0 to +5 V	0	0 V
	1024	1.25 V
	2048	2.50 V
	4096	5.00 V

Bipolar	Decimal	Volts
−10 V to +10 V	0	+10.0 V
	1024	+ 5.0 V
	2048	0 V
	4095	−10.0 V

Data format for the D/A registers is as follows:

Low byte:	D7	D6	D5	D4	D3	D2	D1	D0
Base +0 or 2	B9	B10	B11	B12	x	x	x	x
				(LSB) (x = DON'T CARE)				

High byte:	D7	D6	D5	D4	D3	D2	D1	D0
	B1	B2	B3	B4	B5	B6	B7	B8
	(MSB)							

Writing the low byte stores it in an intermediate register.

Writing the high byte loads the D/A with both the high-byte and the stored low byte data. For 8-bit operation, first write zero to the low byte and all further operations may then be performed with the high byte only. For assembly-language programs, if data is left justified, 16-bit output operations may be used (OUT, DX, AX) since the data sequence is conventional Intel low/high byte.

In addition to its use as a standard DC output D/A, the board may be used with a bipolar or AC reference signal. With an AC reference, if the output is taken from the unipolar outputs, two-quadrant operation is obtained since the reference (which may be positive or negative) is multiplied with a positive-only digital signal.

If the output is taken from the bipolar output, the offset digital input can effectively be positive or negative which together with the possible positive or negative states of the reference results in four-quadrant operation.

Two other parameters are often of interest in AC operation. The first is feed through, the amount of residual signal at digital zero. The feed through which is mainly a function of stray capacitance rises with frequency. At 10 KHz it is typically 5 mV peak to peak with a ±5 V reference.

The second parameter that is a limit at a lower frequency is the accuracy/frequency characteristic. Due to distributed capacitance in the R-2R ladder network, the full 12-bit performance of the D/A falls off as the frequency rises. The board is useful in synchro-digital and resolver applications for sine/cosine generation with 400 Hz reference.

The 4–20 mA current loop output circuit consists of a precision current sink formed by a VMOS power F.E.T. and reverse protection diode as shown in Figure 8-12.

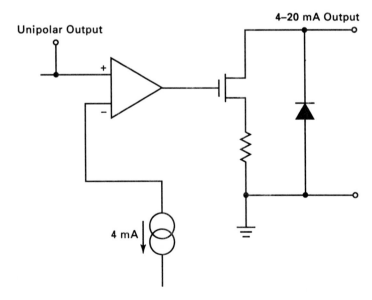

figure 8-12   4–20 mA Current Loop Circuit

8.6.11.4 Typical specifications

Power Supplies	
+5 V	75 mA typ,100 mA max
+12 V	15 mA typ,25 mA max
−12 V	25 mA typ,35mA max
Total power dissipation	0.85 watt typical
I/O address	DIP switch selected on any 8-bit boundary
Resolution	12 bits (1 part in 4095)
Relative accuracy	$\frac{1}{2}$ LSB (0.01%) max
Differential linearity	$\frac{1}{2}$ LSB max
Fixed reference ranges	0 to +5 V (unipolar)
	0 to +10 V (unipolar)
	±5 V (bipolar)
	±10 V (bipolar)
	4–20 mA current loop
Variable reference ranges	±10 V (2 or 4 quadrant)
Reference input resistance	7K ohm min, 11K ohm typ,20K ohm max
Voltage output impedance	<0.1 ohm max
Voltage output	±5 mA min
4–20 mA compliance	8 to 36 V
Environmental	
Temperature coefficient	±25 ppm/°C (with reference)
Of gain	±5 ppm/°C (external reference)
Zero drift	±3 ppm/°C
Operating temp.	0 to 70°C
Storage temp.	−55 to +125°C

8.6.12 Parallel Digital I/O Interface Boards

A typical parallel digital I/O card provides TTL/DTL-compatible digital I/O lines, interrupt input and enable lines, and external connections to the PC's bus power supplies (+5 V, +12 V, −12 V, and −5 V). It is a flexible interface for parallel input/output devices such as instruments and displays and user-constructed systems and equipment.

Digital I/O lines are provided through an 8255 programmable peripheral interface. There are three ports, an 8-bit PA port, an 8-bit PB port, and an 8-bit PC port. The PC port may also be used as two half ports of 4 bits, PC upper (PC4-7), and PC lower (PC0-3).

Each of the ports and half ports may be configured as an input or an output by software control according to the contents of a write-only control register. The PA, PB, and PC ports can be read as well as written to. Other configurations are possible for unidirectional and bidirectional strobed I/O where the PC ports are used for control of data transfer and interrupt generation.

Interrupt handling is done using a tristate drive with separate enable (interrupt enable-active low). This may be connected to any of the interrupt levels 2–7 available on the PC bus by jumpers on the board.

Handling of an interrupt is controlled by the 8259 interrupt controller in the PC. This is set by BIOS system initialization. Users program the 8259 to respond to their requirements and set up corresponding interrupt handlers.

The 8255 uses four I/O address locations which are decoded within the I/O address space of the PC. The base address is set by a DIP switch and can be placed anywhere in I/O address space. Base addresses below FF hex (255 decimal) should be avoided as this address range is used by the internal I/O of the computer. The four locations used are shown here:

Base address	+0	PA port	Read/write
	+1	PB port	Read/write
	+2	PC port	Read/write
	+3	Control	Write only

8.6.12.1 Programming

Programming is commonly done with assembly language or BASIC. The 8255 should be configured in the initialization section of the program by writing to the control register. On power up or reset, all ports are configured as inputs. A variety of configurations is possible by writing the appropriate control code. D7 must be high (= 1) to set the configuration of the ports. There are three possible operating modes: the PA/PC4-7 and PB/PCO-3 groups may be different modes at the same time.

Mode 0. Basic I/O, all ports are I/O ports.

Mode 1. Strobed I/O, part of the PC port controls data transfer.

Mode 2. Bidirectional I/O on PA only, part of PC controls data transfer.

For example, if

1. PA input, PB output, PCO-3 input, PC4-7 output

    Control word = 1001 0001 binary or 91 hex

2. Strobed output on PB, PA output, PCO-3 control, PC4-7 input

    Control word = 1000 1100 binary or 8C hex

To program,

1. First, write to the control register to set configuration in BASIC

    xxxx OUT (Base address +3), &H91

2. Then, to access the ports as required, for example, to read PA

xxxx X% = INP (Base address + 0)

To write to PB,

yyyy OUT (Base address 1), DATA

To read PC,

zzzz Z% = INP (Base address +2)

3. Once the configuration has been set in the initialization, the 8255 will remain in that configuration until a write occurs to the control register. In the 8255 all port registers are cleared by a write to the control register. Repeated changes of configuration require some provision for restoring data to cleared ports.

The following example demonstrates how input bits of the PC port can be used to monitor the status of two points and at a set condition will output a binary value to the PB port.

```
10          OUT &H303, &H89
20          K%=INP(&H302)
30          IF (K% AND 5)=5 THEN OUT &H301,9
40          IF (K% AND 5)=0 THEN OUT &H301,0
50          GOTO 20
```

When input port PC bits 0 and 2 are true, then output A is binary 9 (bits 0 and 3) from the PB port; otherwise, output A is zero.

8.6.12.2 Typical specifications

Logic inputs and outputs	Min	Max
Input logic low voltage	−0.5	0.8 V
Input logic high voltage	2.0	5.0 V
Input load current PA, PB, PC port (0<Vin<5v)	−10	+10 μA
Input low current, interrupts	—	−0.4 mA
Input high current, interrupts	—	20 μA
Output low voltage PA, PB, PC ports (sink = 1.7 mA)	—	0.45 V
Output high voltage PA, PB, PC ports (source = 200 μA)	2.4 V	—

All outputs and inputs are TTL/DTL compatible. Outputs will drive one standard TTL load (74 series) or a 4 LSTTL (74LS) load. CMOS compatibility can be obtained by connecting a 10 Kohm pull-up resistor from the input or output to +5 V.

Power consumption:	170 mA typ, @ +5 V
Environmental	
Operating temp.	0 to 50°C
Storage temp.	−40 to +100°C

8.6.13 High-Speed Parallel Digital Interface Boards

High-speed digital input/output interface boards use 8- or 16-bit direct memory access capability (DMA). Data transfer rates of 250,000 bytes/sec (or 125,000 words/sec) may be attained on the standard 4.77 MHz 8088-based PC, and higher speeds may be obtainable on 8088-2-, 8086-, and 80286-based machines. Normal processor I/O transfers may also be made through the data ports. An on-board counter/timer allows the user to set data transfer rates, or the transfer may be triggered externally.

Applications include interfaces to high-speed peripherals, high-speed memory transfers from other computers, digital I/O control, printer/plotter interfaces, and interfaces to external high-speed A/D and D/A converters.

A BASIC callable software driver allows the user to perform DMA controller setup, timer setup, and data block transfers. Source code is provided allowing the driver to be modified to run with upper-level languages.

These boards usually provide two 8-bit I/O ports, A and B. Each port can be set as an input or output software control. The ports can be addressed as normal I/O locations using programmed transfer, or via an 8237 DMA controller. DMA transfers may be 8 bit (byte) through the A port only or 16 bit (word) using both the A and B ports.

In word mode, double buffering provides a simultaneous update of the A and B ports. Both ports are addressable at any time as normal I/O locations. Two external signals provide the current direction of the ports.

DMA transfers may be initiated by an external or by an internal timer. The internal timer normally consists of a 10 MHz xtal oscillator divided through two sections of an 8254 counter. This provides a clock rate ranging from 2.5 MHz to 0.0023 Hz (about 8 pulses/hr). The choice of external signal or internal clock is via software control. On receipt of a positive edge on a XFER REQUEST input, an XFER ACKNOWLEDGE output goes low. Completion of the transfer to/from memory is acknowledged by a XFER ACKNOWLEDGE output returning to the high state. The operating DMA level is selectable as either level 1 or 3 under software control. The user is required to set up the 8237 DMA controller on the system board before a transfer. A BASIC callable subroutine can be used to do this.

Software control is used to select the active interrupt level (2–7) and choose between a positive or negative edge external interrupt on the INTERRUPT pin, an interrupt from the internal timer, or a terminal interrupt generated by the 8237 DMA controller.

8.6.13.1 Programming

Programming in BASIC is done using a software driver. The driver takes care of all initialization as well as controlling the actual data transfer. The BASIC driver can be modified to be linked to other upper-level languages or assembly code. The I/O structure of the board is described as follows:

8.6.13.2 Register functions

Port A data corresponds directly to the data bus. In word mode, Port A is the least significant byte.

D7	D6	D5	D4	D3	D2	D1	D0
A7	A6	A5	A4	A3	A2	A1	A0

Port B data corresponds directly to the data bus. In word mode, Port B is the most significant byte.

D7	D6	D5	D4	D3	D2	D1	D0
B7	B6	B5	B4	B3	B2	B1	B0

8.6.13.3 DMA control

The DMA control register bits have the following functions:

D7	D6	D5	D4	D3	D2	D1	D0
DMA Enable	DMA Level	AUX2	AUX1	XFER Source 0 = External (XFER REQ 1) 1 = Internal 8254 timer	BYTE /Word	B DIR	A DIR

8.6.13.4 Interrupt control

The interrupt control register bits have the following functions:

D7	D6	D5	D4	D3	D2	D1	D0
INT Enable 0 = Disable 1 = Enable		Interrupt Level 000 = Inactive 001 = Inactive 010 = Level 2 011 = Level 3 100 = Level 4 101 = Level 5 110 = Level 6 111 = Level 7		AUX3	INT 00 = External input 01 = 8237 terminal 10 = 8254 timer 11 = 8237 terminal	Source	Slope 0 = +edge 1 = −edge

8.6.13.5 I/O map

The board uses eight consecutive locations in I/O address space (this does not interfere with memory addressing). The base address is set by a DIP switch and can be on any 8-bit boundary in the decoded address range of 0 to 3 FB hex. One normal useable range is 100 3 F8H. The addresses are mapped as follows:

Address	Function	Type
Base +0	A port	R/W
+1	B port	R/W
+2	DMA control	R/W
+3	Interrupt control	R/W
+4	Counter 0	R/W
+5	Counter 1	R/W
+6	Counter 2	R/W
+7	Control	W
	Status	R
(R = read, W = write)		

The first four addresses correspond to the digital I/O and control, and the last four addresses correspond to the 8254 timer.

8.6.13.6 Typical specifications

Data transfer rate	Up to 125,000 words (16 bit) per second (PC/XT)
	Up to 250,000 bytes (8 bit) per second (PC/XT)
Logic levels	TTL compatible
Input high voltage	2.0 V min
Input low voltage	8 V max
Output high voltage	2.4 V min
Output low voltage	0.5 V max
Power supplies	+5 V/850 mA typ, 1 amp max
Size	$\frac{2}{3}$ slot, will not fit in XT half slots
Environmental	
Operating temp.	0 to 60°C
Storage temp.	−40 to +100°C

8.6.14 Counter/Timer Interface Boards

A counter/timer interface board offers the user general-purpose 16-bit counters. A selection of frequency sources and outputs may be chosen as inputs for individual counters with software selectable (active-high or active-low) input polarities. Each counter may be gated by hardware or software.

The counters can be programmed to count up or down in either binary or BCD. Up to five counters may be concatenated for an 80-bit counter.

The counters have alarm registers and comparators plus logic for operating in a 24-hour time-of-day mode. For real-time applications, the time-of-day logic will operate with 50, 60, or 100 Hz input frequencies.

Each counter has a Load register and a Hold register. The Load register is used to reload the counter to any predefined value controlling the effective count period. The Hold register is used to save count values without disturbing the count process, permitting the processor to read intermediate counts. The Hold register may also be used as a second Load register to generate complex output waveforms.

The board requires one slot in the XT/AT and 16 consecutive address locations in I/O space. Some I/O address locations can be occupied by internal I/O and other peripheral cards, so to provide flexibility in avoiding conflict with these devices the I/O address can be set by a base address DIP switch to be on any 16-bit boundary in the decoded I/O space. This also allows the use of another counter board in the same computer.

8.6.15 Relay Output Boards

A DPDT relay output board offers the programmer electromechanical double-pole double-throw relays for switching of loads by programmed control. Each relay contains two NC and NO contacts for controlling up a load at 120 V RMS. These relays offer zero leakage output currents, compared to a solid-state alternative.

The relays can be energized by applying a 5 V signal level to the appropriate relay channel on the connector located on the board. Another method is to connect the board directly to a digital output board which provides TTL switching capabilities.

This type of interface will permit the user to control loads such as heaters, fans, pumps, solenoid valves, and lights. Annunciator LEDs, one for each relay, light when their associated relay is activated. This feature can aid in troubleshooting.

8.6.15.1 Programming

The following example illustrates how to activate a relay in BASIC using a parallel I/O (PIO) Board:

```
10 OUT &H313, &H80      'sets all PIO ports to outputs
20 OUT &H310, 1         'activates relay 0    (port A, bit 0)
30 OUT &H311, 16        'activates relay 20   (port B, bit 4)
40 OUT &H312, 3         'activates relays 8 and 9 (port C, bits 0
                         and 1)
```

8.6.15.2 Typical specifications

Relays	
Quantity and type	24 DPDT (dual form C)
Contact material	Fold overlay silver
Contact rating	3 A at 28 V dc, resistive
	3 A at 120 V ac, resistive

Operate time	20 ms max, at rated voltage
Release time	10 ms max
Life Expectancy	
Mechanical	10 million ops min
Electrical	100,000 ops min. at rated load
Environmental	
Operating temp.	0 to 60°C
Storage temp.	−40 to +100°C
Power Consumption	
Input power	115 V ac +15% (2 amp fuse)
	230 V ac +15% (1 amp fuse)

8.6.16 Stepper Motor Controller

There is a plug-in two-axis stepper motor and incremental shaft encoder motion control board for the PC. Each stepper channel uses an intelligent controller chip that can execute a variety of motion control commands. Once a command has been loaded, the host computer is not involved in controlling the motion, but it may monitor the status.

The stepper motor may be moved any number of steps up to 24 bits of resolution (16,777,216 steps) either with a controlled acceleration/deceleration profile or constant step rate. Associated with each motor are limit switch inputs as well as a motor enable output. The limit switches provide normal and emergency stop limits at both ends of travel and a home or reference point at any intermediate point.

A normal stop is defined as a normal deceleration to rest without loss of the step count due to inertial effects. An emergency stop is a sudden stop that may lead to run on the motor and hence loss of location from the step count. This would normally require recalibration by return to the reference or home point. In addition to controlling the number of steps traveled by the motor (normal motion), the controller executes the following commands.

An initialization command controls the number of phases driven, logic levels of phase excitation (normal, inverted), internal/external step clock select, and switching excitation at standstill. This command also sets the start-up, acceleration/deceleration, and high-speed run rates. The components of this command that relate to the motor configuration cannot be altered by a further initialization command without resetting the controller.

Other commands include

Move normal. Moves the motor desired number of steps with a controlled rate and acceleration/deceleration.

Move constant. Rotates motor at constant speed for a specified number of steps.

Find limit. Rotates motor to a normal limit switch.

Find high speed limit. Rotates motor to a high-speed or emergency stop limit switch.

Find base point. Rotates motor to home or reference limit point.

Read status. Reads controller status.

Decelerating stop. Stops motor normally.

Emergency stop. Instantly stops motor by removing drive pulses (may lead to loss of true location from step count).

Single step. Single-step or "jog" command.

Reset. This clears the register and sets a command state.

Clock source. This selects internal/external step clock source.

Clock divider. The internal step clock rate is selectable by a programmable divider.

Each stepper channel can provide two different types of outputs. One is a clockwise/counterclockwise (CW/CCW) signal plus a pulse train output corresponding to the number of steps to be moved. This can be used for driving a variety of standard stepper motor translators. The other set of signals consists of five phase outputs which can be used to drive power transistors to switch the stepper motor windings directly. The number of outputs enabled and the stepping sequence are controlled by the initialization command and can be matched to 3, 4, or 5 phase motors.

When the motor is at rest the winding excitation current is at a maximum causing the greatest heating. It is best to select a mode in the initialization that switches the phase outputs at 11 Hz at about a 40% duty cycle. This takes place automatically about 100 μs after standstill and reduces the motor heating without really affecting the holding torque. The logic polarity of all the phase drive outputs can be selected true or inverted.

The step rate is controlled by the clock frequency. The controller has an internal clock of 12.5 KHz plus a programmable divider that can divide by any number in the range 20–255, giving corresponding step rates between 49 to 625 pps (pulses per second).

This can be restrictive so there are external clock sources: a 400 KHz xtal on-board clock with an 8-bit programmable divider or an external user input. The additional 8-bit divider works in conjunction with the internal divider to give step rates ranging from 1.54 pps to 2500 pps and allows the user to vary the step rate during operation or the execution of a command. This allows speeds which are not directly possible with the internal clock. Selection of the clock source is software controlled.

In addition to the stepper motor channels, there are independent incremental shaft encoder channels. These may be ignored in open-loop stepper motor control or used for closed-loop control or setting manual reference positions. The encoder channels are not linked to the stepper motor channels, so it is up to the host computer to intervene in any control utilizing the encoder inputs. Each encoder channel is TTL compatible and consists of a 24-bit quadrature up/down counter for counting single edges with channel A/B output-type incremental encoders. The encoder counters may be cleared and read by the computer. Each encoder input includes a digital noise filter, with a 25 KHz maximum input frequency.

Cascade outputs are provided from the encoder counters to allow the use of additional external counters.

It is possible to program the board using normal I/O port commands such as INP and OUT; however, utility software can simplify the use of the board and save programming time.

8.6.17 IEEE-488 Interface Boards

A GPIB/IEEE-488 interface board is designed to plug directly into an I/O expansion slot inside a PC or compatible. A standard IEEE-488 connector extends out the rear of the PC and connects to any standard IEEE-488/GPIB cable.

The software driver/interpreter for the 488 board is usually on a floppy disk. The driver handles initialization and protocol conversions required for access to all functions covered in the IEEE-488 specification.

The software may be designed as a DOS resident driver which simplifies interfacing the routine to upper-level languages. The software includes routines which allow the software driver to be run from BASIC, FORTRAN, and Turbo-Pascal, and the driver allows the user to interface to the GPIB bus using high-level IEEE-488 commands such as Remote, Local, Enter, and Output.

The GPIB will handle up to 14 other Talker/Listener devices. The controller may be the PC or any of the 14 devices on the bus. The hardware handles all the system timing for Talking, Listening, and Controlling the GPIB bus.

Control information is passed to the software driver in the form of an ASCII command string. Three other parameters must also be passed to the driver. The data transfer requirements are described next.

Command$ includes device addresses or secondary commands and [image terminators]. This is always a String and is decoded by the Command Line Interpreter. Command is separated from the operands (devices) by one or more Spaces, any other delimiters will cause a Syntax error in the command line. The separator for devices is always the comma '','' and secondary address is always a period ''.''. The Image string is identified by brackets ''[].'' The Command Line Interpreter is relatively tolerant of syntax error identification and will send back the appropriate error code to isolate the error. The format is

$$CMD\$ = \text{''COMMAND dev1, dev2, . . . , devn[image]''}$$

The [image] specifier allows the user to specify the variable field operations for the beginning and end of the data transfer variable. The variable may be a variable name, array identifier, numeric data value, or a string.

VAR [$](%) is the data variable output/input to be transferred from/to. Data is transferred as specified by the image terminator/specifier. If the image specifier is not used, the data is treated as an integer. The data may be of String or Integer type.

FLAG% is the transfer status of the CALL statement. If an error occurs, FLAG% will contain a hex number representing the error condition. A set of error and transfer message codes are generated at the completion of each call.

BASADR% is the address of the interface board being used. BASADR% may be 0 or 1, or the actual base address.
Consider the following user commands:

ABORT. Terminates the current selected device and command. If no device is given, the GPIB is cleared and set to the state given in the last CONFIG command. This command is similar to the CLEAR command. The PC must be the active controller or an error message will be generated.
"ABORT dev"

COMMAND$="ABORT"

CLEAR. Clears or resets the selected devices or all devices. If no device is given, the GPIB is cleared and set to the state given in the last CONFIG command. The PC must be the active controller or an error message will be generated.

COMMAND$="CLEAR 10, 11, 14"

(clears devices 10, 11 and 14.)
CONFIG. Configures the IEEE-488 GPIB to the user demands. The GPIB will remain in this state until reconfigured. The variable is not changed with this command. If the TALK-dev1 is omitted the PC is assured the active controller and talker.

COMMAND$="CONFIG TALK=6, LISTEN=12, 14, MLA"

(Device #6 is talker; devices 12 and 14 and PC are listeners.)
ENTER. Inputs GPIB data from selected talker to specified string array. Variable array must have been previously dimensioned. The FLAG% will contain error codes if an error occurs. The PC must have been previously programmed as a listener. If the PC is not the controller, then the ENTER command will wait until the talker sends a message to the PC.

COMMAND$="ENTER 12 [$, 0, 18]"

(Enter from address 12, array element 0 to 18.)
EOI. Sends a data byte on the selected device with EOI asserted. The bus must have been programmed to talk before the command is executed. The variable contains the data to be transferred. It is the user's responsibility to ensure the data and type match.

COMMAND$="EOI 12 [$]"

(Issue an EOI with last byte of the string to listener 12.)
LOCAL. Sets selected devices to the local state. If no device is specified, then all devices on the bus are set to local. The PC must be the active controller, or an error message will be generated.

COMMAND$="LOCAL 10, 11"

(Sets devices 10 and 11 to local state.)
LOCKOUT. A local lockout of the specified device. If no device is given, all devices on the bus will be set to local lockout. The PC must be the active controller, or an error message will be generated. The devices cannot be set to local except by the GPIB controller.

COMMAND$="LOCKOUT 6, 9"

(Lockout of devices 6 and 9.)
OUTPUT. Outputs a selected string to selected listener on GPIB. The variable will contain the data to be transferred. The image specifier will contain the data type and terminators. The FLAG% will contain the error codes if an error occurs. The PC must have been previously programmed as a talker. Devices are separated by commas and secondary commands by a period. Up to 14 devices may be accessed in the list.

COMMAND$="OUTPUT 10, 12 [$E]"

(Outputs an even parity string to listener devices 10 and 12.)
PASCTL. The active control of the GPIB is transferred to the specified device address, and the PC becomes the standard listener/talker but not controller. The PC must be the active controller, or an error will occur. This command may be reissued to allow the PC to be the controller again. If no Listen or Talk is specified, the PC is set to the Listen mode. The PC is not allowed to Talk until programmed by the controller. A request to talk must be specified for the PC to transfer data to a listener when using the OUTPUT command.

COMMAND$="PASCTL 6"

(Device 6 has control of the bus.)
PPCONF. Sets up the desired parallel poll bus configuration for the user. The PC must be the active controller or an error will occur.

COMMAND$="PPCONF 14"

(Parallel poll for device 14.)
PPUNCF. Resets the parallel poll-type configuration of the selected device. The PC must be the active controller or an error will occur.

COMMAND$='PPUNCF 14"

(Remove parallel poll from device 14.)
PARPOL. Reads the 8 status bit messages for the devices on the GPIB which have been set for parallel poll configuration. The integer variable will contain the 8-bit message. The PC must be the active controller or an error will occur.

COMMAND$="PARPOL"

REMOTE. Sets the selected device on the GPIB to go into the remote position. The PC must be the active controller or an error will occur. If an error occurs, the FLAG% will contain the error code.

COMMAND$="REMOTE 10, 12, 14"

(Set devices 10, 12, and 14 to remote.)
REQUEST. Requests service from the active controller on the GPIB. Only used when the PC is not the active controller. The variable% is sent by the PC and is in the range of 00 to 127 decimal in response to a serial poll from the active controller. An error will occur if the PC is already the active controller.

COMMAND$="REQUEST"

(PC is in control.)
STATUS. A serial polled devices status byte is read into the selected variable. The variable% will contain the status byte of the device specified as a serial poll. The PC must be the active controller or an error will occur. Only one device is allowed with one secondary address. If no device is specified an error will occur.

COMMAND$="STATUS 12"

SYSCON. SYStem CONfiguration and initialization of the GPIB. The user must run this command once before using the GPIB. If this is not run first, an error will be generated. If SYSCON.COM is used, the error messages will be displayed on the current screen. BAx is in hex (&H) or decimal.

COMMAND$="SYSCON MAD=dev, CIC=(0/1/2/3), NOB=(1/2),
          BAO=&Hdddd, (BA1=&Hdddd)"

where

    dev = the address of the PC 00 to 30 decimal
    NOB = number of IE488 boards (1 or 2)
    BA1 = base address for board 2
    CIC = controller in charge
    0 = none
    1 = brd 1
    2 = brd 2
    3 = brd 1 and brd 2
    (separate GPIB buses).

COMMAND$="SYCON MAD=3, CIC=1, NOB=1, BAO—&H300"

RXCTL. Receive control of the bus.

COMMAND$="RXCTL"

TIMEOUT. Sets the time and duration when transferring data to/from the device. The variable integer VAR% is set to a number from 0000 to 65000. The approximate time is the VAR%*1.5 seconds for the VAR% *3.5 for the XT. No error flag is returned.

COMMAND$="TIMEOUT"

TRIGGER. Sends a trigger message to the selected device or a group of devices. The PC must be the active controller or an error will occur.

COMMAND$="TRIGGER 11, 12"

(Devices 11 and 12 are triggered at the same time.)

8.6.17.1 Programming

The following list is an example of programming a 488 board in interpreted BASIC.

```
100 PRINT "****** system initialization ******
110 DEF SEG=&H2000
120 BLOAD "488 BIN", 0
130 GPIB=0
140 FLG%=0
150 BRD%=&H300
170 CMD$= "SYSCON MAD=3, CIC=1, NOB=1, BA0-768"
180 CALL GPIB (CMD$, AS, FLG%, BRD%)
190 PRINT "FLAG RETURN CODE FOR SYSTEM INITIALIZATION'HEX$ (FLG%)
200 PRINT "INITIALIZATION COMPLETE"
210 PRINT "** NOW ENTER DATA FROM DEVICE 12 and PRINT IT ON THE
    SCREEN**"
220 B$=SPACES (18)
230 CMD$="REMOTE 12"
```

```
240 CALL GPIB (CMD$, B$, FLG%, BRD%)
250 PRINT "RETURN FLAG= ";HEX$ (FLG%)
260 CMD$= "ENTER 12[$, 0, 17]"
270 CALL GPIB (CMD$, B$, FLG%, BRD%)
280 PRINT "FLAG FOR ENTER COMMAND'"HEX$ (FLG%)
290 PRINT "DATA RECEIVED FROM DEVICE 12= ";B$
300 END
```

8.6.17.2 Base address switch

An IEEE-488 board requires one slot in the PC and 16 consecutive address locations in I/O space. Some I/O address locations will be occupied by internal I/O and other peripheral cards, so to provide flexibility in avoiding conflict with these devices, the IEEE-488 I/O address can be set by the base address DIP switch to be on any 16-bit boundary in the PC decoded I/O space. This also makes possible the use of a second IEEE-488 interface board in the same computer. The user may transfer data to or from the two groups (device to device). This allows the user to have two controllers on line, one for each group. Then data can be transferred among 30 different devices.

8.6.17.3 Typical specifications

Number of devices serviced	15
Maximum number of 488 cards in PC	2
Mating cable required	CGIB-01
Total bus length	20 meters (not exceeding 2× the number of instruments)
Data transfer rate	2KB/sec
DMA data transfer rate	450KB/sec
Max. number of talkers at one time	1
Max. number of listeners at one time	15
Power consumption at +5 V	470 mA typ, 600 mA max
Environmental	
Operating temp.	0 to 50°C
Storage temp.	−40 to +100°C

8.6.18 IEEE-488 Interface Boards with Built-in Interpreter

Some boards for IEEE-488 have a built-in 12KB ROM interpreter which handles all the required initialization and protocol functions. No disk files with driver routines are needed, and the interpreter allows commands to be programmed in conventional high-level IEEE-488 command syntax such as REMOTE or ENTER.

The interpreter is a relocatable 16KB block of code which may be entered via a BASIC CALL statement or via DOS interrupt commands using assembly-language programming. All commands are string coded. The GPIB will handle up to 14 other talker/listener devices. The controller may be the PC or any of the 14 devices.

The IEEE-488 interpreter includes a group of subroutines which may be used to condition the data before data transfer when using assembly-language programs. The IEEE-488 hardware handles all of the system timing for Talking and Listening and Controlling the IEEE-488 GPIB.

8.6.18.1 Programming examples

The following examples illustrate how the IEEE-488 can be used to communicate with IEEE-488 instruments:

```
100    PRINT "******PASS CONTROL TO ANOTHER CONTROLLER******"
110    DEF SEG=&HC000
120    BRD%=&H300
130    CMD$="PASCTL 6"
140    CALL GPIB%(CMD$, X%, FLG%, BRD%)
150    PRINT "FLAG RETURN CODE FOR PASCTL IS = ";HEX$ (FLG%)
160    END
                         *************
100    PRINT "******ENTER DATA FROM DEVICE 12 AND PRINT TO
       SCREEN******"
110    CLS
120    DEF SEG=&HC000
130    'DEFINE GPIB CALL VARIABLES
140    GPIB = 0: FLG% = 0: BRD% = &H300
150    B$ = SPACE$(18)
170    CMD$="REMOTE 12"
180    CALL GPIB(CMD$, B$, FLG%, BRD%)
190    PRINT "FLAG RETURN CODE FOR REMOTE= ":HEX$ (FLG%)
195    CMD$ = "ENTER 12 [$, 0, 17]"
200    CALL GPIB(CMD$, B$, FLG%, BRD%)
210    PRINT "FLAG RETURN CODE FOR ENTER = "HEX$ (FLG%)
220    PRINT "DATA RECEIVED FROM DVM IS —"; LEFT$(B$,14)
230    PRINT "DO YOU WANT TO SCAN THE DATA AGAIN (Y/N)?"
240    YN$ = INKEY$: IF YNS = " " THEN 240
250    IF YN$< > "Y" THEN END ELSE PRINT: GOTO 200
260    END
```

8.6.18.2 Base address

The board requires one slot in the PC and 16 consecutive address locations in I/O space. The board also requires a free 16KB block of memory for the on-board 12KB ROM interpreter and 4KB static RAM. Some I/O address locations will be occupied by internal I/O and other peripheral cards, so to provide flexibility in avoiding conflict with these devices, the I/O address can be set by the base address DIP switch to be on any 16-bit boundary in the PC decoded I/O space.

This also makes possible the use of a second 488 interface board in the same computer. The user may transfer data to or from the two groups (device to device). This allows the user to have two controllers on line, one for each group.

A switch selects the 16KB block of memory on an even 16 KB boundary. The addressing of the switches corresponds to the absolute 20-bit address location in 16KB increments.

Following is a memory layout of the 16KB IEEE-488 interpreter. The GPIB interpreter contains 12KB of ROM and 4KB of static RAM distributed as shown in the following map:

```
                    GPIB IEEE 16 KBYTE INTERPRETER MAP
          ------------------------------------------
0000
                         (12 K ROM INTERPRETER)
0ADB          ASSEMBLY LANGUAGE LINK ROUTINE ADDRESS
0BB8           ASSEMBLY LANGUAGE UTILITY ROUTINES
3000          ------------RAM BUFFER BEGINS-----------
              INTERNAL RAM BUFFERS FOR INTERPRETER
                             2 Kbytes
3800          ------------------------------------------
                  USER RAM AREA FOR SCRATCH PAD
                            2048 bytes
                      NOT USED BY INTERPRETER
3FFF          ------------END OF RAM BUFFERS------------
```

The following IEEE-488 function classifications are allowed:

Basic talker, serial poll, no extended talker
Basic listener, no extended listener function
Source and acceptor handshake capability
Service request capability
Parallel poll remote configuration capability
Remote/local capability
Device clear and device trigger capability

8.6.19 RS-232/422 Expansion Boards

An RS-232/422 I/O expansion board for the PC and compatibles is designed to plug into one I/O slot inside the PC. The board interfaces to the RS-422, RS-232, or current loop serial interface bus through a 25-pin (RS-232 and current loop) or 9-pin (RS-422) D connector. The RS-232 interface includes standard bus control protocols (data set ready, clear to send, data terminal ready) and others. These communication control signals can be disabled if desired. The RS-422 interface can use standard "clear to send" and "request to send" control lines or can be set only to send and receive data. Selection of RS-232 or RS-422 and protocol desired are made with DIP switches on the board.

The board can communicate at speeds up to 56 kiloBaud at distances up to 1.2 kilometers with the RS-422 interface. The data transfer rate is software selectable. The board can be set up as a standard COM1 or COM2 interface, or it can be set at any other I/O address or interrupt level required. The board is based on the 8250 asynchronous communications chip. Even, off, or no parity, and 5, 6, 7, or data bits with 1, $1\frac{1}{2}$ stop bits are software selectable.

The base address is set by DIP switch and can in theory be placed anywhere in the I/O address space. However, in most cases the base address required will be for communication ports COM1 (which is at address hex 3F8) or COM2 (which is at hex 2F8).

There are five different user selectable communication protocols available on the board. These are controlled by a DIP switch on the board. The available protocols are described as follows:

1. RS-232 with standard PC/XT/AT-compatible bus control signals, such as request to send, data terminal ready, clear to send.
2. RS-232 without bus control signals, only data inputs and outputs.
3. Current loop.
4. RS-422 with request to send and clear to send control signals.
5. RS-422 without RTS and CTS control signals.

The board is designed to allow access to all PC interrupt levels. If the board is to be installed as a COM1 or COM2 port, the board must be set to interrupt level 4 or 3. The level selected is set by jumpers.

8.6.19.1 Typical specifications

Power Supplies	
+ 5 V	500 mA typ, 600 mA max
+15 V	30 mA typ, 45 mA max
−15 V	30 mA typ, 45 mA max
Environmental	
Operating temp.	0 to 50°C
Storage temp.	−55 to +125°C

8.6.20 RS-422 Interface Boards

There are also RS-422 interface boards for PC/XT/AT and compatible computers. These boards plug into a slot in the computer, and connections to the external serial buses are made through two 9-pin D connectors. Standard request to send (RTS) and clear to send (CTS) control signals can be used. The board allows communications at speeds up to 57.6 kilobaud at distances up to 4,000 feet. Although most standard PC-based communication routines only allow the board to be set at up to 9600 baud, this limitation can be overridden in most cases.

The ports operate independently, and each has its own base address and interrupt selection controls. A channel can be set at COM1, or COM2, or other desired base address/interrupt level combination. The board may be based on the INS16450 UART which is compatible with the standard 8250. It allows a variety of communications parameters to be selected as well as 5, 6, 7, or 8 data bits. Baud rate may be selected in a range of values from 120 baud up to 57.6 kilobaud.

Each of the communication ports requires the user to set a DIP switch for the base address; jumpers are used to select the port's interrupt level and enable or disable the port's use of the RTS and CTS control signals. The base address is set by a DIP switch, and in theory it can be placed anywhere in the I/O address space of the computer. However, in most cases the two ports will be set as COM1 and COM2.

8.6.20.1 Programming example

The following program assumes that one port has been set as COM1 and the other has been set COM2. An RS-422 cable must be installed between the two ports. This program will not operate properly if more than one communication device is set at the same address or interrupt level.

Lines 60 through 140 of this example program display how (in BASICA or GWBASIC) the communications ports can be set to communicate at faster than the 9600 baud limit in most DOS and BASIC communication routines.

```
10 OPEN "com1:4800" AS #1      'set up standard COM1:
20 OPEN "com2:4800" AS #2      'set up standard COM2:
30 T1$="testing COM1 TX/       'define test transmission data
   COM2 RX"
40 OUT & H3FF,2                'enable COM1:RS-485 driver
50 OUT &H2FF,1                 'enable COM2: RS-485 receiver
60'****start of baud rate override routine****
70 DUMMY=INP(&H3FB)            'read control register
80 OUT &H3FB,128:OUT           'select baud rate control
   &H2FB, 128                   registers
90 OUT &H3F8,2OUT &H3F9,0      'set COM1: at 56 kilobaud
100 OUT &H2F8,2:OUT &H2F9,0    'set COM2: At 56 kilobaud
110                            'note that if selecting 38.4
                                kilobaud
120                            'write a 3 instead of 2 to &H318
130                            'and &H218
140 OUT &H3FB,DUMMY:OUT        'reset control register
    &H2FB,DUMMY

150 PRINT #1, T1s              'transmit data from COM1:
160 INPUT #2,R2$               'receive COM2: data, store in R2$
```

```
170 PRINT R2$                    'print received results
180'
190 IF T1$< >THEN PRINT          "error in transmission"
200'
210 CLOSE                        'close communications ports
220 END
```

8.6.20.2 Typical specifications

Maximum data	
Transfer rate	57.6 kilobaud
Maximum data	
Transfer distance	4000 feet
Power Supplies	
+5 V	850 mA typ, 1 A max
Environmental	
Operating temp.	0 to 50°C
Storage temp.	−55 to +125°C

8.6.21 RS-485 Interface Boards

There is also an RS-485 board that allows IBM PC/XT/AT and compatible computers to be networked over the RS-485 bus. Unlike the RS-422 bus which allows multiple receivers but only a single transmitter on the bus, the RS-485 allows multiple transmitters and receivers to communicate over a 2-wire bus allowing a party-line type of network configuration. The board will allow up to 32 different driver/receiver stations to communicate at 56 kilobaud. Although standard IBM communications software limits the speed to 19.2 kilobaud, these limitations can be overcome. Stations can be located up to 4000 feet away from each other. Applications include networking instruments, scanning, and updating various user input and output devices such as CRTs and keyboards.

8.6.21.1 Programming

The board can be configured as a standard PC or compatible COM1 or COM2 port. The transmitter and receiver are enabled/disabled with a software write to the board's base address +7 (for a COM1, Hex 3FF, and COM2 is at hex 2FF). The least significant bit enables/disables the receiver, and bit 1 controls the transmitter. The following details the enable/disable functions:

BASE ADDRESS +7

B0	B1	B2	B3	B4	B5	B6	B7
RCVR	XMTR	X	X	X	X	X	X

Bit 0	Bit 1	Receiver	Transmitter
0	0	Disabled	Disabled
0	1	Disabled	Enabled
1	0	Enabled	Disabled
1	1	Enabled	Enabled

The base address +7 is a read/write address. Writing controls the XMIT and RCVR input and output enabling, while reading the address returns the current status of the RS-485 driver/receiver.

Although most versions of BASIC (and DOS) do not recognize COM1 or COM2 at communications speeds above 9600 baud (sometimes 19.2 kilobaud), it is possible to override a small portion of the initialization routine and operate the board at 38.4 or 56 kilobaud. This process involves setting the board up as a standard COM1 or COM2 port and then overriding the baud rate registers in the 8250 interface adapter on the board.

The following shows a simple test routine which communicates between two COM-485 boards set as COM1 and COM2. The program is designed to test communication at 56 kilobaud.

```
10 OPEN "com1:4800" AS #1         'set up standard COM1:
20 OPEN "com2:4800" AS #2         'set up standard COM2:
30 T1$ = "testing COM1 TX/COM2 RX" 'define test transmission
                                    data
40 OUT &H3FF,2                    'enable COM1: RS-485 driver
50 OUT &H2FF,1                    'enable COM2: RS-485
                                    receiver
60'****start of baud rate override routine****
70 DUMMY = INP(&H3FB)            'read control register
80 OUT &H3FB, 128:OUT            'select baud rate control
   &H2FB, 128                     registers
90 OUT &H3F8,2:OUT &H3F9,0       'set COM1: at 56 kilobaud
100 OUT &H2F8,2:OUT &H2F9,0      'SET COM2: at 56 kilobaud
110                              'note that if selecting 38.4
                                  Kbaud
120                              'write a 3 instead of 2 to
                                  &H318
130                              'and &H218
140 OUT &H3FB,DUMMY:OUT &H2FB,   'reset control register
    &H2FB,DUMMY
150 PRINT #1, T1$                 'transmit data from COM1:
160 INPUT #2,R2$                  'receive COM2: data, store
                                   in R2$
170 PRINT R2$                     'print received results
180 '
```

```
190 IF T1$ < > R2$ THEN PRINT "error in transmission"
200 '
210 CLOSE                                'close communications ports
220 END
```

8.6.21.2 Base address

The base address is set by a DIP switch and can in theory be placed anywhere in the I/O address space. However, in most cases the base address required will be for communication ports COM1 (which is at address hex 3F8) or COM2 (which is at hex 2F8).

8.6.21.3 Interrupt levels

The board is designed to allow access to all PC interrupt levels. If the board is to be installed as a COM1 or COM2 port, the board must be set to interrupt level 4 or 3, respectively. The level selected is set by jumpers on the IRQ level connector.

8.6.21.4 Typical specifications

Power Supplies	
+ 5 V	500 mA typ, 600 mA max
+15 V	30 mA typ, 45 mA max
−15 V	30 mA typ, 45 mA max
Environmental	
Operating temp.	0 to 50°C
Storage temp.	−55 to +125°C

Other Interface Boards

This chapter shows you how

- Available interface boards for the IBM PS/2 family function
- Commercial interface boards for the IBM PS/2 family can be connected and programmed for data acquisition and control

The boards discussed in this section have been designed for compatibility, being utilized in PS/2 Model 50, 60, and 80 machines. PS/2 Model 25 and 30 computers do not use the Micro-Channel architecture. The products compatible with Models 25 and 30 are products for the PC/XT/AT.

In keeping with the design specifications of the IBM PS/2 Micro-Channel and the POS (programmable option select) rules, there are no dip switches or jumper installations on any of these boards. Base address setting and interrupt-level selection are performed by the software.

9.1 PS/2 INTERFACE BOARDS

A typical input board provides eight analog input channels with 12-bit resolution. In addition, seven digital I/O bits are available, and an on-board counter/timer may be used to set A/D sample rates, count events and measure frequencies.

Another board offers 24 bits of parallel digital I/O. These 24 bits are broken up into three 8-bit ports. Each port can be independently set as input or output. These boards can be used with compatible relay and solid-state I/O module expansion boards.

RS-422 is rapidly becoming a standard in the world of industrial serial communication. More robust than its RS-232 predecessor, RS-422 is capable of communicating at distances of over 4000 feet. A 422 I/O board brings RS-422 communications capability to the PS/2 user.

Another PS/2-compatible board provides the interface to MetraByte's MetraBus industrial control and Monitoring family. The MetraBus can be used for a wide variety of process control and monitoring systems.

9.2 PS/2 ANALOG INPUT BOARDS

The 8-channel, 12-bit analog input board can be used for the PS/2 and other Micro-Channel–based compatible computers. The 8 analog input channels are fully differential, and offer software selectable input ranges of ± 10 V, 0 V, 5 V, 0.05 V, 0.01 V, and 0 to 10 V, 1 V, 0.1 V, and 0.02 V. The board provides 4 digital output bits and 3 digital input bits. A 3-channel counter/timer (INTEL 8254) can be used as an A/D pacer clock, and/or can be used to measure or generate frequency, measure pulse width, and count events. Access to the computer's interrupt bus is available at the I/O connector programs.

There are no dip switches or user adjustments on the board. Base address and interrupt-level selection are performed by the PS/2 setup program. The utility software package has an assembly driver (for BASIC) plus installation and calibration routines. The assembly driver simplifies the programming effort by performing all the actual board I/O commands for the user. The assembly driver is compatible with both compiled and interpreted BASIC.

9.2.1.1 Programming

I/O is accessed via a call to an assembly-level driver. In BASIC the call command is

```
CALL  DAS (MD%, DIO%, FLAG%)
```

where

$$DAS = \text{the data acquisition system}$$
$$MD\% = \text{one of the 22 available modes}$$
$$DIO\% = \text{the DATA}$$
$$FLAG\% = \text{any error conditions}$$

The 23 available modes are described here:

Mode	Function
0	Initialize the board.
1	Set input multiplexer scan limits.
2	Set input multiplexer channel.
3	Read input multiplexer channel number.
4	Perform a single A/D conversion.
5	Perform N conversions after trigger.
6	Enable interrupt operation.
7	Halt/disable interrupt operation.
8	Perform N conversions on interrupt.
9	Move data from memory into BASIC array.
10	Set counter/timer configuration.
11	Load counter/timer.
12	Read counter/timer.
13	Read digital inputs.
14	Write digital outputs.
15	Measure frequency.
16	Measure pulse width.
17	Add channel tag to A/D data.
18	Analog trigger enable.
19	Set PGA gain.
20	Return interrupt status.
21	Perform N conversions in M bursts.
22	Scan on interrupt.

In addition to the assembly-level driver the utility software also provides

- PS/2 address and installation files
- Thermocouple linearization routines
- Setup and installation aids
- A graphics and plotting package for display of data
- A simple data logger program
- A simple strip-chart recorder emulator program

After initializing the board, the following program shows how 4000 samples/sec could be obtained:

```
xxx10  MD%=1                              'set mux scan limits
xxx20  LT%(0)=2                           'start scan on channel 2
xxx30  LT%(1)=5                           'end scan on channel 5
xxx40  CALL DAS (MD%, LT%(0), FLAG%)      'setup
```

```
xxx50  IF FLAG% < > 0 THEN PRINT          'checks
       "ERROR"
xxx60  DIM A% (100)                        'dimension array of 100
xxx70  MD%=5                               'Mode 5
xxx80  TR%(0)=VARPTR (A%(1))               'start as element 1
xxx90  TR%(1)=100                          '100 conversions
xx100  CALL DAS (MD, TR%(0), FLAG%)        'do conversions, load array
xx110  IF FLAG% < > 0 THEN PRINT           'checks for errors
       "ERROR"
```

9.2.1.2 Typical specifications

Analog input	
Resolution	12 bits
Accuracy	0.01% of reading ±1 bit

Input ranges			
Gain	Unipolar	Bipolar	Settling time
			(F.S. step to 0.01%)
1	0 to +10 V	±10 V	15 μs
10	0 to +1 V	±0.5 V	15 μs
100	0 to 0.1 V	±0.05 V	15 μs
500	0 to 0.02 V	±0.01 V	35 μs
Overvoltage Continuous single channel to ±35 V			

A/D	
Type	Successive approximation
Resolution	12 bits
Coding	Offset binary (bipolar ±inputs), true binary (unipolar 0 ± inputs)
Conversion time	35 μs max, 25 typ
Type	Analog devices AD574A or equivalent
Linearity	±1 bit
Zero drift	±10 ppm/°C max
Gain drift	±50 ppm/°C max
Trigger source	External trigger, programmable timer or program command. Software selectable.
Sample Hold	
Acquisition time	4 μs to 0.1% typ for F.S. step input

A/D	
Digital I/O Outputs (standard LSTTL)	
Output port	4 bits
Low voltage	0.5 V max at sink = 8.0 mA
High voltage	2.4 min at source = −0.4 mA
Inputs (IPO-3 and interrupts) (LSTTL)	
Low voltage	0.8 V max
Low current	−0.4 mA max
High voltage	2.0 V min
High current	20 μA max, 2.7 V
Interrupts	
Level	2–7 software selectable
Enable	Via INT of Control register

Interrupts are latched in an internal flip-flop on the board. The state of this flip-flop corresponds to the INT bit in the status register. The flip-flop is cleared by a write to the status register. Service routines should acknowledge and reenable the interrupt flop.

Programmable timer	
Type	8254 programmable interval timer
Counters	3 down counters, 16 bit
Output drive	2.2 mA at 0.454 V (5 LSTTL loads)
Input, gate	TTL/DTL/CMOS compatible
Clock frequency	dc to 10 MHz
Active edge	Negative
Minimum clock pulse width	20 ns high, 50 ns low
Timer range	2.5 MHz to <1 pulse/hr
Power Consumption	
+5 V	800 mA typ, 1 A max
+12 V	2 mA typ, 5 mA max
−12 V	18 mA typ, 30 mA max

9.3 PARALLEL DIGITAL INTERFACE BOARDS

A parallel digital I/O board provides a means of interfacing an IBM PS/2 Model 50, 60 or 80 in a variety of digital I/O applications. In addition to TTL/NMOS/CMOS compatible data lines, it offers access to the PS/2's interrupt lines and allows external connection to the computer's power supplies.

Digital I/O lines are often provided by an Intel 8255 programmable peripheral interface. The 8255 has three separate 8-bit ports (PA, PB, and PC), which may be set independently as inputs or outputs. In addition to operating as a standard 8-bit port, the third port (PC) can be subdivided into two 4-bit ports or can be set to provide handshaking signals for the other two 8-bit ports.

There are no dip switches or user adjustments on some boards. Base address and interrupt-level selection are performed by the PS/2 setup program. The board can plug into any available Micro-Channel expansion slot within the computer.

It can be configured to interface to BCD equipment, monitor switches, and contact closures and control relays. Applications include equipment control, keypad scanning, printer interface, motor control, intruder alarms, and energy management.

The base address is set by installation software routines. The board uses 16 locations in I/O address space as follows:

Location		Function	Type
Base	+0	8255 PA port	Read/write
Address	+1	8255 PB port	Read/write
	+2	8255 PC port	Read/write
	+3	8255 control	Write only
	+4–7	Interrupt status	Read
		Clear interrupt	Write
	+8–15	Not used	

9.3.1.1 Programming

The first four I/O addresses correspond to the 8255 PPI port. All operating modes of the 8255 are supported. The basic input/output mode is called mode 0 operation. In the 8255, mode 1 is strobed input/output and mode 2 is a bidirectional bus configuration. In mode 0 operation the PA and PB ports are bytewide and the direction of all lines within a port is set by the control register. The PC port can also be used as a bytewide port or split into two ports of 4 bits (nibble wide). The directions of the upper and lower ports are independently programmable.

In mode 2 and 3 of PPI operation, the PC port assumes the role of a control or handshaking port and many lines assume fixed functions; however, in mode 0 (basic input/output), the PC lines behave as ports.

Some example control byte codes for mode 0 are shown here:

Control Byte (hex)	Configuration
80	PA, PB, and PC all outputs
81	PA, PB, PC-upper outputs, PC-lower input
82	PA and PC outputs, PB input
8B	PA output, PB, and PC inputs
9B	PA, PB, and PC all inputs

When a port is programmed as an output, you can return the data that the port is outputting by reading the same location. This may not reflect the actual state of the output lines if one or more is shorted, it is a reading back of the state of the output latch, not the buffered output lines.

9.3.1.2 Programming examples

Programming the digital ports is done by setting the 8255 PPI configuration (the examples are in BASIC):

```
xxx00  BASE=&H1000              'assign the base I/O address
xxx10  OUT BASE+3, &H80         'sets all ports to outputs for
                                 example
xxx20  OUT BASE, &H22           'outputs 22 hex to port A
xxx30  OUT BASE + 1, 99         'outputs 99 decimal to port B
xxx40  PRINT INP(BASE +1)       'reads and displays port B data in
                                 decimal
xxx50  PRINT HEX$(8NP(BASE))    'reads and displays port A data in
                                 hex
```

Bit operations can make use of OR, AND, XOR, EQV, IMP, and NOT logical (Boolean) operators to set bit I(I = 0 through 7) in port A to 1 without disturbing the other bits; for example,

```
yyy00  A%=INP(BASE)             'read port A
yyy10  OUT BASE, (A% OR 2^1)    'or in the selected bit
                                 and write back
To clear bit 1:−
yyy20  A%=INP(BASE)             'read port A
yyy30  OUT BASE, (A% AND NOT (2^1^))
```

9.3.1.3 Typical specifications

	Min	Max
Input logic low voltage	−0.5	+0.8 V
Input logic high voltage	2.0	5.0 V
Input load current PA, PB, and PC ports	−10	+10 $\mu\text{Å}$
Input low-current interrupt inputs	—	−0.4 mA
Input high-current interrupt inputs	—	20 μA
Output low-voltage PA, PB, and PC ports (sink = 1.7 mA)	—	0.45 V
Output high-voltage PA, PB, and PC ports	2.4	−V
Output source current PB and PC ports (V_{out} = 1.5 V, 8 outputs max)	−1.0	−4.0 mA

	Min	Max
Power Consumption		
+5 V	600 mA max + any external load	
+12 V	Equal to any external load	
−12 V	6 mA max + any external load	
Environmental		
Operating temp.	0 to 50°C	
Storage temp.	−20 to +70°C	

9.4 RS-232/422 PS/2 INTERFACE BOARDS

An RS-232/422 I/O expansion board for the IBM PS/2 Models 50 through 80 is designed to plug into a Micro-Channel bus slot in the PC. The board interfaces to the RS-232 or RS-422 port through separate 9-pin D connectors, with RS-422 connections made through a female connector and RS-232 made to a male connector. The board can be configured to operate either as an RS-232 or as an RS-422 interface, but not both concurrently. The user can choose to use control protocols (data set ready, clear to send, data terminal ready for RS-232, or clear to send and request to send for RS-422) or to employ only the data transmit and receive lines. Applications include instrument interfaces, industrial controller interfaces, printer/plotter interfaces, and interfaces to networks.

There are no dip switches or user adjustments. The choice of RS-232/RS-422, protocol/no protocol as well as the board base address and interrupt level are set up by the operating system through software at power up. The base address can be placed on any 8-bit boundary in the IBM I/O space below 68828, while the interrupt level can be set at any available level.

The board uses an 8250 UART chip and allows baud rate up to 56 kilobaud. Parity (even, odd, none), numbers of data bits (5, 6, 7, 8) and stop bits (1, $1\frac{1}{2}$, 2) are user programmable. It can communicate up to 56 kilobaud at distances up to 1.2 kilometers with the RS-422 interface.

9.4.1.1 Programming

The board can be configured as any standard COM: port (COM1:). The following BASIC program provides an example of programming. In this example, the computer operator is prompted to enter a command, which is subsequently transmitted. The 422 board waits for a response from the external device, and prints the response on the CRT screen.

```
10 INPUT "Enter Command" CMD$       'get command
20 OPEN "COM1:1200" AS # 1          'open communications at
                                     1,200 baud
30 OUTPUT #1, CMD$                  'send command to external
                                     device
40 INPUTS #1,RTN$                   'input response
50 PRINT "RESPONSE is",RTRNS        'print the response on the
                                     computer screen
```

The following program is a simple communications routine where data is transferred between standard COM1: and COM2: ports:

```
10 OPEN "com1:4800" AS #1          'set up standard COM1:
20 OPEN "com2:4800," As#2          'set up standard COM2:
30 TI$="testing COM1 TX/COM2 RX"   'define test transmission
                                    data

40 REM
50 REM
60'****start of baud rate override routine****
61 OPEN "COM1:1200" AS #1          'open the communications
                                    port

62 D=INP(&H3F8)                    'read the UART control
                                    register

63 OUT &H3F8, 128                  'select UART baud rate
                                    register

64 OUT &H3F8,2:OUT &H3F9,0         'set the baud rate to
                                    57.6 kbaud, note that by
                                    writing a 3 to address
                                    &H3F8 instead of a 2,
                                    the baud rate would be
                                    set at 38.4 kbaud.

65 OUT &H3F8,D                     'reset UART control
                                    register with original
                                    contents

70 DUMMY=INP(&H3F8)                'read control register
80 OUT &H3F8, 128:OUT              'select baud rate control
   &H2FB, 128                       registers
90 OUT &H3F8,2:OUT &H3F9,0         'set COM1: at 56 kilobaud
100 OUT &H3F8,2:OUT                'set COM2: at 56 kilobaud
   &H2F9,0

110                                'note that if selecting
                                    38.4 kilobaud

120                                'write a 3 instead of 2
                                    to &H318

130                                'and &H218
140 OUT &H3F8, DUMMY:OUT           'reset control register
   &H2FB,DUMMY

150 PRINT #1, T1$                  'transmit data from COM1:
160 INPUT #2, R2$                  'receive COM2: data,
                                    store in R2$

170 PRINT R2$                      'print received results
180'
190 IF T1$ <> R2$ THEN PRINT "error in transmission"
200'
210 CLOSE                          'close communications
                                    ports

220 END
```

Normally, a user will not be concerned with the details of the POS rules but the following information may be useful for some applications. During power up the board responds to the following five bytewide addresses:

Address (hex)	Function/Format
100	Returns 2 A, lower board ID byte (read only)
101	Returns 60, upper board ID byte (read only)
102	Control byte (read/write)
	Bits 7 to 4, interrupt level
	Bit 3, control protocol enable/disable
	Bit 2, RS-422 enable/disable
	Bit 1, RS-232 enable/disable
	Bit 0, card enable/disable
103	Top byte base address (read/write)
	Bits 7 to 0 select top bytes of base address
104	Bottom byte base address (read/write)
	Bits 7 to 4 select bits 7 to 4 of base address
	Bits 3 to 0 always zero
105 and up	Not implemented

I/O Address	Function
Base +0	Receiver buffer (read)
	Transmitter register (write)
+1	Interrupt enable
+2	Interrupt identification (read only)
+3	Line control
+4	Modem control
+5	Line status
+6	Modem status
+7	Board control status register (read only)

The byte map of the board control status register is

D7	D6	D5	D4	D3	D2	D1	D0
IL3	IL2	IL1	IL0	PRO	422	232	CDEN

IL0 to IL3 determine the interrupt level (0 to 15). PRO is high if the control protocol is enabled, 422 is high if the RS-422 port is enabled, while 232 is high if the RS-232 port is enabled. CDEN is the card enable and will necessarily be high because the board cannot be read if it is not enabled.

9.4.1.2 Typical specifications

UART type	INS16450 (8250 compatible)
Maximum data Transfer rate	57.6 kilobaud
Maximum data Transfer range	4000 ft (RS-422)
Power Supplies	
+5 V	525 mA typ, 600 mA max
+15 V	30 mA typ, 45 mA max
−15 V	30 mA typ, 45 mA max

9.5 METRABUS BOARDS

The MetraBus concept involves plugging a driver board into an IBM PC/XT/AT, IBM PS/2, MicroVAX, VME-Bus rack or an APPOLLO DM3000. A single cable then connects to between 1 and 32 I/O boards which are mounted in a 19-inch rack or a NEMA enclosure. Field wiring is connected to the detachable screw terminals on the I/O boards.

There are boards for a wide variety of personal or microcomputers. These products are suited for use in production test, incoming inspection, and other applications. A complete system consists of four main parts:

1. *A host computer.* A driver board allows this computer to be an IBM PC/XT/ AT or compatible, an IBM PS/2, a MicroVAX, an Appollo DM3000, or a VME-Bus rack. A serial interface board allows any computer with RS-232 or RS-422 communications capability to serve as a host computer.

2. *A driver board.* Direct plug-in versions of the driver board are available for IBM PC/XT/AT, IBM PS/2, MicroVAX, Appollo DM3000, and VME bus computers. A serial driver board allows a system to be operated from any RS-232/422 port. An intelligent driver board allows the MetraBus to operate as an independent control system. In some cases it can eliminate the need for a host computer.

3. *One or more I/O interface cards.* There are I/O boards with relay outputs, analog inputs, high-voltage digital inputs, and analog outputs. The boards operate independently and allow the system to be customized for the application.

4. *A cable which connects the driver boards and all of the I/O interface boards.*

Each driver board can interface up to 512 digital or 256 analog I/O points to the controlling computer. Large systems can be configured by using additional driver boards. The driver boards offer a parallel architecture that can transfer data in excess of 100 kilobaud.

9.6 METRABUS DRIVER BOARDS

A driver board can interface the MetraBus system to the IBM PC/XT/AT or compatible. It allows a single PC expansion slot to control up to 64 external I/O boards. The board generates all required timing and control signals. It is a half-slot board which can be installed in any PC expansion slot.

A 50-pin connector extends out the rear of the PC and connects to the MetraBus cable. The 50 conductor cable connects the interface boards and power supply to the driver board. The cable carries data, address, and control signals as well as distributing power. Ground conductors are interleaved between all signal lines to increase the system noise immunity.

The system allows cable lengths up to 100 feet. Applications which require communication at distances greater than 100 feet can use a remote driver card.

The board uses four consecutive I/O addresses in the PC. A dip switch on the board allows the base address to be set at any open location in the PC address space. Reading and writing to each of these addresses has a specific function. These are listed here:

I/O address	Read	Write
Base +0	Data in	Data out
+1	Address and status	Address
+2	—	Clear
+3	—	—

There are two steps to reading from or writing to a MetraBus I/O board. The first step selects the address. This selects the desired I/O board on the system. The second step is actually to read and write data to or from the board.

Selecting the address is performed by writing the desired address to the base address +1. The MetraBus address space extends from addresses 0 to 63. Each I/O board on the bus will have one or more distinct addresses on the bus. Once the address is selected it will remain constant until commanded to change. This allows consecutive reads and writes to the same board without requiring the address to be rewritten. Once the address is selected, data from the selected I/O device is transferred by reading and writing to the base address +0. Writing to the base address +2 commands a system wide reset. All output ports are set to zero.

9.6.1.1 Programming

An example of programming in interpreted BASIC is shown here:

```
10 BASEADR=768              'set BASEADR to 768 (hex 300)
20 OUT (BASEADR+2),00       'command system reset
30 OUT (BASEADR+1), 16      'select MetraBus address 16
40 OUT (BASEADR), 55        'write 55 to selected device (at
                             address 16)
50 DD=INP(BASEADR)          'read back address 16 contents
60 IF DD < > 55 THEN        'verify that 55 was received by the
   "ERROR"                   board
70 OUT (BASEADR+1), 00      'select new MetraBus address (00)
80 XX=INP(BASEADR)          'read from new address
90 PRINT XX                 'print the data returned from
                             address 00
```

The address can be read back if desired. To find the current address setting use

```
XX100 A=INP(BASEADR+1)
```

Reading the address also yields 2 bits of status information as well as the address as shown here:

ADDRESS BYTE

D7	D6	D5	D4	D3	D2	D1	D0
BUSY	R/W	A5	A4	A3	A2	A1	A0

The BUSY signal is an additional status signal for slow I/O devices such as A/D converters and stepper motors drivers. Normally both the BUSY and R/W status signals will be zero and the value returned will be identical to the content of the address bus.

For a period of about 100 microseconds after a data output (write) operation on the bus, the R/W status bit will be high. The user cannot read data while the bus is in output mode or perform another output operation until the R/W status returns low.

When programming in interpreted BASIC, it is not necessary to test the R/W status as the interpreter execution delays are longer than the MetraBus write time, but if an interpreted BASIC program is subsequently compiled, or if assembly language or any other compiled language is used, a test should be made of the R/W status before proceeding with the next I/O operation.

9.6.1.2 Power supplies and fusing

Small systems which require only +5 V supplies can be run directly off the PC's power supply. Larger systems require a power supply board. If the system is being run from the PC supply, the fuse on the board should be installed. If a separate power supply is being used, the fuse should be removed.

9.6.1.3 Typical specifications

Number of addressable I/O ports	64
Maximum data transfer rate	80 kilobaud (10,000 8-bit transfers/second)
Maximum drivable cable length	100 feet at full speed
	200 feet at reduced data rates
Power Supplies	
+5 V	250 mA typ, 325 mA max

9.7 OPTICALLY ISOLATED DRIVER BOARDS

There is an optically isolated driver for the MetraBus system. The board interfaces the MetraBus system to the IBM PC/XT/AT or compatible. It plugs directly into an expansion slot within the PC and then can control or monitor up to 512 digital or 256 analog I/O points. A 50 conductor cable carries all data and control signals required by the system as well as distributing power. Ground conductors are interleaved between all signal lines to increase system noise immunity. The maximum recommended cable length is 100 feet.

The board has a programmable counter/timer which can be set to generate periodic system interrupts. This allows the system to be operated in a foreground/background configuration. The board uses eight consecutive I/O addresses in the PC. A dip switch on the board allows the board's base address to be set at any open location in the PC's address space. The functions of each of these is shown here:

I/O address	Read	Write
Base +0	Data in	Data out
+1	Address and status	Address
+2	—	Master clear
+3	—	—
+4	Read counter 0	Load counter 0
+5	Read counter 1	Load counter 1
+6	—	—
+7	—	Counter control

9.7.1.1 Programming

Programming in interpreted BASIC is accomplished using the same commands as a standard driver board as shown here:

```
10 BASEADR=768                'set BASEADR to 768 (hex 300)
20 OUT (BASEADR+2), 00        'command system reset
30 OUT (BASEADR +1), 16       'select MetraBus address 16
40 OUT (BASEADR), 55          'write 55 to selected device (at
                               address 16)
50 DD =INP(BASEADR)           'read back address 16 contents
60 IFF DD < 55 THEN PRINT     'verify that 55 was received by
   "ERROR"                     the board
70 OUT (BASEADR+1),00         'select new MetraBus address (00)
80 xx=INP(BASEADR)            'read from new address
90 PRINT XX                   'print the data returned from
                               address 00
```

The address can be read back if desired by reading the base address + 2. Reading the address returns 2 bits of status information as well as the current address, like a standard driver board as shown:

ADDRESS BYTE

D7	D6	D5	D4	D3	D2	D1	D0
Busy	R/W	A5	A4	A3	A2	A1	A0

Normally both the busy and R/W status signals will be zero, so the value returned will be identical to the content of the address bus.

There are two steps for reading or writing to a MetraBus board. The address must be selected by writing to the base address +1. Then data is transferred by writing and reading from the base address + 0. The address space extends from addresses 0 to 63. Each I/O board will have its own address, which is called the board address. Writing to the base address + 2 commands a systemwide reset. All output points are set to their off (zero) state.

An INTEL 8254 counter/timer chip is connected to the PC's system clock. The counter can be used to generate periodic interrupts on the PC bus. This provides the hardware capability to allow an interrupt service routine to be controlling the MetraBus system in the background while the computer is performing other functions in the foreground. Counter 0 is connected to the system clock in the PC. The output of counter 0 is then cascaded into the input on counter 1. Counter 1's output is brought out to the interrupt jumpers.

9.7.1.2 Typical specifications

Number of addressable I/O ports	64
Maximum data transfer rate	80 kilobaud (10,000 8-bit transfers/second)
Maximum drivable cable length	100 feet at full speed
	200 feet at reduced data rates
Power supplies	
+5 V	250 mA typ, 325 mA max
PC to bus isolation	1000 V (minimum)

9.8 PS/2 DRIVERS

A driver board can also interface IBM PS/2 Models 50 through 80 and other Micro-Channel–compatible computers to the MetraBus. It allows a single expansion slot to control up to 64 external MetraBus I/O boards. Power for the Metra-Bus must be supplied by a separate supply as the IBM PS/2 design specifications limit the amount of power that can be drawn from Micro-Channel bus.

There are no dip switches or user adjustment on the board. Base address setting is performed by the PS/2 setup program on installation. The board is electro-optically coupled to the +15 V line of the MetraBus. If the +15 V is absent, a bit in the Control register will be read high. A low control bit does not ensure that the +15 V is within specification nor that the +5 and −15 V are present. Due to space limitations in the PS/2 backplane, the standard 50-pin MetraBus interface connector is not used. The board uses a 37-pin "D" connector which requires an adaptor cable.

9.9 MICROVAX DRIVERS

A driver board can interface the MetraBus system to Digital Equipment Corp.'s MicroVAX II with a VMS driver. The board is also compatible with the LSI-11–based system 11/73.

The board is a fully isolated dual width Q-bus card allowing access to analog I/O, digital I/O, relay, counter/timer, and other I/O signals from a single Q-bus backplane slot. The board provides optical isolation from the MetraBus and its external power supply with 1 Mbit/sec optical couplers. It is answerable to all standard DEC I/O addresses via user configurable dip switches. The Q-bus hardware interface consists of four DEC DC005 transceivers (w/address decode and vector drive), a DC004 Protocol logic chip, and a DC003 interrupt logic chip for interrupt generation support at all standard vectors.

The interconnection uses a 50-pin header and ribbon cable which carries data, address, and control signals as well as distributing power. Ground conductors are interleaved between all signals I/O lines to increase system noise immunity. The system is designed to allow MetraBus cable lengths up to 100 feet at 80 kilobaud (10,000 8-bit transfers per second) and 200 feet at reduced data rates.

Eight data and control registers are used for all Read/Write Status, and Reset operations. These registers are mapped directly to the DC005 transceivers.

9.9.1.1 Programming

The board uses eight bytewide registers for all Read/Write, Status, and Reset functions. These registers are mapped directly to the DC005 transceivers. The eight registers with their byte offsets are decoded as follows:

Register	Function	Read/write
0	Data	R/W
1	Control Status register	R/W
2	Data	R/W
3	Address	R/W
4	Data (high byte)	R
5	Data (low byte)	R
6	Reset	W
7	Reset	W

Registers 0 and 2 are redundant and used to transfer data to the MetraBus for addressing, outputting analog voltages, and setting bit status. Register 0 may be used in conjunction with register 1 to read data and status in a 16-bit format.

Register 1 contains the following status information:

Bit 0 Power loss interrupt enable (INT vector 1)

Bit 1 Completion interrupt enable (INT vector 2)

Bit 2 MBVAX-64 to MetraBus I/O busy

Bit 3 MetraBus busy

Bit 4 MetraBus Write busy

Bit 5 MetraBus Automatic A/D convert

Bit 6 MetraBus power loss (+5 V dc)

Bit 7 MetraBus power INT request

Register 3 is used to address MetraBus boards as well as to indicate A/D status. It is generally used in conjunction with register 2 for writing the address and data in a word (16-bit) format. Registers 4 and 5 are read only registers containing A/D conversion data. Registers 6 and 7 are redundant registers used to Reset and Clear the MetraBus.

The following example writes address and data to the MetraBus by issuing a system QIQ.

```
; WRITE TO METRABUS
; CALLING SEQUENCE
; CALL (DATA_ADDRESS, CHANNEL_ADDRESS)
```

```
; Macro library calls
      $10DEF
      $SDEF
;Local read only data
      .PSECT  RODATA, NOWRT, NDEXE
;Local read/write data
      .PSECT  RWDATA, WRT, NDEXE
MMCHAN:    .BLKW 1
DATADD:    .BLKW 1
;Executable code:
.PSECT           MBWRTCODE, EXE, NOWRT
.ENTRY           MBWRT, ^M<>
MOVW             @4 (AP) , DATADD        ;Store data (low byte) and
                                         ;address (high byte)
MOVW             @8 (AP) , MMCHAN        ;Store channel assignment
$QIQW_S          CHAN=MMCHAN, -          ;Send request
                 FUNC=#io$_WRITEVBLK, -
                 P1=DATADD
RET
. END
```

DEC Q-bus systems are generally configured in a descending order or priority in the Q-bus backplane. Normally, the CPU is the first card, followed by memory and then option cards. The MetraBus is connected with a 50-pin header and a 50-conductor ribbon cable.

9.9.1.2 Typical specifications

Number of addressable I/O	64
Maximum data transfer rate	80 kilobaud (10,000 8-bit transfers/second)
Maximum drivable cable length	100 feet at full-rated speed
	200 feet at reduced speed
Power supplies	+5 V dc, 1.4 A (max)

9.10 COUNTER/TIMER BOARDS

There is an eight-bit, eight-channel counter/timer board for the MetraBus system. The card accepts inputs from isolated sources and has a debounced input for counting external contact closures. The counters can be cascaded. The board uses eight consecutive addresses on the MetraBus which allows up to eight boards to be connected to a single driver board. Reading each of the addresses will return the current count of that channel. Writing to a counter causes the counter to be cleared. The bus address is controlled by a dip switch on the board.

Seven different crystal-controlled output frequencies between 0.125 and 8 Hz are brought out on screw terminals. These can be used as gating signals in frequency and event counting applications or be used to generate a constant low-frequency output signal.

9.10.1.1 Programming

The card connects to a MetraBus driver card through the MetraBus cable. The driver card is installed in the PC while the MetraBus cards are mounted externally.

There are two different addresses required to program the card. These are

1. The personal computer's I/O address
2. The MetraBus address

The MetraBus driver card controls the transfer of data between the PC and the MetraBus. It uses four consecutive locations in the PC's I/O expansion address space. The function of these addresses is shown here:

I/O Address	Read	Write
Base address + 0	Data in	Data out
Base address + 1	Address and status in	Set address
Base address + 2	—	Master clear
Base address + 3	—	—

The board uses eight consecutive I/O locations in the MetraBus address space. A dip switch on the board allows the board's address to be set on any 8-bit boundary within the MetraBus address space. Each of the eight addresses controls one of the 8-bit counters. A read from the counter returns the current count. A write to any counter causes that counter to be reset to 0. The following program is an example. First, the board is reset; then, the program then goes in a loop waiting for counter 0 to receive a pulse, counter 0 is then reset and counter 7 is read. The driver board is assumed to be at base address 768 (hex 300) and the counter/timer at board address 00.

```
10 BASEADR = 768: BRDADR = 00      'set BASE and BOARD addresses
20 OUT(BASEADR + 2),00             'clear the MetraBus
30 OUT(BASEADR +1), BRDADR         'set current MetraBus address.
                                    This selects Ch. 0
40 CTRO = INP(BASEADR)             'read CTR 0
50 IF CTRO = 0 THEN GOTO 40        'if no count has been received
                                    continue in loop
60 OUT(BASEADR), 00                'a pulse has been received so
                                    clear CTR, 0
70 OUT (BASEADR +1), BRDADR+7      'select CTR 7 address
80 CTR7=INP (BASEADR)              'read CTR 7
90 PRINT "Channel 7 read";CTR7     'print results
```

To cascade counters the TTL output from one counter is connected to a second counter's IN terminal. When the counters are set in a 16-bit mode, the programming is similar. Let counters 0 and 1 cascaded into the 16-bit mode. The following program reads counters 0 and 1 and performs the calculations to obtain a 16-bit count. The driver board is at base address 768 and the counter board is at board address 00.

```
10 BASE ADR = 768 BRDADR=0          'set base and board address
20 OUT (BASEADR + 1), BRDADR        'select CTR 0
30 CTRO = INP(BASEADR)              'read CTR 0
40 OUT (BASEADR + 1), BRDADR +1     'select counter 1
50 CTR1 = INP(BASEADR)              'read counter 1
60 COUNT = CTRO + 256" CTR1         'calculate 16-bit count
70 PRINT "THE count = ",COUNT       'print the results
```

9.10.1.2 Typical specifications

Inputs	
Number of channels	8
Maximum frequency	25 MHz
Trigger edge	Falling
Threshold voltages	
Positive going	1.5 V min
Negative going	1.1 V max
Hysteresis	0.4 V min
Input high current	0.25 mA max
Input low current	0.5 mA
Comparator Inputs	
Maximum frequency	500 KHz
Trigger edge	Falling
Switching threshold	Adjustable 0 to +10 V
Hysteresis	50 mV
Opto-Isolated Inputs	
Isolation	1000 VDC
Maximum frequency	5 MHz (7.5 mA drive current)
Trigger edge	Rising input current
Switching thresholds	(TTL compatible)
Input low	1.5 V (250 mA max
Input high	2.5 V (2 mA) min
Max input voltage	6 V max
Contact Closure Input	
Switching state	Counts on contact closure
Debounce period	10 ms
Maximum rate	100 Hz
Pulsed Outputs	
Output frequency	8, 4, 2, 1, 0.5, 0.25, and 0.125 Hz
Pulse width	$\frac{1}{2}$ of frequency (50% duty cycle)
Output low level	.5 V max at 4 mA max
Output high level	3 V min at 2 mA max
Power Supplies	
+5 V	300 mA typ, 500 mA max
+15 V	10 mA typ, 15 mA max
−15 V	2 mA typ, 4 mA max

	Environmental	
	Operating temp.	0 to 70°C
	Storage temp.	−55 to +125°C

9.11 THERMOCOUPLE I/O BOARDS

There is a 16-channel thermocouple board that provides the computation of temperatures for the MetraBus system. An isolated integrating A/D converter is used for 60 Hz noise rejection. A microprocessor computes the thermocouple temperature from the measured input voltage and a cold-junction compensator (CJC). Data is read by the MetraBus from an on-board memory. Values are updated once per second for all channels. A dip switch is used to set the thermocouple type (J, K, T, E, S, R, or B) in degrees Celsius or Fahrenheit. Digital filtering, a reduced range, and short cycling can also be selected by dip switch. The board may be positioned up to 100 feet from the computer.

9.11.1.1 Programming

The board uses four consecutive addresses in the MetraBus address space. The functions of these addresses are shown here:

MetraBus	Read	Write
Board Address + 0	Chan#/CJC	Chan #/CJC
+ 1	Data (low byte)	Chan #/CJC
+ 2	Data (high byte)	Chan #/CJC
+ 3	Options switch	Chan #/CJC

Writing to the Chan #/CJC selects the desired input channel (or the CJC temperatures). A read from board address + 0 will return the currently selected input channel. In addition to selecting the desired channel, a write to any base address will put the board in its hold condition. The board is constantly performing conversions, without regard to timing in other parts of the system (asynchronous operation). To assure that data cannot be changing during the read cycle a hold mode is used. The board when set into the hold mode during a write will remain in the hold mode until an off-board address is written.

Temperature data is in the form of 2's complement 16-bit binary word that has been divided by 10. This allows temperatures between −3276.8 and 3276.7 to be encoded. Following is the data format of the 16-bit temperature word:

Board address + 2	Board address + 1
B15 B14 B13 B12 B11 B10 B9 B8 MSB	B7 B6 B5 B4 B3 B2 B1 B0 LSB
: :	:	:

Board address + 2		Board address + 1
: 1638.4	25.6	0.1
:		
2's complement sign (1 = minus)		

The process of reading data from the board is illustrated by the following example program written in BASICA:

```
10  CLS                        'driver
20  DRV = 768 BRDADR=16        'set driver base address to 768 and
30                              thermocouple board address to 16
40  LOCATE 1.1
50  FOR I = 1 TO 16            'set up a loop
60  OUT DRV+1.BRDADR           'select thermocouple board ADR + 0
70  OUT DRV                    'select thermocouple # 1's address
80                             'and set thermocouple in hold mode
90  OUT DRV+1.BRDADR+1         'set address to board ADR + 1 (low
100                             'data byte)
110 LOW = INP (DRIVER)         'get low byte
120 OUT DRV+1,BRDADR+2         'point to high byte data register
130 HIGH = INP (DRIVER)        'get high byte
140 OUT DRV+1.0               'drop out of thermocouple hold mode
150 COUNT=(LOW+HIGH '256)      'perform conversion from binary
160                            'to decimal
170 IF COUNT>32767 THEN COUNT=COUNT-65536!
180 TEMP = COUNT/10
190 PRINT "thermocouple";;" reads";TEMP
200 NEXT
210 GOTO 30
```

9.11.1.2 Typical specifications

Thermocouple types	T, S, R, B, J, K, E
Measurement resolution	0.8 to 0.1 degree depending on type and range
Accuracy	0.5°C or twice resolution
Voltage reference error	25 ppm/°C (max)
Readout	Degrees Celsius or Fahrenheit or mV
CJC accuracy	0.5°C
A/D converter type	Integrating for one 60 Hz period
Full-scale ranges	76.4, 25, 15, or 5 mV
A/D resolution	12 bits plus sign
A/D accuracy	±1 bit
Update rate	1/sec (16 channels), 4/sec (4 channels)
Isolation	500 V dc thermocouples share a common ground
Power required	+5 V @ 500 mA
Operating temperature	0 to 70°C
Storage temperature	−40 to +100°C

9.12 ANALOG OUTPUT BOARDS

A typical analog output board for the MetraBus system has eight independent output channels, each with 8-bit (1 part in 256) resolution. There are switch selectable output voltage ranges, or the board can be set to output 4–20 mA. The installation of additional resistors allows user-programmable gains to be selected. Applications include control process control equipment with 4–20 mA outputs, variable voltage sources, servo controllers, function generators, and digital attenuators. The board uses eight consecutive addresses in the MetraBus address space. This allows up to eight boards to be controlled by a single driver card. A dip switch allows the board address to be set on any 8-bit boundary within the address space.

9.12.1.1 Programming

A driver card controls the transfer of data between the PC and the MetraBus. It uses four consecutive locations in the PC's I/O expansion address space. The functions of these I/O addresses are shown here:

I/O Address	Read	Write
Base address + 0	Data in	Data out
Base address + 1	Address and status in	Set address
Base address + 2	—	Master clear
Base address + 3	—	—

Each of the eight I/O locations controls one of the analog output channels. A dip switch allows the board's address to be set on any 8-bit boundary in the MetraBus address space. A write (an OUT statement in BASIC) to any of these locations loads an 8-bit latch which controls the D/A converter. A read (an INP statement in BASIC) from any of these locations retrieves the data on the latch without changing it. This allows the data being written to the D/A converter to be verified. A system clear from the card resets all D/A converters to zero.

Data is written in straight binary format in unipolar modes and offset binary in bipolar modes. The data formats are shown here:

Data bits								Output byte	Unipolar output	Bipolar output
B7	B6	B5	B4	B3	B2	B1	B0			
1	1	1	1	1	1	1	1	255	+ Full scale	+ Full scale
1	0	0	0	0	0	0	0	128	+ Half scale	Zero output
0	0	0	0	0	0	0	0	0	Zero output	− Full scale

The following program will reset the system, set channel 0 to half scale, and set channels 6 and 7 to plus full scale. The driver card is at base address 768 (hex 300) and the analog and board address 16 (hex 10).

```
10  BASEADR=768 BRDADR=16              'set base and board addresses
20  OUT (BASEADR + 2), 00             'clear the MetraBus
30  OUT (BASEADR +1), BRDADR          'set current MetraBus address
                                       to 16.
                                      'This selects channel 0
40  OUT (BASEADR), 128                'set channel 0 to half scale
50  OUT (BASEADR + 1), BRDADR+6       'select channel 6
60  OUT (BASEADR), 255                'set channel 6 to full scale
70  OUT (BASEADR + 1), BRDADR+7       'select channel 7
80  OUT (BASEADR), 255                'set channel 7 to full scale
90  D=INP (BASEADR)                   'read back data sent to
                                       channel 7
100 IF D<>255 THEN PRINT "ERROR"      'if data was not correct
                                       print error
```

9.12.1.2 Typical specifications

Power supplies	
+5 V	330 mA typ, 535 mA max
+15 V	54 mA typ, 88 mA max
−15 V	75 mA typ, 105 mA max
Outputs	
Resolution	8 bits
Relative accuracy	0.5%
Linearity error	$\frac{1}{4}$ LSB max
Temperature coefficient	±75 ppm/°C (internal reference)
	±10 ppm/°C (external reference)
Output ranges	0 to +5 V, 0 to +10 V, ±5 V, ±10 V
	4 to 20 mA current loop
Voltage output impedance	0.1 ohm max
Voltage output drive current	±5 mA max
4–20 mA compliance	8 to 36 V
Environmental	
Operating temp.	0 to 70°C
Storage temp.	−55 to +125°C

9.13 ANALOG INPUT BOARDS

There is also a 16-channel, 8- or 12-bit analog input board for the MetraBus system. The board has four software or hardware selectable input ranges. The addition of a user-installable resistor allows other input ranges for special applications.

The board uses 4 consecutive MetraBus addresses. This allows up to 16 (256 analog input points) to be controlled by a single driver board. Writing to the addresses initiates conversions, controls input ranges, and selects the channel to sample. Reading from the board address + 0 will return the MSBs of the conversion while reading the board address + 1 will return the LSBs. Applications include voltage and current measurement, interface to temperature, pressure, flow rate and other transducers, monitoring 4–20 mA outputs, data logging, and signal analysis. Jumpers allow the hardware selection of input range if software control is not desired. Annunciator LEDs on each input show which channel is being scanned.

9.13.1.1 Programming

The board uses four consecutive addresses in the MetraBus address space. A dip switch on the board selects the board address. Reading from and writing to the board address and board address +1, +2, and +3 select the input channels, set the input range, initiate A to D conversions, and transfer the data. The functions of each address are shown here:

Board address	Read	Write
+0	A/D MSB data	Start 12-bit Conversion
+1	A/D LSB data	Start 8-bit Conversion
+2	—	Gain/chan select
+3	—	—

A three-step process is used to read the analog inputs. These steps are summarized here:

1. Select channel to scan and desired input range.
2. Start the analog-to-digital conversion.
3. Read the data.

Selecting the input channel and input range is performed by writing to the board address +2. The gain/channel select byte is written as

MSB-----	-------	-------	-------	-------	-------	-------	-----LSB
128	64	32	16	8	4	2	1
—	—	G1	G0	CS3	CS2	CS1	CS0

Where the 2 MSBs are not used, the next two bits (G0 and G1) control the input range and the 4 LSBs (CS0 through CS3) select the channel to scan.

G1	G0	Input range
0	0	±10 V F.S.
0	1	±5 V F.S.
1	0	±2.5 V F.S.
1	1	±1.25 V F.S.

The channel selection bits decode as follows:

CS3	CS2	CS1	CSA0	Channel
0	0	0	0	0
0	0	0	1	1
0	0	1	0	2
0	0	1	1	3
.	.	.	.	.
.	.	.	.	.
1	1	1	1	15

The following is an example of how to select channel 7 and set the input range to +5 V. The example is written in BASIC, the driver board is at base address 768, and the analog board is at board address 00 for all examples.

```
xx10 BASEADR=768: BRDADR=0          'set BASE and board address
xx20 OUT(BASEADR+1), BRDADR+2       'select the gain and channel
                                     select address
xx30 OUT (BASEADR), 26              'select channel 10 with a +5V
                                     input range
```

The number 26 in binary is 0001 1010. Bits CS0 and CS2 are 0, CS1 and CS3 are 1 thus selecting channel 10, G1 is 0, G0 is 1, which selects the ±5 V input range.

Once the channel and input range are selected the A/D converter must be commanded to perform a conversion. Writing to the board address + 0 starts a 12-bit conversion while writing to the board address + 1 initiates an 8-bit conversion. An example of a 12-bit conversion is shown here:

```
xx40 OUT(BASEADR+1),BRDADR          'select driver board ADDRESS+0
XX50 OUT  (BASEADR),00              'start a 12-bit conversion
```

The data may be read after commanding a conversion. The most significant 8 bits (MSBs) of a 12-bit conversion or all bits of an 8-bit conversion are read from board address + 0. The least significant 4 bits are read from board address + 1. The data format is shown here:

READ FROM BOARD ADDRESS

+0	+1
B11 B10 B9 B8 B7 B6 B5 B4	B3 B2 B1 B0 0 0 0 0
MSB	LSB

The data format is offset binary and is shown here:

Input	B11	B10	B9	B8	B7	B6	B5	B4	B3	B2	B1	B0
+Full scale	1	1	1	1	1	1	1	1	1	1	1	1
0 Volts	1	0	0	0	0	0	0	0	0	0	0	0
−Full scale	0	0	0	0	0	0	0	0	0	0	0	0

An example of a BASIC routine to read the 12-bit data and print out the input voltage follows:

```
xx60 OUT (BASEADR+1), BRDADR          'select MSB's address
xx70 MSB=INP(BASEADR)                 'read MSBs
xx80 OUT(BASEADR+1), BRDADR+1         'select LSB's address
xx90 LSB=INP(BASEADR)                 'read LSBs
X100 VIN=MSB*16+LSB/16                'combine both bytes
x110 VFS=-5                           'set VFS equal to full scale
                                       input range (selected in line
                                       xx30 above)
x120 VOLTS=VFS+VIN*FFS/2048          'convert VIN to voltage
x130 PRINT "INPUT VOLTAGE";VOLTS     'print the result
```

When running compiled or assembly programs, a few precautions are required. Reading the MetraBus address will return the current address as well as two status bytes. This read can be performed by reading from the base address + 1. The address is returned as

ADDRESS BYTE

D7	D6	D5	D4	D3	D2	D1	D0
Busy	R/W	A5	A4	A3	A2	A1	A0

Usually both the Busy and R/W status signals will be zero so the number returned will be identical to the content of the address bus. However, for a period of about 100 microseconds after a data output (write) operation on the bus, the R/W status bit will be higher. Also, while the A/D converter is converting, the Busy bit will be low. When programming in interpreted BASIC, it is not necessary to test the status bits as the interpreter execution delay is longer than the conversion and write times. If the program is written in a compiled language, however, the R/W and the Busy line should be tested before reading or writing to the board.

The example program following performs a scan on all channels of the board and then prints the results as voltages. All channels are read as 12 bit, with ±5 V input ranges.

```
10   BASEADR=768;  BRDADR=0      'set base and board address
20   FOR i=0 TO 15               'start 16-channel loop
30 OUT(BASEADR+1),BRDADR+2       'select gain/channel set address
40 OUT(BASEADR), 16 OR I         'I is the channel number, it is
50                               'OR'd with 16 because the 16's
                                  bit
60                               'on with the 32's bit off selects
70                               'the ±5 volt input range
80 OUT(BASEADR+1),BRDADR         'select board address +0 location
90                               'for 12 bit conversion
100 OUT(BASEADR),0               'start 12-bit conversion
110 MSB=INP(BASEADR)             'read MSBs
120 OUT(BASEADR+1),BRDADR+1      'choose LSB's data address
130 LSB=INP(BASEADR)             'read MSBS
140 VIN=MSB*16+LSB/16            'combine MSBs and LSBs
150 VFS=5                        'set full-scale variable to +5
160 VOLTS=-VFSVIN*VFS/2048       'convert to volts
170 PRINT "channel ; I;reads"; VOLTS;"
    volts"
180 NEXT I
```

The standard input stage contains a 50 Hz single-pole, low-pass filter. The filter cutoff frequency can be changed, or the filter may be removed entirely. Figure 9-1 shows the circuit diagram of the input section of one of the channels.

The input to the A/D converter is set at +5 V. Input gains should be selected such that the maximum input voltage times the gain should be less than or equal to 5 V for proper operation. This is the gain while the +10 V software selected input

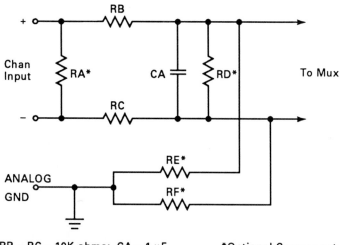

RB = RC = 10K ohms; CA = 1 µF   *Optional Component.

Figure 9-1 Analog Input Connections

range. Selecting +5 V, +2.5 V, or +1.25 V will multiply this gain by an additional 2, 4, or 8. Lower gains are possible by installing a resistor divider.

9.13.1.2 Typical specifications

Input ranges	±10 V, ±5 V, ±2.5 V, or ±1.25 V F.S.
Converter type	12-bit successive approximation
Conversion time	35 μsec max
Accuracy	0.01% ± 1 bit
Temperature coefficient	+45 ppm/°C
Data format	Offset binary
Input bias current	2 nA typ, 6 nA max
Input impedance	100 megohms
Common-mode voltage	±10 V max
Input overvoltage	30 V continuous max
Reference	
Voltage	+10.0 ± 10.1 V
Drive current	10 mA max
Power Supplies	
+5 V	180 mA typ, 220 mA max
+15 V	33 mA typ, 40 mA max
−15 V	44 mA typ, 50 mA max
Environmental	
Operating temp.	0 to 70°C
Storage temp.	−40 to +100°C

9.14 VME DRIVER BOARDS

A driver board can interface the MetraBus to any VME bus computer system. It allows a single VME expansion slot to control up to 64 external MetraBus I/O boards, 512 digital or 256 analog I/O points. The VME board generates all required timing and control signals. It is a single-width board which can be installed in any VME expansion slot. A 50-pin connector extends out the front of the VME card cage and connects to the MetraBus cable. The 50-conductor cable connects the MetraBus interface boards and power supply to the driver board. The cable carries data, address, and control signals as well as distributing power on the MetraBus. Ground conductors are interleaved between all signal lines to increase the system noise immunity.

It is IEEE P1014 compatible and can be used with VersaDOS- and UNIX/ "C"-based systems. A switch-selectable base address allows custom addressing. Switch-selectable standard or short VME addressing modes are allowed, and it uses supervisory or nonprivileged data space.

Applications include energy management, process control, product testing, laboratory automation, and product test and/or inspection. The MetraBus system allows cable lengths up to 100 feet. Applications which require communication at distances greater than 100 feet require a remote driver card. One version can be set to generate a VME interrupt when data from the MetraBus system becomes available or on a periodic interrupt from a timer.

9.14.1.1 Programming

The board uses 32 consecutive addresses in the VME I/O address space. Reading and writing to each of these addresses has a specific function as shown here:

I/O Address	Read	Write
Base + 1	Data in	Data out
+ 3	Address and status	MetraBus address
+ 5	Reserved	MetraBus Clear
+ 7	Reserved	Reserved
+ 9	Timer/counter 0	Timer/counter 0
+11	Timer/counter 1	Timer/counter 1
+13	Timer/counter 2	Timer/counter 2
+15	Reserved	Timer/counter control
+17	BIM Control reg. 0	BIM Control reg. 0
+19	BIM Control reg. 1	BIM Control reg. 1
+21	BIM Control reg. 2	BIM Control reg. 2
+23	BIM Control reg. 3	BIM Control reg. 3
+25	BIM Vector reg. 0	BIM Vector reg. 0
+27	BIM Vector reg. 1	BIM Vector reg. 1
+29	BIM Vector reg. 2	BIM Vector reg. 2
+31	BIM Vector reg. 3	BIM Vector reg. 3

BIM Control and Vector registers are defined as follows:

> Vector and Control reg. 0, MetraBus IRQ
>
> Vector and Control reg. 1, not used
>
> Vector and Control reg. 2, Timer 1 IRQ
>
> Vector and Control reg. 3, Timer 2 IRQ

There are two steps to reading from or writing to a MetraBus I/O board. The first step selects the MetraBus address. This selects the desired I/O board on the system. The second step is actually to read and write data from or to the board.

Selecting the MetraBus address is performed by writing the desired address to the VME base address +3. The MetraBus address space extends from addresses 0 to 63. Each MetraBus I/O board on the bus will have one or more addresses. Once the MetraBus address is selected it will remain constant until commanded to change. This allows consecutive reads and writes to the same board without requiring the MetraBus address to be rewritten.

Once the MetraBus address is selected, data from the selected I/O device is transferred by reading and writing to the VME base address + 1. Writing to the base address + 5 commands a systemwide reset. All output ports are set to zero.

An example of programming the driver VME board in 68000 assembler code is shown.

Base I/O address must be known to system MMU if present. In VersaDos use the "GETSEG" command. In Univ/"C"-based systems the SAZLLOC command should be used.

```
        MOVEA.L    #$380000,A0      BASE ADDRESS
        MOVE.B     #0,5(A0)         CLEAR ALL METRABUS DEVICES
        MOVEQ.L    #10,D0           WAIT FOR CLEAR TO COMPLETE
                                    (10 μSECs)
        DBF        DO,*
WRITE
        MOVE.B     #16,3(A0)        SELECT METRABUS DEVICE AT
                                    ADDRESS=16
        MOVE.B     #$55.1(A0)       WRITE $55 TO SELECT DEVICE
.001    BTST.B     #6,3(A0)         TEST FOR WRITE COMPLETED
        BNE.S      .001
READ
CHANGES THE CURRENT ADDRESS IN THE NEXT THREE STEPS.
        MOVE.B     #17.3(A0)        SELECT METRABUS DEVICE AT
                                    ADDRESS=17
        MOVEO.L    #10.D0           WAIT FOR ADDRESS TO SETTLE
                                    (10 μSECs)
        DBF        DO,*
.002    BTST.B     #7.3(A0)         CHECK IF SELECTED DEVICE
                                    IS STILL BUSY
        BNE.S      002
        MOVE.B     (1(A0),DO        SAVE DATA INTO REGISTER DO
        END
```

The MetraBus address can be read back if desired. Reading the address yields two bits of status information as well as the current MetraBus address as shown here:

ADDRESS BYTE

D7	D6	D5	D4	D3	D2	D1	D0
Busy	R/W	A5	A4	A3	A2	A1	A0

Normally both the busy and R/W status signals will be zero and the value returned will be identical to the currently selected MetraBus address.

For a period of about 10 microseconds after a data output (write) operation the R/W status bit will be high. A read while the R/W status bit is high will return the data just output and not the addressed devices data. Another output operation should not be initiated until the previous operation is completed. After an address change, a read operation should be executed only after a 10-microsecond delay.

Switch functions include an address modifier select switch which is used to select the VME addressing mode. It selects between regular and short addressing modes. This switch is mapped directly to the VME AM4 bit. Standard addressing uses address lines up to A23 while the short addressing mode uses addresses up to A15. Regardless of which addressing mode is selected, the board only responds to supervisory or nonprivileged data access.

The version with counter and interrupt capability uses an Intel 8254 counter/timer with the system clock connected to counter 0. Counter 0's output is then cascaded to the clock input of counter 1. Counter 1's output is then cascaded to the input of counter 2. Either counter 1 or 2 may be used to generate interrupts.

The cascaded configuration allows the board to generate interrupts from 4 microseconds to 1.19 hours in any 1-microsecond interval. The counters may be programmed to generate a single interrupt or periodic interrupts.

Interrupt generation and control are handled by the BIM (MC68153). This device handles the interrupt handshake signals for the VME bus. It is necessary to program this device prior to generating interrupts. Each of the three interrupting devices may interrupt at the same or a different interrupt level, and each may use a distinct or equal interrupt autovector. The interrupt map is shown here:

Register	Function
0	MetraBus operation complete
1	Not used
2	Counter/timer 1 interrupt
3	Counter/timer 2 interrupt

9.14.1.2 Typical specifications

Maximum data transfer rate	800 kilobaud
	(100,000 8-bit transfers per second)
Maximum MetraBus cable length	100 feet at full speed
	200 feet at reduced rate
Power supplies	
+5 V	1.5 A typ, 2 A max
Environmental	
Operating temp.	0 to 70°C
Storage temp.	−40 to +100°C

9.15 REMOTE SERIAL DRIVER BOARDS

There is an interface board for connecting a MetraBus industrial control/data acquisition system to any standard RS-232 or RS-422 serial data port. The serial control information is brought in through a 25 (RS-232)- or 9 (RS-422)-pin D connector. The board then interfaces to the MetraBus system with MetraBus 50-pin ribbon cable. A multidrop/party-line scheme is implemented allowing up to 16 independent systems per serial communications port. Use of the RS-422 bus allows a single computer to control MetraBus systems up to 5000 feet away. The command syntax consists of eight ASCII characters. These eight commands sent over the RS-232 or RS-422 bus provide access to MetraBus boards and functions. A set of dip switches on the board allows the user to set RS-232 or RS-422 operation, which bus control signals to enable/disable baud rates, parity, and board addresses. A watchdog timer system is used to assure that the board is operating properly.

The eight ASCII command codes are used to provide access to MetraBus functions. The command codes can be sent in upper- or lowercase. The transmission of illegal commands generates an error message describing the type of error made such as unrecognized command syntax or data out of range. The command list is shown here:

Command	Function
BXX	Board Select—Allows the selection of any one of the possible 16 driver boards. XX can be any number from 0 to 15 boards.
AXX	MetraBus Address—Selects the MetraBus address to set. XX can be any number in the MetraBus address space (0 to 63).
WXXX	Write Data—Writes XXX to the currently selected MetraBus address. XXX can range from 0 to 255.
R	Read Data—Tells the driver board to transmit the data on the currently selected MetraBus address.
C	Clear—Generates a system clear command. All MetraBus boards connected to the driver board are reset.
S	Status—Return status. Status information includes current MetraBus address plus condition of Read/Write, Wstrobe, and Busy lines.
D	Decimal—Sets driver board in decimal mode. All driver commands which contain numbers are decoded in decimal. Decimal is the default condition.
H	Hex—Sets driver command interpreter to consider all numbers as hexadecimal. The default setting for the hex/decimal control is decimal.

XX and XXX as used here stand for two- and three-digit ASCII numbers.

The multidrop/party-line design allows up to 16 independent-based I/O drops to be controlled by a single serial port. Each board will be set at a distinct board address. All driver boards in the system are always monitoring the serial bus, but only the active board as set by the last board address command decodes the system commands and enables its transmitter stage. Board addresses can range from 0 to 15 and are set by a dip switch.

A protocol select switch allows the user to select baud rate, parity, number of data bits, echo on/off, and enabled/disabled bus control lines. In the RS-232 mode the switches select between all standard asynchronous adapter control lines enabled, and only DATA IN/DATA OUT enabled. In the RS-422 mode the selection is between CLEAR TO SEND, READY TO SEND, enabled and DATA IN/DATA OUT.

9.15.1.1 Typical specifications

Power Supplies	
+5 V	285 mA typ, 325 mA max
+15 V	30 mA typ, 45 mA max
−15 V	30 mA typ, 45 mA max
Environmental	
Operating temp.	0 to 70°C
Storage temp.	−55 to +125°C

Software for Process Control

This chapter shows you how

- Available software packages operate for data acquisition, logging, and other functions
- Today's software packages are used in typical applications

Process control packages are offered by a number of software vendors. One example is the Genesis program series, a graphics-oriented control package designed for IBM PC/AT and compatibles that incorporates many functions found previously only on large process control systems. Genesis is a multifunction package for process modeling, control system design and checkout, operator training real-time data acquisition or control, and plant or process information management. Another example is FIX, which is an integrated process monitoring and control system providing data acquisition and interactive graphics for the IBM PC. Scanning, alarm, and control are performed in a background mode, so that other programs can be run online. Up to 50 programs can be run at once, including an online spreadsheet program. FIX connects to a variety of process I/O subsystems, data highways, and programmable controllers. The system has options such as direct data base access from user-written programs, historical archiving with trend playback, and the ability to monitor up to 2000 I/O points.

10.1 DATA ACQUISITION AND OTHER PACKAGES

Data acquisition software packages that are compatible with the IBM PC/AT/XT are available for laboratory and industrial applications. Labtech Notebook, for example, can perform data analysis, charting, and output to a Lotus spreadsheet. This package also has a process control function for automatic linearization of strain and temperature inputs. Other packages such as the Controllograph data logger support type J, K, and T thermocouples and include cold junction compensation and linearization. Engineering unit conversions or arithmetic functions can be configured. The program outputs to a file in Lotus format. There are other software packages for the IBM PC and Apple Macintosh computers that use a spreadsheet approach to acquisition and control applications. Maccontrol and Icontrol use a standard spreadsheet such as Excel, Lotus, or Multiplan to define an application. Hart Scientific offers data acquisition and control software with acquisition rates to 30,000 points per second. This integrated package requires no programming, but still allows users to specify routines for acquiring, graphing, manipulating, storing, and transferring data.

There are other data acquisition software packages for industrial PCs such as the View Workstation Software package. This is a real-time menu-driven multitasking software link to data loggers. There are also interface drivers for connecting systems to PLC networks like MODBUS and TiWay. Kits that allow the IBM PC to access signals in real time through plug-in I/O cards are available from Analogic Devices and others. There is also data acquisition and control hardware and software conforming to CAMAC (IEEE-583).

Action Instruments offers industrial operations management software consisting of a set of IBM PC/XT-based routines for logging, graphics, spreadsheet, and executive functions for computer-aided engineering (CAE). ASYST and ASYSTANT+ are data acquisition/analysis and graphics software packages that run on the IBM PC/XT/AT and compatibles. ASYSTANT+ is menu driven and supports functions such as FFT, power spectrum, matrix inversion, and smoothing, as well as basic arithmetic and trigonometric functions. Other menus support curve fitting, presentation graphics, statistics, polynomials, differential equations, file I/O, and automatic waveform generation.

PARAGON Control is a package in which the PC is used as a process control station. The user can configure the station for interactive process monitoring and control. The software package may also be used for diagnostics, simulation, and operator training.

Meters for industrial, commercial, and utility use can be monitored by EASYBILL. A standard interface is used which can be accessed by an IBM PC or unit. Software functions include meter polling and report printing.

PC-based data acquisition software is also useful for vibration data capture. The Dynamic Data Manager can monitor steady-state dynamic vibration data upon alert or danger alarm conditions on different types of rotating machinery. The data may be used immediately or accessed later for predictive maintenance. Another tool is the Machinery Diagnostic Expert (DXPERT) which uses artificial intelligence (AI) techniques to solve vibration-related rotating machinery problems. DXPERT executes on IBM PCs or compatibles and has six general knowl-edge bases from which to solve machinery problems: pumps, motors, gearboxes, turbines, fans, and compressors. Users can create their own knowledge bases which rely on specific plant history data.

Software for vibration-monitoring systems is available from Vitec. One package is designed for analysis, trending, warning levels, fast Fourier trans-forms, and predictive maintenance programs.

Other companies such as GSE offer microcomputer-based statistical process control software packages. These packages provide data storage and reporting capabilities and run on the IBM PC/AT and compatibles. The programs store the incoming data while simultaneously allowing the user to run statistical process control charts and other reports. GSE's software enables multiple monitoring stations to be linked into a plantwide statistical process control network. In a typical application, several monitors may measure a parameter such as torque. The data is then transferred to the PC for storage and the development of statisti-cal reports.

Distributed control system manufacturers have made possible the integra-tion of the PC into their proprietary networks by developing necessary packaged interfaces. For example, Foxboro has a package which allows interfacing to the company's unit controllers. Functions for feedback, feedforward, cascade, logic, and match can be configured in block tasks. Moore Products, Leeds & Northrup, Honeywell, and Bailey Controls also offer computer interface components for PC-based workstations.

Documentation, modeling, and design software is also available for the per-sonal computer. ONSPEC is a software package developed for modeling systems on a personal computer. Online displays for status, trend analysis, and manage-ment may be planned and implemented.

Several vendors offer packages for the programming of PLCs. ProDoc/Pro-Draft is a family of PLC program development, documentation, and support software. It can be used with the IBM PC, DEC MicroVax, and Unix systems. Allen Bradley and Gould also support software for ladder design and documen-tation.

Applications software for computer-aided design are also available. AutoCAD is a popular computer-aided design and drafting program. It can be used with utilities to prepare process, piping, and instrument diagrams.

Programs are also available for engineering economics, physical properties, fluid flow/heat transfer, and mass transfer and are compatible with IBM and Apple II PCs.

Artificial intelligence software is a growing segment of the PC software market. Development tools are available to the end user for developing an AI-based application. Most of the major process control companies have integrated AI into their control structure in some way. There is the Teknowledge program for the IBM PC/AT/XT family for designing, building, and running knowledge-based systems. Tektronix also has a system which supports the Smalltalk-80 AI language, LISP, and PROLOG.

10.2 I/O BOARD UTILITY SOFTWARE

Since it is necessary initially to set the base address of the analog and digital I/O interface to an unused address, the installation program will draw the base address switch on the CRT's screen upon entry of the decimal or hex value requested. The program will also create an address file as shown:

```
Desired Base Address (Decimal or &H--)? &H300
Closest Base Address on a 16-Bit Boundary is 768 Decimal
(Hex 300)
Do You Wish to Generate an Address File ‹Y,N›?
FOR ADDRESS 768 (HEX 300) SET SWITCHES AS SHOWN
```

There are a number of utility software packages available for plug-in interface boards. Utility software packages are designed to emphasize the ease of use of the product and to assist the programmer in the writing of software programs. They also tend to minimize the time required to utilize a particular product.

The following section is a descriptive list with illustrations of software packages included with interface boards. Due to the characteristics of the various data acquisition and control interface boards available, some boards do not require and/or support the entire list of software packages discussed.

10.2.1 Call Statements

To minimize the amount of programming required in the writing of data acquisition and control programs, a CALL routine is available. Call statements on some boards have up to 18 modes of operation. A binary driver source listing is available and can be used to link the Call routine to other languages such as FORTRAN, Pascal, or C.

The following example demonstrates how the CALL statement is used. The three lines of BASIC tell the A/D to perform a conversion and print out its value in volts.

```
180 MD% = 4' DO A/D CONVERSION
190 CALL DASH8 (MD%, CH%, FLAG%)
200 PRINT CH% *0.00244." VOLTS
(WHERE 1 BIT = 0.00244 VOLTS)
```

10.2.2 Data Loggers

A data logger software package stores the date and time at set user selectable intervals along with their associated decimal analog and digital input values (Table 10-1). The data can be recalled from floppy or hard disk and sent either to the CRT or printer. If the program is written in BASIC, it is a simple task to modify the program and tailor it to specific applications. For example, it might be desired to

TABLE 10-1 DATA LOGGER PRINTOUT

Data	Time	Ch. 0	Ch. 1	Ch. 2	Ch. 3	PC 3	PC 2	PC 1	PC 0
09-17-88	17:49:18	22	−226	16	85	0	0	0	0
09-17-88	17:49:19	23	−224	15	86	0	0	0	1
09-17-88	17:49:20	25	−228	15	86	1	0	0	0
09-17-88	17:49:21	23	−224	15	85	1	0	0	0
09-17-88	17:49:22	22	−226	15	87	1	0	0	0
09-17-88	17:49:23	18	−227	15	85	0	0	0	0
09-17-88	17:49:24	25	−224	16	86	0	1	0	0
09-17-88	17:49:25	24	−226	15	86	0	0	1	0
09-17-88	17:49:26	22	−227	16	86	0	0	0	0

End of file
Number of records = 9
Ok

change the decimal value in bits listed to the actual pressure in pounds or the temperature in degrees. The user can choose from the following options:

```
<1> - Display and log data to disk.
<2> - Display data from disk data file.
<3> - Print out data from disk data file.
Choose option (1-3):   1
Name of data file (e.g., B:MYFILE.DAT)? 1.dat
```

10.2.3 Data Streamers

A data streamer is a high-speed data acquisition and control software package for use with analog/digital expansion boards. The streamer allows A/D conversions to be stored on hard disk at sample rates of up to 62,000 samples per second. The package also allows data streaming from hard disk to one or both of the D/A channels on the board. A streamer package allows digital inputs or outputs to be streamed to or from hard disk in either 8- or 16-bit modes.

The streamer utilizes the DMA capability of the I/O boards to collect data and store it in the computer's memory. The streamer software concurrently takes this data and writes it out to a data file on disk. The data is taken from hard disk and written to memory while the I/O board's DMA capability is concurrently taking the data from memory and writing to the outside. These capabilities allow continuous high-speed sampling over long periods of time, limited only by the capacity of the disk.

Streamer software is usually completely menu driven. The menu allows the user to select sample rate, data file name, channels to scan, and trigger mode. The program includes error-checking routines that warn the user of probable errors. A batch operation mode allows a number of stream operations to be performed without requiring constant menu updates.

To maximize the speed of the disk write process, it is necessary to have the data file on the hard disk stored in contiguous sections of the disk. This minimizes the amount the disk must seek other sections during the write routine and maximizes speed. However, MS-DOS files are not always contiguous and may have sections of data scattered over the disk. This disk fragmentation occurs with normal use. A disk optimizer package goes through the hard disk and places all files in contiguous sectors. Optimizing the disk will not only make the stream operate better, but will speed up all disk access functions.

To maximize speed in the disk write sequence, it is necessary to create the data files before actually writing data to them. This eliminates the need for complex file allocation operations during the data streaming procedure. The streamer package allows this file to be created by running a MKFILE program.

Before running the data streamer, it is necessary to provide the software with some information about the hardware setup. There are four pieces of information the streamer needs to know. These are the base address, the interrupt level, the DMA channel, and the clock speed. A program like DSINSTALL asks the user for these four pieces of information and then writes them to a file that the data streamer can read.

Once a compatible file has been created and the hardware setup has been entered, the next task is to go ahead and take data. To start the streamer type

C>STREAM <cr>

This will bring up the streamer's menu.

Moving the cursor through the menu and entering the desired information allows the data acquisition run to be set up. Once the parameters are set, press F1 or @, and the run is started.

The data is stored on disk in binary form. Although this is a compact storage method, most analysis packages are not able to read this type of file. A format conversion may be necessary. An unpack utility can take the binary formatted data and create an ASCII format file which is suitable for analysis by other programs such as 1-2-3 and Asyst.

10.2.4 Measure

Measure software from Lotus adds a powerful, easy-to-use data acquisition capability to the popular Lotus 1-2-3 program. It measures interfaces directly connected to analog input signals and can be interfaced to a variety of RS-232 or RS-422 instruments with serial communication boards. Measure allows experimental data to be acquired, transformed, and stored directly in a 1-2-3 worksheet. Reduction, analysis, and graphic display of the data are possible using 1-2-3's mathematics and graphics functions. The measure program is menu driven with the same menu formats as 1-2-3. When loaded, measure becomes a part of 1-2-3, and the data acquisition menus can be brought up using the ALT and F8 keys concurrently.

   Measure acquires the data directly into 1-2-3 worksheet cells. It uses macros
and allows collection of data from different channels at different rates of speed.
The program can acquire up to 64 channels of incoming data simultaneously and
convert the inputs into engineering units. Up to 16 channels can be displayed and
converted into engineering units in real time.
   Users familiar with 1-2-3 will recognize the standard command menu that
allows access to 1-2-3 functions:

```
     A1:                                                        MENU
Worksheet Range Copy Move File Print Graph Data System Quit
Global,Insert,Delete,Column,Erase,Titles,Window,Status,Page
      A       B        C        D      E       F       G       H

1
2
3
4
5
6
7
8
```

   The measure menu that follows is similar to the standard 1-2-3 menu. The
measure menu may be accessed from the 1-2-3 program by concurrently pressing
the ALT and F8 keys.

```
A1:                                                         MENU
Go   Verify   Observe   ID Setting   Stage Settings   Quit
Acquire data with the DAS
A        B        C        D         E        F        G        H
1
2
3
4
5
```

   The Go command starts the data acquisition run that has been set up. Verify
checks the current setup and assures that the entries made have been valid. The
observe command allows the user to view up to 16 channels in real time, allowing
a quick check for system functions. The ID-setting and stage-setting commands
are used for the actual setup of the data acquisition run.
   The ID menu allows access to the two menus shown following. The first is
the hardware setup menu. This menu allows several boards to be installed at
various base addresses and interrupt levels.

```
A1                                                              MENU
Board   Interrupt   Clear    Quit
Enter hardware configuration
     Board           Address
       0              0300H            Interrupt Level:   7
       1              0310H
       2              0330H
       3              0340H
```

The second menu allows the user to configure an input channel. The channel name, type (analog or digital), input board, and channel number, along with where in the spreadsheet the data is to be placed, are set up with this menu.

```
A1                                              MENU
Type  Board  Channel  Range  Formula  Gain View Duplicate
Next-ID  Quit
Switch to next ID in alphabetical order
ID-Name:            TEMP1
                   Type:  Analog        Range: A1..A32
           Board Number:  0             Size : 32
         Channel Number:  0
                   Gain:  None
                   View:  Yes
     Formula:
```

The final menu to set up before running the acquisition program is the stage-setting menu that follows. This menu allows the selection of inputs, to sample, sample rate, number of samples, and type of trigger to be set.

```
A1:                                                    MENU
1   2   3   4   5   6   7   8 Clear  Rate  Number  Trigger  ( ) Quit
Enter an ID or Group on line 1
               Stage One        Stage Two        Stage Three
          Divisor ID/Group Divisor ID/Group  Divisor ID/Group
1            1      TEMP1
2            1      TEMP2
3
4
5
6
7
8
Sampling Rate:        500/sec
Number of Samples:    32
Stage total:          64
Trigger:          Keyboard         None         None
Grand Total:  64       Additional Loops:  0    Start Stage:   1
                                               End Stage:     1
```

Measure allows three separate consecutive data acquisition runs to be per-formed. Each run is called a stage and the setups for all three stages are selected by the foregoing menu. The divisor column allows the sample rate for each chan-nel or groups of channels to be selected independently. The sampling rate (in this case 500 samples/sec) is divided by the divisor column to determine the actual channel rate.

Specifications

    Max number of channels   64

    Max number of channels displayed   16

    Real time

    Max sampling rate   3,000 samples/sec

Supported hardware

    Analog input boards

    Serial communications adapters

    Any other serial communications adapter configurable as COM1: or COM2:

Computer requirements

    Lotus 1-2-3, Release 2.0 or higher

    DOS 2.0 or higher

    IBM PC/XT/AT or compatible

    512K RAM (minimum)

    Hercules, IBM, CGA, IBM EGA graphics cards, or 100% compatibles.

10.2.5 Labtech Notebook

Labtech Notebook is an integrated software package for data acquisition, moni-toring, and real-time control. It runs on the PC compatibles. Notebook operates with a hardware analog/digital interface but insulates the user from the low-level instructions the interface usually requires. It replaces laboratory notebooks and the hand keying of data in the same way that spreadsheet programs such as Lotus 1-2-3 replaced paper spreadsheets in business offices.

Labtech Notebook is menu driven. The conditions which define the current run are displayed on the screen and can be easily modified. All of the conditions pertaining to a run can be saved or recalled as a group. Labtech Notebook can reduce data acquisition and control procedures to single-button operations, so repetitive tests or process-monitoring activities are simplified. Data can be col-lected at rates up to 50,000 KHz and continuously streamed to disk at up to 400 Hz. Data can also be collected at very slow rates, with runs lasting weeks or months, if desired.

Each channel can be set up with different characteristics. Sampling rates may vary from channel to channel, and on each channel the sampling rate may vary at different times during a run. Open- and closed-loop control algorithms can be implemented. In open-loop mode, the user defines one period of waveform.

The signal is then clocked out automatically during the run. For closed-loop control, both PID (proportional-integral-derivative) and bang-bang (on/off) loops can be set up.

The curve-fitting function uses an iterative routine to fit a model of up to 10 parameters to the collected data. This routine can be set up to take advantage of the PC's optional 8087 chip. The 8087 and the IEEE floating point standard allow 80-bit real number processing, which reduces round-off error and provides faster computations. Notebook data files may be automatically imported into Lotus for reduction and analysis.

Labtech Real Time Access is a data pipeline continuously communicating real-time information between Notebook and the user's selected data analysis and display package. This option is an outgrowth of Notebook's foreground/background operations, where Notebook can continuously acquire real-time data off screen while the user can run an MS-DOS application on screen. Real Time Access forms a software link that allows Notebook and another MS-DOS application package operating concurrently to exchange data in real time. It transforms MS-DOS operating systems for multitasking, and off-the-shelf or user-written custom software into real-time analysis and display packages. Real Time Access reads data samples as they are acquired in background mode from Notebook's RAM memory buffers, directly into spreadsheet, statistical data analysis, database management, and display programs.

10.2.6 ASYST

ASYST is a scientific software package that turns an IBM PC/XT/AT or compatible into a scientific workstation. The ASYST package is comprised of four integrated modules:

10.2.6.1 MODULE 1 (system/graphics/statistics)

MODULE 1 establishes the ASYST environment. It provides the following functions.

1. *Arithmetic operations and special functions:*
   +, −, *, /, **, min, max, neg, abs, inv, sqrt, In, exp, conj, sin, cos, tan, sec, csc, cot, sinh, cosh, tanh, sech, scsh, coth, asin, acos, atan, asec, acsc, acot, asinh, acosh, atanh, acoth. All arithmetic operators work directly (without loops) on all elements of an array.
2. *Statistical functions:*
   Mean, variance, mode, median, moments, standard deviation, cumulative distributions, Gaussian, Chi-square, Student-T distributions, random number generators, and an index and sort function.
3. Built-in full-screen, text editor, and an array editor. Input and outputs from/to standard text files, saving and loading workspace images to disk, direct array I/O to packed binary disk files, ASCII files, and BASIC files.

10.2.6.2 MODULE 2 (analysis)

1. *Polynomial mathematics:*
   Polynomial multiplication, synthetic division, integration and differentiation, shifting, and root extraction.
2. *Vectors and Matrices:*
   Matrix inversion, matrix determinants, QR factorization, Gram-Schmidt orthogonalization, eigenvalues, eigenvectors, eigensystems for Hermitian matrices, and reductions of a general matrix to Hessenberg or Triangular form.
3. *Regression analysis:*
   Least squares polynomials, multilinear regressions, parametric, curve fitting, weighted least squared, exponential and logarithmic fits, orthogonal polynomials.
4. *Frequency analysis:*
   Fast Fourier transform, 2-D FFT, and inverse FFT.
5. Solutions to simultaneous equations, data smoothing, differentiation and integration, peak detection, convolutions, and filtering.

10.2.6.3 MODULE 3 (data acquisition)

Allows actual data acquisition with the personal computer. This requires that an I/O board be installed in the PC.

1. *Analog I/O:*
   Single- or multiple-input channel sampling, signal generation, up to 50 KHz sample rate.
2. *Digital I/O:*
   High-level addressing down to individual bits, read, write, set, reset, and pulse capabilities (requires MetraByte PIO-12 board).
3. *Real-time synchronization:*
   External trigger, clock-initialized trigger, timer-initiated acquisition.
4. *Background data acquisition:*
   Allows data to be acquired in the background while other computer functions are being performed in the foreground.
5. *Array handling functions:*
   Subarrays, reversal of indices, transposition of dimension, lesser dimension subsets, individual elements, catenation, lamination, inner and outer products and matrix multiplication.
6. *Graphics:*
   Multiple window graphics, autoplotting (with array versus indices, X array versus Y array, superposition of data plots, polar plots, autoscaling and data fitting, linear and logarithmic display on either axis), and hidden lines. Most graphics commands work on plotters as well as on video displays.

7. *Control structures and programming functions:*
if . . . else . . . then, begin . . . until . . . begin . . . while . . . repeat, do . . . loop. Comparisons available for =, <, <, >, >, ><, not, and, or, xor.

10.2.6.4 Specifications for module 3

Analog inputs	Up to 16
Precision	12 bit
Fastest sample rate	50,000 samples per sec
Trigger methods	External or internal triggers accepted
Analog outputs	2
Precision	12 bit
Digital bits	24 (in three 8-bit ports)
	Configurable as inputs or outputs in groups of 8
Number of devices controlled	15
Data transfer rate	2 kHz in standard mode
	300 kHz in DMA mode

10.2.6.5 MODULE 4 (IEEE-488)

Module 4 allows the user to read or write data to IEEE-448 controlled equipment. The software allows communications on a number of levels.

Hardware Required

IBM PC/XT/AT or compatible (DOS 1.10 or above)

640K of memory

Two or more disk drives (including at least one DSDD floppy drive), 8087 or 80287 coprocessor

10.2.7 CODAS

A computer-based oscillograph and data acquisition system (CODAS) hardware/ software package can be combined with an analog input board to form a data acquisition, storage, and real-time display system. A waveform scroller board included with the CODAS system makes possible real-time data display at speeds faster than software alone can provide.

CODAS allows continuous data streaming to floppy or hard disk and simultaneous display to the screen at sample rates of 2000 samples per second on the XT and other 4.77 MHz machines and 5000 per second on the AT and compatibles. CODAS functions are controlled with simple keystroke commands, no programming is required. The display can be set in smooth scroll (chart recorder) or triggered sweep (oscilloscope) modes. Up to eight channels may be simultaneously plotted on the computer's monitor. The real-time display is independent of disk storage activity.

Included with the CODAS package is a waveform analysis package allowing the review and qualification of data previously acquired on disk. Specific waveform voltages can be measured as well as timing intervals on one or more channels. Scrolling through the data set may be done in either a positive or negative time direction in a manner similar to reviewing the paper of a chart recorder. A copy and paste utility is provided allowing either entire data sets or bits and pieces to be pasted to separate disk files for further analysis with packages like Lotus 1-2-3 or ASYST.

The graphics accelerator card disk streaming software routines allow display/storage at speeds usually unobtainable with a PC-based system. The following compares the total time required to acquire, display, and store data using CODAS and the graphics accelerator board versus systems not using a special-purpose graphics board and disk streaming software. All benchmarks assume an AT or equivalent computer.

	Data acquisition and display without CODAS	Data acquisition and display with CODAS
ADC conversion time	30 μs	30 μs
Monitor plotting time		
Smooth scrolling	320,000 μs	64 μs
Nonsmooth scrolling	1,000 μs	64 μs
Continuous storage to disk	9,000 μs	106 μs
Total data acquisition and display time		
Smooth scrolling	329,030 μs	200 μs
Nonsmooth scrolling	10,030 μs	200 μs
Maximum sample rate		
Smooth scrolling	3 Hz	5000 Hz
Nonsmooth scrolling	100 Hz	5000 Hz

The following chart describes the main CODAS commands and the functions they perform.

Command	Action
CODAS B:DATACO.DAT 200K	Issued from the DOS level, this command invokes the CODAS software package and opens a 204,800 byte target data acquisition file named DATACO.DAT on drive B. The monitor is cleared and replaced with the default CODAS screen: 1. ADC channel one enabled and displayed as a continuous smooth scrolling plot through the graphics accelerator card. 2. Data acquisition to disk is disabled. 3. Sample rate set to 100 samples per second.

Command	Action
→Left Arrow	Pressing the left arrow cursor key increments the sample rate. The real-time display will update at a faster rate reflecting this change.
←Right Arrow	Pressing the right arrow cursor control key decrements the sample rate. The real-time display will update at a slower rate.
Up Arrow, PgUp, Down Arrow, PgDn	Using these cursor control keys, the user can dynamically scale and offset each real-time display channel independently. Only raw ADC data (unscaled) is sent to disk. Any scale and offset adjustments are annotated on the screen and the real-time plot reflects the changes.
F2 2	Pressing the F2 key and then the 2 key will enable two ADC channels for acquisition.
Shift 5	Pressing the shift and 5 keys together will enable display format 5 to display both ADC channels simultaneously.
F5	Press the F5 key to display time per division annotation.
F10	Pressing the F10 key enables data acquisition to disk file DATACO.DAT. The real-time display remains active during acquisition.
F9	The F9 key disables acquisition to disk leaving the real-time display active. Acquisition may be enabled or disabled as many times as needed.
Specifications	
Supported monitors	Monochrome, RGB color, EGA
Supported video	Separate sync and video (noncomposite).
Supported graphics cards	Any compatible with the given monitors.
Pixel resolution	Selectable 640×350, 640×200.
Waveform display modes	Selectable continuous smooth scroll or triggered sweep
Trigger conditions	+slope selectable, selectable trigger level, and source
Maximum continuous throughput	2000 Hz(PC/ST), 5000 Hz (PC/AT).
Number of input ADC channels	Eight channels single ended or differential.
Measurement range	Selectable ± 10 V, ± 5 V, ± 2.5 V, ± 1 V, ± 0.5 V F.S.
Graphics Accelerator Card Specifications	
Vector draw rate	15,000 vectors per second
Pixel draw rate	5.25×10 pixels per second
Number of waveform channels	Eight
Waveform display modes	Continuous smooth scroll (horizontal pan); triggered sweep (retrace plotting upon valid trigger conditions)

Minimum Computer Requirements

PC/XT/AT or compatible
128K of memory
One DSDD or SSDD floppy disk drive, hard disk optional

Any IBM-compatible graphics card or monochrome display and printer adaptor (graphics not necessary)

IBM-compatible monochrome or color monitor (noncomposite)

10.2.8 ASYSTANT+

ASYSTANT+ is a menu-driven version of the ASYST software package. The product is suitable for a range of applications and requires no programming. Data reduction capabilities include FFT, smoothing, integration/differentiation, data set averaging, polynomial scaling, rise time, peak width, area under curve, envelope detection, interactive zoom and scroll graphics, and automatic file processing for the reduction of large data sets. Analysis capabilities include curve fitting with automatic display of raw data, fitted curves and residuals, statistics, differential equations, and matrix and polynomial operations. Graphics include line, scatter, polar, log, semilog, axonometric, and contour plotting.

Data acquisition capabilities include real-time data display, automatic thermocouple linearization (including cold-junction compensation), conversion to engineering units, interactive graphics base waveform editor, signal averaging, alarm conditions plus real-time operator control of A/D sample rate, digital outputs, and D/A range. The package can also simulate traditional laboratory instruments such as strip-chart, transient, and XY recorders.

Hardware Required:

IBM PC/XT/AT, AT&T PC6300, or compatible

DOS 2.0 or above

Two or more disk drives (DSDD) hard disk drive recommended

640K of memory

8087 or 80287 coprocessor

IBM color enhanced color graphics board or compatible

10.2.9 Labtech Acquire

Acquire is a package designed for those needing to use the PC as a data logger. The package allows up to four channels of time-stamped data to be written to disk. It is menu driven. The operating environment is described through an installation menu. A single menu is used to set up the data acquisition. The user can control start-up, data rates, run duration, and display and file writing parameters from this single menu. The system supports up to four channels of analog input and one digital input channel. The user can also time-stamped data as an aid to later data analysis.

The incoming data, measured in volts, can be scaled using scale and offset factors defined in the menu. This allows for triggering, display, and storage of values in engineering units and for converting two signals to the same scale for comparison displays.

Data acquisition can be started immediately upon the start of the program, or later, when a trigger occurs. The trigger may occur when a key on the system's keyboard is depressed, or when the value of one of the analog channels is less than or greater than a threshold value. The data that is being acquired can be displayed in real time in one to four windows on the screen. Multiple signals can be shown in a single window. At the same time the data is displayed, it can be written to a disk file. All five channels can be written, as well as the elapsed time of the acquisition. The system will automatically write the time and date of the start of acquisition in the first two records of the file. Data is written as an ASCII real file. The ability to save setups by name and recall them for later use is useful since you don't have to restate the parameters each time you use the system. This makes it easy to switch from one experiment to another.

Specifications

Number of analog channels sampled	Up to 4
Number of digital channels sampled	1
Maximum scan rate (8 MHz AT)	50 Hz per channel
Maximum time between samples	11.5 days
Maximum number of samples per run	Disk limited
Trigger type	Immediate, analog, or keyboard
Number of analog channels displayed	Up to 4
Number of windows	Up to 4
Supported display types	CGA, EGA, Hercules
Real-time file type	ACSII real

10.2.10 Snapshot Storage Scope

Snapshot Storage Scope is a menu-driven digital storage oscilloscope software package for PC/XT/AT and compatibles. It is designed for users whose primary needs are real-time collection, display, and storage of analog data. It can both acquire and display data in virtual real time up to the maximum sampling speed of the boards. Capabilities include digital- or analog-triggered acquisitions of 16 channels; display of any 8 channels along with dual cursor readouts; time and magnitude readouts in engineering units; channel labels; X and Y zooming and offset; A/D, D/A, and digital output; selective recording of data to disk; and regraphing stored data. Minimum, maximum, and average of a waveform is calculated. Successive waveforms can be averaged to reduce noise.

Commands and parameters are issued through menus, and the software displays the range of acceptable answers for each parameter and provides feedback for the current parameter entry. User-defined files specify the setup parameters. Both the display and data files list the necessary setup parameters such as the number of points collected, sampling rate, date, time, title, sweep time, and sensitivity of each channel. Data file options include exponential and compressed formats.

Users can store either continuous sets of data or selected snapshots of data. Real-time acquisition of 32,000 data points with 12 bits accuracy (0.024%) is supported with a selectable sampling rate range from fewer than four samples per hour to 130,000 per second. Data is displayed graphically or in tabular format.

SNAP-FFT is a frequency spectrum analysis software package that converts time domain data acquired with Snapshot Storage Scope to the frequency domain using a fast Fourier transform algorithm. SNAP-FFT is menu driven and requires no programming. It calculates amplitude and phase for four channels of data. The amplitude ratio of any two sets of channels and the difference in phase angle is also calculated to provide the transfer function, impedance, transmissibility, and frequency response. The power spectral density along with the relative power within specified frequency bands is determined. The results can be in either a tabular or graphical format and can be displayed on screen, stored on disk, or sent to the printer. Graphs can be plotted on either a linear or log (Bode) format. The user may select a portion of time data to be analyzed in the frequency domain as well as the starting point and the number of points to be analyzed. Menu selections are used to change the analysis parameters. The user can save menu settings and then recall them to rerun various sets of data.

SNAP-CAL C is a software package to analyze and display acquired test data. Mathematical operations include calculation of arithmetic, trigonometric, calculus, logic, correlation, and statistical functions. It analyzes waveforms, not just single data points. Equations are defined in a user-friendly, algebraic manner. Data can be processed immediately after it is acquired (concurrent processing) or after it is acquired and stored in a file (postprocessing). Concurrent processing provides immediate results; postprocessing is used to analyze previously collected data. These two approaches can be used in combination in the postprocessing mode.

Single keystroke commands (SKC) define equations in a calculatorlike manner. Shift keys are not required since capital and lowercase letters have the same meaning. Single keystroke commands are defined alphabetically and usually use the first letter of the corresponding operator. Functions, equations, or subroutines that are frequently used can be saved, recalled as macros, and displayed for reference.

Specifications

Number of channels sampled	Up to 16
Number of channels displayed	Up to 8
Maximum scan rate	100,000 samples per second
Minimum scan rate	1 sample per minute
Maximum number of samples per scan	32,000
Trigger type	Internal (free run) or external (analog or digital)
Computer Requirements	
IBM PC/XT/AT or compatible	384KB RAM
PC DOS 2.0 or greater	DSDD or hard disk drives
CGA, EGA, or Hercules card	

10.2.11 UnkelScope

UnkelScope is a general-purpose data acquisition and control software package for the PC/XT/AT or compatibles. It is divided into two levels. Level 1 allows the personal computer to emulate an oscilloscope, a chart recorder, or an X-Y plotter. Level 1 provides the capability required to acquire, display, print, and store up to four analog inputs simultaneously. Level 2 adds proportional and PID control capabilities. Level 2 also provides data analysis and manipulation capabilities including FFT or power spectrum analysis, digital filtering (low, high, and band pass), integration, differentiation, and mathematical functions such as log, exponential, squares, and square roots. UnkelScope is menu driven. It can produce data files which can be read by most of the major spreadsheet and data reduction packages such as Lotus 1-2-3 or Symphony.

Specifications

Maximum number of channels sampled	4
Maximum number of channels displayed	2
Fastest sampling rate	50,000 Hz
Slowest sampling rate	Once per 500 sec
Horizontal trace selections	Time or analog input
Maximum number of samples per scan	1024
Computer requirements	
IBM PC/XT/AT or compatible	
256K of memory	
One DSDD floppy disk drive	
Graphics adapter	
IBM graphics printer or equivalent	
DOS version 1.10 or greater	

10.2.12 UnkelScope Junior

UnkelScope Junior is a low-cost, data acquisition tool for use with the PC/XT/AT and an analog input board. It supports sampling on up to four channels, with a sample size of up to 1024 points each and can also be set to acquire 4096 points from two channels, or 8192 points from a single-channel scan. It uses the same menu style as UnkelScope. The controls on the screen are designed to look and act like the familiar controls on an oscilloscope strip-chart recorder or X-Y plotter. A useful feature is the ability to plot one input against another. Once the setup parameters are selected, the data is acquired and displayed on the screen. Once displayed, the data can then be stored on disk for further study and analysis. The package includes a graphical editing/analyzing capability. Graphical editing allows scrolling two cursors through the data and displaying the differences between the two cursors.

Specifications

Maximum number of channels acquired	4
Maximum number of channels displayed	2
Minimum sample rate	One sample per 500 sec
Maximum sample rate	Hardware limited (up to 100,000 samples per second)
Maximum samples per scan	4 channels—1024 per channel
	2 Channels—4096 per channel
	1 Channel—8192 samples
System requirements	
IBM PC/XT/AT or compatible	
DOS 2.0 or greater	
256K RAM	
2 DSDD floppy drives or hard disk	
CGA, Hercules Graphics card, or compatibles	

10.2.13 MBC-BASIC

MBC-BASIC offers programming features that are not available in other versions of BASIC. MBC-BASIC syntax is virtually 100% compatible with GWBASIC and BASICA. For the programmer that is used to more structured languages such as C, MBC-BASIC offers the capability to create organized programs which use procedures and functions. Variables may be declared as local (within a procedure) or global (external). Many forms of BASIC do not allow this type of structure which is illustrated next.

```
PROCEDURE/FUNCTION
      PROCEDURE XXYZX
```

or

```
      INTEGER FUNCTION IFUNCT
```

An argument list can also be declared.

```
ARGUMENT PASSING
      INTEGER ARG: X
      STRING ARG: A$
      KEYWORD ARG: K1    ON    OFF
```

This argument list would require three arguments to be passed when calling the procedure/function. They would be referred to as X, A$, and K1. The first must be a numeric, which MBC-Basic would convert to an integer if one were not given. The second argument would be a string (A$), and the third would be a keyword that must be either ON or OFF. If ON is given, K1 will have a value of 1, and if OFF is given, K1 would have a value of 2. LOCAL/GLOBAL variables and other procedures/functions can be declared global with the EXTERNAL statement.

```
EXTERNAL A, B, C, DOUBLE
Local Variables can be predefined . . .
INTEGER Y, Z
STRING: W$ [ 20 ]
```

Here two local integer variables are defined and 1 local string variable with a MAX size of 20 characters.

MBC-BASIC allows the definition of up to 5 windows. Each window includes independent scrolling, borders, titles, foreground color, background color, and character attributes. Window may display up to eight colors on the screen at a single time. A number of examples describing MBC-BASIC's use of windows are shown here:

```
10 DEFINE WINDOW 1 5, 10, 20, 60 RED on BLACK
```

Here window 1 is defined with its upper left-hand corner to be at row 5, column 10, and its lower right-hand corner at row 20, column 60. Any outputting to this window will result in red on black characters.

```
20 FRAME WINDOW 1 CYAN ON RED
```

The statement will place a frame around window 1 with a foreground color of cyan and a background color of red.

The programmer can place headers in a window centered on the first line of the window.

```
30 HEADER 1, "THIS IS WINDOW 1" WHITE ON BLACK BLINKING
```

Here the text "THIS IS WINDOW 1" will be centered on line 1 of window 1 in blinking white on black characters.

Colors in the selected window may be changed as in GW-BASIC or by name.

```
40 COLOR 3, 1
```

or

```
40 Color CYAN ON BLUE
```

will set the window colors as cyan on blue.

SELECTing a window is accomplished by

```
60 SELECT 2                              'Places one in window 2
```

User-defined keywords allow the user to tailor the language to the application's specific needs. The Make Module command converts procedures and functions in memory into a module that can be added to the configuration file. Keywords are useful in many data acquisition and control applications. MBC-BASIC also provides for the creation of libraries. This ability to create reusable code allows programmers to store pretested, error-free procedures for repeated use in different programs.

MBC-BASIC allows programmers to use the entire 640KB memory space that is available to DOS. The programmer is not limited to the 64KB available in most BASIC languages. Dimensioning and operating on large arrays and vectors are not limited by having to coexist with the actual program all within 64KB.

To aid in the programming of MetraBus cards, MDC-BASIC statements configure the system and execute input or output operations.

To configure a driver card

```
Config drivername ({Driver Index,},Base Address})
Config cardname ({Drive Index,Card Index,}MetraBus Address)
```

where

drivername	Name of the driver used
cardname	One of the MetraBus card names
Driver Index	This is an optional argument, which defaults to zero. It declares the value of a Driver Card which can in a future statement be used to associate with a MetraBus card.
Card Index	This is an optional argument, which defaults to zero. It declares the value of the I/O Card which can in a future statement be used to associate with a MetraBus Card.
Base Address	The base address through base address $+4$ is used by the card for I/O operations. If there is a conflict with another card already configured, a runtime error (base address already in use) will be issued.
MetraBus Address	This is the address the I/O card occupies on the MetraBus. It is assumed that the address given matches the switch settings on the board.

The general form for I/O statements is very similar to the OUT and INP statements of GW-BASIC.

```
Output form...
    card anem({Card Index},I/O Index, {Operation},N
Input form...
    X=card name ({Card Index},I/O Index)
```

where

    I/O Index   For most cards an index of 0 indicates the I/O is to take place on bits 0–7 and index of 1 bits 8–15.

    Operation   This is an optional argument for digital ouput operations only.

The following is an example of programming the MetraBus in MBC-Basic. To force the outputs of bits 0–7 of a card to go the opposite state they are currently in

```
10 CARD (0,XOR),&HFF
```

Specifications

Hardware requirements	
CPU	IBM PC, XT, AT, COMPAQ, and compatibles
Memory	256KB min
Display	Monochrome or color
Disk drive	One $5\frac{1}{4}$'' floppy, single or double sided
Operating system	MS-DOS 1.1 and up
Data types	
Numeric data	
BYTE, range	0 to +255
INTEGER, range	−32768 to +32767
REAL, range	Single precision 8.43×10^{37} to 3.37×10^{38}
	Double precision 4.19×10^{307} to 1.67×10^{308}
String data	Variable from 0 to 32767 characters in size.
Record variables	

Allows grouping of dissimilar data types into a single logical variable. Elements of a record are addressed as fields and can be of any type, including array, record, and pointer.

Array variables

N-dimensional arrays of any type, including array, record, and pointer.
Dynamic arrays like PC-BASICA.

Pointer variables

Allows indirect reference to any data type. Can be used with record variable to create linked lists or to create relational data structures.

10.2.14 RTM 1000

RTM 1000 is a menu-driven extension of PC-DOS that allows an operator of a PC/ XT/AT or compatible computer to receive, display (digitally or in graphic form), and log (to disk or printer) data acquired from the MetraBus family of I/O boards. Acquisition, analysis, and display are performed in real time. The foreground/background capability of the package allows the user to be using the computer for a task in the foreground, while the process control, monitoring, and data logging continue in the background.

The package maintains a real-time database that is divided into columns that are referred to as display cells or slots. In addition to the current values, 15 cells of historical data are also maintained and can be operated on by other cells, or can be logged to disk or printer in case of an alarm condition. Each slot can represent an input channel (analog or digital), a function, or an output. Data is scaled into engineering units (via a $Y = MX + B$ scaling formula) and checked for alarm conditions before it is placed in its respective cell.

There are 15 mathematical functions that can be used for intercell manipulations. A standard cell function is in the form

```
Cslot = (Aslot OPER1 bslot) OPER2 Const.
```

where

C is the identification number of the cell to receive the data
A and B are IDs of cells to be operated on
OPER1 and OPER2 will be one of the available functions listed here:

OPER1	OPER2
+ Addition	+ Addition
− Subtraction	− Subtraction
· Multiplication	· Multiplication
/ Division	/ Division
A Average of N reading	
D First order digital filter	
E Exponential e(X)	
G Log base 10	
L Natural log	
N Minimum value	
P Power of 10	
R Running average	
S Square root	
T Totalizer	
X Maximum value	

Cells are identified by a single four- or five-digit numeral, and like many programmable controller interfaces, different types of cells fall in different ranges (communications cells are between 1001 and 2000, MetraBus input cells fall between 10,000 and 20,000). The package allows for a maximum of 512 total cells (plus the 14×512 historical cells) and performs system updates at least once per second. Smaller systems can be operated at higher speeds.

Cell inputs can be derived from

1. Analog or digital input boards
2. Serial communications ports
3. Results of calculations performed on one or more other cells
4. Keyboard inputs
5. Computer real-time clocks
6. Alphanumeric alarm messages
7. Concurrently operating user programs

System outputs can be provided in

1. Analog or digital output boards
2. Spreadsheet real-time displays
3. Bar graph real-time displays
4. Trend graph real-time displays
5. Separate disk files that may operate on any subset of cells at independent update rates
6. Alarm logs to either disk or printer

Specifications

Hardware requirements
    IBM PC, XT, AT, or compatible computer
    Hard disk drive
    Real-time clock
    512K RAM
    IBM PC-DOS 3.1 or equivalent
    Color display high-resolution CRT, Princeton Graphic Systems model
    HX-12E or equivalent
    Epson FX-286E printer or equivalent when hard copy is to be generated
    Enhanced graphics adapter
Software specifications

Nominal screen update rate	1 second
Maximum number of simultaneous disk files	4
System size	512 display slots
Tagging per display slot	4 lines of 8 characters each
Maximum numeric display slot size	8 characters

System automatically upranges to scientific notation as required

Alarming on discrete limits, assignable on a display slot basis

Individual input scaling ($y = mx + b$) on a per display slot basis

Multiple input/display slot assignment

Complete real-time database access

Fourteen-function real-time calculator

10.2.15 Paragon Control

The Paragon Control software package is an industrial control software package for use with a PC/XT/AT computer and a variety of I/O boards. The package is divided into two sections. The configuration section allows the user to set up the control algorithms, set alarm conditions, and design a custom display. Runtime routines actually perform the control and screen display functions after the system is set up using the mouse-driven, icon-based configurator.

Proportional, integral, derivative analog controls are allowed. The real-time customized display shows the system status. Up to 30 control loops can be run at $\frac{1}{4}$ second update rates, larger systems are possible at slower speeds. A data historian saves real-time process conditions to disk in Lotus 1-2-3– and Symphony-compatible data files. A process simulation feature allows control strategies to be tested and optimized. An expert system checker reports errors and inconsistencies and recommends solutions. Applications include process control, batch system control, data acquisition, and real-time displays.

Control strategy configuration is achieved graphically by selecting icons that represent the building blocks of the strategy. The package provides 35 built-in block types for designing control strategies with up to 300 blocks. A mouse is used to select the blocks in a strategy, and connections are made by drawing the lines that link selected elements in the process database. Configuration editing capabilities include

1. Multiple-screen control worksheets for strategy configuration with off-screen scrolling and pan and zoom.
2. Block specifications entered through interactive configuration menus.
3. Tuning parameters, setpoints, and logic inputs may be externally assigned.
4. Diagnostics including connection tracing.

Users build their own operator graphic displays using an icon-based interface similar to the one used for control configuration. Shapes and alphanumerics are either selected from a library or defined by the user. Graphic symbols can be static or dynamic. Features include

1. Cut and paste or replication of graphic symbols.
2. Free-form pen-type icon for user-created valves, motors, pumps, and other items.

3. User-created symbols may be saved in a library.

4. Dynamic selections include size and color changes, or interactive data entry or display.

5. Creation of up to 49 operator displays for viewing in real time.

6. Graphical connection of symbols.

A runtime module provides two operating modes, one of which is password protected. The unprotected mode allows process monitoring through user-selected displays and permits some tuning. The protected mode offers a range of interactive displays and access to internally defined values. In either mode, there is a split-screen interface for viewing the displays while simultaneously modifying tuning parameters. Features include

1. Displays that can be accessed without disturbing the process or affecting speed.

2. Built-in trends with variable time scales and selective point zoom, selective alarm activation, and reporting.

3. Reports that feature event and shift summaries and historian for recording selected data on disk.

4. Block point displays to view and modify tuning values and other parameters.

5. A drive capability for zooming into the point displays of blocks from the control strategy display, operator graphics, trend points, and alarm summaries.

6. Variable scan rates for individual blocks range from 0.25 to 30 seconds.

7. Control functions divided into prioritized tasks with individual scan rates.

8. Search by attribute for the selection of data.

9. Single keystroke switching between operator displays, trends, alarm summaries, and control strategies.

10.2.16 Compatible I/O Boards

16-channel single-ended/8-channel differential analog input boards
24-bit digital I/O boards
8-channel analog output boards
8- and 32-channel relay boards
32-channel digital input boards
16- and 32-channel solid-state I/O module boards
32-channel logic-level output boards

Minimum Configuration Requirements

IBM PC/XT/AT or compatible
512K RAM

10M hard disk

360K disk drive

EGA with 128K memory or compatible; also supports Tecmar color graphics card, Sigma Graphics, and other non-EGA boards

Enhanced graphics monitor or compatible

8087/80287 coprocessor microchip

Mouse systems mouse or equivalent

RS232 serial board

MS-DOS 3.0 or higher

10.3 ONSPEC CONTROL SOFTWARE*

This software runs on 286/386 personal computers such as the PC AT, PS/2 Models 50, 60, and 80, and compatibles. It is also available for the DEC VMS environment on the DEC MicroVAX, DEC 2000, DEC 3500, and DEC VAX series.

It contains a multitasking operating system, Pascal compiler, spreadsheet, and editor. There are process control programs for the preparation of diagrams, lists, specifications, and reports; for modeling and simulation; and for process control displays, alarms, trends, and historical reporting. Displays are created using a process control character set. All the variable information is stored in data tables using fill-in-the-blank data entry.

The 286 version is designed for 640K RAM and math coprocessor. An EGA or VGA color graphics board is required. Another version supports the EEMS standard for extended memory. It is capable of supporting extended memory up to 8MB on compatible 286 and 8086 family machines with the addition of an extended memory card.

The 386 version supports the speed and memory capabilities of computers that use the Intel 80386 with the 80387 numeric coprocessor. It supports 16 MB of RAM and accesses virtual memory.

ONSPEC can be used with Foxboro Spec 200 Micro controller cards to allow the personal computer to function as a distributed supervisory control system. The Spec 200 Micro is a control card for the regulatory and logic control functions for a wide variety of control systems. ONSPEC provides the operator with trending, monitoring, alarming, control optimization, historical data archiving, and reporting.

A template allows ONSPEC to interface to control cards through an HPIL loop. The setpoint, measurement, output, and alarm status can be polled every 5 seconds for 180 loops. Parameters in a control block can be read and written.

* The following material was supplied by Heuristics, Inc., Sacramento, CA, and is used with permission.

I/O templates (drivers) provide an interface between the computer and instruments, allowing ONSPEC to monitor and control a process. The template configuration file defines the functions to be performed, such as how often to poll a point in the device, where to send the data, what kind of data conversion to use, or special commands. More complex templates use a configurator to create this file.

Many of the templates support user-definable conversions, variable polling speed, COM1 and COM2 selection in banked memory, and serial interfaces. Polling 30 to 100 points per second is possible in an AT computer. Interfaces include RS-232, RS-422, RS-485, HPIL, HPIB (IEEE-488), and analog/digital I/O.

A draw command offers displays using a predefined set of ovals, lines, and other shapes. A Soft Key operator interface allows push-button response to operating changes and alarm conditions.

The Editor can be used for shift logs, reports, and programs; batch files; and the definition of variables. The Historian can be used for compressed and time-stamped data logging with status arranged by time series for analog and digital values.

PID control blocks and other common control elements suitable for supervisory control are available. Schedule-activated reports can be triggered by event or time of day.

A table extractor locates data for manipulation in a real-time spreadsheet and trending package. Trends of process variables can be combined with graphic or tabular displays. Alarms can be prioritized with messages, history file, display attributes, and user-defined alarm logic. A block alarm scheme allows up to 500 alarms per system.

The following I/O templates are available.

Allen Bradley Data Highway.   Provides an interface for the Allen Bradley Data Highway KG, KF, KF2, KE, and KA modules (KA needs a KF). It can interface to the PLC-2, PLC-3, and PLC-5 families of controllers. All 2 byte file types can be read and written. Block reads are supported. Linkage is RS-232.

Analog Devices Micromac.   Uses either Analog Devices MCCOM protocol or the ONSPEC protocol to interface to the MACBASIC running in MAC 5000 or 6000 computers. It includes a terminal emulation program for MACBASIC programming or up and downloading of files. The linkage is RS-232.

Bailey Net-90.   Interfaces ONSPEC to Bailey Network-90 through the computer interface unit (CIU). It can make the CIU establish points for the variables connecting to the network. Then it can read or write these points from or to the CIU. Linkage is RS-232.

Eagle Signal.   Provides an interface to Eagle Signal Eptak 7000, 700, 215, 225, and 245 controllers. It can read and write 8- or 16-bit registers. Block read is supported. Linkage is RS-422 through an Eagle Signal CP-2082 programmer interface card and a special cable. Eptak 700 requires a CP718 module.

Fischer & Porter.   Interfaces to F&P Chameleon directly or through a Supervisor. It can access the main database, any of the 90 control templates, and any of the 24 parameter templates. Linkages through Supervisor, RS-232. Requires F&P DCI data link device.

Fluke Helios I.   Provides interface to the Fluke Helios I Data Acquisition Unit. It can read and write to a single channel in the Helios. It can also read contiguous block or noncontiguous blocks of data. Linkage is RS-232.

Foxboro M/760,761.   Interfaces to Foxboro 760 or 761 single-station controllers. The setpoint, measurement, output, A/M, R/L, W/P status, and alarm byte of 31 controllers can be polled every 5 seconds. The setpoint, output, A/M, R/L can be changed from the computer. Memory locations in the 761 can be addressed from the computer. Linkage is RS-485. A Foxboro RS-232 to RS485 converter or an Opto 22 AC-24 card is required.

General Electric Series 6.   Interfaces to GE Series 6 using a CCM2 communication module. All Series 6 registers allowed by the CCM2 can be accessed. Block reads are supported and up to 89 controllers can be linked in a multidrop configuration. Linkage is RS-232.

Gould Modicon.   Interfaces to Modicon 84, 384, 484, 584, 884, 984 (ASCII or RTU). It can be configured to read/write coil status, holding registers, and read input status and input registers. The registers can be read or written to, one at a time or in contiguous blocks. Linkage is RS-232.

Hewlett-Packard 3852.   Interfaces to HP 3852 data acquisition unit. Different types of data points can be read or written. Block read is also supported. Linkage is HPIB (IEEE-488).

Honeywell TDC/PCSI.   Interfaces to the Honeywell PCSI (Personal Computer Serial Interface) which acts as a gateway into the TDC 2000 or 3000 data highway. Communicates to Honeywell Multifunction Controllers, Basic Controllers, Extended Controllers, and Process Interface Units located on the TDC 3000 highway. Linkage is RS-232 to PCSI.

Honeywell Gateway 300/400/500.   Interfaces to UDC 5000 and VersaPak 94 through Gateway 300/400/500. Linkage is RS-232.

OPTO 22 Optomux and LC2.   Interfaces to Optomux analog or digital boards directly or through LC2 controllers. It can do block reads and supports the PID loop software for the LC2 controller (PIDWARE). Linkage is RS-422.

Square D SY/MAX.   Interfaces to the Square D SY/MAX PLC family. It can connect directly to Model 300 or 500 controllers or through the network interface modules (NIM). All registers can be read and written. Block read is also available. Linkage is RS-232/Current loop.

Texas Instrument Tiway.   Interfaces to TITIWAY I Host Adapter through the network interface module to TI controller Models 510, 520, 530, 550, 565, and 5TI. Linkage is RS-232.

Texas Instrument 530.   Interfaces to one TI530 controller through the computer interface module (CIM). Block reads are supported. Linkage is RS-232.

Toshiba.   Interfaces to Toshiba TOSDIC Mini System through the MCAU (MC-Bus Linkage Adapter Unit) to TOSDIC 200 series single-loop controllers. Linkage is RS-232.

Westinghouse Numa-Logic and HPPC.   Interfaces to Numa-Logic 700, 900, and 1100 PLCs and HPPC. Linkage is RS-232.

10.3.1 Program Modules

The Superintendent is an expert system designed to capture the human thought process. The user accesses a real-time environment and defines a set of rules governing the process. This knowledge base is used by the Superintendent in making inferences about the process. The user creates the knowledge base using an interactive knowledge base builder which resembles a spreadsheet. Each rule or event-action procedure can be brought up with a single keystroke. The superintendent determines actions to be taken for the possibilities yes, no, and unknown. Inferences can be based on standard Boolean or algebraic operations, and resultant actions can be control outputs, operator notification, report generation, the calling of other programs, or the branching to further inference cells. Unknown responses can cause the superintendent to query the operator for additional information or cause the superintendent to continue and attempt to infer the answer through inductive reasoning.

SQC/SPC is a function key and menu-driven program for statistical quality/process control on personal computers or VAX environments. Real-time data can be retrieved online through a template. Historical data can be extracted from historical files, and lab data can be entered manually. The data can be manipulated so that control charts, histograms (frequency distributions), sample data tables, archive files, and alarms can be generated. The package provides two- and three-dimensional graphics, data archiving, user-selectable alarm criteria and limits, event- or batch-based sampling, and passwords. Up to 99 online variables can be configured in a PC system.

Control blocks are a set of preprogrammed control blocks for implementing control strategies on personal computers. A set of mnemonic commands allows the user to develop and change control information. A fill-in-the-screen format is used to establish blocks and form control loops.

The modular blocks compute feedback, feedforward, and batch algorithms and perform status, switching, setpoint, and failure alarming. Several control loops can be serviced by a common equation set based on closed loop algorithms for direct digital control and supervisory control. There are feedforward, lead/lag, dead time, and computational blocks. Batch control blocks can perform ramp, override, and cutoff functions.

A self-tuner uses adaptive control techniques to provide a closed-loop, self-tuning, PID control system. It can interface to many PID controllers to tune them online.

This menu-driven program operates in real time and interfaces with the external PID controllers through a template. The control loops in the system are always closed and can be tuned at the same time. Three sets of PID tuning parameters for each loop can be saved for initial start-up in batch applications.

The batch toolkit is a collection of programs used for controlling or monitoring batch processes. The programs in this package provide capabilities for batch sequencing, batch reporting, recipe management, and power failure recovery.

Batch language is used for controlling sequential batch processes. The sequences are developed in a special process control language which uses simple commands such as Open, Close, Wait, and When.

An example of coding for filling a tank to a level specified is shown here:

```
OPEN AV1001
REPEAT
 WAIT 1 SECOND
UNTIL LT 1001 GE TARGET1
CLOSE AV1001
```

The batch language can reference any point in the system either by tag, as shown, or by direct table name.

The batch collector and reporter gathers batch information such as minimum value, maximum value, and average on a batch-by-batch basis. The data files are managed using a database management system which permits the user to design report formats. Reports can be selected by indexes such as unit number, batch number, or recipe (grade) identification.

10.3.2 Applications

Henderson Mine & Mill in Colorado uses up to 30,000,000 kilowatt-hours and reaches peak demands of 64 megawatts of electric power. ONSPEC is used to monitor and control power usage.

A Cutler-Hammer D520 multiplexer monitors and controls fans and pumps spread throughout 150 miles of underground sites. Taylor, LM Erikson, and Westinghouse Numa-Logic systems are used. The three mill I/O systems were connected to a Westinghouse PLC communicating with ONSPEC.

An IBM AT monitors overall project power usage with a graphic process window while monitoring and controlling power. Monthly peaks were minimized without adversely impacting equipment maintenance. ONNET is used to transmit critical analog power readings between sites.

The city of Sacramento uses ONSPEC systems. Remote terminals located at water storage facilities communicate with the main plant via modems. The main plant collects data from remote facilities such as elevation heights, system pressure in water pipes, monitoring on/off states of pumps, valves, and other plant equipment, as well as chemical parameters such as chlorine residuals, turbidity, and PH.

Pacific Gas Transmission uses ONSPEC to monitor compressor variables, emergency parameters, power status, and alarming. The long-term historical trending feature is used for maintenance scheduling. Compressor operation is monitored by the collection of operating parameters such as suction, interstage, and discharge pressures and displayed on a per-compressor basis. Overview displays show start and stop permissives, pressure permissives, and timers used for pressure, purge, and full gas purge. Differential pressure and percentage of surge are displayed next to the compressor graphic.

A paper manufacturer uses ONSPEC on the DEC MicroVAX II interfaced to an Accuray measurement instrument for data gathering and a Bailey Net-90 for control and to provide a window to the process. The Accuray scans the paper rolling on the paper machine for moisture, caliper, formation, and texture. Each scan reads 96 points on the paper and combines them as profiles which are saved in a microfile on the Accuray. The microfile is uploaded to the MicroVAX II, where profiles can be shown on the displays. Points are processed for quality control using SQC/SPC. Three-dimensional SQC control charts and profiles are generated. Control variables from the Bailey Net-90 are sent to ONSPEC for monitoring, trending, and alarming. Fifteen IBM ATs connected to the MicroVAX provide terminals to access parts of the process that are of concern.

The ONSPEC superintendent can be used in applications such as sequencing, safety operations, and control. It is suited to applications where a large volume of critical information must be evaluated quickly and accurately to provide analysis prediction of system faults.

For example, a complex boiler system is run using three Allen-Bradley PLCs interfaced to ONSPEC Control Software. Each stage of the process impacts the later sequences. Events leading to a critical situation can occur too quickly for a human operator to understand and make a decision. The superintendent is used to analyze the information coming into the data tables.

A product called the gamma-metric coal analyzer incorporates ONSPEC to provide analysis reports of the different elements in coal such as the percentages of sulphur, ash, carbon, hydrogen, moisture, nitrogen, chlorine, and oxygen. The ash is analyzed to determine silicon dioxide, aluminum oxide, calcium oxide, titanium dioxide, potassium oxide, and trace element contents. The Btu/lb and total pounds of sulphur dioxide over tons analyzed is reported. Function keys have been assigned to allow the operator to generate a weighted average batch report by entering a start and end time. Status displays provide coal levels, analyzer flow rate, plant flow rate, belt speed, and top and bottom densities. Ash fusion and blend control options provide control to achieve cumulative as well as continuous targets by controlling the feeders.

Supertrends is used by a plastic manufacturer. The points plotted include temperature, flow, level, and pressure. Any of the plant variables can be selected for trend recording.

Ledesma of Argentina makes paper out of sugar, alcohol, and fructose. ONSPEC is used to monitor the preparation and boiling of the liquor and to

TABLE 10-2 PROCESS MONITORING/CONTROL AND DATA ACQUISITION SOFTWARE

Company/product	Function		Capacity			Features	Cost
	PMC	DA	Max# I/O points monitor	Max# discrete control	Max# PID loops		
Acrosystem							
Acrolog		X	128			CMWSP, CWLC, AL, RTU, SSP, SC,	LO
Action Instruments							
CIM-PAC	X	X	250	50	100	CMWSP, CWLC, AL,	LO
ADAC							
Genesis/4000XT	X	X	700	50	50	CWLC, AL, RTU,	HI
Adatek							
CMAX	X		1176	1176	8	CMWSP, CWLC, AL, RTU, SSP, SC	LO
System 10	X		1176	1176	8	CMWSP, CWLC, AL, RTU, SSP, SC	MED
Allen-Bradley							
AB CAMM	X	X	250			CMWSP, CWLC, AL, RTU, SSP, SOC/SPC	HI
Anatec							
I/Onyx System	X	X	750	100	100	CMWSP, CWLC, AL, RTU, SSP, CCB, SOC/SPC SC	
Automation Solutions							
Production Monitoring	X	X	1250			AL, RTU, SSP	LO
Bristol Babcock							
Troitbak-PC ver. 3.0	X	X	1600			CMWSP, CWLC, AL, RTU, SSP, CCB, SC	HI
Burr-Brown							
LabTech Notebook	X	X	208	80	24	CMWSP, CWLC, AL, RTU, SSP	LO
Loopworks 100	X	X	50	32	4	CMWSP, CWLC, AL, RTU, SSP, CCB, SC	LO
PCI ControloGraph	X	X	56	8		AL, RTU, SSP	LO

Company / Product						Features	Rating
Computer Methods Alert	X	X	2000			CMWSP, CWLC, AL, RTU, SOC/SPC, SC	HI
Computer Products SysteMyzer	X	X	500	200	200	CMWSP, CWLC, AL, RTU, SSP, CCB, SC	HI
Computer Systems PC-Control	X	X	64	32	12	CMWSP, CWLC, AL, RTU, SSP, CCB, SOC/SPC, SC	LO
Cyborg Loggernaut	X	X	64	32		AL, RTU, SSP	HI
Daedal Systems Statnet Workstation	X	X				CMWSP, AL, RTU	LO
Daytronic Corp LoggerPAC		X	400				MED
Digtronics Sixnet 10MUX	X	X	16	256	64	CMWSP, CWLC, AL, RTU, SSP, CCB, SPC/SPC, SC	MED
DYAD Technology PC/VRTX		X		256	256	CWLC, AL, RTU, SSP, CCB, SC	MED
ECP Flex Gage	X	X	64			CWLC, AL, RTU, SSP, SOC/SPC	HI
Gage Master	X	X	128			AL, RTU, SSP, SOC/SPC, SOC/SPC	HI
Elexor Associates PL/1000/MACS	X	X	32	2	2	CMWSP, AL, RTU, SSP	LO
Equinox Data Loopworks 100	X	X	100	33	4	CMWSP, CWLC, AL, RTU, SSP, CCB, SPC/SPC, SC	LO
Loopworks 300	X	X	300	100	75	CMWSP, CWLC, AL, RTU, SSP, CCB, SPC/SPC, SC	HI

TABLE 10-2 PROCESS MONITORING/CONTROL AND DATA ACQUISITION SOFTWARE (cont.)

Company/product	Function		Capacity			Features	Cost
	PMC	DA	Max# I/O points monitor	Max# discrete control	Max# PID loops		
Loopworks 3000	X	X	3000	1000	640	CMWSP, CWLC, AL, RTU, SSP, CCB, SOC/SPC, SC	HI
Eurothem							
Eurovis		X				AL	MED
HEM Data							
Snapshot Storage Scope		X				SSP	LO
Herco							
APRS	X	X				AL, RTU	HI
SCADA	X	X				AL, RTU, SSP	HI
Heuristics							
On Spec	X		4696			CMWSP, CWLC, AL, RTU	HI
Holmor							
Plant-View (Indelec)	X	X	4800	600	600	CMWSP, CWLC, AL, RTU, SSP, CCB, SPC/SPC, SC	HI
Iconics							
Genesis	X	X	800	200	200	CMWSP, CWLC, AL, RTU, SSP	HI
Intec Controls							
Paragon-Control	X		1000	500	200	CMWSP, CWLC, AL, RTU, SSP, CCB, SC	HI
Paragon-Data Acquisition		X	1000	500	500	CWLC, AL, RTU, CCB	HI
Intellution							
The Fix ver. 2.1	X	X	3000	3000	1000	CWSP, CWLC, AL, RTU, SSP, CCB, SPOC/SPC, SC	HI

Company / Product							Cost
Interactive Microware							
OMNISENSE		X	196			AL, RTU	LO
OMNISENSE-PLUS	X	X	244	96	32	CMWSP, CWLC, AL, RTU, SSP, CCB	LO
Kaye Instruments							
KView Workstation Software	X		1024			CMWSP, CWLC, AL, RTU, SSP, CCB, SC	HI
Kinetic Systems							
P CAM	X	X	500	64	64	CMWSP, CWLC, AL, RTU, SSP, CCB, SPC/SPC, SC	HI
Laboratory Tech.							
LabTech Notebook Ver. 4	X		800	400	400	CMWSP, CWLC, AL, RTU, SSP, CCB	LO
Lawson Labs							
PC 64 Version C4	X	X	64			AL, RTU, SSP	LO
Macmillan Software							
Asystant	X					RTU	LO
MCC Systems							
MicroMast-MT	X	X	5000			CWLC, AL, RTU, SSP	HI
MicroMast ST	X	X	3000			CMWSP, CWLC, AL, RTU	HI
Megasystems							
MIDAS	X		8000	256	256	CMWSP, CWLC, AL, RTU, SSP, CCB, SPC/SPC, SC	HI
MetraByte							
DAS-16	X	X	256			AL, RTU, SSP	LO
MetraBus	X	X	2000	1000	100	AL, RTU, SSP	LO
Microtie							
Microtie-1200 PC	X		58K			CMWSP, CWLC, AL, RTU, SSP, SOC/SPC	HI
Microtie-2000	X		58K			CMWSP, CWLC, AL, RTU, SSP, SOC/SPC	HI

TABLE 10-2 PROCESS MONITORING/CONTROL AND DATA ACQUISITION SOFTWARE (cont.)

Company/product	Function PMC	Function DA	Max# I/O points monitor	Max# discrete control	Max# PID loops	Features	Cost
Neff Instrument							
System 470	X	X	512			RTU, SSP	HI
Pioneering Controls							
Scadix	X	X				CMWSP, CWLC, AL, RTU, SSP, CCB	HI
R C Electronics							
IS 16	X	X	16			RTU, SSP	HI
Solartron							
359571 Impulse	X	X	600			AL, RTU, SSP	MED
Straightforward							
Fortyone Transfer System		X				CMWSP, CWLC, AL, RTU, SSP, CCB	LO
Strawberry Tree							
Analog Connection PC	X	X	240	240		CMWSP, CWLC, AL, RTU, SSP, SC	
Texas Instruments							
ICC5000 SCADA System	X	X	1000			CMWSP, AL, RTU, SSP	HI
Micro Monitoring Station	X	X	250			AL, RTU, SSP	HI
The Automation Group							
MDL-16	X	X	59			AL, RTU, SSP, CCB, SC	LO

MDL-22	X	X	38			AL, RTU, SSP, SC	LO
Tumbull Control Tactican T2000	X	X	256	128	128	CMWSP, CWLC, AL, RTU, SSP, CCB, SPC/SPC, SC	MED
Unkel Software UnkelScope Level 2+	X	X	8	1	1	RTU, SSP, SC	LO
Western Telecomputing DMS Ver. 2	X	X	112	16	16	CMWSP, CWLC, AL, RTU, SSP, CCB	LO
Xcel Controls Xpress Link Ver. 2.1	X	X	600	600		CMWSP, AL, RTU, SSP, CCB	MED
Zydeco LogLink	X	X	60	8	2	CMWSP, CWLC, AL, RTU, SSP, CCB, SQC/SPC, SC	MED

AL = Alarming
CCB = Chain control books
CMWSP = Control maturity with set points
CWLC = Control with logic calculations
DA = Data acquisition
PMC = Process monitor control
RTU = Real-time update
SC = Sequencing control
SQC/SPC = Statistical quality control/statistical process control
SSP = Selectable scan period

control and monitor the total process of digestion. The plant uses pressed sugar cane pulp (bargasse). ONSPEC on an IBM XT is interfaced to a Foxboro 99 UCB for data gathering and outputs.

The Aircraft Supply Supervision and Control System at the Guarulhos Airport in Sao Paulo, Brazil, uses ONSPEC to maintain the pressure of hydrant valves used for supplying fuel to the aircraft. The system supervises the operational conditions of the tanking, filtering, and fuel pumping set.

The package is interfaced to a MIC-1000 supervisor and control unit manufactured by SISCO of Brazil. The following functions are supplied:

1. The automatic control of pumps
2. The monitoring of pumping capacity
3. The automation of storage operations including tank exchange and refiltering
4. Operating changes such as pump start-ups and tank allocation
5. Emergency procedures for alarm conditions

Table 10-2 summarizes characteristics of a number of available representative industrial software packages.

Transducers

The terms transducer, sensor, and pickup, as applied to instrumentation, indicate a device or system in which the magnitude of an applied input is converted into a useful output which is proportional to the quantity of the input stimulus. The energy transmitted by these devices may take various forms, such as electrical, mechanical, or acoustical, and it may be of the same form or different forms in the various input and output systems. This definition includes devices which convert electrical power into mechanical force or displacement. However, the term is not primarily concerned with such inverse relationships.

The nature of the output from the transducer depends on the basic principle involved in its design. The output may be an analog, digital, or frequency-modulated electrical signal. Transducer design can be based on almost any combination of the following mechanical and electrical examples.

Capacitor.   A force applied to a diaphragm or mass displaces one plate of a simple capacitor. This type of transducer may be used as part of an RC or LC network in oscillators. It may also be used as a reactive element in ac bridges. When used in an oscillator circuit, the output which it provides may be RF, DC, digital, or phase shift.

Advantages	Disadvantages
Excellent frequency response	Motion of connecting cables, or long lead
Simple to construct and inexpensive to produce	length, can cause distortion and/or erratic signals
Low shock response	High impedance output

Advantages	Disadvantages
Measures either static or dynamic phenomena Minimum diaphragm mass Small volumetric displacement Continuous resolution	Must be reactively and resistively balanced Can be sensitive to temperature variations

Magnetic.   The force being measured displaces a magnetic core inside a differential transformer. In "E" core arrangements, the armature may be rotated by the applied force. The core itself may constitute the mass in an accelerometer. This principle is best suited for relatively large displacements. The output signal is greater than in strain gauges but lower than in potentiometer type devices.

Advantages	Disadvantages
Continuous resolution High output Low hysteresis	Must be excited with ac only Receiving circuits operate on ac signals, or a demodulator network must be used for dc output Low natural frequency Large displacement required Sensitive to vibration

Inductance.   The measurement of a force is accomplished by the change in the inductance ratio of a coil or pair of coils. The force being measured in the two-coil arrangement changes the magnetic coupling path upon displacement of the armature. Hysteresis errors are almost entirely limited to mechanical components. In a pressure transducer, the diaphragm itself is often used as part of the inductive loop. In this arrangement, the desired mechanical characteristics of the diaphragm must be compromised to improve the magnetic performance. The "E" core construction is often used to maintain good balance and low phase shift.

Advantages	Disadvantages
Responds to static or dynamic measurements Continuous resolution High output (>40 mV/V) High signal-to-noise ratio	Must be excited with ac Must be reactively and resistively balanced Frequency response is normally limited by construction Large volumetric displacement Proximity to magnetic objects, or fields, can cause erratic performance

Ionization.   An ionization transducer consists of a glass envelope with two internal electrodes. The envelope is filled with inert gases under reduced pressure. The gas is ionized by a radio frequency source on the electrodes. Ions and electrons are produced or liberated in this way. The space charge that is created may be controlled by electromagnetic or electrostatic fields.

Advantages	Disadvantages
High output may be provided	Must be excited by RF source
High sensitivity	Requires complex accessory equipment
Measures static or dynamic conditions	
Free of mechanical friction	
High frequency response	

Magnetostriction.   This refers to a property of certain materials (similar to the piezoelectric effect) in which the magnetic characteristics of the material change due to the application of stress or strain. The use of this principle is generally restricted to relatively high power levels and ultrasonic frequencies. This principle is used in underwater sound equipment (hydrophone) and high-intensity, high-frequency microphones.

Photoelectric.   Displacement of a force-summing member can be used to modulate the quantity of light incident upon a photosensitive element. The photomissive properties will be changed at a rate dependent on the displacement. A stable source or AC-modulated (pulsed) light can be used.

Advantages	Disadvantages
High output	Limited temperature range
High electrical efficiencies	
Simple to construct	
Static or dynamic conditions can be measured	

Piezoelectric.   An asymmetrical crystalline material produces an electrical potential with the application of strain or stress. The most common piezoelectric crystals are quartz, tourmaline, Rochell salt, and barium titanite. Although hydrophones and pressure and strain transducers are based on the piezoelectric principle, a principal application is high-frequency accelerometers.

Advantages	Disadvantages
High output	Sensitive to temperature changes
High frequency response	Cannot be used to measure static conditions
Self-generating	High impedance output
Negligible phase shift	Sensitive to cross-accelerations
Small size	Usually requires impedance-matching amplifier
Rugged construction	Long cables can generate noise or spurious response
	Extreme shocks can cause permanent effects

Potentiometric.   These are electromechanical devices containing a resistance element which is contacted by a movable slider. Motion of the slider results in resistance change that can be linear, sine, cosine, logarithmic, hyperbolic, or exponential, depending on the manner in which the resistance is formed. Deposited carbon and platinum film are among the materials used to provide the resistive element. The potentiometer principle is widely used despite its many limitations. Its electrical efficiency is extremely high. It provides a sufficient output to permit many control operations without amplification.

Advantages	Disadvantages
High output	Usually large size
Inexpensive	The resolution is finite in most cases
Easily serviced	High mechanical friction
Easy to excite and install	Limited life
May be excited with ac or dc	Sensitive to vibration
Wide range of functions	Develops high noise levels with wear
No amplification or impedance matching is	Requires a large force-summing member
necessary	Low frequency response

Strain.   The force being measured displaces and changes the length of a member to which the strain gauge is attached. The strain gauge possesses a property known as a gauge factor which produces a change in resistance proportional to the change in length. Strain gauges are often arranged in the form of a Wheatstone bridge circuit with one to four of the bridge legs being active. Strain gauge transducers can be classified as unbonded and bonded. The unbonded strain gauge has one end fixed while the other end is movable and attached to the force collector. The bonded strain gauge, however, is attached by an adhesive to the member whose strain is to be measured.

Strain gauges may be made from metal and metal alloys, semiconductor materials (silicon), and thin film materials.

Advantages	Disadvantages
High accuracy	Low output (higher output available with
Static and dynamic response	silicon strain gauges with some loss of
May be excited with ac or dc	thermal and stability characteristics)
Low sensitivity to shock and vibration for	Low range limitation for bonded types
bonded types	
Continuous resolution	

Moving Coil.   This type of pickup is often used for the measurement of velocities developed in a linear, sinusoidal, or random manner. A voltage is generated by the motion of a small coil in a magnetic field. The output is proportional to the velocity of the coil. Damping is obtained electrically.

Moving Core.   A permanent magnet core is displaced by the applied force inside a concentric induction coil. The voltage generated varies linearly as a function of core velocity.

Noise Considerations

B.1 NOISE

Electrical noise refers to any unwanted and interfering voltage developed within, or external to, a system that reduces the performance of that system. Interfering noise can be reduced by brute force filtering, which stops the noise after it enters the system. This method is expensive but reasonably effective for systems that are not too large or complex. High information rates and frequencies as well as low-level analog or digital pulse systems require a different approach. Filtering produces excessive deterioration of the desired pulse waveforms or inaccuracies and distortion of analog signal voltages. Noise reduction is best accomplished by keeping the noise out of the system. This can be done by installing noise-rejecting cables and applying equipment isolation and grounding techniques.

Most electronic equipment does not produce random noise, but when connected to other equipment to form a system, unwanted noise is picked up by the interconnecting wiring due to ground loops, common-mode returns, and capacitive or inductive pickup of radiated fields. A desired signal in one circuit can be noise to another. This noise can be produced by local circuits in the system or from equipment external to the system. Cables can radiate the signal they are carrying into adjacent circuits. The problems are compounded by poor cable to equipment impedance matching which produces signal reflections and high standing wave ratios. The lower the signal voltage level, the greater is the susceptibility to any interference.

B.1.1 Noise Sources

B.1.1.1 Inductive pickup from power sources

This includes 60 Hz noise from power lines, 120 Hz noise from fluorescent lighting, and higher frequencies from electric arcs and pulse-transmitting devices.

B.1.1.2 Electrostatic coupling to ac signals

Distributed capacitance between signal conductors, and from signal conductors to ground, affords low-impedance ac paths for cross-talk and signal contamination. The internal capacitance of power transformers also causes voltage fluctuations and electrical transients in power lines to be conducted into electronic systems via the ac power cord.

B.1.1.3 Common impedance coupling—ground loops

Placing more than one ground on a signal circuit produces a ground loop. This is a closed path or loop which can generate enough 60 Hz noise from circulating 60 Hz currents to obscure the signal.

B.1.1.4 Inadequate common-mode rejection

Common-mode signals (common-mode voltages and in-phase signals) are signals that appear simultaneously at both amplifier input terminals. These signals must be rejected without disturbing the useful signal, which is the difference in voltage across the input terminals of the amplifier.

B.1.2 Amplifier Configurations and Ground Loops

Figure B-1 shows the three most critical mutual capacitances between an amplifier and its shield enclosure conductor 3. The input-signal reference is called the signal reference conductor or zero-signal reference conductor. It is common to the input and output.

      Figure B-2 is the equivalent circuit of Figure B-1. It shows how the three mutual capacitances of Figure B-1 form a feedback circuit from output to input,

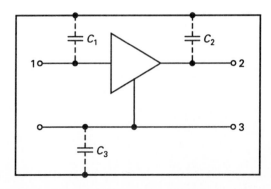

Figure B-1

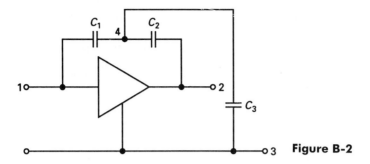

Figure B-2

providing a source for instability and noise. Capacitor c_3 is eliminated by connecting the signal reference (3) to the shield, as shown in Figure B-3.

Voltages between separate ground points are known as ground-loop potentials (V_{gl}) which cause ground-loop currents. A ground loop exists when a current has more than one ground reference point. This can be an earth ground or current ground. The path 3-4-5-6 provides a ground loop (Figure B-4).

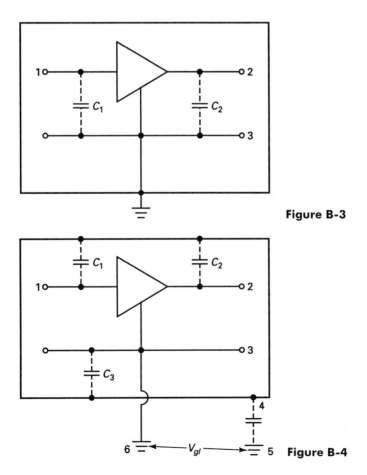

Figure B-3

Figure B-4

B.2 SHIELDING AND GROUNDING

A shielding enclosure shields the contained volume by terminating the electric field lines or charges that are supplied by some source through the ground point for the shield. The motion of these charges is current, which flows in the shield. It is essential that the currents in the shield do not flow in the sensitive input lines to the amplifier. This is done by connecting the shield to only one point which is the signal reference point as shown in Figure B-3.

When the shield is split in sections, all shield sections should be connected in series, and then connected to the signal-reference point at the signal-earth point. If it is not possible to do this, loop currents should be confined to the high-signal-level portions of the circuit.

Power entry lines to the amplifier can cause shielding and pickup problems unless batteries are used. One side of the power line is usually at its own ground reference which is not the same as the signal reference. Avoid bringing the power-supply reference into the amplifier circuit because of the potential difference that exists between the power ground and the circuit ground.

Although disturbances in the amplifier shield will cause unwanted signals at the amplifier reference, this is usually less than the pickup resulting from induction effects along a long line to the signal reference point.

The single-ended amplifier requires a reference line that is common to both inputs and outputs, and the shield and all current return paths must be connected to only one point—the signal reference point. This requires that no more than one ground reference point be used for sensors, amplifiers, and output devices, which is often difficult.

Some of these problems can be solved by the use of differential amplifiers instead of single-ended amplifiers. The differential amplifier allows the signal to be developed at one ground reference and measured at another ground reference. Up to now we have considered the amplifier to be single ended with only one input line for the signal. The other line is the reference or ground line, which functions as the return path for the signal.

A differential amplifier has two input lines and the amplifier response only to the difference between the two input signals. The differential amplifier is insensitive to common-mode signals, those signals that appear simultaneously at both of its inputs.

In addition to this insensitivity to common-mode signal, the differential amplifier provides reduced ground-loop problems since the input reference and the output reference can be separated. A signal appearing simultaneously at both inputs to an amplifier is called a common-mode signal since it is common to both inputs. In a single-ended amplifier the signal appears only on one input to the amplifier, with the return being the signal reference point. The desired signal is actually the difference in voltage between the two amplifier input terminals, but one is used as the zero reference in the single-ended amplifier.

The reactance of this path can exceed 1000 megohms. If the impedance of the circuit carrying the unwanted noise signal is 1000 megohms or greater, the circulating ground-loop current will be in the nanoamp range, and the noise signal it produces should be tolerable for most applications. This can be done by using amplifiers with an input impedance of this order of magnitude.

Floating inputs should be avoided or treated with caution. The shield should be connected to the signal reference point, and grounding a shield does not satisfy this requirement if the signal is floating. A ground system can float without earth contact such as in aircraft. The system ground point should be connected to an earthed conductor at only one point (Figure B-3). Each ground and earth point develops currents, so shorting ground points together is not usually helpful.

Differential amplifiers, unlike single-ended amplifiers, use two signal reference potentials. If one is grounded, the other can assume any potential as determined by the ambient E and H fields and parasitic currents. It is better to define this point than to permit it to find its own level by floating. A floating reference can also be a hazard if the floating line contacts an unknown conductor with a high voltage.

B.3 SYSTEMS WIRING AND CABLING

After buying the equipment, many systems engineers have difficulty in determining the best methods of cabling, interconnections, and the routing of signals from place to place, with the minimum of loss, degradation, and noise pickup. Often, simple solutions such as selection of the correct cable, eliminating common-mode grounds, and separating long runs of parallel cables will make the difference needed for a reliable system. These practices must be implemented at the time of initial design since they become difficult to install after the system is in place.

These interface problems are generally of two types: signal degradation and noise. First, there should be a study of the systems parameters and the noise environment. Consideration should be given to

- Signal frequencies
- Voltage and power levels
- Tolerable losses or degradation
- Pickup of noise from direct contact common-mode, ground-loop returns, and radiated magnetic fields

All low-voltage-level wiring should be shielded regardless of the frequency to be transmitted. Coax cable, although primarily designed to carry high frequencies, is useful for low-frequency shielded wire since it is relatively inexpensive and many types of connectors are available. For higher frequencies, coax should be used for point-to-point wiring since it has the transmission characteristics, flexibility, and economy needed for most systems. Coax cable is available in 50 and 75 ohm versions. A 93 ohm cable was developed due to the need for low-capacitance instrumentation coax cable. By removing some of the coax dielectric and substituting air in RG-59, the distributed capacitance was lowered, resulting in a lower loss voltage transmission medium RG-62. Cables and connectors of twinax, triax, and quadrax are also available to improve external noise rejection or to contain classified signals and prevent them from becoming a security compromise.

In a signal transmission system, the signals must move with minimum signal degradation and loss. It is necessary to reduce unwanted external noise to an acceptable level.

B.4 CABLE CONSIDERATIONS

Signal degradation in any transmission medium may consist of voltage amplitude reductions, wave shape changes, phase or delay changes, or power losses where power is transmitted. Since the interconnecting cable is the longest transmission path in most systems, its selection should be carefully considered. It is important to consider the length of the cable run, heat exposure, frequency, and power to be transmitted and compare these to the acceptable losses inherent in the cable, the external noise fields and frequencies to be encountered, and the availability of connectors to terminate the cable. Too small a cable can result in excessive losses. Fast rise time digital pulses will have the leading edge distorted due to the high-resistance skin effect of small coax cables. When selecting a cable for a long run, consider the insertion loss to ensure that the signals reach the destination without excessive loss. When in doubt, select a bigger cable. Incomplete coverage in the outer braid of the cable can cause transmission line losses as well as cable susceptibility to signal leakage or noise pickup.

During installation, be careful that the cable does not support equipment or is subject to prolonged heat. Do not bundle cables tightly so as to cause cross-talk or bend beyond the manufacturer's recommended radius of bend which could produce cable discontinuities. When routing cables, try to separate signal and power circuits.

Signal cables are often manufactured with polyethylene. High heat or chemical action can attack polyethylene cables, and Teflon™ cable should be used for these applications.

B.4.1 Coax Connectors

Connectors should be able to make interconnections with a low dc series resistance of less than 10 milliohms. The ac impedance of a connector is not critical below 300 MHz since the connector does not contribute to the circuit performance until its length approaches about a 1/20th of the wavelength. Thus, 50 ohm connectors can be attached to 75 ohm cables with no major effect at lower frequency. Above about 300 MHz, coax connectors should be impedance matched to the cable impedance.

Many cable systems were designed for specific problem solutions or proprietory products. The connector letters listed on the next page have gained wide acceptance due to their simplicity of design and performance.

Nominal cable O.D.	Connector Size	Quick Disconnect	Threaded
0.3 to 0.425"	Medium	C	N
0.10 to 0.3"	Miniature	BNC	TNC
0.10 to 0.242"	Subminiature	TPS	SMA

The choice of one series of connectors over another is usually economic or performance related. Crimping is usually done when time is important or where there is a lack of available soldering iron power. Crimping requires an expensive crimping tool that can be improperly used. Crimped contacts can corrode over a period of time particularly in chemical or salt environments. Soldered connections will not corrode if correctly done. Many coax connectors can be used again with proper care. This is an advantage in field locations where spare parts or special tools are not always available.

Glossary

access time   The time between the instant that an address is sent to a memory and the instant the data returns. Since the access time to different locations may be different, the access time specified is the path that takes the longest time.

accumulator   The register and related circuits that hold one operand for the arithmetic and logical operations.

address   The digital number used by the CPU to specify a location in memory.

addressing modes   See memory addressing modes.

ALU   Arithmetic-logic unit. The part of the CPU that performs adds, subtracts, shifts, ANDs, ORs, and other arithmetic or logical operations.

architecture   The organizational structure of a computing system.

assembler   The software that converts an assembly-language program into machine language. The assembler assigns locations in storage for successive instructions and replaces the symbolic addresses by machine-language equivalents. If the assembler runs on a computer other than that for which it creates the machine language, it is called a cross-assembler.

assembly language   An English-like language which limits the problem of remembering the bit patterns for instruction. It also relieves the necessity to keep track of locations of data and instructions in the program. In an assembler each phrase of the language translates directly into a specific machine-language word, as contrasted with a high-level language.

assembly listing   A printed listing made by the assembler to document an assembly operation. It shows how the assembler interpreted the assembly-language program in a line-by-line fashion.

asynchronous operation   An operation that does not use a common timing source. Each operation is terminated and the next operation is initiated by a return signal from the destination. Contrast with synchronous operation.

BASIC   Beginner's All-purpose Symbolic Instruction Code. A language developed for beginners.

baud   A measure of serial data transmission rate; loosely, refers to bits per second but may include character-framing start and stop bits.

benchmark program   A sample program used to evaluate and compare processors. In general, two processors will not use the same number of instructions, memory words, or cycles to solve the same benchmark program.

bit   An abbreviation for binary digit.

bootstrap   A technique or device for loading the first instructions or words of a routine into memory. Then, these instructions are used to bring in the rest of the routine.

branch   See jump.

branch instruction   A decision-making instruction that uses conditions to force a new address into the program counter. The conditions may be zero result, overflow on add, or an external flag. One of two alternate program segments in the memory are chosen, depending on the results.

breakpoint   A location at which program execution is to terminate. Used as an aid in locating program errors.

bus   A group of wires usually used for communications.

byte   A sequence of 8 bits operated upon as a unit.

call routine   See subroutine.

clock   A device or circuit that sends out timing pulses to synchronize the actions of the processor.

COBOL   Common Business-Oriented Language. A language developed for business applications.

compiler   Software used to convert a program in a high-level language into an assembly-language or machine-language program. It usually performs this operation for the complete program listing.

cross-assembler   A symbolic language translator that runs on one type of computer to produce machine code for another type of computer. See assembler.

CPU   Central processing unit. The section of a processor that controls the interpretation and execution of instructions. The CPU may contain the following: arithmetic-logic unit (ALU), timing and control, accumulator, scratch-
pad memory, program counter and address stack, instruction register and
decoder, parallel data and input/output bus, memory, and input/output
control.

cycle stealing   A memory cycle taken or stolen from the normal CPU operation
for a DMA operation. See DMA.

cycle time   The timer interval at which a set of operations is repeated regularly in
the same sequence.

data pointer   A register holding the memory address of the data to be used by an
instruction. The register then points to the memory location of the data.

data register   A register used to hold data.

debug   To eliminate programming mistakes, including any omissions, from a
computer program.

debug programs   Programs that help the programmer to find and correct errors in
other programs while they are running on the computer.

diagnostic program   A program used to check the hardware parts of a system for
proper operation. CPU diagnostics may check the CPU, and memory diagnostics may check the memory.

direct addressing   The address of an instruction or operand is completely specified in an instruction without reference to a base register or index register.

DMA   Direct memory access. A mechanism that allows an input/output device
to take control of the CPU for one or more memory cycles in order to write
to or read from memory. The order of executing the program instructions
remains unchanged in the DMA mode.

editor   Programs used to manipulate text material. These programs may also be
called text editors.

execute   The process of interpreting an instruction and performing the indicated
operations.

fetch   The process of addressing memory and reading into the CPU the word, or
byte, stored at the addressed location. Fetch usually refers to the reading
out of an instruction from memory.

firmware   Software that is implemented in ROMs.

fixed memory   See ROM.

flag lines   Alarm inputs to a microprocessor usually controlled and tested by
branch instructions.

FORTRAN   A high-level programming language expressed using algebraic notation. From FORmula TRANslator.

hardware   The physical equipment forming a computer system.

hexadecimal   A number system using 0, 1, . . . , 9, A, B, C, D, E, F to represent
the possible values of a 4-bit digit. The decimal equivalent is 0 to 15. Two
hexadecimal digits can specify a byte.

high-level language   A programming language that generates machine codes from
problem-oriented statements. FORTRAN, COBOL, and BASIC are three
common high-level languages. A single statement may translate into a series
of instructions or subroutines in machine language in contrast to a low-level
or assembly language in which statements translate via a one-for-one basis.

immediate addressing   The method of addressing an instruction in which the
operand is located in the instruction itself or in memory location immediately following the instruction.

immediate data   Data that follows an instruction in memory and is used as an
operand by that instruction.

indexed addressing   An addressing mode in which the address part of an instruction is modified by the contents in an auxiliary or index register during the
execution of the instruction.

index register   A register that contains data that can be used to modify a memory
address.

indirect addressing   A mode of addressing in which the address of the operand is
specified by an auxiliary register or a memory location specified by the
instruction rather than by the bits in the instruction.

input/output   A general term for the equipment used to communicate with a
CPU, or the data involved in the communication. Abbreviated I/O.

input/output controller   The electronics required to interface an input/output
device to a CPU. The usefulness of a CPU is closely associated with the
range of input/output devices that can be connected to it. The complexity
and cost of the controller is determined by both the hardware and software
input/output architecture of the CPU.

input/output interface   See input/output controller.

input/output port   A connection to a CPU that is configured or programmed to
provide a data path between the CPU and the external devices. An input/
output port may be an input or an output port, or it may be bidirectional.

instruction   A structured set of bits used to define a computer operation. A command that may move data, do arithmetic and logic functions, control input/
output devices, or make a decision for which instruction to execute next.

instruction cycle   The process of fetching an instruction from memory and executing it.

instruction length   The number of words needed to store an instruction. It is usually one word in most computers, but some use multiple words to form a single instruction. Multiple-word instructions may have different instruction execution times depending on their length.

instruction set   The set of instructions available with a given computer. The number of instructions only partially indicates the quality of an instruction set. Some instructions may be slightly different from one another; others rarely may be used.

instruction time   The time required to fetch an instruction from memory and execute it.

interpreter   A program that translates and executes instructions written in a higher-level language. It usually does this one line at a time. Contrast with compiler.

interrupt mask   A mechanism to allow the program to specify whether or not interrupt requests will be accepted.

interrupt request   A signal that temporarily suspends the normal sequence and transfers control to a special routine. Operation is resumed from this point later. The ability to handle interrupts is useful in many applications since it allows the microprocessor to service many channels.

interrupt service routine   A routine or program to store away to the stack the present status of the machine in order to respond to an interrupt request, then perform the work required by the interrupt, restore the status of the machine, and then resume operation of the interrupted program.

jump   A departure from the normal single-step incrementing of the program counter. By forcing a new value or address into the program counter, the next instruction can be fetched from location either farther ahead or back.

linkage   See subroutine.

loader   A program used to read a program from an input device into RAM. It may be a part of the package of utility programs.

load facility   A hardware facility to allow program loading using the DMA. It makes a bootstrap unnecessary.

loop   A self-contained series of instructions in which the last instruction can cause repetition of the series until a terminal condition is reached. Branch instructions can be used to test the conditions in the loop to determine if the repetition should be continued or terminated.

low-level language   See assembly language.

machine   A term for a computer or processor.

machine code See machine language.

machine cycle The basic CPU cycle. In one machine cycle an address may be sent to memory and one word read or written. Or in one machine cycle a fetched instruction can be executed.

machine language A numeric form of specifying instructions which is ready for loading into memory and execution by the machine; the lowest-level language in which to write programs. The value of every bit in each instruction in the program is specified by giving a string of binary, octal, or hexadecimal digits for the contents of each word.

machine state See state code.

macroinstruction A symbolic source language statement that is expanded by the assembler into one or more machine-language instructions. This relieves the user of having to write out frequently occurring instruction sequences.

memory The section of a computer that holds data and instructions. Each instruction is assigned a unique address that is used by the CPU when fetching or storing the data or instruction.

memory addressing mode The method used to specify the memory location of an operand. Addressing modes include direct, immediate, relative, indexed, and indirect.

memory address register A CPU register that holds the address of the memory location being accessed.

microcomputer A small computer with a CPU which is a microprocessor. The microcomputer is a system with microprocessor, memory, and input/output devices.

microprocessor An integrated circuit capable of performing the essential functions of a computer CPU.

mnemonics Symbolic names or abbreviations for instructions, registers, or memory locations. A technical aid used to improve the efficiency of the human memory.

multiple processing Configuring two or more processors in a single system, which operates with a common memory. The system execution of as many programs as there are processors.

nesting Subroutines which are called by other subroutines. The nesting level is the number of times the nesting can be repeated.

nibble A sequence of 4 bits operated upon as a unit. Also see byte.

object program A program that is the output of an automatic coding system, such as an assembler. The object program is often a machine-language program ready for execution.

op code   A code that represents specific operations of an instruction. Also called operation code.

operating system   The software for controlling the overall operation of a computer system, including the tasks of memory allocation, input and output, interrupt processing, and scheduling.

page   A grouping of memory locations by higher-order address bits. In an 8-bit microprocessor, $2^8 = 256$ consecutive bytes may constitute a page. Then the words on the same page may only differ in the lower-order 8 address bits.

Pascal   A structured programming language developed in the 1970's.

pointer   A register in the CPU that contains memory addresses. See program counter and data pointer.

program   A group of instructions ordered to perform particular tasks.

program counter   A register that specifies the address of the next instruction to be fetched and executed. It may be incremented each time an instruction is fetched.

PROM   Programmable read-only memory. An integrated circuit that has a specific bit pattern written into it by the user. Some PROMs called EPROMs (erasable programmable read-only memory) can be erased and reprogrammed by the user.

RAM   Random access memory. A memory that has both read and write capability. The time required to read from or to write into the memory is independent of the location of the memory where data was most recently read from or written into. Contrast with a serial access memory in which this time is variable.

register   A circuit used to store bits or words in the CPU. In many computers the efficiency of execution is related to the number of registers available.

relative addressing   A data address which uses the address given in the instruction plus another number. The number may be the address of the instruction, the address of the first location of the current memory page, or a number stored in a register. Relative addressing allows the CPU to relocate a program or a block of data by changing only one number.

return routine   See subroutine.

ROM   Read-only memory. A fixed memory that cannot be readily rewritten. ROMs require a masking operation during production to record the data patterns permanently. The data is stored on a permanent basis and used repetitively. ROMs are used for programs or tables of data that are to remain fixed.

routine   A subprogram where the task performed is less complex. A program can include many routines. See program.

scratch-pad memory   RAM or registers that are used to store temporary results.

serial access memory   A memory in which the time required to read from or write into the memory is dependent on the location in the memory. A wait occurs while nondesired memory locations are accessed. Examples include paper tape, disk, and magnetic tape.

snapshots   A capture of the state of a machine such as memory contents, registers, or flags.

software   A set of computer programs.

source program   A program written in a language designed for ease of expression by humans. It may be symbolic or algebraic.

stack   A sequence of registers or locations which is used in a LIFO (last-in, first-out) manner. A stack pointer is used to specify the last-in entry or where the next-in entry will be placed.

stack pointer   A counter or register used to address a stack in the memory. See stack.

subroutine   A group of instructions that is reached from more than one place in a main program. The process of passing control from the main program to a subroutine is a subroutine call, and the mechanism is called a subroutine linkage. Data or data addresses are made available by the main program to the subroutine, and the process of returning control from subroutine to main program is a subroutine return. The linkage may automatically return control to the original position in the main program or to another subroutine. See nesting.

subroutine linkage   See subroutine.

synchronous operation   The use of a common timing source or clock to time circuit or data transfer operations. Contrast with asynchronous operation.

syntax   A formal structure of rules governing sentence structure in a language such as an assembly language.

test and branch   See branch instruction.

Turbo-Pascal   A version of Pascal that reduces programming time, see Pascal.

utility program   A program for providing user or programmer conveniences, such as the capability for loading and saving programs, for observing and saving programs, for observing and changing values in a program, and for initiating program execution.

word   The basic group of bits that is manipulated by the computer in a single step. Two types of words are used in microprocessor programming, data words and instruction words. Data words contain the information to be manipulated while instruction words allow the machine to execute a particular operation.

word length   The number of bits in a word. The longer the word length, the greater the precision due to the number of significant digits. The longer the word length, the more varied the addressing modes of the computer are likely to be.

BIBLIOGRAPHY

AARONS, RICHARD. "BASIC." *PC Magazine*, October 1985, 117–119.

ABBOTT, K. W. "Plan and Control Projects with a Personal Computer." *Hydrocarbon Processing*, December 1983, 63–68.

ADAMS, L. F. *Engineering Measurements and Instrumentation*. London: English Universities Press, 1975.

ALTMAN, L., ed. *Microprocessors*. New York: Electronic Magazine Book Series, 1975.

ANDREWS, M. *Principles of Firmware Engineering in Microprogram Control*. London: Computer Science Press, 1980.

ASAOKA, S., SHINO, K., NORIMURA, K., AND YOSHIOKA, M. "Operation of a 1.3 GeV Electron Synchrotron with a Personal Computer," Report INS-TH-149. Tokyo Uni Institute for Nuclear Studies (Tokyo, Japan), July 2, 1982.

ASOHIMA, N. "Personal Computer Based Signal Compression Method Applied to the Measurement of the Sound Field in a Pipe." *Journal of the Acoustical Society of Japan*, March 1984, 146–151.

ATHANS, M., AND FALB, P. *Optimal Control: An Introduction to the Theory and Its Applications*. New York: McGraw-Hill, 1966.

BADE, P., ENGGEBRETSON, A. M., HEIDBREDER, A. F., AND NIEMOELLER, A. F. "Use of a Personal Computer to Model the Electroacoustics of Hearing Aids." *Journal of the Acoustical Society of America*, February 1984, 617–620.

BAILY, S. J. "Personal Computers Frugal Path to Specialized Control Systems." *Control Engineering*, July 1984.

BARTOGIAK, G. "Guide to Thermocouples." *Instruments and Control Systems*, November 1978.

BATTISTA, FRED F. "A Toolkit Approach to Operator Interface Systems." Proceedings of the North Coast Conference, Instrument Society of America, Research Triangle Park, N.C., May 1986.

BELL, C., AND NEWELL, A. *Computer Structures*. New York: McGraw-Hill, 1970.

BELL, L. H., AND STOUT, J. L. "Future of the Personal Computer as an Interactive Geological Graphics Workstation." *American Association of Petroleum Geologists Bulletin*, April 1984.

BENEDICT, R. P. *Fundamentals of Temperature, Pressure and Flow Measurements*. New York: John Wiley, 1969.

BERGER, J., AND TANNHAUSER, D. S. "Personal Computer as an Inexpensive Lock-in Analyzer Operating at Very Low Frequencies." *Review of Scientific Instruments*, December 1983, 1781–1783.

BEVERIDGE, G. S. G., AND SCHECHTER, R. S. *Optimization: Theory and Practice*. New York: McGraw-Hill Series in Chemical Engineering, 1970.

BEYCHOK, M. R. "Selecting a Personal Computer." *Chemical Engineering*, October 3, 1983, 103–104.

BLASSO, L. "Flow Measurement Under any Conditions." *Instruments and Control Systems*, February 1975.

BONE, T., AND STOFFER, J. O. "Use of the Apple II Personal Computer for GPC Data Collection and Analysis." *Journal of Water Borne Coatings*, August 1983, 24–31.

BREUER, M. A., AND GRIEDMAN, A. D. *Diagnosis and Reliable Design of Digital Systems*. Woodland Hills, CA: Computer Science Press, 1976.

BROOKS, F. P. *The Mythical Man-month, Essays on Software Engineering*. Reading, MA: Addison-Wesley, 1975.

BROOKS, F. P. "An Overview of Microcomputer Architecture and Software." *Micro Architecture*, EUROMICRO 1976 Proceedings, Europe.

BUCKLEY, P. S. *Techniques of Process Control*. New York: John Wiley, 1964.

BURTON, D. P. "Handle Microcomputer I/O Efficiently." *Electronic Design*, June 21, 1978.

BURZIO, G. "Operating Systems Enhance μCs." *Electronic Design*, June 21, 1978.

CAINE, K. E. "Personal Computer as an Engineering Tool." *Iron and Steelmaker*, April 1984, 12–16.

CALDWELL, W. I., COON, G. A., AND ZOSS, L. M. *Frequency Response for Process Control*. New York: McGraw-Hill, 1959.

CAMENZIND, H. R. *Electronic Integrated System Design*. New York: Van Nostrand Reinhold, 1972.

CARO, RICHARD H. "Programming for Batch Process Control." *Advances in Instrumentation* Vol. 40, 883–889. Research Triangle Park, NC: Instrument Society of America, 1985.

CHANDY, K. M., AND REISER, M., eds. *Computer Performance*. Amsterdam: North-Holland, 1977.

CHANG, C. Y., KSU, W. C., UANG, C. M., FANG, Y. K., LIU, W. C., AND WU, B. S. "Personal Computer-Based Automatic Measurement System Applicable to Deep-Level Transient Spectroscopy." *Review of Scientific Instruments*, April 1984, 637–639.

CHINTAPPALI, P. S., AND AHLUWALIA, M. S. "The Use of Personal Computers for Process Control." *Energy Progress*, June 1984.

CHINTAPALLI, P. S., AND STEELY, R. K. "Microcomputers as Productivity Tools in Plant Operations." Paper presented at the AIChE National Meeting, Anaheim, California, May 1984.

CHORNIK, B. "Application of a Personal Computer for Control and Data Acquisition in an Auger Electron Spectrometer." *Review of Scientific Instruments*, January 1983, 80–84.

CHU, Y. *Computer Organization and Microprogramming*. Englewood Cliffs, NJ: Prentice Hall, 1972.

COFFEE, M. B. "Common-mode Rejection Techniques for Low-Level Data Acquisition." *Instrumentation Technology*, July 1977.

COLLIER, D. "Personal Computers in Industrial Control." *Microelectronics and Reliability* (UK), Vol. 21, 1981, 461–465.

COMBS, C. F., ed. *Basic Electronic Instrument Handbook*. New York: McGraw-Hill, 1972.

CONSIDINE, D. M. *Process Instruments and Controls Handbook*. New York: McGraw-Hill, 1957.

CORWIN, T. K., CLARKE, P., AND FREDERICK, E. R. "Field Application of a Personal Computer for Data Collection and Reduction." Proceedings of the Specialty Conference on Continuous Emission Monitoring Design, Operation, and Experience, Air Pollution Control Association, Denver, Colorado, 1982, 293–302.

CRICK, A. "Scheduling and Controlling I/O Operations." *Data Processing*, May–June 1974.

CRONIN, D. P. "The Personal Computer as an Energy Management System." *Energy Technology*, June 1983, 388–396.

DANNENBERG, R. B. "Resource Sharing in a Network of Personal Computers," Ph.D. Thesis, CMU-CS-82-152. Work performed at Carnegie Mellon University (Pittsburgh, PA), December 1982.

DAVIS, A., AND MOLINARI, F. "Personal Computer Additions Can Speed Your R&D Projects." *Industrial Research & Development*, February 1983, 178–180.

DAVIS, D. B. "Personal Computer Networks Go OnLine." *High Technology*, March 1984, 62–68.

DESCHOOLMEESTER, D. "The Personal Computer: A Necessary Instrument or a Management Toy." *Informatie* (The Netherlands), January 1984, 37–43.

DIEFENDERFER, A. J. *Principles of Electronic Instrumentation*. Philadelphia: W. B. Saunders, 1972.

DIJKSTRA, E. W. *A Discipline of Programming*. Englewood Cliffs, NJ: Prentice Hall, 1976.

DODDS, D. E. "Home Energy Simulation Using Personal Computers." Proceedings of ENERGEX '83, Solar Energy Society of Canada (Winnipeg, Manitoba), 1982, 1020–1025.

DOEBELIN, E. O. *Measurement System—Application and Design*. New York: McGraw-Hill, 1975.

DONOVAN, J. J. *Systems Programming*. New York: McGraw-Hill, 1972.

DOW, J. "One File-Transfer Protocol Serves All Personal Computers." *Electronics*, August 11, 1983, 114–115.

DOWNEY, R. M. "Communicating Between the IBM Personal Computer and the Wang Word-Processing System," Report UCID-19889. Lawrence Livermore Laboratory (Livermore, CA), September 7, 1983.

ECKHOUSE, R. J., JR. *Minicomputer Systems*. Englewood Cliffs, NJ: Prentice Hall, 1975.

ECKMAN, D. P. *Automatic Process Control*. New York: John Wiley, 1958.

E.E.U.A. *Installation of Instrumentation and Process Control Systems*. Handbook No. 34. London: Constable and Co., 1973.

EISENBERG, J., AND HILL, J. "Using Natural-Language Systems on Personal Computers." *Byte*, January 1984.

ELLIOTT, T. C. "Temperature, Pressure, Level, Flow-key Measurements in Power and Process." *Power*, September 1975.

ENGEL, S., AND GRANDA, R. *Guidelines for Man/Display Interfaces*, Technical Report TR 00.2720. Poughkeepsie, NY: IBM, 1975.

ENGLEMANN, B., AND ABRAHAM, M. "Personal Computer Signal Processing." *Byte*, April 1984, 94–110.

EVANS, F. L., JR. *Equipment Design Handbook for Refineries and Chemical Plants*. Houston, TX: Gulf, 1971.

FABRYCKY, W. J., GHARE, P. M., AND TORGERSEN. P. E. *Industrial Operations Research*. Englewood Cliffs, NJ: Prentice Hall, 1972.

FARNBACH, W. A. "Bring Up your μP Bit-by-Bit." Electronic Design, Vol. 24, no. 15, July 19, 1976.

FEINER, S., NAGY, S., AND VAN DAM, A. "An Integrated System for Creating and Presenting Complex Computer-Based Documents." Proceedings 1981 SIGGRAPH Conference, published as *Computer Graphics*, Vol. 15, no. 3, August 1981.

FOLEY, C., AND LAMB, J. "Use of a Personal Computer and DFT to Extract Data from Noisy Signals." EDN, April 5, 1984.

FOLEY, J. D. "Evaluation of Small Computers and Display Controls for Computer Graphics." *Computer Group News*, Vol. 3, no. 1, January–February 1970.

FOSKETT, R. "Torque Measuring Transducers." *Instruments and Control Systems*, November 1968.

FOSTER, C. C. *Computer Architecture*. New York: Van Nostrand Reinhold, 1970.

FREEDMAN, M. D. *Principles of Digital Computer Operation*. New York: John Wiley, 1972.

FRIEDMAN, A. D., AND MEMON, P. R. *Fault Detection in Digital Circuits*. Englewood Cliffs, NJ: Prentice Hall, 1971.

FUNG, K. T., AND TOONG, H. D., "On the Analysis of Memory Conflicts and Bus Contentions in a Multiple-Microprocessor System." *IEEE Trans. Computers*, Vol. C-27, no. 1, January 1979.

GAMMILL, R. C. "Personal Computers for Science in the 1980s." Report P5954. The RAND Corp. (Santa Monica, CA), February 1978.

GARLAND, H. *Introduction to Microprocessor System Design*. New York: McGraw-Hill, 1979.

GEAR, C. W. *Computer Organization and Programming*. New York: McGraw-Hill, 1974.

GRANT, E., AND LEAVENWORTH, R. S. *Statistical Quality Control*. New York: McGraw-Hill, 1972.

GREGORY, B. A. *An Introduction to Electrical Instrumentation*. New York: Macmillan, 1973.

GRIMSDALE, R. L., AND JOHNSON, D. M. "A Modular Executive for Multiprocessor Systems." *Trends in On-Line Computer Control Systems* (Sheffield, England), April 1972.

GROFF, G. K., AND MUTH, I. F. *Operations Management: Analysis for Decisions.* Homewood, IL.: Richard D. Irwin, 1972.

GUEDJ, R., et al., ed. *Methodology of Interaction.* Amsterdam: North-Holland, 1980.

GUNASHINGHAM, H., ANG, K. P., MOK, J. L., AND THIAK, P. C. "Design of a pH Titrator as a Component Part of a Personal Computer." *Microprocessors and Microsystems,* July–August 1984, 274–279.

HALL, J. "Flowmeters—Matching Applications and Devices." *Instruments & Control Systems,* February 1978.

HALL, J. "Solving Tough Flow Monitoring Problems." *Instruments & Control Systems,* February 1980.

HAMANN, J. C., AND JACQUOT, R. G. "Analog Simulation on the Personal Digital Computer." *CoED* (journal of the Computers in Education Division of ASEE), April–June 1985, 12–15.

HAMILTON, M., AND ZELDIN, S. "Higher Order Software—A Methodology for Defining Software." *IEEE Transactions on Software Engineering,* Vol. SE-2, no. 1, March 1976.

HANNEMYR, G. "High Quality Document Production on a Personal Computer." *Microprocessing and Microprogramming* (Netherlands), March–April 1983, 233–242.

HARRIOTT, P. *Process Control.* New York: McGraw-Hill, 1964.

HAYES, P., BALL, E., AND REDDY, R. "Breaking the Man-Machine Communication Barrier." *Computer,* Vol. 14, no. 3, March 1981.

"Hearing on National Centers for Personal Computers in Education," House of Representatives, Committee on Education and Labor (Washington, DC), April 21, 1983.

HEATON, J. E. *The Personal Computer as a Controller.* Ann Arbor, MI: Oracle.

HELMERS, C. T., ed. *Robotics Age, in the Beginning.* Rochelle Park, NJ: Hayden, 1983.

HERRICK, C. N. *Instrumentation and Measurement for Electronics.* New York: McGraw-Hill, 1972.

"Hewlett-Packard Personal and Portable Computers, 1979–1986, Citations from the INSPEC Data Base," Report PB86-857042/XAB. National Technical Information Service (Springfield, VA), January 1986.

HILL, F. J., AND PETERSON, G. R. *Digital Systems: Hardware Organization and Design.* New York: John Wiley, 1973.

HNATEK, E. R. *A User's Handbook of Semiconductor Memories.* New York: John Wiley, 1977.

HNATEK, E. R. "Current Semiconductor Memories." *Computer Design,* April 1978.

HODGES, D. A. *Semiconductor Memories.* New York: IEEE Press, 1972.

HOLTON, M. J. "Programmable Input/Output System Prevents Communication Bottlenecks." *Advances in Instrumentation,* Vol. 39, 1001–1010. Research Triangle Park, NC: Instrument Society of America, 1984.

HORDESKI, M. F. "Digital Control of Microprocessors." *Electronic Design,* December 6, 1975.

———. "Digital Sensors Simplify Digital Measurements." *Measurements and Data,* May–June 1976.

————. "When Should You Use Pneumatics, When Electronics?" *Instruments & Control Systems*, November 1976.

————. "Guide to Digital Instrumentation for Temperature, Pressure Instruments." *Oil, Gas and Petrochem Equipment*, November 1976.

————. "Digital Instrumentation for Pressure, Temperature/Pressure, Readout Instruments." *Oil, Gas and Petrochem Equipment*, December 1976.

————. "Innovative Design: Microprocessors." *Digital Design*, December 1976.

————. "Passive Sensors for Temperature Measurement." *Instrumentation Technology*, February 1977.

————. "Adapting Electric Actuators to Digital Control." *Instrumentation Technology*, March 1977.

————. "Fundamentals of Digital Control Loops and Factors in Choosing Pneumatic or Electronic Instruments." Presentation at the SCMA Instrumentation Short Course, Los Angeles, California, April 6, 1977.

————. "Balancing Microprocessor-Interface Tradeoffs." *Digital Design*, April 1977.

————. "Digital Position Encoders for Linear Applications." *Measurements and Control*, July–August 1977.

————. "Future Microprocessor Software." *Digital Design*. August 1977.

————. "Radiation and Stored Data." *Digital Design*, September 1977.

————. "Microprocessor Chips." *Instrumentation Technology*, September 1977.

————. "Process Controls Are Evolving Fast." *Electronic Design*, November 22, 1977.

————. "Fundamentals of Digital Control Loops." *Measurements & Control*, February 1978.

————. "Using Microprocessors." *Measurements & Control*, June 1978.

————. *Illustrated Dictionary of Micro Computer Terminology*. Blue Ridge Summit, PA: Tab, 1978.

————. *Microprocessor Cookbook*. Blue Ridge Summit, PA: Tab, 1979.

————. "Selecting Test Strategies for Microprocessor Systems." ATE Seminar Proceedings, Pasadena, California, January 1982 (New York: Morgan-Grampian).

————. "Selection of a Test Strategy for MPU Systems." *Electronics Test*, February 1982.

————. "Trends in Displacement Sensors." Sensors and Systems Conference Proceedings, Pasadena, California, May 1982 (Campbell, CA: Network Exhibitions).

————. "The Impact of 16-Bit Microprocessors." Instrumentation Symposium Proceedings, Las Vegas, May 1982 (Research Triangle Park, NC: Instrument Society of America).

————. "Diagnostic Strategies for Microprocessor Systems." ATE Seminar Proceedings, Anaheim, California, January 1983 (New York: Morgan-Grampian).

————. *Microprocessors in Industry*. New York: Van Nostrand Reinhold, 1984.

————. *The Design of Microprocessor Sensor and Control Systems*. Reston, VA: Reston, 1984.

————. "CAD/CAM Equipment Reliability." Paper presented at the Western Design Engineering Show and ASME Conference, San Francisco, December 5, 1984.

————. "Specifying and Selecting CAD/CAM Equipment." CADCON West, Anaheim, California, January 14–17, 1985 (New York: Morgan-Grampian).

———. "A Tutorial on CIM/Factory Automation." Paper presented at the Western Design Engineering Show and ASME Conference, Anaheim, California, December 12, 1985.

———. *CAD/CAM Techniques*. Reston, VA: Reston, 1986.

———. *Microcomputer Design*. Reston, VA: Reston, 1986.

———. *Transducers for Automation*. New York: Van Nostrand Reinhold, 1987.

HORNBUCKLE, G. D. "The Computer Graphics/User Interface." *IEEE Trans.*, Vol. HFE-8. no. 1, March 1967.

HOUGEN, J. O. *Measurements and Control Applications*. Research Triangle Park, NC: Instrument Society of America, 1979.

HUGHES, J. S. "Personal Computers: If You Don't Have One Now, You Soon Will." *InTech*, February 1985, 45–47.

HUGHES, J. S. "Personal Computers in Process Control." *Advances in Instrumentation*, Vol. 40. Research Triangle Park, NC: Instrument Society of America, 1985.

"IBM Personal Computers and Compatible Equipment, 1975–1983, Citations from the INSPEC Data Base," Report PB84-855956. National Technical Information Service (Springfield, VA), December 1983.

"IBM Personal Computers and Compatible Equipment, January–September 1984, Citations from the INSPEC Data Base," Report PB84-875145. National Technical Information Service (Springfield, VA), September 1984.

"IBM PC Multiuser and Networking Systems, 1983–1986, Citations from the INSPEC Data Base," Report PB8 6-856853/XAB. National Technical Information Service (Springfield, VA), January 1986.

"IBM Personal Computers and Compatible Equipment, April 1985–March 1986, Citations from the INSPEC Data Base," Report PB86-859022/XAB. National Technical Information Service (Springfield, VA), March 1986.

Intel Corp. *8086 User's Guide*. Santa Clara, CA: Intel, 1976.

ISAACSON, P. "Ask Portia . . ." *Computer Retail News*. June 25, 1984, 23.

IVANOV, V. V., MORENKOV, A. D., AND OLEINKKOV, A. Y. "Personal Computers and Measurement-Computation Complexes for Automation of Large-Scale Laboratory Experiments." *Instruments and Experimental Techniques* (English Translation of *Pribory I Teknika Eksperimenta*), September–October 1984, 1106–1109.

IWAIK, T., IMAI, Y., ONO, M., OKAMOTO, T., KOBAYASHI, M., MATSUI, M. TAKEO, Y., AND KAWAMORI, Y. "The Personal Computer for Measuring Controller." *Anritsu Technical Bulletin* (Japan), May 1979, 82–94.

JACKSON, M. A. *Principles of Program Design*. New York: Academic Press, 1975.

JAMES, D. R., AND GRIERSON, J. B. "Evaluating Personal Computers for Process Control." *InTech*, January 1984, 49–51.

JAMES, D. R., AND GRITERSON, J. B. "Evaluating Personal Computers for Use in Process Control." *Advances in Instrumentation*, Vol. 38, 707. Research Triangle Park, NC: Instrument Society of America, 1983.

JOHNSON, S., AND LESK, M. "Language Development Tools." *The Bell System Technical Journal*, Vol. 57, nos. 6, 2, July–August 1978.

JONES, B. E. *Instrumentation, Measurement and Feedback*. New York: McGraw-Hill, 1977.

JONES, J. C. *Design Methods*. New York: Wiley-Interscience, 1970.

JUTILA, J. M. "Temperature Instrumentation." *Instrumentation Technology*, February 1980.

KAY, ALAN C. "Microelectronics and the Personal Computer." *Scientific American*, Vol. 237, no. 3, September 1977.

KEENE, B. "Solving Mechanical Problems with Personal Computers." *Machine Design*, February 10, 1983, 121–125.

KLINGMAN, E. E. *Microprocessor Systems Design*. Englewood Cliffs, NJ: Prentice Hall, 1977.

KLIPEC, B. "How to Avoid Noise Pickup on Wire and Cables." *Instruments & Control Systems*, December 1977.

KOBAYASHI, K., WATANABE, K., ICHIKAWA, R., AND KATO, A. "Personal Computer." In C & C (Computing and Communications), *Proceedings of the IEEE*, March 1983, 352–362.

KRAKOWSKY, A. M. "Cost Savings Resulting from Standardization and Support of Personal Computers," Report UCID-19969. Lawrence Livermore Laboratory (Livermore, CA), December 14, 1983.

KRAMPER, B., AND MacKINNON, B. "EPICS Personal Computer Evaluation," Report FERMILAB/TM-1225. Fermi National Accelerator Lab (Batavia, IL), February 1984.

KRIGMAN, A. "Selecting Peripherals for Process I/O." *InTech*, April 1984, 49.

KLOPF, P., VAN RHEE, L. A., AND STUBER, W. "An Autonomous CAMAC Crate Controlled by a Personal Computer." *Nuclear Instrumentation and Methods of Physical Research* (Netherlands), August 15, 1981, 435–441.

KNUTH, D. E. *The Art of Computer Programming. Volume 1: Fundamental Algorithms*. Reading, MA: Addison-Wesley, 1973.

KOFLER, G. "Personal Instrumentation, A Personal Computer as Part of a Measuring System." *Elekronkschau* (Austria), June 1983, 46–47.

KOHONEN, T. *Digital Circuits and Devices*. Englewood Cliffs, NJ: Prentice Hall, 1972.

KOTELLY, G. "Personal Computer Networks." *EDN*, March 3, 1983.

KRAMPER, B., AND MacKINNON, B. "EPICS Personal Computer Evaluation." Report FERMILAB/TM-1255. Fermi National Accelerator Lab (Batavia, IL), February 1984.

KUCK, D. J. *The Structure of Computers and Computations*. Vol. 1. New York: John Wiley, 1978.

KUENNING, M. K. "Programmable Controllers: Configuration and Programming." *Automated Manufacturing* (Greenville, SC), March 19–22, 1984.

KWAKERNAAK, H., AND SWAN, R. *Linear Optimal Control Systems*. New York: John Wiley, 1972.

LAWRENCE, S., AND MARCUS, L. S. "Designing PC Boards with a Centralized Database." *Computer Graphics World*, March 1984.

LEE, H. "Use of the Personal Computer to Design Processing Conditions for Improving the Accuracy of RTV Silicone/Epoxy Resin Replicas." *SAMPE Journal*, September–October 1985, 22–24.

LEVENSPIEL, O. *Chemical Reaction Engineering*. New York: John Wiley, 1962.

LEVENTHAL, L. V. *Microprocessors: Software, Hardware, Programming*. Englewood Cliffs, NJ: Prentice Hall, 1978.

LIGHTMAN, S. "Personal Computer Instruments and Personal Preferences." *Test & Measurement World*, March 1985, 93–102.

LIPTAK, B. G. *Instrument Engineers' Handbook*. Radnor, PA: Chilton, Vol. I, 1969, Vol. II, 1970, Supplement, 1972.

LIPTAK, B. G. *Instrumentation in the Processing Industries*. Radnor, PA: Chilton, 1973.

LIPTAK, B. G. *Environmental Engineers' Handbook*, Vols. I–III. Radnor, PA: Chilton, 1974.

LIPTAK, B. G. "Ultrasonic Instruments." *Instrumentation Technology*, September 1974.

LIPTAK, B. G., ed. *Instrument Engineers' Handbook on Process Measurement*. Radnor, PA: Chilton, 1980.

LORIN, H. *Parallelism in Hardware and Software*. Englewood Cliffs, NJ: Prentice Hall, 1972.

LUPFER, D. E., AND JOHNSON, M. L. "Automatic Control of Distillation Columns to Achieve Optimum Operation." *ISA Trans*. Pittsburgh, PA: Instrument Society of America, 1974.

MADNICK, S. F., AND DONOVAN, J. L. *Operating Systems*. New York: McGraw-Hill, 1974.

MANOFF, M. "Control Software Comes to Personal Computers." *Control Engineering*, March 1984, 66–68.

MARTIN, D. P., *Microcomputer Design*. Chicago: Martin Research, 1975.

MARTIN, J. *Design of Man-Computer Dialogues*. Englewood Cliffs, NJ: Prentice Hall, 1973.

MARUBAYASHI, K., MATSUMOTO, Y., AND TAWARA, H. "Low Cost Personal Computer System for Controlling an X-ray Crystal Spectrometer in Use for Collision Experiments." *Nuclear Instrumentation and Methods of Physical Research* (Netherlands), December 1, 1982, 571–576.

MAZUR, T. "Microprocessor Basics." Part 4, "The Motorola 6800." *Electronic Design*, July 19, 1976.

MCARTHUR, L. "Automate Your Instrument Maintenance with a Personal Computer." *InTech*, November 1983, 41–42.

MCDERMOTT, J. "Personal Computer Add-ons and Add-ins." *EDN*, January 20, 1983, 62–82.

MCGIRT, F. "REMOTE Modem Communicator Program for the IBM Personal Computer." Report LA-10143-MS. Los Alamos National Lab (Los Alamos, NM), June 1984.

MCGLYNN, D. R. *Microprocessors*. New York: John Wiley, 1976.

MCKENZIE, K., AND NICHOLS, A. J. "Build a Compact Microcomputer." *Electronic Design*, Vol. 24, no. 10, May 10, 1976.

MCMAHON, W. J. "Development Tool Helps Write Integrated Software for Personal Computers." *Electronic Design*, August 9, 1984, 171–180.

MEDITCH, J. S. *Stochastic Optimal Linear Estimation and Control*. New York: McGraw-Hill, 1969.

MERRITT, K., AND PERSUN, T. "Personal Computers Move into Process Control." *Instruments & Control Systems*, June 1983.

METCALFE, B. "Controller/Transceiver Board Drives Ethernet into PC Domain." *Mini-Micro Systems*, January 1983.

MEYER, J. AND JAYARAMAN, R. "Simulating Robotic Applications on a Personal Computer." *Computers in Mechanical Engineering*. July 1983, 15–18.

MILLS, J. "Use Your Personal Computer for Measurement and Control." *Analog Dialog*, Vol. 16, no. 2 (Analog Devices, Norwood, MA), 1982.

MILLS, M. "Memory Cards: A New Concept in Personal Computing." *Byte*, January 1984.

MILNE, B. "Personal Computers: Instruments." *Electronic Design*, September 29, 1983.

Moss, C. E. "Sophisticated Gamma-Ray Data Acquisition System Based on an IBM PC/XT Computer." Report LA-UR-85-3755. *Proceedings of the IEEE Nuclear Science Symposium*. October 23, 1985.

Moss, D "Multiprocessing Adds Muscle to uPs." *Electronic Design II*, May 24, 1978.

MOTOROLA SEMICONDUCTOR. *M6800 Microprocessor Applications Manual*. Phoenix, AZ: Motorola, 1975.

MOTOROLA SEMICONDUCTOR. *MC68000 Microprocessor User's Manual*. Austin, TX: Motorola, 1979.

MULLINS, M. "Instrument Controllers—Evaluating Cost and Function." *Test & Measurement World*, April 1984.

MURRILL, P. W. *Automatic Control of Processes*. Scranton, PA: International Textbook, 1967.

MYERS, G. J. *Reliable Software Through Composite Design*. New York: Petrocelli Charter, 1975.

NICK, J. R. "Using Schottky 3-State Outputs in Bus-Organized Systems." *Electronic Design News*, Vol. 19, no. 23, December 5, 1974.

NILES, J. M., CARLSON, F. R., GRAY, P., HAYES, J. P., AND HOLMEN, M. G. "Technical Assessment of Personal Computers (Vols. I–III)." Report NSF/PRA-7805647(1–3). UCLA Office of Interdisciplinary Programs (Los Angeles), September 1980.

NORTON, H. N. *Handbook of Transducers for Electronic Measuring Systems*. Englewood Cliffs, NJ: Prentice Hall, 1969.

OFFEREINS, R. P., AND MEERMAN, J. W. "Simulation Program (BASIM) for Personal Computers." *Proceedings of the 3rd IFAC/IFIP Symposium on Software for Computer Control*, 409–413. Oxford: Pergamon Press, 1983.

OHKUBO, T., AND NAKAMURA, T. "Automated Data Acquisition System of Environmental Radiation Monitor with a Personal Computer." Report INS-TS-24. Tokyo University (Japan), Institute for Nuclear Study, May 1984.

OLIVER, B. M., AND CAGE, J. M. *Electronic Measurements and Instrumentation*. New York: McGraw-Hill, 1971.

OLMSTEAD, K. "The Future Factor—A First Report." *Test & Measurement World*, December 1983.

OTTINGER, L. "Using Robots in Flexible Manufacturing Cells/Facilities." *Automated Manufacturing* (Greenville, SC), March 19–22, 1984.

PARISI, V. M. "Development of a Computer Aided Design Package for Control System Design and Analysis for Use on a Personal Computer." Report AFIT/GE/EE83D-53. Air Force Institute of Technology (Wright Patterson, AFB OH), December 1983.

PARK, R. M. "Applying the Systems Concept to Thermocouples." *Instrumentation Technology*, August 1973.

PATTERSON, D. A., AND SEGUIN, C. H. "Design Considerations for Single-Chip Computers of the Future." *IEEE Trans. Comp.*, Vol. C-29, February 1980.

"Personal Computers in Japan: The Most Up-to-Date Information on Japanese Computer Industries." Report PB84-176510. Work performed at PB Co., Ltd (Tokyo), National Technical Information Service (Springfield, VA), December 1983.

PETERS, L. J., AND TRIPP, L. L. "Is Software Wicked?" *Datamation*, Vol. 22, no. 6, June 1976.

PEUTO, B. L., AND SHUSTEK, L. J. "Current Issues in the Architecture of Microprocessors." *Computer*, February 1977.

PINTO, J. J. "Evolution of the Industrial Process Measurement and Control Computer." *Advances in Instrumentation*, Vol. 38. Research Triangle Park, NC: Instrument Society of America, 1983.

PINTO, J. J. "Software for Industrial Microcomputer Applications." *Advances in Instrumentation*, Vol. 40. Research Triangle Park, NC: Instrument Society of America, 1985.

PLUMB, H. H. *Temperature: Its Measurement and Control in Science Industry*. Research Triangle Park, NC: Instrument Society of America, 1972.

PRITTY, D. W. "The Potential of Personal Computers in Laboratory Control Applications." *Journal of Microcomputer Applications* (UK), January 1983, 47–57.

"Process Control by Personal Computers." *Wireless World* (UK), September 1983, 54–59.

RIBLET, G. P. "A Personal Computer Based System for the Rapid Display of Smith Chart Curves Using 6-Ports." *Proceedings of the Colloquium on Advances in S-Parameter Measurement at Microwavelengths*, IEEE (London), 1983.

RILEY, J. "Process Control for a PWB Facility." *Automated Manufacturing* (Greenville, SC), March 19–22, 1984.

ROMPELMAN, O., SNIJDERS, J. B. I. M., AND VAN SPRONSEN, C. J. "The Measurement of Heart Rate Variability Spectra with the Help of the Personal Computer." *IEEE Transactions on Biomedical Engineering*, July 1982, 503–510.

ROSS, C. A. "Automation Policies, Practices and Procedures." *Automated Manufacturing* (Greenville, SC), March 19–22, 1984.

ROTH, G. "Integrated Test Functions Aid in Process Control." *Test & Measurement World*, December 1983.

SANDBERG, U. "Personal Computers in Control and Regulatory Systems: Dream or Nightmare." *Industrielle Dataknik* (Sweden), Vol. 47, June 1984.

SANDBERG, U., AND FAXER, M. "Personal Computers for Real-Time Control of Power System Distribution Networks." *IEEE Transactions on Power Apparatus and Systems*, July 1984, 1720–1724.

SAXENA, P., AND GUPTA, L. K. "PCs Provide Low Cost Process Monitoring." *Proceedings of the North Coast Conference*. Research Triangle Park, NC: Instrument Society of America, 1986.

SCHAEFFER, E. J., AND WILLIAMS, T. J. "An Analysis of Fault Detection Correction and Prevention in Industrial Computer Systems." Purdue Laboratory for Applied Industrial Control, Purdue University (Lafayette, IN), October 1977.

SCHGOR, G. "Personal Computers in the Control of Industrial Plants." *Automazione y Strumentazone* (Italy), November 1983, 93–96.

SCHWARTZ, P. "When Personal Computers Become Measuring Instruments." *Electronique Industrielle* (France), May 1983, 49–53.

SCHWIDERSKI, G. "Personal Computers—A New Computer Technology for the Steel Industry." *Stahl und Eisen* (West Germany), February 23, 1985, 39–46.

SHEINGOLD, D. H. *Analog-Digital Conversion Handbook*. Norwood, MA: Analog Devices, 1972.

SHINSKEY, F. G. *Process Control Systems*. New York: McGraw-Hill, 1979.

SHNEIDERMAN, B. "Human Factors Experiments in Designing Interactive Systems." *Computer*, Vol. 12 , no. 12, December 1979.

SIGMA INSTRUMENTS. *Stepping Motor Handbook*. Braintree, MA: Sigma Instruments, 1972.

SINGER, A., AND RONY, P. "Controlling Robots with Personal Computers." *Machine Design*, September 23, 1982, 78–82.

SINHA, N. K. "Control System Design with Personal Computers." *Proceedings of the 1983 International Electrical and Electronics Conference* IEEE, New York, 1983, 420–423.

SKROKOV, M. R., ed. *Mini and Microcomputer Control in Industrial Processes*. New York: Van Nostrand Reinhold, 1980.

SLOMIANA, M. "Selecting Differential Pressure Instruments." *Instrumentation Technology*, August 1979.

SMITH, W. D. "An EEG Monitoring System on a Personal Computer." *Proceedings of the 1983 AAMSI Congress* (American Association of Medical Systems and Informatics, Bethseda, MD), 1983, 315–317.

SOISSON, H. E. *Instrumentation in Industry*. New York: John Wiley, 1975.

SORIANO, S. "Simulation by Means of a Personal Computer of a PID Regulator Controlled Process." *Automaziane y Strumentazione* (Italy), June 1984, 159–165.

SOUCEK, B. *Microprocessors and Microcomputers*. New York: John Wiley, 1976.

SROCZYNSKI, C. "3D Modeling in Process and Power Plant Design." CADCON East 84, Boston, June 12, 1984 (New York: Morgan-Grampian).

STONE, H. S. Introduction to Computer Architecture. New York: McGraw-Hill, 1975.

SYLVAN, J. "Industrial Monitoring with Personal Computers." *Machine Design*, October 6, 1983, 91–95.

SYLVAN, J. "Personal Computers in Distributed Measurement and Control." *Advances on Instrumentation*, Vol. 40. Research Triangle Park, NC: Instrument Society of America, 1985.

TAKANISHI, I., TOMOKIYO, O., AND YOKOUCHI, N. "Personal Computer for Measurement and Control." *Hitachi Zosen Technical Review* (Japan), March 1983, 56–63.

"Take Measurements with Your Personal Computer." *Measures* (France), September 13, 1983, 27–29.

TALYOR, A. P. "Getting a Handle on Factory Automation." *Computer-Aided Engineering*, May–June 1983.

Technical Data Book—Petroleum Refining. Washington, D.C.: American Petroleum Institute, 1970.

TER HAAR ROMNEY, B. M., NUIJEN, W. C., AND MAGIELSE, A. D. L. "Single Fibre Electromyography with a Personal Computer." *Medical Biology and Engineering Computation*, May 1984, 240–244.

TESCHLER, L. "Engineering Software for Personal Computers." *Machine Design*, January 26, 1984, 64–69.

TEXAS INSTRUMENTS. *The TTL Data Book for Design Engineers*. Dallas, TX: Texas Instruments, 1973.

TEXAS INSTRUMENTS. *The Microprocessor Handbook*. Houston, TX: Texas Instruments, 1975.

TEXAS INSTRUMENTS. *TMS 9900 Microprocessor Data Manual*. Dallas, TX: Texas Instruments, 1978.

"The Personal Computer as a Measuring Instrument." *Regulación y Mendo Automatico* (Spain), December 1983, 55–56.

THOMAS, T. B., AND ARBUCKLE, W. L. "Multiprocessor Software: Two Approaches." Paper presented at Conference on the Use of Digital Computers in Process Control, Baton Rouge, Louisianna, February 1971.

TIPPIE, J. W., AND KULAGA, J. E. "Design Considerations for a Multiprocessor-Based Data Acquisition System." *IEEE Transactions on Nuclear Science*, August 1979.

TOONG, H. D., AND GUPTA, A. "An Architectural Comparison of Contemporary 16-Bit Microprocessors." *IEEE Micro*, May 1981.

TOONG, H., AND GUPTA, A "New Direction in Personal Computer Software." *Proceedings of the IEEE*, March 1983, 377–388.

TORRERO, E. A. "Focus on Microprocessors." *Electronic Design*, September 1, 1974.

TORRERO, E. A., ed. *Microprocessors: New Directions for Designers*. Rochelle Park, NJ: Hayden, 1975.

TOTARO, L. "Personal Computer and a Quality Control." *Electronica Oggi* (Italy), March 1983, 167–192.

USEDA, K., AND KINOSHITA, K. "Data Processing System for the Measurement of Thermal Desorption Spectra Using a Personal Computer," *Journal of the Vacuum Society of Japan*, Vol. 26, no. 10, 1983, 784–788.

VACROUX, A. G. "Explore Microcomputer I/O Capabilities." *Electronic Design*, May 10, 1975.

VAN WINKLE, M. *Distillation*. New York: McGraw-Hill, 1967.

VOELCKER, H. B., AND REQUICHA, A. G. "Geometric Modelling of Mechanical Parts and Processes." *Computer*, December 1977.

WALLACE, V. L. "The Semantics of Graphic Input Devices." Proceedings SIGGRAPH/SIGPLAN Conference on Graphics Languages, published as *Computer Graphics*, Vol. 10, no. 1, April 1976.

WARNER, J.R. "Device-Independent Tool Systems." *Computer Graphics World*, February 1984.

WEGNER, W., ed. *Research Directions in Software Technology*. Cambridge, MA: MIT Press, 1978.

WEIR, J. D., AND WEIR, C. J. "Personal Computers for Machine and Process Control: Fast, Inexpensive, Easy Automation." *Elastromerics*, August 1983, 17–18.

WEISBERG, D. E. "Performance and Productivity in CAD." *Computer Graphics World*, June 1983.

WEISS, B. "Evaluating Graph and Chart Output." *Computer Graphics World*, February 1984.

WESTERHOFF, T. "Software in the Future Factory." *Test & Measurements World*, December 1983.

WIGHTMAN, E. J. *Instrumentation in Process Control*. Woburn, MA: Butterworth, 1972.

WOLF, S. *Guide to Electronic Measurements and Laboratory Practice*. Englewood Cliffs, NJ: Prentice Hall, 1973.

YOURDON, E., AND CONSTANTINE, L. L. *Structured Design*. New York: Yourdon, 1975.

ZAKS, R. *Microprocessors*. Berkeley, CA: Sybex, 1979.

ZILOG CORP. *Z8000 User's Guide*. Cupertino, CA: Zilog Corp, 1980.

Index